The Interpretive Turn

The Interpretive Turn

PHILOSOPHY, SCIENCE, CULTURE

EDITED BY

David R. Hiley, James F. Bohman,
and Richard Shusterman

Cornell University Press

Ithaca and London

First published 1991 by Cornell University Press.

International Standard Book Number 0-8014-2549-2 (cloth)
International Standard Book Number 0-8014-9785-x (paper)
Library of Congress Catalog Card Number 91-55061
Printed in the United States of America
Librarians: Library of Congress cataloging information
appears on the last page of the book.

⊗ The paper in this book meets the minimum requirements
of the American National Standard for Information Sciences—
Permanence of Paper for Printed Library Materials, ANSI Z39.48-1984.

For all the philosophy campers

Contents

PART THREE
Interpretation

Preface

In the summer of 1988, beneath the redwoods overlooking the Pacific, we gathered at the University of California at Santa Cruz to consider the theme "Interpretation and the Human Sciences." The meeting was an institute sponsored by the National Endowment for the Humanities Division of Education Programs, and organized by David Hoy and Hubert Dreyfus. David and Bert were joined by a staff that included Thomas Kuhn, Charles Taylor, Richard Rorty, Stanley Cavell, Alexander Nehamas, and Clifford Geertz. Twenty-two people—from philosophy, literature, law, and political science—were invited to participate in the six-week institute. As with every other distinction that confronted the group during that summer, the distinction between staff and participant soon collapsed, and what emerged was a community in the fullest sense. This is not to say that consensus was reached on any topic. There was none. But through the formal seminar, ad hoc working groups, lunches, beach parties, jazz clubs, funky restaurants, hikes in the redwoods, late night conversations, Sunday brunches, wine tours, and encounters with dreamers and dowsers who shared the UCSC campus that summer, something special emerged. The intense and stimulating summer was followed by two "reunion" meetings, first in Philadelphia in February 1989, and then in Memphis in October 1989. Those who were able to attend spent each meeting working together through papers that had resulted from the institute. Some of those papers form this volume.

Not everyone could be included here. Constraints of space, other commitments, and the organization of this volume meant that a selection had to be made. It is our hope, however, that the essays included

here convey the intellectual excitement, the variety of interests, and
the quality of discussion that were characteristic of the institute, and
that this book will be a credit to the entire group. Though these essays
differ and disagree in fundamental ways, they are products of a collaborative process and each is better for it.

   Those participating in the institute that summer in Santa Cruz were
Frank Adler, Gordon Bearn, James Bohman, Eloise Buker, Ronald Car-
son, Stanley Cavell, John Connolly, Stephen Doty, Hubert Dreyfus,
Marilyn Frye, Clifford Geertz, Judith Genova, Charles Guignon, David
Hiley, David Hoy, Henry Kariel, Thomas Kent, Judy Koffler, Michael
Krausz, Thomas Kuhn, Alexander Nehamas, Joseph Prabhu, Richard
Rorty, Paul Roth, Joseph Rouse, Richard Shusterman, John Valauri,
Samuel Wheeler, and Kathleen Wright.

                                                              D. H.
Auburn, Alabama
                                                              J. B.
St. Louis, Missouri
                                                              R. S.
Paris

The Interpretive Turn

The Interpretive Turn

James F. Bohman, David R. Hiley, and Richard Shusterman

It is now popular to mark shifts in philosophical method and preoccupation as "turns." In the modern period, for example, philosophy turned from its previous preoccupation with metaphysical questions to a primary concern with the possibility and nature of knowledge. This "epistemological turn" was to dominate philosophy for two centuries, only to be replaced in the early part of this century, at least for Anglo-American philosophy, by a "linguistic turn." By analyzing language, it sought to achieve many of the same goals that epistemology seeks in analyzing the mind. The linguistic turn has been characterized by preoccupations with the structure of language, word-world relationships, and the analysis of meaning. Recently, however, the views about the foundations of knowledge and the knowing subject that were the basis for the epistemological turn have been called into question, and it has seemed to many philosophers that language and meaning cannot bear the kind of weight the linguistic turn required.

These challenges have been joined by developments in the philosophy of sciences and the hermeneutic tradition, pointing toward a new direction in philosophy characterized by an interest in interpretive activities. This "interpretive turn" has benefited from the interpretive practices of such disciplines as literary criticism, cultural anthropology, jurisprudence, historiography, and feminist theory. With philosophy's redirection of attention to the interpretive disciplines, however, the concept of interpretation itself has become the source for controversy. The more philosophy and the interpretive disciplines proclaim the importance of interpretation in all of inquiry, the less there is agreement about what it is, what interpretive practices presuppose, and how to judge interpretive successes and failures.

1

The papers that make up this volume grew out of an institute, sponsored by the National Endowment for the Humanities, in which participants were to address the problems that emerge when philosophy and other disciplines take the interpretive turn. The institute was organized by David Hoy and Hubert Dreyfus around the following questions:

(1) What is interpretation? As the old logical division of labor between explanation and understanding is abandoned and interpretation comes to characterize the whole field of human endeavor, what, if anything, is the "contrast class" to interpretation?

(2) What makes an interpretation correct or better than another interpretation? As one answers this question, does the interpretive turn simply reintroduce older epistemological questions about truth and validity in a new guise?

(3) If interpretations are fallible and circular and if there is nothing to appeal to that is not an interpretation, is the interpretive turn relativistic and ethnocentric?

(4) If interpretive practices do not presuppose standards of universal reason and neutral evidence, do they become nihilistic or the result of sheer power and authority?

The essays collected here have been guided by discussion of these questions during the institute. They, like that discussion, quickly move beyond the older debate about the relationship between the natural and human sciences to issues about the "epistemology" of interpretation and the implications of the interpretive turn. As the essays will show, these questions about interpretation cannot be discussed without raising fundamental issues in epistemology, ontology, the philosophy of science, ethics, and political philosophy, and, consequently, without redrawing the boundaries of knowledge and the methods of various disciplines. In collecting these essays and, thereby, capturing something of the conversations of the institute, we hope to advance discussion on these important issues.

(1)   For most of the modern period philosophy has drawn its authority from epistemology, from its claim to provide the foundations for the rest of inquiry. Epistemology reigned as "the tribunal of pure reason," the high priest of culture that could authorize some intellectual endeavors and condemn others. In the heyday of epistemology a fundamental distinction was drawn between explanation and inter-

pretation. In the terms of the distinction, the real business of inquiry was explanation, whereas interpretive practices were confined to the special domain of the human sciences, the traditional *Geisteswissenschaften.* For much of this century, positivist philosophy of science reinforced the distinction through its view of the unity of science, which demanded a reduction of all sciences, including the social and behavioral sciences, to the ontology and methods of physics. The result was a clear demarcation of the scientific enterprise and interpretive disciplines. The distinction also implied a normative distinction that served to privilege the views about reason, knowledge, and the knowing subject inherent in the positivist view of science.

The recent impetus for rejecting the demarcation of the natural and human sciences has come initially from within the philosophy of the natural sciences, in challenges to positivism by the postempiricist philosophers of science such as Thomas Kuhn, Mary Hesse, and Paul Feyerabend. For positivism, the standard list of differences between the sciences and other forms of inquiry had derived from a view of the natural sciences that turned on the supposed neutrality of observation, the "givenness" of experience, the independence of empirical data from theoretical frameworks, the ideal of a univocal language, and belief in the rational progress of science. With the rejection of positivism and its thesis of the unity of science, many of the historic reasons for drawing a line between the natural and human sciences simply disappeared; distinctions between the disciplines were blurred by the suggestion of a much looser and interpretive conception of natural scientific inquiry. But the interpretive turn is having repercussions within the more traditional interpretive disciplines as well.

Within the human sciences themselves it was once thought that interpretation was called for primarily when one wanted to understand exotic cultures and historically distant texts. However, recent views in the philosophy of language—W. V. O. Quine's indeterminacy of translation thesis and Donald Davidson's view about radical interpretation—suggest that our understanding of speakers in our own culture and even our understanding of ourselves raise the same sorts of interpretive problems as those posed in our attempts to understanding exotic cultures and the distant past. As with recent philosophy of science, this issue has served to expand the scope and interest in questions about the nature of interpretive practices. Furthermore, Quine's and Davidson's arguments against a key distinction of the linguistic turn, that between the conceptual and the empirical, has served to undermine many of the presuppositions of the linguistic turn itself. The result is that recent directions in the philosophy of science and the philosophy of language are merging with the hermeneutical tradition and developments in the various interpretive disciplines to bring questions about interpretation to the center of philosophical discussion.

The turn to interpretation raises questions the answers to which inform the varied perspectives that make up this volume. The essays in Part One take up the debate about the relationship between the human and the natural sciences. We begin with this debate because it is through it that many of us, in the past few years, have been led to larger questions about the nature and role of interpretation. Ironically, it is among the friends of the human sciences, not from old-guard positivists, that one now finds the most heated arguments for a difference between the human and natural sciences. From the point of view of the human sciences, the claim of the uniqueness of interpretive methods not only protected them from the imperialism of natural scientific method but also involved important ontological, moral, and political convictions having to do with human freedom, agency, and power. How or whether one draws a line between the natural and human sciences is a debate involving interrelated methodological, ontological, and pragmatic considerations. This became clear to American philosophers as a result of an important exchange among Charles Taylor, Hubert Dreyfus, and Richard Rorty that appeared in the *Review of Metaphysics* in 1980, and their exchange is continued and extended in this volume. Since their views form part of the background for the institute and for the essays that follow, it is useful to summarize them.[1]

Despite the direction of postpositivist philosophy of science, Taylor and Dreyfus have remained staunch defenders of a fundamental distinction between the natural and human sciences. Rorty, however, has argued that it is a distinction that has outlived any usefulness it once may have had. Taylor's and Dreyfus's refusal to abandon the distinction is motivated by their desire to retain *both* a realist account of the natural sciences and essentialist claims about human beings. While holding that the natural sciences constitute a social practice like any other and that the history of this practice is one of Kuhnian conceptual revolutions, Taylor and Dreyfus insist that it is nonethe-

---

[1] This exchange should be read as background for the essays in Part One. See *Review of Metaphysics* 33 (1980).

less the social practice whose goal it is to gain access to subject-independent reality—to decontextualize beliefs from the web of purposes and practices, to "un-world" them, in the Heideggerian idiom. As Taylor puts it, science does not grasp things merely as they are relevant to our purposes and practices, but rather "as they are, outside of the immediate perspective of our goals, desires and activities."[2]

Thomas Kuhn opens this volume with an essay clarifying his own position in relation to Taylor's view of the natural sciences. Kuhn believes with Taylor that the natural and human sciences are not of the same sort, but he disagrees with Taylor about where to draw the line between them. Unlike Taylor, he believes that the concepts of natural science shape the natural world just as much as the concepts of the human sciences shape our social world. In returning to his familiar example from *The Structure of Scientific Revolutions* of people with different theories about the heavens inhabiting different worlds, he remarks, "I really do believe some—though by no means all—of the nonsense attributed to me." In the second essay Dreyfus takes up this aspect of the debate, offering an interpretation of Martin Heidegger's philosophy of science as a basis for what he calls "hermeneutic realism." Although he believes that Heidegger correctly undermines the illegitimate authority of the natural sciences and recognizes that science is a cultural practice, he nonetheless claims that Heidegger holds that the natural sciences can tell us truths about objective reality. Joseph Rouse, in the following essay, claims that arguments such as Taylor's and Dreyfus's not only fail to appreciate the full implications of postpositivist philosophy of science, they obscure the fact that the "objectivity" of science is politically laden.

This debate over interpretation in the natural and human sciences is further complicated because the human sciences are "doubly hermeneutic." They do not just give interpretations, they are interpretations of interpretations. What follows from this recognition for Taylor, and for Jürgen Habermas as well, is that the human sciences involve a radical reflexivity not found in the natural sciences. For Habermas, however, the double hermeneutic of the human sciences is only a guiding moral and methodological principle. But for Taylor and Dreyfus it is also ontological. It establishes something about who we are as *Dasein* or self-interpreting beings.

---

[2]Charles Taylor, "Rationality," in *Philosophical Papers*, vol. 2 (Cambridge: Cambridge University Press, 1985), p. 136.

For his part, Taylor wishes to maintain the distinction between the natural and human sciences because of this essentialist view about human agency in addition to his view about the natural sciences. He has argued that there is something about human agency, bound up with the fact that we are self-interpreting beings, that would be lost in the reduction of the human to the natural sciences. Because humans are self-interpreting beings, the meaning of human actions are always for an agent—the beings-for-whom they are meaningful. As such, the goal of the human sciences, according to Taylor, is not to achieve objectivity as in the natural sciences, but to grasp what these meanings are for agents.

Critics of Taylor such as Rorty and Paul Roth are quick to object that such a view implies "meaning realism," the belief that there is a "fact of the matter" about what agents believe; or at least it presupposes the belief that there is one determinate, correct interpretation. In his essay in Part Two, Rorty suggests that we give up such dualisms as "belief and that about which it is a belief," and he argues for a thoroughgoing anti-essentialism. The result is that the difference between the natural and human sciences is merely sociological, not methodological and philosophical. Charles Guignon's essay in Part Two pits Taylor's stance on human agency against Rorty's pragmatism, siding, finally, with a hermeneutic account of everyday human agency against Rorty.

In the final essay in this volume Taylor offers an elaboration of his view about human agency implicit in the discussion about the relationship between the natural and human sciences. In this essay he claims that what is perennial about human life is that human beings always have a sense of self that situates them in ethical space, though how that space is constituted varies through history. His concern is to reject the modern, monological, and disengaged version of the self because it fails to capture how human agency is constituted by the irreducibly social, dialogical nature of action. He ends the essay alluding to M. M. Bakhtin's insight that human beings are constituted in conversation. The implication, he thinks, is that this places dialogue at the center of human life and that a science of human beings must strive for an ideal of expanded intersubjectivity between agents who interpret themselves and others. In the essay preceding Taylor's, Thomas Kent also turns to Bakhtin's work, but for more deconstructive purposes.

(2) In the background of the debate over the relationship between the natural and human sciences is a series of epistemological issues

that make up the subject matter of Part Two and inform the interpretations of Part Three. The questions at issue turn, in one way or another, on the possibility of interpretive validity and the scope of interpretation. Once epistemological notions of objectivity and truth provide neither a fruitful contrast nor an analogue for interpretive practices, how can we decide whether or not an interpretation is adequate or truthful? Once the interpretive field is rid of putatively contrast inquiries such as the natural sciences, is interpretation the only game in town? If it is, what are the consequences of the ubiquity of interpretation? Taylor once characterized Rorty's hermeneutic universalism with the quip that he and other "old-guard Diltheyeans, their shoulders hunched from years-long resistance against the encroaching pressures of positivist natural science, [will now] suddenly pitch forward on their faces as all opposition ceases to the reign of universal hermeneutics."[3] Rorty, in his essay in Part Two, returns to this quip, drawing the conclusion that with the reign of universal hermeneutics, the very idea of hermeneutics might disappear. Others in Part Two, however, are not so willing to indulge in Rorty's "fantasy." For them, the ubiquity of interpretation raises serious questions that must be addressed: On what are interpretations based? Do they refer to nothing but other interpretations? How can they be assessed or justified? What are the political implications of offering or accepting one interpretation over another?

As one deals with these questions, it is important to note that "universal hermeneutics" has always been an ambiguous term. Two different elements of it need to be distinguished, each raising a distinct set of problems for the epistemology of interpretation. The first element may be called "hermeneutic universalism," the claim that interpretation is a universal and ubiquitous feature of all human activity. This strand of universal hermeneutics is captured in Dreyfus's phrase that we are "interpretation all the way down." There can be no appeal to experience, meaning, or evidence that is independent of interpretation or more basic than it. The second, related strand may be called "hermeneutic contextualism," the claim that interpretation always takes place within some context or background—such as webs of belief, a complex of social relations, tradition, or the practices of a form of life. This claim has a positive and a negative formula-

[3]Charles Taylor, "Understanding in the Human Sciences," *Review of Metaphysics* 34 (1980): 26.

tion. Positively, it implies holism, that is, that anything must be understood within some presupposed context, whole, or "hermeneutic circle." Negatively, it denies atomism, the view that something could be understood by itself independent of such contexts and could somehow be the incorrigible and foundational building blocks for knowledge. Opposing the atomism typical of much modern epistemology, contextualism holds that all justification is circular. If universalism entails that everything is interpretation, contextualism implies that truth is relative to some interpretive circle or other and that there are no external or outside grounds that would warrant stronger justification and validity for interpretations.

Both these basically epistemological elements of universal hermeneutics have powerful social and political implications. That interpretation takes place within a context or background of beliefs and practices implies that it is social, and hence that it is infused with political relations of power and domination. If there is nothing that is not an interpretation against which to judge, choices among competing interpretations—especially interpretations of other people and cultures—raise important moral and political issues about the relationship between interpreters and the subjects of their interpretations.

Each of the epistemological elements of universal hermeneutics involves philosophical difficulties that are addressed in Shusterman's, Bohman's, and Hoy's essays in Part Two, and that inform various essays on particular interpretive practices in Part Three. First, there are obvious skeptical issues following from the circularity of interpretation. The inevitability of the hermeneutic circle undermines the positivist conception of inquiry, but it may also undermine any knowledge claim whatsoever. This implication of contextualism is the issue that Bohman's essay examines. Shusterman's concern with universal hermeneutics is somewhat different. He argues that we can overcome foundationalist epistemology without maintaining the ubiquity of interpretation. Not only is it wrong to think that interpretation exhausts the realm of meaningful experience, but such a view fosters an overly cognitivist conception of human being-in-the-world.

The hermeneutic tradition has always been dogged by charges of relativism and skepticism, but the holistic nature of the interpretive turn poses the deeper problem of ethnocentrism. Rorty wants to make a virtue of this by taking the curse off ethnocentrism and being "frank" about it. "We" can understand "them" only in light of our postmodern bourgeois liberal values. David Hoy, in his essay, insists that ethnocentrism can be overcome by critical pluralism, the recognition that there may be many equally acceptable interpretations.

The issue of ethnocentrism straddles epistemological concerns about skepticism and relativism, and political concerns about dogmatism and domination. The possibility of interpretation assumes that we share a large and unspecifiable set of beliefs and practices with others with whom we communicate and engage in common activities. Some advocates of universal hermeneutics take this assumption to be relatively unproblematic. This is the case with Rorty who, drawing on the work of Donald Davidson, describes truth as what our peers let us get away with saying. But others, like Samuel Wheeler in his essay in Part Three, see its political threat. Indebted to Davidson as well as to Friedrich Nietzsche and Michel Foucault, Wheeler suggests that sharing a language and controlling its processes of metaphoric innovation are matters of force and fraud. From the direction of feminist theory, Eloise Buker also addresses the issue of the relationship between language, power, and the political consequences of how "we" constitute subjects and objects and allocate value and status to them through discourse. Rorty, Wheeler, and Buker demonstrate the importance of grasping the complex processes by which shared practices are maintained and reproduced, enforced and contested in social life. But they do this on the basis of very different views of how power affects interpretation.

These political issues show that the relation between power and community remains an unresolved problem for philosophers and political theorists who have taken the interpretive turn. On the one hand, hermeneutics has been traditionally associated with an apolitical notion of interpretive communities. According to Ludwig Wittgenstein and Hans-Georg Gadamer, societies consist of sets of shared practices that are held together by cultural consensus. On the other hand, newer theories of interpretation have tended to be more political and to take into account how culture is a product of domination. Philosophers such as Nietzsche and Foucault have seen existing interpretive practices as the contingent result of relations of power that are held together more by force than agreement. Both views are problematic. The first view makes society seem too unified to permit political disputes about interpretations, but the second puts in question the minimal unity of interpretations necessary to permit any common social life. Between the horns of the dilemma of an apolitical conception of community and an asocial conception of power politics lies the most plausible alternative: that interpretation is both a social and a political practice.

(3)   In taking the interpretive turn and thereby distancing itself from the authoritative appeal of foundational epistemology, philosophy has not condemned itself to lonely isolation. On the contrary, it has gained the enthusiastic attention and support of a growing number of disciplines that have come to recognize the centrality and inelimi- nability of interpretation in their cognitive practices. Their interest in hermeneutic philosophy is motivated by real practical concerns. For it is one thing to agree on the essential role of interpretation, but quite another to agree on the form and direction that role should take. Thus within an incontestably interpretive discipline like literary criticism or legal interpretation we find divergent interpretive meth- ods and aims, and the proper way to interpret is a very fiercely contested issue. Such disciplines tend to look to philosophy to clarify or help resolve this issue. There is a natural desire to seek agreement on interpretive method since that might facilitate cooperative work by different practitioners and contribute to cumulative consistency and commensurability of interpretations. Consensus on method, if not also on results, would make the interpretive disciplines seem closer to normal science and thus more cognitively respectable. More- over, if we construe correctness in terms of consensus rather than mirroring representation, such consensus becomes crucial for any objective results in these fields.

The philosophy of interpretation is, thus, eagerly pursued to help achieve some consensus of interpretive methods or at least to see the degree to which it can be expected or desired. The motivating idea of such a view is that if we know what interpretation is, we can better determine the way it should be practiced, establish its legitimate methods, aims, and limits. The assumption behind this idea is that philosophical theorizing could provide the general, authoritative tem- plate for interpretation, which the various hermeneutic disciplines could then apply, making whatever elaborations and adjustments might be necessary to account for their different subject matters and orientations.

There is, however, something misleading about this way of con- struing the interpretive turn in philosophy and its relation to the interpretive disciplines. It suggests a sharp distinction between the theory of interpretation and its application. The idea of "applied hermeneutics," however, falsely implies that there is some sort of hermeneutics that is not applied. But interpretation is always applied to something, because it is always an interpretation of something, even if that something is itself a prior interpretation. Furthermore, "applied hermeneutics" suggests that outside those disciplines where interpretation has become distinctly self-conscious and theoretically thematized, serious interpretive issues do not arise. But interpretive possibilities are far more pervasive than the scope of the tradi ional hermeneutic disciplines would suggest. Features of popular culture we might think unworthy of interpretive attention can be shown to reward it, as Alexander Nehamas, in his essay in Part Three, demonstrates with respect to the television series "St. Elsewhere."

Finally, "applied hermeneutics" implies a mistaken hierarchy of inquiry, where philosophy, as "pure" theory, determines a priori the legitimate form of interpretive practice. Certainly theoretical reflection informs interpretive practice, but it is wrong to assume that philosophical light about the nature of interpretive validity emanates only in one direction. Gadamer had already noted the importance of legal interpretation for hermeneutics, and in Part Three John Valauri takes up Gadamer's insight in order to show how American constitutional law presents striking instances of some central hermeneutical problems. Thus, just as theory can clarify and reform interpretive practice, it itself can be enlightened and reshaped by that practice. Paul Roth's interpretation of psychoanalytic practice, for example, casts fresh light on two long-standing issues about the difference between explanation and understanding and the effectiveness of therapy. More important, theory in fact always depends on a background of entrenched interpretive practices that initially get it going and continue to orient it. Theory emerges from practice and is judged pragmatically by its fruits in the practice that it can help reshape and sustain. The "Interpretations" of Part Three exemplify this interdependence of theory and practice.

Philosophy's interpretive turn is, thus, a practical turn, one that insists on the philosophical centrality of practice. Gadamer and Rorty make Aristotelian *phronesis* (practical wisdom) rather than *theoria* the model for philosophical understanding. Dreyfus argues for practical holism over theoretical holism. Taylor insists that theory is itself a practice. In the Continental tradition, this practico-interpretive turn is identified as philosophical hermeneutics, and in Anglo-American philosophy it sees itself as a renewal of pragmatism.

At least four reasons may be given why interpretation always implies application and the practical. First, there is the intentional aspect of interpretation already noted. It is always directed at or applied to some intentional object. (That this could be argued of all thought, even theory, is a consequence both hermeneutics and pragmatism will readily accept.) Second, it applies a particular perspective to what it interprets, a perspective that shapes in large part the interpretandum. Third, interpretation is always context bound. This is not merely to say that it always takes place in some specific situation. For the same could be said of a general law or principle in physics applied uniformly to different specific cases. Rather, with interpretation the contextuality is formative; the specific situation is what determines the very form and direction interpretation will take. Gadamer claims that interpretive understanding is always already application, since the situation that prestructures interpretation always calls for an application, always demands some response from us in the pursuit of the purposes through which we encounter the situation. For as purposive agents, we always have motives and needs in the situations we face. What and how we choose to interpret is always guided by those motives and needs with the aim of furthering our purposes. Indeed, one could say that the motives and needs we carry are themselves part of the applicational situation that prestructures interpretation. This purposiveness, implicit in all the situations in which we find ourselves interpreting, is a fourth reason why interpretation is intrinsically practical and applied.

Thus, not only so-called applied hermeneutics is practical. Interpretive theory, the philosophical interpretation of interpretation, also occurs within a concrete situation and, as such, is motivated by specific purposes that help to define it. Among the motives of current interpretive theory is the desire to clarify and improve interpretive practice, to establish some order and more convergence among a multitude of divergent methods and aims. Another motive is the desire to establish interpretation more firmly as a legitimate and fruitful methodological orientation in the human and natural sciences, so as to extend their scope and explanatory power. Part of this task of legitimation is to present interpretation as a theoretically convincing and well-reasoned alternative model to traditional foundationalist accounts of scientific explanation, the rigid conformity to which would badly constrain scientific practice and progress. Interpretive theory, then, like all interpretation (and this includes philosophy itself as a general interpretation of the world of human experience) is shot through with practical motives; it is founded on practice and itself constitutes a practice.

Does theory then not ultimately collapse into practice and the practical? In breaking down old boundaries between theory and practice, the transcendent and the situational, the interpretive turn raises serious questions about the status or role of theory. Once we recognize the primacy of practice and insist on the situated and perspectival character of all understanding, what remains of theory's claim to guide and transform practice? When one rejects *theoria* for *phronesis*, what remains for theory to be or do? One is tempted to scrap the whole idea of theory as a vestige of transcendental foundationalist thinking, which the interpretive turn has sought to undermine. As T. W. Adorno warned, "from the primacy of practical reason it was always only a step to hatred of theory."[4] And having made the interpretive turn, some, like Stanley Fish, have taken that further step, rejecting theory as "an impossible project" providing "no consequences" or guidance for practice.[5] Yet the primacy of practice and the rejection of theory's transcendental claims of cognitive privilege do not mean that theory no longer has an instructive role to play with respect to practice. All that follows is that the foundationalist concept of theory has to go, and that "theory," like "understanding," "truth," and "knowledge," needs to be reinterpreted in the light of the interpretive, postfoundationalist turn. It needs to be understood as critical reflection on practice. Moreover, though always rooted in a given practice, theory involves imaginative reflection on possible modifications of that practice. And though imagination is always constrained by established practice, it is not confined to slavish, mechanical repetition. Changing circumstances and encounters with other practices can nourish the imagination; and since no practice is defined for all possible situations, there is always need for imaginative projections and creative decisions in pursuing a practice, which again raises second-order problems of how to justify those decisions. As long as our practices present us with such problems and admit of improvement, theory will be not only possible but necessary.

In this pragmatic sense, theories are instruments for transforming reality, rather than mirroring representations of its putative essential and invariable features. So conceived, theory is not extinguished but encouraged by the interpretive turn. For once we give up foundationalism's picture of invariable essences and its hope of apodictic, per-

---

[4]T. W. Adorno, *Minima Moralia* (London: Verso, 1978), p. 88.
[5]See Stanley Fish, "Consequences" in W. J. T. Mitchell, ed., *Against Theory* (Chicago: University of Chicago Press, 1985), pp. 110, 115. See also "Changes" in his recent collection *Doing What Comes Naturally* (Durham, N.C.: Duke University Press, 1989).

manent justification for everything, once we see our practices as contingent products whose encounter with changing situations has necessitated continual adjustment, clarification, and justification, only then is theory's role of critical reflection on practice secure and ineliminable. Philosophy remains perennial, though with a new sense of its role.

PART ONE

THE INTERPRETIVE TURN IN THE NATURAL AND HUMAN SCIENCES

CHAPTER 1

The Natural and the Human Sciences

Thomas S. Kuhn

Let me begin with a fragment of autobiography. Forty years ago, when I first began to develop heterodox ideas about the nature of natural science, especially physical science, I came upon a few pieces of the Continental literature on the methodology of social science. In particular, if memory serves, I read a couple of Max Weber's methodological essays, then recently translated by Talcott Parsons and Edward Shils, as well as some relevant chapters from Ernst Cassirer's *Essay on Man*. What I found in them thrilled and encouraged me. These eminent authors were describing the social sciences in ways that closely paralleled the sort of description I hoped to provide for the physical sciences. Perhaps I really was onto something worthwhile.

My euphoria was, however, regularly damped by the closing paragraphs of these discussions, which reminded readers that their analyses applied only to the *Geisteswissenschaften*, the social sciences. "Die Naturwissenschaften," their authors loudly proclaimed, "sind ganz anders." (The natural sciences are entirely different.) What then followed was a relatively standard, quasi-positivist, empiricist account of natural science, just the image that I hoped to set aside.

Under those circumstances, I promptly returned to my own knitting, the materials for which were the physical sciences in which I had taken my Ph.D. Then and now, my acquaintance with the social sciences was extremely limited. My present topic—the relation of the

Remarks delivered on 11 February 1989 at a panel discussion held at LaSalle University and sponsored by the Greater Philadelphia Philosophy Consortium.

natural and human sciences—is not one I have thought a great deal about, nor do I have the background to do so. Nevertheless, though maintaining my distance from the social sciences, I've from time to time encountered other papers to which I reacted as I had to Weber's and Cassirer's. Brilliant, penetrating essays on the social or human sciences, they seemed to me, but papers that apparently needed to define their position by using as foil an image of the natural sciences to which I remain deeply opposed. One such essay supplies the reason for my presence here.

That paper is Charles Taylor's "Interpretation and the Sciences of Man."[1] For me it's a special favorite: I've read it often, learned a great deal from it, and used it regularly in my teaching. As a result, I took particular pleasure in the opportunity to participate with its author in an NEH Summer Institute on Interpretation held during the summer of 1988. The two of us had not had the opportunity to talk together before, but we quickly started a spirited dialogue, and we undertook to continue it before this panel. As I planned my introductory contribution, I was confident of a lively and fruitful exchange to follow. Professor Taylor's forced withdrawal has been correspondingly disappointing, but by the time it occurred, it was too late for a radical change of plans. Though I'm reluctant to talk about Professor Taylor behind his back, I've had no alternative but to play a role close to the one for which I was originally cast.

To avoid confusion, I shall start by locating what Taylor and I, in our discussions at the 1988 institute, primarily differed about. It was not the question whether the human and natural sciences were of the same kind. He insisted they were not, and I, though a bit of an agnostic, was inclined to agree. But we did differ, often sharply, about how the line between the two enterprises might be drawn. I did not think his way would do at all. But my notions of how to replace it—about which I shall later have just a bit to say—remained extremely vague and uncertain.

To make our difference more concrete, let me start from a too simple version of what most of you know. For Taylor, human actions constitute a text written in behavioral characters. To understand the actions, recover the meaning of the behavior, requires hermeneutic interpretation, and the interpretation appropriate to a particular piece

---

[1]Charles Taylor, "Interpretation and the Sciences of Man," in his *Philosophy and the Human Sciences* (Cambridge: Cambridge University Press, 1985).

of behavior will, Taylor emphasizes, differ systematically from culture to culture, sometimes even from individual to individual. It is this characteristic—the intentionality of behavior—that, in Taylor's view, distinguishes the study of human actions from that of natural phenomena. Early in the classic paper to which I previously referred, he says, for example, that even objects like rock patterns and snow crystals, though they have a coherent pattern, have no meaning, nothing that they express. And later in the same essay he insists that the heavens are the same for all cultures, say for the Japanese and for us. Nothing like hermeneutic interpretation, Taylor insists, is required to study objects like these. If they can properly be said to have meaning, those meanings are the same for all. They are, as he has more recently put it, absolute, independent of interpretation by human subjects.

That viewpoint seems to me mistaken. To suggest why, I shall also use the example of the heavens, which, as it happens, I had used also in the set of manuscript lectures that provided my primary text at the 1988 institute. It is not perhaps, the most conclusive example, but it is surely the least complex and thus the most suitable for brief presentation. I did not and cannot compare our heavens with those of the Japanese, but I did and will here insist that ours are different from the ancient Greeks'. More particularly, I want to emphasize that we and Greeks divided the population of the heavens into different kinds, different categories of things. Our celestial taxonomies are systematically distinct. For the Greeks, heavenly objects divided into three categories: stars, planets, and meteors. We have categories with those names, but what the Greeks put into theirs was very different from what we put into ours. The sun and moon went into the same category as Jupiter, Mars, Mercury, Saturn, and Venus. For them these bodies were like each other, and unlike members of the categories 'star' and 'meteor'. On the other hand, they placed the Milky Way, which for us is populated by stars, in the same category as the rainbow, rings round the moon, shooting stars and other meteors. There are other similar classificatory differences. Things like each other in one system were unlike in the other. Since Greek antiquity, the taxonomy of the heavens, the patterns of celestial similarity and difference, have systematically changed.

Many of you will, I know, wish to join Charles Taylor in telling me that these are merely differences in beliefs about objects that themselves remained the same for the Greeks as for us—something that could be shown, for example, by getting observers to point at them or to describe their relative positions. This is not the place for me to try very seriously to talk you out of that plausible position. But given more time, I would certainly make the attempt, and I want here to indicate what the structure of my argument would be.

It would begin with some points about which Charles Taylor and I agree. Concepts—whether of the natural or social world—are the possession of communities (cultures or subcultures). At any given time they are largely shared by members of the community, and their transmission from generation to generation (sometimes with changes) plays a key role in the process by which the community accredits new members. What I take "sharing a concept" to be must here remain mysterious, but I am at one with Taylor in vehemently rejecting a long-standard view. To have grasped a concept—of planets or stars, on the one hand, of equity or negotiation, on the other— is not to have internalized a set of features that provide necessary and sufficient conditions for the concept's application. Though any- one who understands a concept must know *some* salient features of the objects or situations that fall under it, those features may vary from individual to individual, and no one of them need be shared to permit the concept's proper application. Two people could, that is, share a concept without sharing a single belief about the feature or features of the objects or situations to which it applied. I don't sup- pose that often occurs, but in principle it could.

This much is largely common ground for Taylor and me. We part company, however, when he insists that, though social concepts shape the world to which they are applied, concepts of the natural world do not. For him but not for me, the heavens are culture- independent. To make that point, he would, I believe, emphasize that an American or European can, for example, point out planets or stars to a Japanese but cannot do the same for equity or negotiation. I would counter that one can point only to individual exemplifications of a concept—to this star or that planet, this episode of negotiation or that of equity—and that the difficulties involved in doing so are of the same nature in the natural and social worlds.

For the social world Taylor has himself supplied the arguments. For the natural world the basic arguments are supplied by David Wiggins in, among other places, *Sameness and Substance*.[2] To point usefully, informatively, to a particular planet or star, one must be

2David Wiggins, *Sameness and Substance* (Cambridge: Harvard University Press, 1980).

able to point to it more than once, to pick out the same individual object again. And this one cannot do unless one has already grasped the sortal concept under which the individual falls. Hesperus and Phosphorus are the same *planet*, but it is only under that description, only as planets, that they can be recognized as one and the same. Until identity can be made out, there is nothing to be learned (or taught) by pointing. As in the case of equity or negotiation, neither the presentation nor the study of examples can begin until the concept of the object to be exemplified or studied is available. And what makes it available, whether in the natural or the social sciences, is a culture, within which it is transmitted by exemplification, sometimes in altered form, from one generation to the next.

I do, in short, really believe some—though by no means all—of the nonsense attributed to me. The heavens of the Greeks were irreducibly different from ours. The nature of the difference is the same as that Taylor so brilliantly describes between the social practices of different cultures. In both cases the difference is rooted in conceptual vocabulary. In neither can it be bridged by description in a brute data, behavioral vocabulary. And in the absence of a brute data vocabulary, any attempt to describe one set of practices in the conceptual vocabulary, the meaning system, used to express the other, can only do violence. That does not mean that one cannot, with sufficient patience and effort, discover the categories of another culture or of an earlier stage of one's own. But it does indicate that discovery is required and that hermeneutic interpretation—whether by the anthropologist or the historian—is how such discovering is done. No more in the natural than in the human sciences is there some neutral, culture-independent, set of categories within which the population—whether of objects or of actions—can be described.

Most of you will long since have recognized these theses as redevelopments of themes to be found in my *Structure of Scientific Revolutions* and related writings. Letting a single example serve for all, the gap that I have here described as separating the Greek heavens from our own is the sort that could only have resulted from what I earlier called a scientific revolution. The violence and misrepresentation consequent on describing their heavens in the conceptual vocabulary required to describe our own is an example of what I then called incommensurability. And the shock generated by substituting their conceptual spectacles for our own is the one I ascribed, however inadequately, to their living in a different world. Where the social world of another culture is at issue, we have learned, against our own deep-seated ethnocentric resistance, to take shock for granted. We can, and in my view must, learn to do the same for their natural worlds.

What does all of this, supposing it cogent, have to tell us about the natural and human sciences? Does it indicate that they are alike except perhaps in their degree of maturity? Certainly it reopens that possibility, but it need not force that conclusion. My disagreement with Taylor was not, I remind you, about the existence of a line between natural and human sciences, but rather about the way in which that line may be drawn. Though the classic way to draw it is unavailable to those who take the viewpoint developed here, another way to draw the line emerges clearly. What I'm uncertain about is not whether differences exist, but whether they are principled or merely a consequence of the relative states of development of the two sets of fields.

Let me therefore conclude these reflections with a few tentative remarks about this alternate way of line-drawing. My argument has so far been that the natural sciences of any period are grounded in a set of concepts that the current generation of practitioners inherit from their immediate predecessors. That set of concepts is a historical product, embedded in the culture to which current practitioners are initiated by training, and it is accessible to nonmembers only through the hermeneutic techniques by which historians and anthropologists come to understand other modes of thought. Sometimes I have spoken of it as the hermeneutic basis for the science of a particular period, and you may note that it bears a considerable resemblance to one of the senses of what I once called a paradigm. Though I seldom use that term these days, having totally lost control of it, I shall for brevity sometimes use it here.

If one adopts the viewpoint I've been describing toward the natural sciences, it is striking that what their practitioners mostly do, given a paradigm or hermeneutic basis, is not ordinarily hermeneutic. Rather, they put to use the paradigm received from their teachers in an endeavor I've spoken of as normal science, an enterprise that attempts to solve puzzles like those of improving and extending the match between theory and experiment at the advancing forefront of the field. The social sciences, on the other hand—at least for scholars like Taylor, for whose view I have the deepest respect—appear to be hermeneutic, interpretive, through and through. Very little of what goes on in them at all resembles the normal puzzle-solving research of the natural sciences. Their aim is, or should be in Taylor's view, to understand behavior, not to discover the laws, if any, that govern it. That difference has a converse that seems to me equally striking. In the natural sciences the practice of research does occasionally produce new paradigms, new ways of understanding nature, of reading its texts. But the people responsible for those changes were not looking for them. The reinterpretation that resulted from their work was involuntary, often the work of the next generation. The people responsible typically failed to recognize the nature of what they had done. Contrast that pattern with the one normal to Taylor's social sciences. In the latter, new and deeper interpretations are the recognized object of the game.

The natural sciences, therefore, though they may require what I have called a hermeneutic base, are not themselves hermeneutic enterprises. The human sciences, on the other hand, often are, and they may have no alternative. Even if that's right, however, one may still reasonably ask whether they are restricted to the hermeneutic, to interpretation. Isn't it possible that here and there, over time, an increasing number of specialties will find paradigms that can support normal, puzzle-solving research?

About the answer to that question, I am totally uncertain. But I shall venture two remarks, pointing in opposite directions. First, I'm aware of no principle that bars the possibility that one or another part of some human science might find a paradigm capable of supporting normal, puzzle-solving research. And the likelihood of that transition's occurring is for me increased by a strong sense of déjà vu. Much of what is ordinarily said to argue the impossibility of puzzle-solving research in the human sciences was said two centuries ago to bar the possibility of a science of chemistry and was repeated a century later to show the impossibility of a science of living things. Very probably the transition I'm suggesting is already under way in some current specialties within the human sciences. My impression is that in parts of economics and psychology, the case might already be made.

On the other hand, in some major parts of the human sciences there is a strong and well-known argument against the possibility of anything quite like normal, puzzle-solving research. I earlier insisted that the Greek heavens were different from ours. I should now also insist that the transition between them was relatively sudden, that it resulted from research done on the prior version of the heavens, and that the heavens remained the same while that research was under way. Without that stability, the research responsible for the change could not have occurred. But stability of that sort cannot be expected when the unit under study is a social or political system. No lasting base for normal, puzzle-solving science need be available to those who investigate them; hermeneutic reinterpretation may constantly be required. Where that is the case, the line that Charles Taylor seeks between the human and the natural sciences may be firmly in place. I expect that in some areas it may forever remain there.

CHAPTER 2

Heidegger's Hermeneutic Realism

HUBERT L. DREYFUS

The status of the entities supposedly discovered by natural science, and the correlated question of the special authority of science in our culture—a question posed two decades ago by Thomas Kuhn's *Structure of Scientific Revolutions*—has recently become a central issue of debate. Literary theorists, social scientists, and feminists, each for their own reasons, have found themselves allied with Kuhn in their attack on the special claim of the natural sciences to tell us the truth about objective reality. The literary theorists would like to one-up the sciences by showing that scientific theories are after all just interpretive texts and therefore fall into the domain of the humanities. Similarly, social scientists, by pointing out that scientific truth is a product of shared practices, seek to annex science to the domain of sociology and anthropology. Feminists would like to undermine the authority of the scientific establishment, which they regard as a bastion of male domination. All these groups would like to believe that natural science is just one more interpretive practice that has somehow conned our culture into thinking that it alone has access to the real. The stakes are high. As Evelyn Fox Keller recently put it: "The question of whether scientific knowledge is objective or relative is at least in part a question about the claim of scientists to absolute authority. If there is only one truth, and scientists are privy to it . . . then the authority of science is unassailable. But if truth is relative, if science

This paper is a slightly revised version of a chapter of Hubert Dreyfus, *Being-in-the-World: A Commentary on Division I of "Being and Time"* (Cambridge: MIT Press, 1991) and appears with the permission of MIT Press.

is divorced from nature and married instead to culture then the privileged status of that authority is fatally undermined."[1]

There is, indeed, something wrong with our culture's worship of natural science, as if what science tells us about the fundamental particles has fundamental importance for all aspects of life. The success of books like Fritjof Capra's *Tao of Physics*, which tells us that we can breathe easier because science is no longer atomist and materialist but is now holist and works with energy fields, shows that many people believe that science tells us the final truth about reality. But the attempt to limit the influence of science by denying that it discovers anything at all—as the title of a recent book, *Constructing Quarks*,[2] implies—is clearly an overreaction. It is a non sequitur to claim that because the development of physical theories depends upon scientists' practices and that the authority of science is constituted by way of broader social practices, physics does not discover truths about nature and so has no legitimate authority. If one wants to undermine the illegitimate authority of natural science, especially physics, in our culture, it would be sufficient to demonstrate that although natural science can tell us the truth about the causal powers of nature, it does not have special access to the truth about ultimate reality. This is exactly what Martin Heidegger attempts to show.

Many interpreters, however, understand Heidegger as holding the instrumentalist view that scientific entities are social constructions essentially related to human purposes, or else a form of operationalism equating scientific entities with their intraworldly effects or measurements. Such forms of antirealism, as Arthur Fine puts it, "accept the behaviorist idea that the working practices of conceptual exchange exhaust the meaning of the exchange, giving it its significance and providing it with its content."[3] But Heidegger never concluded from the fact that our practices are necessary for *access* to theoretical entities that these entities must be *defined in terms of* our access practices. I will seek to show that in *Being and Time* Heidegger is what

[1]Evelyn Fox Keller, "The Gender/Science System: or, Is Sex to Gender as Nature Is to Science?" *Hypatia* 2 (Fall 1987): 45.

[2]Andrew Pickering, *Constructing Quarks* (Chicago: University of Chicago Press, 1984).

[3]Arthur Fine, *The Shaky Game: Einstein, Realism and the Quantum Theory* (Chicago: University of Chicago Press, 1986), p. 140. See Joseph Rouse, *Knowledge and Power: Toward a Political Philosophy of Science* (Ithaca: Cornell University Press, 1987), and Mark Okrent, *Heidegger's Pragmatism: Understanding, Being, and the Critique of Metaphysics* (Ithaca: Cornell University Press, 1988). Both these authors seem to think that Heidegger holds or should hold that the entities scientists discover are defined in terms of the practices that disclose them.

one might call a minimal hermeneutic realist concerning nature and the objects of natural science, and that he remained such in his later work, even when he became severely critical of the understanding of being underlying scientific research and technology.

To begin with, Heidegger is not an instrumentalist. Unlike the pragmatists, Heidegger accepts the Greek view that human beings are capable of a mood of pure wonder in which they can form theories that do not have any necessary relation to their needs and purposes. In his course on Kant, contemporaneous with the publication of *Being and Time*, Heidegger describes scientific discipline (*Wissenschaft*) as follows:

> *Scientific* knowing presupposes that existing Dasein[4] takes as a freely chosen task the revealing of the entity it approaches *for the sake of revealing it*. . . . Thereby are discontinued all behavioral goals which aim at the application of the uncovered and known; and all those boundaries fall away that confine the investigation within planned technical purposes—the struggle is solely directed to the entity itself and solely in order to free it from its hiddenness and precisely thereby to help it into what is proper to it, i.e. to let it be the entity which it is in itself.[5]

Heidegger remained an anti-instrumentalist in this sense all his life. In 1954 he wrote: "Even where, as in modern atomic physics, theory—for essential reasons—necessarily becomes the opposite of direct viewing, its aim is to make atoms exhibit themselves for sensory perception, even if this self-exhibiting of elementary particles happens only very indirectly and in a way that technically involves a multiplicity of intermediaries."[6]

To understand Heidegger's position, it helps to compare it to a view recently defended by Fine. Fine starts with the observation that the scientist "believes in the existence of those entities to which his theories refer."[7] He calls this the Natural Ontological Attitude (NOA). In this attitude, he tells us, one "accepts the evidence of

---

[4]*Dasein* in colloquial German can mean "everyday human existence." The best way to understand what Heidegger means by *Dasein* is to think of our term "human being," which can refer to a way of being that is characteristic of all people, or to a specific person—a human being.

[5]Martin Heidegger, *Gesamtausgabe*, vol. 25 (Frankfurt: Vittorio Klossman, 1977), p. 2.

[6]Martin Heidegger, "Science and Reflection," *The Question Concerning Technology and Other Essays* (New York: Harper & Row, 1977), p. 173.

[7]Fine, *The Shaky Game*, p. 130.

one's senses [with regard to the existence and features of everyday objects] and . . . accepts, *in the same way,* the confirmed results of science.''[8] He then adds:

> NOA helps us to see that realism differs from various antirealisms in this way: realism adds an *outer* direction to NOA, that is, the external world and the correspondence relation of approximate truth; antirealisms add an *inner* direction, that is, human-oriented reductions of truth, or concepts, or explanations. NOA suggests that the legitimate features of these additions are already contained in the presumed equal status of everyday truths with scientific ones, and in our accepting them both as *truths.* No other additions are legitimate, and none are required.[9]

Heidegger, like Fine, wants to remain true to the understanding in scientific background practices—whatever scientists take for granted in their scientific activity. Let us call this view hermeneutic realism. Hermeneutic realists hold that scientists' background realism cannot be used to *justify* the claim that the objects of science exist independently of the activity of the scientists, nor can this understanding *dictate* what methods or operating assumptions a science must accept. Rather, the role of the hermeneutic philosopher of science is (1) to spell out what everyday scientific practice takes for granted—in the case of natural science, that there is a nature independent of us and that current science is giving us a better and better explanation of how that nature works, and (2) to show that the self-understanding of the science is both internally coherent and compatible with the ontological implications of our everyday practices.

According to the hermeneutic realist, the background realism of natural science is compatible with neither metaphysical realism nor antirealism. Scientists work within social practices that neither they nor philosophers can transcend, so science cannot justify a metaphysical realism that claims to have an *argument* that there is a nature in itself, and that science is converging on the one true account of this independent reality. Yet scientists take for granted they *can* discover the truth about nature as it is independent of scientific practices, so antirealism in the form of metaphysical idealism or of instrumentalism is also unacceptable.

In *The Basic Problems of Phenomenology* Heidegger makes an ontological place for the realistic view that besides the way nature shows up

[8]Ibid., p. 127.
[9]Ibid., p. 133.

in our world there is a way nature is in itself whether or not *Dasein* exists.

> An example of an intraworldly entity is nature. It is indifferent in this connection how far nature is or is not scientifically uncovered, indifferent whether we think this being in a theoretical, physico-chemical way or think of it in the sense in which we speak of "nature out there", hill, woods, meadow. . . . Nonetheless, intraworldliness does not belong to nature's being. Rather, in commerce with this being, nature in the broadest sense, we understand that this being *is* as something occurrent[10] . . . which on its own part always already is. It is, even if we do not uncover it, without our encountering it within our world. Being within the world *devolves upon* this being, nature, solely when it is *uncovered* as a being.[11]

Heidegger's hermeneutic realism concerning natural entities such as trees and dinosaurs and presumably even quarks is also evident in *Being and Time*: "Entities *are*, quite independently of the experience by which they are disclosed, the acquaintance in which they are discovered, and the grasping in which they nature is ascertained" (p. 228).[12] But this passage continues: "being 'is' only in the understanding of those entities to whose being something like an understanding of being belongs" (p. 228). It seems that although natural entities are independent of us, the being of nature depends upon us. "It must be stated that the entity as an entity is 'in itself' and independent of any apprehension of it; yet, the being of the entity is found only in encounter and can be explained, made understandable, only from the phenomenal exhibition and interpretation of the structure of encounter.[13] The basic point Heidegger wants to make—that nature *is* in itself and yet it is illegitimate to ask about "being" in itself—

---

[10]I have modified all translations. The terms *Zuhandenheit* and *Vorhandenheit* are standardly translated as "readiness-to-hand" and "presence-at-hand." These are the ways of being of equipment in use and of objects merely contemplated, respectively. "Availableness" and "occurrentness" convey a better sense of these two ways of being. The entities that have these ways of being are called "available" and "occurrent."

[11]Martin Heidegger, *The Basic Problems of Phenomenology* (Bloomington: Indiana University Press, 1982), pp. 168–69.

[12]Page references to Martin Heidegger, *Being and Time*, trans. John Macquarrie and Edward Robinson (New York: Harper & Row, 1962), will appear in parentheses after the quotation.

[13]Martin Heidegger, *The History of the Concept of Time* (Bloomington: Indiana University Press, 1985), p. 217.

is summed up in two paradoxical propositions: "1) Beings are in themselves the kinds of entities they are, and in the way they are, even if . . . Dasein does not exist. 2) Being "is" not, but there is being, insofar as Dasein exists."[14]

Getting this point sorted out requires getting clear about how Heidegger is using his terms. Only *Dasein* makes sense of things. So the intelligibility of each kind of thing, or the understanding of the way of being of each, including natural things, depends upon *Dasein*. But nature as *a* being, or as an ensemble of beings, need not depend on us, for one way *Dasein* can make sense of things—find them intelligible—is as occurrent, that is, as not related to our everyday practices. As Heidegger says succinctly: "The cosmos can be without human beings inhabiting the earth, and the cosmos was long before human beings ever existed."[15]

Occurrent beings are revealed when *Dasein* takes a detached attitude toward things and decontextualizes them—in Heidegger's terms, deworlds them. Then things show up as independent of human purposes and even as independent of human existence. Deworlding takes place in two stages. First, we use skills and instruments to decontextualize things and their properties, which then appear as meaningless objects, colors, shapes, sounds, and so forth. Such data are independent of our purposes but not independent of our senses. We then invent theories in which the occurrent data are taken up as evidence for quasars and quarks and other entities we cannot directly experience. These theoretical entities need not conform at all to our everyday understanding of objects, space, time, and causality. Yet our current theory tells us that these entities belong to natural kinds—types of things in nature like water, gold, iron, and so forth—and if correct, the theory describes the causal powers of these natural kinds. There is no way to stand outside current science and give it metaphysical support by arguing that there must be natural kinds or that these are what our science must be about. All that hermeneutic phenomenology can do is show the coherence of the natural scientist's current practices for dealing with natural kinds as the way nature is in itself.

Of course, this understanding is achieved by human beings. If it were not for *Dasein* as a clearing in which entities could be encountered, the question of whether there could be entities independent

---

[14]Ibid., p. 153.

[15]Martin Heidegger, *The Metaphysical Foundations of Logic* (Bloomington: Indiana University Press, 1984), p. 169.

of *Dasein* could not be asked, and more important, without *Dasein's* giving meaning to the occurrent way of being, the question would not even make sense. However, since human beings do exist and have an understanding of occurrentness as a way of being, we can make sense of the questions, What was here before we started to exist? and even, What would be left of nature if *Dasein* ceased to exist or *had never existed*? Indeed, the counterfactuals licensed by scientific laws require us to take such questions as legitimate.

Still, we must ask our questions from within that understanding of being that alone gives sense to the questions. We cannot meaningfully ask, What would have been the case if *Dasein had never existed*? if by that we mean, if the above questions made no sense? That would be to treat being—intelligibility—as if it were in itself. When Heidegger considers this move, he warns: "Of course only as long as Dasein *is* (that is, only as long as an understanding of being is ontically possible), 'is there' being. When Dasein does not exist, 'independence' 'is' not either, nor 'is' the 'in-itself' " (p. 255). There is no intelligibility in itself. We cannot ask whether things were intelligible before we were around, or if they would go on being intelligible if we ceased to exist. Intelligibility is not a property of things; it is relative to *Dasein*. When *Dasein* does not exist, things are neither intelligible nor unintelligible. If *Dasein* does not exist, entities are not revealed as anything, not even as occurrent. *"In such a case* it cannot be said that entities are, nor can it be said that they are not. But *now*, as long as there is an understanding of being and therefore an understanding of occurrentness, it can indeed be said that *in this case* entities will still continue to be [i.e., be occurrent]" (p. 255; my gloss in brackets). Since we do exist and make sense of entities as occurrent, we can make sense of things as being independent of us, even though this mode of intelligibility, that is, this understanding of being, like any other depends on us. In short, making sense of reality as independent is something that we do, but what there independently is does not depend on us. "The fact that reality is ontologically grounded in the being of Dasein, does not signify that only when Dasein exists and as long as Dasein exists, can the real be as that which in itself it is" (p. 255).

If we encountered entities only in using them, never in detachedly reflecting on them, so that *availableness* was the only way of being we knew, we would not be able to make the notion of entities in themselves intelligible. But since we understand *occurrentness*, we can understand that occurrent entities would have been even if *Dasein* had never existed. Indeed, given our understanding of occurrentness, we *must* understand things this way. An example will help us to see the importance of the contrast between the available and the occurrent here. What it is to be a hammer essentially depends upon *Dasein* and its cultural artifacts. It belongs to the being of a hammer that it is used to pound in nails for building houses, and so forth. In a culture that always tied things together, there could be no hammers, because there would be nothing that it was to be a hammer. But there could, nonetheless, be pieces of wood with iron blobs on the end, since wood and iron are natural kinds, and their being and causal powers make no essential reference to human purposes.

Joseph Rouse, in defense of what he takes to be Heidegger's social constructivism, argues convincingly that what counts as an electron and even what counts as a physical cause depends on current scientific instruments and practices. Heidegger would agree. He would of course further agree that once our practices define what counts as an X, we must still determine whether there are any Xs. Heidegger would even accept that if the Xs in question are available like hammers, then when we find out that there are Xs, we find entities that exist only relative to our practices. He would point out, however, that if what counts as an X has occurrentness as its way of being, then when we find that there are Xs, we find at the same time that these Xs exist independently of us and of our scientific instruments and practices. This is what Heidegger means when he says, "Intraworldliness does not belong to the essence of occurrent things as such, but it is only the transcendental condition . . . for the possibility of occurrent things being able to emerge as they are."[16]

In the years immediately following the publication of *Being and Time* Heidegger suggests that the "evidence" that there is a nature independent of us is provided not by science but by anxiety. Joseph Fell points out that in a footnote in *The Essence of Reasons* Heidegger claims that "nature is primordially manifest in Dasein because Dasein exists as attuned and affected in the midst of beings," and, in *What is Metaphysics,* he adds that anxiety "discloses beings in their full but heretofore concealed strangeness as the pure other."[17]

---

[16]Heidegger, *Basic Problems,* p. 194.

[17]See Martin Heidegger, *The Essence of Reasons* (Evanston, Ill.: Northwestern University Press, 1969), p. 83, and "What Is Metaphysics?" *Basic Writings* (New York: Harper & Row, 1977), p. 105, quoted by Joseph Fell in "The Familiar and the Strange: On the Limits of Praxis in the Early Heidegger," in *Heidegger: A Critical Reader,* ed. H. Dreyfus and H. Hall (Cambridge, Mass.: Basil Blackwell, 1991).

Such pronouncements must have been taken to be reminiscent of Fichte, according to whom the ego *posits* nature as its pure other, for in his book on Schelling, Heidegger feels called upon to repudiate the idea that pure otherness is a meaning given by human beings.

> *Being & Time* has also among other things been equated with Fichte's basic position and interpreted by it, whereas if there is any possibility of comparison at all here, the most extreme opposition is dominant. But "opposition" is already false since the thinking in *Being & Time* is not just "realistic" in contrast to the unconditional "egoistic" idealism of Fichte. . . . According to Fichte the ego throws forth the world . . . according to *Being & Time* . . . *Da-sein* is the thrown.[18]

Dasein is presumably thrown into nature, and the nature *Dasein* is thrown into need not be thought of as an unstructured, viscous being-in-itself, as in Sartre. Anxiety reveals nature as pure otherness, but this does not imply that nature has no ontic structure.

Still, there is a further problem that makes Heidegger seem to be, if not a Fichtian, at least a Kantian, idealist. Since time, understood as a sequence of nows, before and after some present now, depends upon *Dasein*'s temporality, it might seem to follow that nature cannot be in time. Heidegger seems to assert as much when he says, "There is no nature-time, since all time belongs essentially to Dasein."[19] And he repeats this claim as late as 1935: "Strictly speaking we cannot say: There was a time when man *was* not. At all *times* man was and is and will be, because time temporalizes itself only insofar as man is."[20] This, however, still leaves open the possibility that, just as in the case of spatiality "the homogeneous space of nature shows itself only when the entities we encounter are discovered in such a way that the worldly character of the available gets specifically deprived of its worldliness" (p. 147), so when temporality is detemporalized, a pure sequence of natural events would remain. In his discussion of space Heidegger adds: "The fact that space essentially shows itself in a world is not yet decisive for the kind of being which it possesses. It need not have the kind of being characteristic of something which is itself spatially available or occurrent" (p. 147). Likewise, natural time need not even be occurrent; still, some sort of pure sequential

[18]Martin Heidegger, *Schelling's Treatise on the Essence of Human Freedom* (Athens, Ohio: Ohio University Press, 1985), pp. 187–88.

[19]Heidegger, *Basic Problems*, p. 262.

[20]Martin Heidegger, *Introduction to Metaphysics* (New York: Doubleday, 1961), p. 71.

ordering of events might well remain. This would allow us to make sense of what Heidegger calls the Cosmos and of a nature in itself revealed by science. Perhaps these unresolved tensions were troubling Heidegger when, in a 1929 lecture, he admitted: "The question of the extent to which one might conceive the interpretation of Dasein as temporality in a universal-ontological way is a question which I myself am not able to decide—one which is still completely unclear to me."[21]

Whatever Heidegger's answer, it must not contradict his claim that natural entities do not depend for their structure upon the world or upon human temporality. As Heidegger says in *Basic Problems*: "Occurrent things are . . . the kinds of things they are, even if they do not become intraworldly, even if world-entry does not happen to them and there is no occasion for it at all."[22] After all, we do know substantive facts about nature. We know not only that dinosaurs existed, but that they were born, grew up, and died. That is why Heidegger calls nature "the cosmos" and not X or the thing in itself.

If it allows a sequence of natural events, Heidegger's account is compatible with holding that science is converging on getting it right about natural kinds like gold and water and their causal powers.[23] But even though Heidegger presumably thinks that physical science is progressing in its understanding of physical nature, he does not think that this progress shows that the scientific approach to reality is the only right one, or even that physical science has the right approach to nature. In his lectures of 1928 he remarks: "Beings have stages of discoverability, diverse possibilities in which they manifest themselves in themselves. . . . One cannot say that, for example, physics has the genuine knowledge of the solar sphere, in contrast to our natural grasp of the sun."[24]

Thus even though Heidegger is a realist with respect to the entities discovered by natural science, he is not a physicalist, reductionist, or materialist. He argues at length in Sections 19, 20, and 21 of *Being and Time* that worldliness, and *Dasein*'s correlative ability to make ways of being intelligible and thus to disclose beings, cannot be un-

[21]Heidegger, *The Metaphysical Foundations of Logic*, p. 210.

[22]Heidegger, *Basic Problems*, p. 194.

[23]If these kinds of things turn out not to have the properties predicted and the natural kind terms referring to them have to be dropped from the lexicon of science, as phlogiston was, then some other system of natural kind terms might, in principle, still be found which do refer to the natural kinds there really are—although, of course, we would never know for certain we had the final account.

[24]Heidegger, *The Metaphysical Foundations of Logic*, p. 167.

derstood in terms of the occurrent, and that therefore the occurrent, even recontextualized in a successful science of nature, cannot provide the fundamental building blocks of reality. A theory of the causal power of natural kinds tells us only what is *causally* real; it cannot account for *Dasein*'s ability to make intelligible various ways of being, thereby disclosing various beings including the entities described by physical science. Thus science cannot be a theory of *ultimate* reality. This is Heidegger's reason for rejecting all forms of *metaphysical* realism. "Realism tries to explain reality ontically by real connections of interaction between things that are real. . . . [But] being can never be explained by entities but is already that which is 'transcendental' for every entity" (p. 251). Thus he can say:

> If we consider the work of Descartes in relation to the constitution of the mathematical sciences of nature and to the elaboration of mathematical physics in particular, these considerations then naturally assume a fundamentally positive significance. But if they are regarded in the context of a general theory of the reality of the world, it then becomes apparent that from this point on the fateful constriction of the inquiry into reality sets in, which to the present day has not yet been overcome.[25]

Heidegger further holds that modern science is not even the only way of revealing nature. If, like Aristotle, one wants to relate a wide variety of phenomena rather than to predict and control them, one may find final causes rather than the sort of causal powers discovered by modern physics. Thus there may be only one right answer to the search for physical causes, but many different projections can reveal nature as it is in itself.

> What is represented by physics is indeed nature itself, but undeniably it is only nature as the object-area, whose objectness is first defined and determined through the refining that is characteristic of physics and is

---

[25]Heidegger, *The History of the Concept of Time*, pp. 184–85. Alexander Nehamas finds what I take to be Heidegger's view of science already in Nietzsche. "[Nietzsche] does not object to science itself . . . but rather to an interpretation which refuses to acknowledge that science itself is an interpretation in the sense that it provides a revisable description of a part of the world which is no more [ultimately] real than any other. The problem has been that the methods of science have been assumed to be better than any others, and its objects have been considered to be more real or ultimate than anything else. Nietzsche attacks only this privileging of the methods and objects of science and not its methods or objects themselves." A. Nehamas, *Nietzsche: Life as Literature* (Cambridge: Harvard University Press, 1985), p. 65.

expressly set forth in that refining. Nature, in its objectness for modern physical science, is only *one* way in which what presences—which from of old has been named *physis* —reveals itself.[26]

Heidegger would thus deny that modern physics has found *the* right vocabulary for describing nature so that its vocabulary could be used for a foundational ontology. This, I presume, is the meaning of his Kuhn-like remark in 1938:

[We cannot] say that the Galilean doctrine of freely falling bodies is true and that Aristotle's teaching, that light bodies strive upward, is false; for the Greek understanding of the essence of body and place and of the relation between the two rests upon a different interpretation of entities and hence conditions a correspondingly different kind of seeing and questioning of natural events. No one would presume to maintain that Shakespeare's poetry is more advanced than that of Aeschylus. It is still more impossible to say that the modern understanding of whatever is, is more correct than that of the Greeks.[27]

Here Heidegger is obviously trying to counter the claim that Galileo has refuted Aristotle. He is doing so, not as Kuhn does, by holding that neither theory is true of nature, but rather by holding that *both* are true. This could be the innocuous observation that both are "illuminating," but in the context of the remark just quoted that "what is represented by physics is indeed nature itself," it must be the stronger claim that different theories can reveal different aspects of nature. Of course, if one thinks of Aristotle's theory of natural place as an account of *physical* causality meant to explain, for example, why rocks fall, in the same sense that modern physics claims to explain the same phenomenon, this position is untenable. As an account of physical causality, modern physics, as far as we know, is right and Aristotle is simply wrong. Heidegger, however, clearly holds that Aristotle and Galileo were asking *different kinds of questions,* and so the answer each gives could be right about a different aspect of nature.

If one is interested neither in physical causality nor in final causes but prefers to recontextualize the occurrent in a theory about the cosmic mind, that might be true, too. It would not give one control of nature nor a way of finding one's interests reflected in the cosmos,

[26]Heidegger, "Science and Reflection," pp. 173–74.
[27]Martin Heidegger, "The Age of the World Picture," *The Question Concerning Technology and Other Essays,* p. 117.

but it might give one an insight into enlightenment. Likewise, if one does not want to base one's account of ultimate reality on our ability to decontextualize, but, like the Navajo, one is able to see the everyday world as sacred or full of gods (as long as these are not thought of as having physical powers), that might well allow sacred beings to show up.[28] Physics does not show Buddhism or the Navajo to be wrong, nor does it contradict Christianity. It can have no view on the ultimate meaning of reality. The ultimate *physical* power might well reside in quarks, but the ultimate *saving* power, for example, might be the Christ. The physical properties of iron are essential for making effective hammers but are irrelevant when it comes to making powerful crucifixes.

What counts as real for a culture depends upon the interpretation in its practices, but this does not make what is thus understood any less real. Where ultimate reality is concerned, later Heidegger could be called a *plural realist*. For a plural realist there is no point of view from which one can ask and answer the metaphysical question concerning the one true nature of ultimate reality. Given the dependence of the intelligibility of all ways of being on *Dasein*'s being the question makes no sense. But does this not lead us back to antirealism? No. A plural realist looks like an idealist or a relativist only if one thinks that only one system of description could correspond to the way things really are. For Heidegger, however, as we have seen, different understandings of being reveal different realities or domains of intelligibility, and since no one way of revealing is exclusively true, accepting one does not commit us to rejecting the others. There is a deep similarity between Heidegger and Donald Davidson on this point. Both would agree that if we are right in our claims about reality under various descriptions, then what we are right about has whatever properties it has even if these descriptions are not reducible to a single description, and both would further agree that physical reality has whatever properties it has whether we describers and our ways of describing things exist or not.[29]

[28]The way of being of the sacred is neither the way of being of equipment defined by its place in an equipmental whole, nor is it the way of being of the occurrent defined by its nonrelation to cultural practices. Heidegger notes in *Being and Time* that "perhaps even availableness and equipment have nothing to contribute as ontological clues in interpreting the primitive world; and certainly the ontology of thinghood does even less" (p. 113). Later, Heidegger develops this idea in his account of the ways of being of the sacred, of things, and of works of art. See, e.g., "The Origin of the Work of Art," *Poetry, Language, Thought* (New York: Harper & Row, 1971).

[29]See Donald Davidson, "Mental Events," in *Essays on Actions and Events* (New York: Oxford University Press, 1980).

Just as different cultural practices free different aspects of nature, so they free different sorts of cultural entities. Such historical entities have their own ontological status. Their way of being is not the de-worlded being of the occurrent.

> There are entities . . . to whose being intraworldliness belongs in a certain way. Such entities are all those we call *historical* entities . . . all the things that the human being, who is historical and exists historically in the strict and proper sense, creates, shapes, cultivates: all his culture and works. Beings of this kind *are* only or, more exactly, arise only and come into being only *as* intraworldly Culture *is* not in the way that nature is.[30]

Of course, not just any cultural interpretation will disclose entities. If, instead of encountering heroes or saints, a culture begins to develop practices for encountering aliens that are round and give out beams of light, it may well be that nothing will show up at all. But there are no clear limits as to what kinds of cultural entities can be encountered. In physical science, however, there seems to be one right answer as far as physical causality is concerned. Radically different theories than those proposed by modern science presumably would not reveal physical causal powers. Heidegger notes this difference between a cultural and a scientific interpretation: "The spiritual . . . offers less resistance than in the field of natural science, where nature immediately takes its revenge on a wrongheaded approach."[31] This sentence suggests how Heidegger would respond to scientific relativists like Richard Rorty who scoff at the idea of science's learning nature's own language. Granted that we can never completely decontextualize our data and that therefore our scientific theories are always to some extent parasitical upon our cultural practices and language, still, once we discover that we have practices that can reveal meaningless occurrent data divorced from reference to our purposes, we can use recontextualization in theories to distance our scientific theories further and further from the everyday world. Our Newtonian theories seemed to reveal a universe similar to our everyday experience of occurrent space and time, but our interaction with nature has led us to replace these theories with relativistic and quantum indeterministic theories. It is as if nature *is* teaching the natural scientist, not *nature's own language*, since only a Platonist thinks that

---

[30]Heidegger, *Basic Problems*, p. 169.
[31]Heidegger, *The History of the Concept of Time*, p. 203.

representations exist independently of meaningful practices, but, rather, nature is leading natural scientists to improve *their* language for representing her under an objectified aspect.

In any case, as we have noted, once we have established what counts as real, we must still find out what specific things there are. The Greeks stood in awe of the gods their practices revealed, and we have to *discover* the elementary particles—we do not construct them. The understanding of being establishes what can count as a fact in whatever domain, but it does not determine what the facts are. As Heidegger says: "Being (not beings) is dependent upon the understanding of being; that is to say, reality (not the real) is dependent upon care [i.e., *Dasein*]" (p. 255).

Heidegger thus holds a subtle and plausible position beyond metaphysical realism and antirealism. *Nature* is whatever it is and has whatever causal properties it has independently of us. Different questions, such as Aristotle's and Galileo's, reveal different natural kinds and different kinds of causal properties. Different cultural interpretations of reality reveal different aspects of the real, too. But there is no right answer to the question, What is the ultimate reality in terms of which everything else becomes intelligible? The only answer to this metaphysical question is that *Dasein*, because it is the source of sense and so of the understanding of being and of reality, is the being in terms of whose practices all aspects of the real show up.

Heidegger's emphasis on scientific practices is remarkably similar to Kuhn's in *The Structure of Scientific Revolutions*, but they draw opposed conclusions from their shared insights. For Kuhn, once one sees that the background practices determine what counts as true, it looks as if truth must be relative to current scientific practices, so there can be no truth about how things are in themselves. Kuhn argues persuasively in his Sherman lectures[32] that a given scientific lexicon of natural kind terms determines what can count as true, so that for Aristotle, for example, it was true that the sun was a planet and that there could not be a void, whereas for us, Aristotle's assertions are neither true nor false because "planet" and "void" have different meanings in the lexicon of modern science. Kuhn concludes that in general the assertions picking out the sort of things taken to exist at each stage of a science can be true at that stage, but are neither true nor false at some other stage in some other system of

---

[32]Thomas Kuhn, "Sherman Memorial Lectures," University College, London, November 23–25, 1987, unpublished.

terms. Thus assertions are never true of things as they are in themselves.

Heidegger would, I think, agree with Kuhn's elegant argument that true statements in science can be made only relative to a lexicon. But the strong relativistic claim that no lexicon can be true of physical reality does not follow from the fact of incommensurate lexicons. Nor does relativism follow from Heidegger's acknowledgment that our practices are a more primordial form of truth that makes truth as agreement possible. On the contrary, it follows from Heidegger's account that several incompatible lexicons can be true, that is to say, agree with how things are in themselves. In each case there is something the theory claims to be true of, and in each case the theory either points out its referent as it is in itself or it is false. As Heidegger notes, once we see that Newton's laws are true, we see that they were true at the time of Aristotle. Conversely, if Aristotle's terms successfully picked out natural kinds (relative to final causes), his account is still true today.

Why doesn't Kuhn share this conclusion? Perhaps because he implicitly accepts the traditional view that in principle only one lexicon can point out the kinds in nature, and, since he has discovered that relative to different lexicons incompatible theoretical assertions count as true, he concludes that none can correspond to how things are in themselves. For Heidegger, on the contrary, as finite beings capable of discovering truth, we work out many perspectives—many lexicons—and thus reveal many ways things as they are in themselves. And just because we can reveal things from many perspectives, no single perspective can be *the* right one.

We can conclude by comparing Heidegger and Rorty once again, since their views on metaphysical realism are strikingly similar. Both argue that the real can show up differently given different practices (vocabularies, Rorty would say), and neither wants to allow that there is a way that ultimate reality is in itself so that there is a privileged description that founds all the others. Anyone who claims to have a description of ultimate reality claims a point of view outside of all particular, finite interpretations, and both Heidegger and Rorty think, given their understanding of understanding, that the very idea of such an interpretation-free understanding of what ultimately is does not make sense. But Rorty thinks that this is an argument against accepting even a minimal hermeneutic realism where natural science is concerned, whereas Heidegger shows how one can reject the claim that there is *a* correct description of reality and still hold that there can be *many* correct descriptions, including a correct causal description of objectified physical nature. Natural science can be getting it righter and righter about how things *work* even if there is no one right answer to how things *are*.

CHAPTER 3

Interpretation in Natural and Human Science

JOSEPH ROUSE

In recent years there has been considerable controversy over whether the notion of interpretation, and the hermeneutic circle that interpretation invokes, belong distinctively to the human sciences. An influential tradition in the philosophy of social science, going back at least to Wilhelm Dilthey and Max Weber, insists that what calls for interpretation in the strong sense is human action. Interpretation is necessary, according to this tradition, because actions (including speech acts) are meaningful, and their identity and significance as actions can be disclosed only by uncovering and clarifying the meaning expressed by or through those actions. The meaningfulness of action has been variously situated in actors' intentions, rules constitutive of their behavior, background practices that provide the context within which action is intelligible, and so forth. All such views, however, suggest important methodological and epistemological differences between human and natural science, along with ontological differences in kind between nature and the "social world."

This hermeneutic tradition in the philosophy of the social sciences acquired new momentum from the widespread criticism since the late 1950s of positivist demands for unity of method throughout the sciences; indeed, its defenders prominently contributed to the critique of positivism. Nevertheless, the critique of positivism also generated controversy about the epistemological locus of interpretation,

An earlier version of this paper was presented at LaSalle University, 11 February 1989, to a Conference on the Human Studies sponsored by the Greater Philadelphia Philosophy Consortium.

for prevailing accounts of the natural sciences were also radically revised. A number of prominent philosophers, most notably Thomas Kuhn, Richard Rorty, and Mary Hesse, noted deep similarities between the image of natural science emerging from the critique of positivism and the various accounts of interpretive social science. Postpositivist philosophy of science thus threatened to abolish any fundamental differences between natural and human science, or between nature and society as objects of knowledge. Defenders of hermeneutic social science responded quickly by proposing important differences between the interpretation of nature and the interpretation of human beings, differences that were thought to restore the alleged methodological and ontological distinctions between two kinds of science.

I have argued extensively elsewhere that no such interesting differences in kind between natural and human science can be sustained on the basis of a need to interpret meaningful action that is absent from our dealings with the natural world.[1] I am led to further discussion of the issue by reflecting on two features of these debates. First, the views of some critics of the natural science–human science distinction, such as Thomas Kuhn and myself, are substantially indebted to the work of its defenders, notably, Charles Taylor and Hubert Dreyfus. The very arguments that are supposed to establish the uniqueness of the human sciences have contributed to our accounts of natural science, thereby further undercutting the distinction. Second, Rorty and Kuhn, while giving up the attempt to distinguish the human sciences as hermeneutical, have nevertheless tried to retain the idea that hermeneutics, or "hermeneutic interpretation" in Kuhn's phrase, is distinct from other forms of inquiry. I think this distinction is also untenable; ironically, Charles Taylor's account of interpretation helps us see why this is so.

I would like to begin by outlining what I take to be the important areas of disagreement among Taylor, Kuhn, and myself. The most prominent issue, clearly, is whether there is a philosophically interesting difference in kind between the natural and the human sciences. Taylor believes there is such a difference, manifest in the inescapably hermeneutical character of the human sciences. The crucial turn in his version of the claim is that the objects of the human sciences are *essentially* self-interpreting agents for whom their actions

[1] Joseph Rouse, *Knowledge and Power: Toward a Political Philosophy of Science* (Ithaca: Cornell University Press, 1987), esp. chap. 6.

are significant, whereas the natural sciences deal with objects that need not be, indeed should not be, understood as self-interpreting. Thus, even if one wanted to say that the natural sciences were interpretive in some sense, one would have to conclude that the human sciences are *doubly* interpretive, interpretations of interpretations. Taylor goes on to argue that this difference restores the important methodological and epistemological differences between natural and human science.

Thomas Kuhn's investigations of the historical development of the natural sciences have led him to question Taylor's way of drawing this distinction. Kuhn has figured most prominently among those philosophers and historians who have reminded us that we never encounter the natural world unmediated by previous understanding. Our knowledge of nature is a response to prior knowledge and the successes and failures it engendered. The result is that there are conflicts of interpretation over such things as voltaic cells, classical resonators or quantum oscillators, and chemical reactions that parallel the interpretive issues which Taylor thinks characteristic of human activity alone. The reason is straightforward: cells, oscillators, and reactions belong to a meaningful field of human activity, with a history, and a significance that cannot be disentangled from that history. Making sense of these objects and their interactions is inextricable from understanding scientific practices.

This initial disagreement points to a second issue lurking behind the dispute over the natural and the human sciences, namely, the question of realism. Take realism to be the view that beliefs within some domain are true or false depending upon the real properties of objects in that domain, that is, properties they possess regardless of anyone's beliefs, practices, or standards. Taylor wants to be a realist in this sense about the objects of natural science, even while insisting that a realist construal of "social reality" is unintelligible. Kuhn, of course, has mounted a powerful attack upon realism in the natural sciences, with his insistence upon the incommensurability of competing scientific practices and standards, and his denial that we can make any sense of what the world is "really" like independently of any reference to a history of scientific interpretation.

On these first two conflicts, Kuhn and I line up on one side, and Charles Taylor on the other. There is, however, a third issue among us on which the lines do not show up quite so neatly. This issue concerns whether there is an epistemologically distinct activity appropriately called "interpretation," which is characteristic of some activities or disciplines rather than others. Taylor insists that despite the sense in which the natural sciences involve interpretation because data are always theory laden, there is a stronger sense in which interpretation is specific to the human sciences. He has memorably objected to the currency of more expansive accounts of interpretation, ironically noting how "old-time Diltheyans, their shoulders hunched from years-long resistance against the encroaching pressure of positivist natural science, suddenly pitch forward on their faces as all opposition ceases to the reign of universal hermeneutics."[2] But Kuhn also believes that there is a distinctive activity of interpretation, which concerns what we do when confronted with texts or practices that are unfamiliar or puzzling. Thus, on Kuhn's view, historians and ethnographers must frequently engage in interpretation, whereas physicists or economists typically do not.[3]

It should not be hard to see that Kuhn and Taylor do not draw the line between interpretive and noninterpretive activities in quite the same place, and they certainly do not do so in the same way. Indeed, it is critical to Taylor's account that interpretation in the human sciences is continuous with interpretation in everyday life, in which meanings need not be explicitly articulated. The human sciences must be interpretive, on Taylor's view, because human beings are already "self-interpreting animals," in just the *same* sense of 'interpretation'. The practices in which we try to get clear about unfamiliar meanings are just a subset of our quite varied interpretive activities. In this dispute I am going to come down on Taylor's side rather than

[2]Charles Taylor, "Understanding in Human Science," *Review of Metaphysics* 34 (1980): 26.

[3]In some ways, Kuhn's distinction resembles Richard Rorty's distinction between hermeneutics and normal discourse (in *Philosophy and the Mirror of Nature* [Princeton: Princeton University Press, 1979], in which normal discourse proceeds within a shared vocabulary and taken for granted epistemic standards, whereas hermeneutics is the attempt to converse across differing standards and vocabularies without reducing them to a common framework. This resemblance should not be surprising, since Rorty's distinction is an extension of Kuhn's earlier notions of normal and revolutionary science. Kuhn's and Rorty's positions are not quite the same, however, because Kuhn thinks that the space of "hermeneutic interpretation" has relatively stable disciplinary boundaries, whereas Rorty takes the boundary between normal and hermeneutical conversations to be contingent upon the evolving history of inquiry. I nevertheless think that Rorty's distinction is vulnerable to the same sorts of arguments I raise against Kuhn. Working this out in detail seems inappropriate here, since Rorty has abandoned this version of the distinction. Criticizing its analogue in his most recent work (*Contingency, Irony, and Solidarity* [Cambridge: Cambridge University Press, 1989]), which is the difference between private irony and liberal hope and solidarity, would take us too far afield of the other concerns of this essay.

Kuhn's, but when Taylor's position is combined with Kuhn's views about realism and the natural sciences, it leads to a denial of there being any epistemically distinctive domain or activity of interpretation. This is a conclusion that I happily endorse, but neither Kuhn nor Taylor is likely to join me in so doing.

A good place to begin discussion of these three issues is with what I have learned from Charles Taylor about the natural sciences, and about the work of Thomas Kuhn. This account will provide an important background to my arguments against Taylor's attempts to preserve some version of Dilthey's difference in kind between the *Geistes-* and the *Naturwissenschaften*. As will become clear, my objections have much more to do with his understanding of the natural sciences than it does with the consequences he thinks this distinction has for the human sciences themselves.

There are three important points that I at least think I learned from the work of Charles Taylor, and that I take to be very important for understanding scientific inquiry. Taylor was not the only possible source for these points, which could undoubtedly be extracted from Ludwig Wittgenstein or Martin Heidegger, but he articulated them more clearly and powerfully than I had seen before. The first point explicitly concerns how to read Kuhn's *Structure of Scientific Revolutions*. Many critics of that book understood Kuhn to be saying that research communities in the natural sciences are, and perhaps ought to be, united by an enforced consensus about fundamental issues of ontology, method, and value. Charles Taylor taught me to see the difference between consensus, an agreement in belief between individuals who each hold that belief separately, and what he once called the sharing of "intersubjective meanings." He had in mind the way in which understanding a common language and participating in the social practices, institutions, and norms associated with that language shape the intelligible possibilities for individual belief and thereby make *either* consensus or dissensus possible. Ever since reading Taylor, I have understood Kuhnian paradigms to be "ways of experiencing action in society which are expressed in the language and descriptions constitutive of institutions and practices."[4] Paradigms, that is, are shared fields of activity rather than shared beliefs.

The second point I took from Taylor is that Kuhn's views do not entail the claim that language is somehow constitutive of the world;

[4]Charles Taylor, "Interpretation and the Sciences of Man," in *Philosophy and the Human Sciences: Philosophical Papers, 2* (Cambridge: Cambridge University Press, 1985), p. 38.

it would be better to say that language and the real are mutually dependent. Taylor pointed me in this direction with his emphasis upon the inseparability of language and social practice. Linguistic distinctions and ways of employing them are embedded in larger contexts of social practice, which in turn could not exist without the appropriate linguistic resources. Taylor took this to mean that one could not characterize "social reality" apart from the language and practices that constitute it, and vice versa. But in the case of scientific inquiry, the relevant practices include ways of encountering, responding to, and being resisted by the things scientists are dealing with. The intertwining of language, social practice, and reality cannot be neatly bounded at the points where we run up against the natural world, for our encounters with the world, and indeed the very boundaries between self and world, belong to our interpretive social practices. I will have more to say about this later.

The third point I learned from Taylor took me in a different direction from anything I found explicitly in Kuhn's work, but it has been very important for my own thinking about the natural sciences. In the extended example that was the focus of "Interpretation and the Sciences of Man," Taylor was concerned to show that an empiricist political science will seriously misunderstand some politically important phenomena when it limits itself to considering only political action identifiable *within* a given configuration of "intersubjective meanings" and "common meanings." Political conflict can occur over the shaping of that field of meaningful action itself. Taylor found this phenomenon exemplified in the 1960s counterculture challenge to "the vision of society as a large-scale enterprise of production," and to the politics of negotiation, which is "bound up with the distinct identity and autonomy of the parties and with the willed nature of their relations."[5] Such conflicts are especially tricky, because the very language in which to characterize what is at issue in the conflict is part of what is at issue. The result is that the conflict is easily misrepresented or trivialized by those who occupy the position of the dominant field of action.

Taylor thought that this was a serious problem with mainstream political science. Such is also the situation, I believe, in the case of feminist, postmodernist, and neo-Romantic criticisms of the dominant culture of "technoscience," to use Bruno Latour's term for that mobilization of social resources that continually breaks down any

[5]Ibid., pp. 46, 32.

boundaries between science and society.[6] There is an understanding of natural science, and of nature as the object of scientific knowledge, that represents not just the consensus of many people within the industrialized West; it shapes what they—we—understand as intelligible possibilities for action. Indeed, the ideals of objectivity and rationality that inform that understanding of science are part of the common meaning through which the dominant community identifies itself to itself. Conflict over such ideals was precisely the sort of conflict that Taylor thought would be obscured unless it was understood hermeneutically.

We can now turn to my more detailed response to Taylor's attempt to preserve an epistemologically significant difference in kind between the natural and the human sciences. There are three lines of argument that I want to develop against Taylor's view. The first is a point I simply take from Thomas Kuhn. Charles Taylor's descriptions of the way in which social reality cannot be identified ''in abstraction from the language we use to describe, invoke, or carry out'' various social practices[7] also aptly characterizes physical reality as the object of natural scientific research. Kuhn reminded us that scientists do not and could not achieve knowledge of things independently of particular historically contingent categories and practices. They always encounter nature as a configuration of significant possibilities for research activities. This is why Kuhn first identified ''normal science'' as a kind of social *practice*, and why he said that ''after discovering oxygen Lavoisier *worked* in a different world.''[8] Taylor thought that the human sciences had to be interpretive because what they were trying to understand was a field of meaningful human action, which was constituted by a shared understanding of what would count as intelligible and significant action within that context. Kuhn insisted that learning how to practice research within a scientific field is very much like being socialized into a culture, while trying as an outsider to understand that research activity *and the world it reveals* is very much like the work of an ethnographer. If it still seems odd to you to think of electrons and tectonic plates as belonging inescapably to social reality in Taylor's sense, remember that the social world on Taylor's account certainly includes the various sorts of equipment that people use in their activities. One cannot make

[6]Bruno Latour, *Science in Action* (Cambridge: Harvard University Press, 1987).
[7]Taylor, ''Interpretation and the Sciences of Man,'' p. 33.
[8]Thomas Kuhn, *The Structure of Scientific Revolutions*, 2d ed. (Chicago: University of Chicago Press, 1970), p. 118.

sense of those activities without understanding what that equipment is, what it is for, and how it is used. Kuhn's argument is that a field of natural scientific research is a work world in which the objects of research are understood as equipment, and they make sense only through the ways we deal with them in research and development.[9] Hence the appropriateness of his famous analogy between scientists who too readily abandon a paradigm in the face of anomaly and carpenters who blame their tools.

Taylor recognizes the affinity between Kuhn's account of the way scientific knowledge is always mediated by previous understanding and his own account of interpretation in the human sciences, but he still insists there is an important difference. As he claimed in response to Richard Rorty, "The understanding which is relevant to the sciences of man is something more than this implicit grasp on things. . . . We are talking here of what you could call human understanding, understanding what makes someone tick, or how he feels or acts as a human being."[10] I will not discuss here the particular way Taylor tries to explicate the relevant difference in understanding in terms of "desirability-characterizations," a point that has been extensively criticized elsewhere. My concern, which makes up my second line of argument, is that however Taylor tries to work out the notion of "understanding a human being," it will not support his point about the natural and human sciences unless there were an extensional correspondence between two distinctions that in fact do not match neatly at all. The boundary between natural and social reality, which also supposedly demarcates the boundary between the objects of natural and human science, needs to match up with the distinction between those areas of inquiry in which our self-understanding as human agents is at issue in the inquiry, and those areas in which it is not. Any such match is at best historically contingent, but I want to argue that it does not occur at all.

We need to remember that drawing the relevant line between the human sciences and the natural sciences is not just a simple matter of ascertaining the objects of the various sciences. Taylor certainly wants to exclude human biology from the interpretive human sciences, and he may well want to include some aspects of primatology or other studies of animal behavior among them. Hence the line depends upon there being a fairly sharp split between the categories

[9]This reading of Kuhn is developed in my *Knowledge and Power*, chap. 2, and extended beyond Kuhn's own treatment in chap. 4.
[10]Taylor, "Understanding in Human Science," p. 30.

in which human action is meaningful, and the categories through which we appear merely as physical objects. The difficulty is that this distinction is itself a contestable point of human self-understanding. Whether there is such a distinction, and where it lies, is inescapably part of our sense of who we are and what it means for us to act. It is no accident that anthropologists study cosmology as an inescapable part of culture. Human beings understand themselves as much through their understanding of nature as anything else. We should also not forget how much the disenchantment of the natural world, the Darwinian account of natural selection, or the turn from qualitative and perfectionist to compositional accounts of substances is integrated into our own self-understanding as agents.

Nor can one try to sustain Taylor's distinction by claiming that the understanding of nature influences our self-understanding, but that nature itself must be understood to be independent of the ways we understand it.[11] Taylor himself attempts such a strategy by insisting upon the importance of what he calls an "absolute" conception of the world, freed from "the meanings it might have for human subjects, or of how it figures in their experience."[12] But the project of such an "absolute" conception is quite remote from what actually goes on in the natural sciences. As Mary Hesse once noted (responding not to Taylor, but to Jürgen Habermas): "It is impossible in studying theories of evolution, ecology, or genetics, to separate a mode of knowledge relating to technical control from a mode relating to the self-understanding of man . . . [since] the very categories of these theories, such as functionality, selection, survival, are infected by man's view of himself."[13] Even the most basic ontological distinctions, for example, between an organism and its environment in evolutionary theory are problematically engaged with our conceptions of individuation and agency.[14] These difficulties are not confined to the biological sciences. Evelyn Fox Keller has suggestively described how the notion that chemical processes are "regulated" or "controlled" by "master molecules" implicates a gendered conception of

[11]I am grateful to William Blattner for showing that I must deal directly with this objection.
[12]Taylor, "Understanding in Human Science," p. 31.
[13]Mary Hesse, *Revolutions and Reconstructions in the Philosophy of Science* (Bloomington: Indiana University Press, 1980), p. 186.
[14]Richard Levins and Richard Lewontin, *The Dialectical Biologist* (Cambridge: Harvard University Press, 1985), part I.

human agency.[15] The attempt to characterize the "state" of a physical system in quantum mechanics and to interpret what it means for a system to have a definite (possibly indeterminate or probabilistic or both) state is likewise difficult to disentangle from our self-conception.[16] The point is not just to suggest that scientific theory is debilitatingly ideological, although that is sometimes the case. Commonly, the opposite point is apropos: natural science proceeds quite well without needing to try to eliminate aspects of our self-understanding from scientific interpretations of the natural world.

An interesting connection between Taylor's view that only the human sciences interpret the self-understanding of human agents and his communitarian political arguments against liberal individual conceptions of the self may help show what is wrong with the former view. Taylor argues that it is a serious mistake to draw the boundaries of the self at a point short of our social relations with others. There are irreducibly social dimensions to our self-understanding, and there are irreducibly social goods that cannot be reduced to individual preferences. Taylor objects, rightly, to those approaches to the human sciences that rule out on methodological grounds the possibility of an irreducibly social dimension to human life, and that regard all of our social relations instrumentally: "the ontology of mainstream social science," he argues, "lacks the notion of meaning as not simply for an individual subject; of a subject who can be a 'we' as well as an 'I'."[17] Yet Taylor is similarly ruling out on methodological grounds the idea that the boundaries of self-understanding extend beyond our social relations in the narrowest sense to encompass our dealings with the natural world.

The result is a remarkably Whiggish interpretation of the history of science since the seventeenth century. On Taylor's view, it was unequivocally progressive to interpret nature as dead and noncommunicative, such that our dealings with it can be only instrumental (of value only with respect to societal "preferences," to maintain the analogy to his critique of liberal individualism). Taylor believes that the further extension of atomistic and mechanistic understanding to a liberal utilitarianism was a mistake, of course, but that has now

---

[15]Evelyn Fox Keller, *Reflections on Gender and Science* (New Haven: Yale University Press, 1985), chap. 8.

[16]Keller (ibid., chap. 7) also offers a useful account of how the issues surrounding the interpretation of the Schrödinger equation display the entanglement of self-understanding and the interpretation of nature.

[17]Taylor, "Interpretation and the Sciences of Man," p. 40.

presumably been exposed. We have now learned to replace the dualism between the mental as the realm of meaning and physical nature as what is unaffected by how it is meant with a more adequate dualism between social practice as the realm of meaningful interpretation and physical nature. Well, maybe. Perhaps we have also learned from the unfortunate political history of the distinction between nature and society, which has been used to justify social hierarchies of race, gender, culture, and class, so that we will no longer make those mistakes. But I remain suspicious of the sort of history of science that Taylor's distinction may compel us to accept.

My suspicions are heightened when I cast about for examples where it would make a difference to follow Taylor in denying that our understanding of nature involves interpretation in his strong sense. I cannot resist beginning with the example Taylor himself offers in defense of his view. Taylor says of traditional Japanese society that "they live under the same heavens as we do, only understand it differently, but it is not true that they have the same kind of bargaining as we do."[18] Perhaps it is just a remediable slip that he takes "living under the heavens" to capture a meaning-independent reality identifiable apart from how we understand our own lives, but I do not think so. I am worried that Taylor's lack of self-consciousness in so regarding that phrase reflects a complacent identification with the ascendancy of a contentious interpretation of science and nature comparable to the 1950s understanding of the ascendancy of liberal pluralism as the "end of ideology."

We can see this in the way Taylor's distinction between the natural and human sciences bears upon some recent intellectual and political controversies. Feminist interpretations of the gendering of scientific knowledge and of nature as the object of such knowledge offer one important group of examples. Taylor's view can accommodate those feminist philosophers and scientists for whom the discovery of gender in science is the discovery of a bias to be eliminated in accord with an unchanged notion of scientific objectivity. But his view rules out on methodological grounds any stronger feminist account of natural scientific knowledge as gendered. Thus, I believe Taylor must reject out of hand the idea, suggested by Nancy Chodorow and Evelyn Fox Keller, that the separation between self and nature, which he thinks essentially characterizes natural science, is the product of male psychodynamics in societies where women nurture infants. He

[18]Ibid., p. 33.

must also reject the idea, put forward in rather different ways by G. H. von Wright and Keller, and illustrated in Keller's example of "master molecules," that causality is not conceptually separable from how we understand ourselves as agents. For it is important to Taylor that efficient causality be a real relation in nature, and not a part of the intersubjective meanings of a particular historical culture. If scientists like Barbara McClintock or the pseudonymous Anna Brito find it appropriate to interpret their understanding of maize or lymphocytes in terms of friendship or love,[19] this must at best be metaphorical or merely psychological. These are not the sorts of interactions that can really be reciprocal relations, so they must be reduced to something else in much the same way the individualist reduces social relations to individual subjective values or preferences. On Taylor's view, such accounts can only concern a kind of attunement to the world that we must regard as separable from theoretical understanding, even if the scientists themselves somehow fail to see this.

A related sort of example is suggested by the various attempts to create an ecological politics that would take noninstrumental relations to the natural world as irreducible goods. Social ecologists, deep ecologists, ecological feminists, Marcusean critical theorists, and perhaps some defenders of animals are engaged in precisely the sort of challenge to the common and intersubjective meanings of our culture that Taylor recognized in the counterculture of the 1960s. To insist that they and their political concerns must be understood within the parameters of the dominant understanding of scientific rationality seems to me comparable to the attempt, which Taylor deplores, to impose the vision of a society of work and the social practices of negotiation as the horizon within which we must make sense of the protests of the 1960s. My point in raising these examples is not to endorse any or all of these views, any more than Taylor wanted unequivocally to endorse the protests of the 1960s. Indeed, the parallel is a strong one. Taylor thought that a social science and social reality constituted by political and methodological individualism was incapable of understanding what was at issue in those debates. I similarly want to argue that a conception of natural science and the natural world constituted by a sharp separation between the social and the natural is incapable of grasping much of our current political

[19]Evelyn Fox Keller, *A Feeling for the Organism* (San Francisco: W. H. Freeman, 1983); June Goodfield, *An Imagined World* (New York: Harper & Row, 1981).

situation. My first line of argument suggested that Taylor's distinction between the human and natural sciences could not accommodate what we have learned from Thomas Kuhn and others about natural science. Now, this second line of argument suggests that the distinction also cannot accommodate the kind of political insight that is rightly associated with the work of Charles Taylor.

There is a third line of argument against Taylor's distinction which I cannot really develop here, but which I want to mention because I think it explains much of the intuitive appeal which that distinction continues to possess. Taylor sees a deep connection between his view of the human sciences and his views about what it is to be a human agent. The human sciences must be interpretive in a stronger sense than is true of the natural sciences, because they have as their objects human agents who are in an important sense constituted by their interpretive activities. A human science that left out of account the self-interpretive dimension of human beings would be radically incomplete or misguided about its own object, whereas this would not be true of the natural sciences. Unfortunately, this argument involves a mistaken inference, which was first brought to my attention by Mark Okrent.[20] From the fact that all human understanding takes place within a field of intersubjective meanings, as Taylor rightly insists, it does not follow that this is a fact about human beings *as objects* which must always be taken into account in the human sciences. The point parallels Kant's Paralogisms of the Soul: conditions on the possibility of knowledge are not facts about knowers now taken as objects of knowledge. The argument from human beings as self-interpreting subjects to the human sciences as interpretive in Taylor's strong sense is a non sequitur.

We can now turn to the last issue I promised to address. There might still be an interesting group of activities that are distinctively "interpretive," even if its boundaries do not map onto those usually drawn between the natural and the human sciences. Kuhn, for example, still holds onto the idea that there is a characteristic activity of interpretation typically engaged in by historians, ethnographers, literary critics, and the like, in their encounters with the unfamiliar. We engage in interpretation in this sense when we try to get inside an alien culture or text, learn our way about, and eventually perhaps explicate what is going on there. This is fundamentally different,

[20]Mark Okrent, "Hermeneutics, Transcendental Philosophy, and Social Science," *Inquiry* 27 (1984): 23–49.

Kuhn wants to argue, from the ways in which we live more or less unproblematically within a culture that is very much our own, including our own scientific cultures.

Taylor helps us to understand what is wrong with this view. He insisted that "already to be a living agent is to experience one's situation in terms of certain meanings; and this in a sense can be thought of as a sort of proto-'interpretation'."[21] The reason for this claim is twofold: first, making sense of one's own culture and even clarifying one's own sense of the situation one is in are more reflective and interpretive than a sharp distinction between understanding familiar and alien meanings would suggest; and second, there is less homogeneity and more room for construal and misconstrual even within a familiar and shared field of activity than is often assumed. After all, it was Thomas Kuhn who taught us that even the shared practices of normal science incorporate multiple interpretations of that practice. Scientists usually "read" one another's work in ways that largely manage to smooth over those differences, and it is not clear why these readings are different in kind from making sense of practices one explicitly recognizes to be puzzling or alien. I am happy to accept the insight that I believe Kuhn is trying to capture, namely, that there are times when it is important to be attentive to the possibility that others are using words or things in ways that do not neatly fit our own assumptions, and other times when we can safely make those assumptions for the time being. But I insist that this difference is a pragmatic one, which does not demarcate real and intrinsic differences between the alien and the familiar; that even this pragmatic difference does not neatly divide disciplines; and that the need to be alert for a possible breakdown of commensurability can sometimes arise in the midst of what we took to be familiar surroundings. There is undoubtedly much more to say on this topic. But I believe the outcome would not fundamentally change: interpretation, characterized by the hermeneutic circle, and the entanglement of understanding with self-understanding, does not demarcate a particular domain of activity or inquiry (or its objects), but is a general characteristic of how things become manifest.

Let me conclude by attempting to head off one serious misunderstanding of what I have been trying to say about the relation between natural and human science. Taylor's defense of a strongly interpretive account of the human sciences was directed against the logical

---

[21]Taylor, "Interpretation and the Sciences of Man," p. 27.

positivists' insistence upon the methodological unity of science, and against the construction of mainstream American social science to accord with positivist demands. So when I reject his view that human and natural science are different in kind, I might be read as resurrecting the view that there is only one kind of science, now perhaps modeled upon the human sciences rather than physics. This would be a mistake. What I am arguing instead is that neither natural nor human science forms a natural kind. There are many interesting and important differences among the various scientific disciplines. Paleontology or meteorology may be as interestingly different from one another and from high-energy physics as they are from macroeconomics or political science. All have been shaped by a history of internal development and interaction with other scientific fields and other social practices. I follow Friedrich Nietzsche in insisting that "only that which has no history is definable"[22]; successful practice in the various sciences always has and will continue to escape the constraints and typologies placed upon them by methodologists armed with the latest account of what a science must be like in order to be successful.

[22]Friedrich Nietzsche, *On the Genealogy of Morals,* trans. Walter Kaufmann and R. J. Hollingdale (New York: Random House, 1967), p. 80.

PART TWO

INTERPRETATION AND EPISTEMOLOGY

CHAPTER 4

Inquiry as Recontextualization: An Anti-Dualist Account of Interpretation

RICHARD RORTY

Think of human minds as webs of beliefs and desires, of sentential attitudes—webs that continually reweave themselves so as to accommodate new sentential attitudes. Do not ask where the new beliefs and desires come from. Forget, for the moment, about the external world, as well as about that dubious interface between self and world called "perceptual experience." Just assume that new ones keep popping up, and that some of them put strains on old beliefs and desires. We call some of these strains "contradictions" and others "tensions." We alleviate both by various techniques. For example, we may simply drop an old belief or desire. Or we may create a whole host of new beliefs and desires in order to encapsulate the disturbing intruder, reducing the strain that the old beliefs and desires put on it and that it puts on them. Or we may just unstitch, and thus erase, a whole range of beliefs and desires—we may stop *having* attitudes toward sentences that use a certain word (a word like "God" or "phlogiston," say).

By a familiar trick, you can treat desires as if they were beliefs. You do this by treating the imperative attitude toward the sentence S "Would that it were the case that S!" as the indicative attitude "It would be better that S should be the case than that not-S should be." So from here on I shall save space by leaving out "and desires" and just talk about beliefs. I can do this with an easier conscience because, as a good pragmatist, I follow Alexander Bain and Charles Peirce in

This paper appears with the permission of Cambridge University Press, publishers of *The Philosophical Papers of Richard Rorty*, vol. 2 (1991).

seeing beliefs as habits of action. That is, I regard beliefs as states attributed to organisms of a certain complexity—attributions that enable the attributor to predict or retrodict (mostly retrodict) the behavior of that organism. So the web of belief should be regarded not just as a self-reweaving mechanism but as one that produces movements in the organism's muscles—movements that kick the organism itself into action. These actions, by shoving items in the environment around, produce new beliefs to be woven in, which in turn produce new actions, and so on for as long as the organism survives.

I say "mechanism" because I want to emphasize that there is no self distinct from this self-reweaving web. All there is to the human self is just that web. To view beliefs as habits of action is to view the self from the outside. So viewed, there is no distinction between mind and body other than the Rylean one between the organism's movements and the interior states of the organism which you need to posit in order to explain and predict those movements. Some of these states are states of muscles or heart or kidneys; others are states of mind. But to call them "mental" is just to say that they are intentional states, which is just to say that they are beliefs.

If one takes this Deweyan stance, one will naturally make a distinction between what John Dewey called "habit" and what he called "inquiry." This is, like all of Dewey's distinctions, one of degree. At one end of a spectrum are situations where minimal reweaving is required—as when one moves one's left hand to pick up the fork, comes to believe that it is not there but rather on the other side of the plate, and so moves one's right hand. The reweaving involved in assimilating the novel belief "The fork is on the wrong side" is usually too minimal to deserve the name of "inquiry." But sometimes, in special situations, the acquisition of that belief will provoke the sort of large-scale, conscious, deliberate reweaving that does deserve that name. It might, for instance, lead one to realize that one's host is not who he claims to be, but a daring foreign imposter— a revelation that leads one to rethink one's long-term plans and, ultimately, the meaning of one's life. The same goes for the incursion of the belief that there are unexpected patterns of mold in a petri dish, or unexpected flecks on a telescopic image. They may lead to "reflex" actions or they may initiate scientific breakthroughs. Which they do is a matter of what *other* beliefs happen to make up the mechanism that is reweaving itself.

As one moves along the spectrum from habit to inquiry—from instinctive revision of intentions through routine calculation toward revolutionary science or politics—the number of beliefs added to or subtracted from the web increases. At a certain point in this process it becomes useful to speak of "recontextualization." The more widespread the changes, the more use we have for the notion of "a new context." This new context can be a new explanatory theory, a new comparison class, a new descriptive vocabulary, a new private or political purpose, the latest book one has read, the last person one talked to; the possibilities are endless.

One can, however, divide all contexts into two kinds: (a) a new set of attitudes toward some of the sentences previously in one's repertoire, and (b) the acquisition of attitudes toward new truth-value candidates, sentences toward which one had previously had no attitudes. This distinction between two senses of "context" is roughly coincident with the distinction between inference and imagination, and also with the distinction between translation and language learning. We speak of inference when logical space remains fixed, when no new candidates for belief are introduced. Paradigms of inference are adding up a column of figures, or running through a sorites, or down a flow chart. Paradigms of imagination are the new, metaphorical use of old words (for example, *gravitas*), the invention of neologisms (for example, "gene"), and the colligation of hitherto unrelated texts (for example, Hegel and Genet [Jacques Derrida], Donne and Laforgue [T. S. Eliot], Aristotle and the Scriptures [the Schoolmen], Emerson and the Gnostics [Harold Bloom], Emerson and the skeptics [Stanley Cavell], cockfights and Northrop Frye [Clifford Geertz], Nietzsche and Proust [Alexander Nehamas]).[1]

Again, however, this is a distinction of degree, and it will be drawn differently by people with different concerns. Consider an accountant recontextualizing the figures on a corporate income tax return, provoked to do so by the thought that a certain depreciable item might plausibly be listed on Schedule H rather than on Schedule M. This belief will eventually lead him to infer to a different bottom line. We usually think of this process as clever rearrangement of antecedent material, clever inference from antecedent beliefs about the contents of the tax laws. But there is of course a touch of imagination in it (as is suggested by the term "creative accounting"). Again, admirers of

---

[1] Successful colligation of this sort is an example of rapid and unconscious reweaving, produced by laying one set of beliefs on top of another and finding that, magically, they have interpenetrated and become warp and woof of a new, vividly polychrome fabric. I take this as analogous to what happens in dreams, and that analogy as the point of Donald Davidson's remark "Metaphor is the dreamwork of language."

Derrida like myself think of Derrida's recontextualization of western metaphysics, his neologistic redescription of it as "phallogocentrism," as a paradigm of creative imagination. But hostile critics of Derrida think of this as merely rearranging old themes and slogans— just shoving the old pieces around the old board, to no good purpose.

The distinction between "rationality" and something else has traditionally been drawn so as to coincide roughly with this distinction between inference and imagination. We are being rational, so the story goes, insofar as we stick to the logical space given at the beginning of the inquiry and so long as we can offer an argument for the beliefs held at the end of the inquiry by referring back to the beliefs held at its beginning. Before the arrival of Thomas Kuhn, Stephen Toulmin, Paul Feyerabend, and Norwood Russell Hanson, it was often thought that the physical sciences were, in this sense, paradigmatically rational areas of culture. The scientists were thought of as going up or down flow charts labeled "the logic of conformation" or "the logic of explanation" and as operating within a logical space in which, magically, all possible descriptions of everything were already at hand. Insofar as this logical space was unavailable, or not clearly seen, it was the job of "conceptual analysis" to make it available and visible—to translate every unclear locution into a clear one, where "clear" meant something like "accessible to every rational inquirer."

On this view, proto-Kuhnian suggestions that we might have to learn a new language to do history of science, or anthropology, or that we might have to invent a new language to make scientific or political progress, were thought of as "irrationalist." In pre-Kuhnian times, rational inquiry was a matter of putting everything into a single, widely available, familiar context—translating everything into the vocabulary provided by a set of sentences that any rational inquirer would agree to be truth-value candidates. The human sciences were urged to get inside this context, while the arts were allowed to escape this requirement of "rationality." The idea was that there is a rough equivalence between being scientific and being rational. So being scientific is a matter of sticking within a logical space that formed an intrinsically privileged context.[2]

---

[2] This pre-Kuhnian notion of what it is to be scientific is criticized by Dewey at the end of "The Influence of Darwin on Philosophy" (*The Middle Works of John Dewey*, vol. 4, ed. Jo Ann Boydston [Carbondale: Southern Illinois University Press, 1977], p. 14): "conviction persists—though history shows it to be an hallucination—that all the questions that the human mind has asked are questions that can be answered in

We enlightened post-Kuhnians are free from this idea, but we are not yet free from what I shall call "realism." This is the idea that inquiry is a matter of finding out the nature of something that lies outside the web of beliefs and desires. On this view, inquiry has a goal that is not simply the equilibrium state of the reweaving machine—a state that coincides with the satisfaction of the desires of the organism which contains that machine. For realists there is some sense in which the object of inquiry—what lies outside the organism—has a context of its own, a context that is privileged by virtue of being the object's rather than the inquirer's. This realism is found in both the hard and the soft sciences—among anthropologists who dislike ethnocentrism,[3] literary critics who dislike deconstruction, Heideggerians who distrust Derrida,[4] as much as among those who prize the "absoluteness" of natural science's description of the world.[5]

For us pragmatists, by contrast, the object of inquiry is "constituted" by inquiry only in the following sense: We shall answer the questions "What are you talking about?" and "What is it that you want to find about?" by listing some of the more important beliefs we hold at the current stage of inquiry, and saying that we are talking about *whatever these beliefs are true of*. The model here is the familiar contextualist claim that a non-Euclidean space is whatever certain

---

terms of the alternatives that the questions themselves present. But in fact intellectual progress usually occurs through sheer abandonment of questions together with both of the alternatives they assume—an abandonment that results from their decreasing vitality and a change of urgent interest. We do not solve them; we get over them."

[3]See Clifford Geertz's "The Uses of Diversity," *Michigan Quarterly Review* 25 (1986), and my "On Ethnocentrism: A Reply to Clifford Geertz," *Michigan Quarterly Review* 25 (1986).

[4]Hubert Dreyfus and John Caputo are examples. See Dreyfus, "Holism and Hermeneutics," *Review of Metaphysics* 34 (1980), and Caputo, "The Thought of Being and the Conversation of Mankind: The Case of Heidegger and Rorty," *Review of Metaphysics* 36 (1983): 661–83. Both articles are reprinted in Robert Hollinger, ed., *Hermeneutics and Praxis* (Notre Dame: Notre Dame University Press, 1985).

[5]See Charles Taylor's insistence on this absoluteness in his "Understanding in the Human Sciences," immediately following Dreyfus's "Holism and Hermeneutics" in *Review of Metaphysics* 34 (1980). These two papers are followed by a paper of mine called "A Reply to Dreyfus and Taylor" and by debate among Dreyfus, Taylor, and myself. There I object to the notion of "absoluteness," which Taylor, like Bernard Williams, ascribes to the descriptions offered by natural science. For criticism of the positions that Dreyfus and I adopt in the aforementioned debate, see Mark Okrent, "Hermeneutics, Transcendental Philosophy and Social Science," *Inquiry* 27 (1984): 23–49

axioms are true of.[6] We pragmatists hear the question "But is there *really* any such thing?" as an awkward way of putting the question "Are there other beliefs which we ought to have?" The latter question can be answered only by enumerating and recommending such other beliefs. So we do not countenance any *generalized* skepticism about other minds or cultures, or the external world, but only detailed skepticism about this or that belief or cluster of beliefs—detailed suggestions about how to reweave.[7]

One way of formulating the pragmatist position is to say that the pragmatist recognizes relations of *justification* holding between beliefs and desires, and relations of *causation* holding between these beliefs and desires and other items in the universe, but no relations of *representation*. Beliefs do not represent nonbeliefs. There are, to be sure, relations of *aboutness*, in the attenuated sense in which G. F. D. Riemann's axioms are about Riemannian space, Alexius Meinong talks about round squares, and Shakespeare's play is about Hamlet. But in this vegetarian sense of aboutness, there is no problem about how a belief can be about the unreal or the impossible. For aboutness is not a matter of pointing outside the web. Rather, we use the term "about" as a way of directing attention to the beliefs that are relevant to the justification of other beliefs, not as a way of directing attention to nonbeliefs.

We pragmatists must object to, or reinterpret, two traditional methodological questions: "What context is appropriate to this object?" and "What is it that we are putting in context?" For us, all objects are always already contextualized.[8] They all come with contexts

---

[6]On the importance of non-Euclidean geometry for the anti-essentialist, increasingly playful, tone of twentieth-century philosophy, see my "From Logic to Language to Play," *Proceedings and Addresses of the American Philosophical Association* 59 (1986): 747–53.

[7]For criticism of the attitude toward generalized skepticism that I share with Davidson, see Colin McGinn, "Radical Interpretation and Epistemology," in *Truth and Interpretation: Perspectives on the Philosophy of Donald Davidson*, ed. Ernest LePore (Oxford: Oxford University Press, 1986). McGinn shares Thomas Nagel's anti-Wittgensteinian and anti-Peircian view that there are aspects of experience that escape language, and thus escape contextualization. For a more general, very penetrating, discussion of generalized skepticism, and in particular of the attitude toward skepticism shared by Nagel, Barry Stroud, and McGinn, see Michael Williams, *Unnatural Doubts* (Oxford: Basil Blackwell, 1991).

[8]Contrast, e.g., Anthony Giddens's claim that "sociology, unlike natural science, deals with a pre-interpreted world where the creation and reproduction of meaning-frames is a very condition of that which it seeks to analyze, namely human social conduct: this is why there is a double hermeneutic in the social sciences" (*New Rules of Sociological Method* [New York: Basic, 1976], p. 158). This passage is quoted approv-

attached, just as Riemannian space comes with axioms attached. So there is no question of taking an object out of its old context and examining it, all by itself, to see what new context might suit it. There is only a question about which other regions of the web we might look to to find ways of eliminating the residual tensions in the region currently under strain. Nor is there an answer to the question of what it is that is being put in context except, boringly and trivially, "beliefs." All talk about doing things to objects must, in a pragmatic account of inquiry "into" objects, be paraphrasable as talk about reweaving beliefs. Nothing but efficiency will be lost in such translation, any more than anything else is lost if, with Peirce, we paraphrase talk about the object as talk about the practical effects that the object will have on our conduct.

Once one drops the traditional opposition between context and thing contextualized, there is no way to divide things up into those that are what they are independent of context and those that are context dependent—no way to divide the world up into hard lumps and squishy texts, for example. Or, to put it another way, there is no way to divide the world up into internal and external relations, nor into intrinsic versus extrinsic properties—nor, indeed, into things that are intrinsically relations and things that are intrinsically terms of relations. For once one sees inquiry as reweaving beliefs rather than discovering the natures of objects, there are no candidates for self-subsistent, independent entities save individual beliefs—individual sentential attitudes. But these are very bad candidates indeed. For a belief is what it is only by virtue of its position in a web. Once

---

ingly by Jürgen Habermas (*Theory of Communicative Action*, vol. 1, trans. Thomas McCarthy [Boston: Beacon, 1985], p. 110). Habermas glosses it by saying, "Giddens speaks of a 'double' hermeneutic because in the social sciences problems of interpretive understanding do not come into play only through the theory-dependency of data description and the paradigm-dependency of theory-languages; there is already a problem of understanding below the threshold of theory construction, namely in *obtaining* data and not first in *theoretically describing* them; for the everyday experience that can be *transformed* into scientific operations is, for its part, already symbolically structured and inaccessible to mere observation."

My reaction to Habermas's gloss is that it is precisely "the theory-dependency of data-description" that makes "mere observation" an *equally* useless notion in the *Natur-* and in the *Geisteswissenschaften*. I can no more see the point of Giddens's "double" hermeneutics than that of its near relative, W. V. O. Quine's "double" indeterminacy of translation. (The latter notion has been criticized in detail by Noam Chomsky, Hilary Putnam, and others, and by me in "Indeterminacy of Translation and of Truth," *Synthese* 23 [1972]: 443–62.)

we view the "representation" and "aboutness" relations (which some philosophers have supposed to "fix the content" of belief) as fallout from a given contextualization of those beliefs, a belief becomes simply a position in a web. It is a disposition on the part of the web to react to certain additions or deletions in certain ways. In this respect it is like a thing's value or its valence—it is just a disposition to respond in various ways to various stimuli.[9]

If this dissolution of inquiry into a self-reweaving web of beliefs seems wacky to you, consider that such a dissolution is a natural and easy consequence of a generalized anti-essentialism. Anti-essentialism is, as Samuel Wheeler has noted,[10] the principal point of convergence between analytic philosophy and Continental philosophy. The same movement of thought that led A. N. Whitehead and W. V. O. Quine to sneer at Aristotle, and to relativize the substance-property distinction, led Martin Heidegger to say that the West began to forget Being when the Greeks started distinguishing "that" from "what," and appearance from reality.[11] This same line of thought leads Gareth

---

[9]I owe the analogy between doxastic content and value to Daniel Dennett. See Dennett, *The Intentional Stance* (Cambridge: MIT Press, 1987), p. 208: "Propositions, as ways of 'measuring' semantic information by the topic-ful, *turn out to be more like dollars than like numbers.* Just as 'what is that worth in U.S. dollars?' asks a usefully unifying question in spite of the frequent occasions when the answer distorts the reality in which we are interested, so 'what proposition (in Standard Scheme P) does that store/transmit/express?' might exploit a valuable, somewhat systematic if often procrustean testbed. Only naive Americans confuse the former question with 'What is that worth in *real* money?' and it would be similarly naive to consider a proposition-fixing standard, however well established, to be even an approximation of the way semantic information is *really* parcelled out. *There are no real, natural, universal units of either economic value or semantic information.*"

Think of the question "What is that worth in *real* money?" as parallel to the equally naive questions "What sentence in the *real* language—the Language of Reason, or the Language of Nature, or the Language of Observation—is that behavioral disposition an attitude toward?" or "What piece of reality—reality as it *really* is—is that behavioral disposition directed toward?" or "What context does that disposition *really* belong in?"

[10]See Samuel Wheeler, "The Extension of Deconstruction," *The Monist* 69 (1986): 3–21, esp. p. 10: "In a way, the most striking expression of the thought common to Quine and Derrida is that all thought can be at most brain-writing or spirit-writing, both of which modes of inscription yield texts with at least the hermeneutical problems of other texts." When this point is separated, by Davidson, from Quine's adventitious physicalism, the convergence between Derrida and Davidson becomes clear. See Wheeler, "Indeterminacy of French Translation: Derrida and Davidson," in *Truth and Interpretation*, pp. 477–94.

[11]Martin Heidegger, *Nietzsche*, vol. 26 (Pfullingem: Neske, 1962), pp. 14–15. "The what (*das Was-sein, to ti estin*) and the that (*das Dass-sein, to estin*) reveal themselves in

Evans, followed by Dennett and others, to repudiate Russell's Principle (viz.: "it is not possible to make a judgment about an object [or: to have a belief about an object] without knowing what object you are making a judgment [having a belief] about)."[12]

The anti-essentialist philosopher looks forward to the day when all the pseudo-problems created by the essentialist tradition—problems about the relation of appearance to reality, of mind to body, of language to fact—will be dissolved. She thinks that all these traditional dualisms collapse, like so many dominoes, once the distinction between essence and accident is collapsed. She sees the distinction between reality and appearance as a way of suggesting that some set of relations, some context, is intrinsically privileged. She sees the mind-body distinction as a way of suggesting that human beings have an inside that is beyond the reach of language (Thomas Nagel, Colin McGinn), or possess an intrinsic intentionality (John Searle), a kind that escapes recontextualization. She sees the distinction between language and fact as a way of intimating that some bits of language bear a special relation—that of accurate representation—to something that is what it is apart from language, apart from any description.

The essentialist philosopher, the one who wants to hold on to the notion of "intrinsic, context-independent property," says that the "it" that inquiry puts in context has to be something precontextual. The anti-essentialist rejoins by insisting that it is contexts all the way down. She does so by saying that we can inquire after things only under a description, that describing something is a matter of relating it to other things, and that "grasping the thing itself" is not something that precedes contextualization, but is at best a *focus imaginarius*. The latter is the idea of a simultaneous grasp of all the possible descriptions that the thing might be given, of all the possible contexts in which it might be placed. This is the impossible idea of comparing

---

their difference along with the difference on which metaphysics everywhere reposes—the one which establishes itself firstly and in its finality (although capable of transmutation to the point of unrecognizability) in the Platonic distinction between true being (ontōs on) and non-being (mē on)." At the bottom of p. 15 Heidegger says: "The what and the that volatilize themselves, with the growing unquestionability of the identification of Being with the beingness of beings (die wachsende Fraglosigkeit der Seiendheit), into empty 'concepts of reflection' and thus acquire ever greater strength, in proportion as metaphysics itself becomes more and more taken for granted."

[12]See Gareth Evans, *The Varieties of Reference* (Oxford: Clarendon Press, 1982), p. 89. See Dennett, *The Intentional Stance*, pp. 200, 210.

and contrasting all the infinitely many possible beliefs that, under some possible interpretation, might be viewed as beliefs about that thing.[13]

The essentialist rejoins by saying that although the descriptions may vary depending on the describer, the thing described does not. He accuses the anti-essentialist of having confused the order of being with the order of knowing, of being a "verificationist." So he continues to press his question: what is it that is being related to what? Relativizing and contextualizing, he says, are all very well, but relations require terms. Sooner or later we have to be told what these terms are, what they *intrinsically* are. Once we are told *that*, we shall have to acknowledge the need for the traditional dualisms. For we shall have a clue to what is real rather than apparent, what it is that language attempts to represent accurately, what mind and body *intrinsically* are and how they are *really* related.

To evade this question about what the terms of all these relations are, about what sort of thing it is that gets endlessly recontextualized, the anti-essentialist has to say that anything *can* be treated as a term of a relation *or* can be dissolved into a set of relations to other things, depending on one's current purposes. There will always be terms that are related, but which terms these are depends upon the purpose of the recontextualization currently being undertaken. You can dissolve macrostructure into microstructure—stars and tables into atoms—but you can also view microstructural entities as devices for predicting macrostructural behavior. You can dissolve a substance into a sequence of Whiteheadian events, but you can also treat events as relations between Aristotelian substances. You can dissolve persons into webs of beliefs and desires, but you can also dissolve a belief into the attitude a person has toward a sentence. You can dissolve a sentence into a pattern of words, but you can go on to remark that only in the context of a sentence does a word have meaning. The anti-essentialist specializes in creating this hall-of-mirrors effect—in getting us to stop asking which is the real thing and which the image, and to settle for an ever-expanding choice of images, of Goodmanian "worlds."

This anti-essentialist strategy thus seems to get rid of the *objects* of inquiry—of the things that get reflected in all those mirrors. But there

---

[13]See Hilary Putnam, *Representation and Reality* (Cambridge: MIT Press, 1988), p. 89: "To ask a human being in a time-bound culture to survey all modes of human linguistic existence—including those that will transcend his own—is to ask for an impossible Archimedean point."

is something dubious about the idea that it is mirrors all the way down. So the essentialist, at this stage of the argument, begins to call himself a "realist" and to call his opponent a "linguistic idealist." She is speaking, he says, as if there were nothing to do but rearrange our mental representations into pleasing or useful patterns—as if there were nothing for them to represent. The anti-essentialist rejoins that her position has nothing in common with idealism save an acknowledgment that inquiry does not consist in confrontation between beliefs and objects, but rather in the quest for a coherent set of beliefs. She is a coherentist but not an idealist. For she believes, as strongly as does any realist, that there are objects that are *causally* independent of human beliefs and desires.

The realist rejoins that the anti-essentialist must be saying that objects are unknowable as they are in themselves—that she must, therefore, be some newfangled kind of transcendental idealist. She replies that she can find no use for the notion "as they are in themselves," nor for the distinction between "as they are" and "as we describe them." We do in fact describe most objects as causally independent of us, and that is *all* that is required to satisfy our realistic intuitions. We are not also required to say that our descriptions *represent* objects. Representation is, on her view, a fifth wheel. If we have relations of justification between our beliefs and desires, and relations of causation between those and the rest of the universe, those are all the mind-world or language-world relations we need.

At this point one can imagine the realist saying: If you give up the notion of *representing* objects, then you had better give up the claim to be recontextualizing *objects*. You had better admit that all your conception of inquiry allows you to do is to recontextualize your beliefs and desires. You do not find out anything about objects at all—you just find out about how your web of beliefs and desires can be rewoven so as to accommodate new beliefs and desires. You never get outside your own head.

What I have been saying amounts to accepting this gambit. The anti-essentialist should admit that what she calls "recontextualizing objects" could just as well be called "recontextualizing beliefs." Reweaving a web of beliefs is, if you like, all she does—all anybody can do. But, she will add, this is not as bad as the realist makes it sound. In the first place, one of her more central, difficult to imagine revising, beliefs is that lots of objects she does not control are continually causing her to have new and surprising beliefs, beliefs that often require hasty and drastic reweaving on her part. She is no more free from pressure from outside, no more tempted to be "arbitrary," than anyone else. She is free from the questions "Are you representing accurately?" and "Are you getting at the way the object *really, intrinsically,* is?" but *not* from questions like "Can you fit in the belief that the litmus paper turned red (or that there are nonstellar sources of radiation, or that your lover has deceived you) with the rest of your beliefs?" In the second place, she is not stuck within her own head. At worst, the community of inquirers to which she belongs, the one that shares most of her beliefs, is stuck, for the time being, within its own vocabulary. But bemoaning this fact is like bemoaning the fact that we are, for the time being, stuck in our own solar system. Human finitude is not an objection to a philosophical view.

I turn now from this large debate between the essentialist and the anti-essentialist to the topic of interpretation. Interpretation has become a theme for philosophers largely as a result of the attempt to split the difference between the essentialist and the anti-essentialist. For "interpretation" is an exciting notion only as long as it contrasts with something harder, firmer, less controversial—something like "explanation" or "natural science." The contrast effect is typically attained by saying that essentialism is true on the hard side of the line but not on the soft side.

Typically, those who take up the subject of interpretation divide culture into two areas—in one of which interpretations, recontextualizations, go all the way down and in another of which they do not. When we are told that a certain activity should be viewed as *interpretive,* we are usually being told that we should not, perhaps contrary to our earlier expectations, expect this activity to produce either knock-down arguments or a consensus among experts. We should not expect it to have a natural starting point, nor a method. Perhaps we should not even expect it to provide "objective truth." We should be prepared to settle for recontextualizing what lies to hand, and then playing various recontextualizations off against each other. But advising us to settle for this fuzziness is only interesting insofar as we have reason to think that other people, in other areas of culture, manage to be *less* fuzzy than this.

Suppose we are anti-essentialist all the way. Then we shall say that *all* inquiry is interpretation, that *all* thought consists in recontextualization, that we have never done anything else and never will. We shall not grant that there is useful contrast to be drawn between topics about which there is objective truth and topics about which there is not. We shall not grant that there is *any* area of culture in which the essentialist has a point. So, if we use it at all, we shall have to stretch the term "interpretation" to cover what stockbrokers, geologists, actuaries, and carpenters do. A notion stretched that thin, deprived of contrastive and polemical force, loses its pizzazz. If we had all been raised from the cradles to be anti-essentialists, "interpretation" would never have been inscribed on the banners of a philosophical movement. Wilhelm Dilthey, Hans-Georg Gadamer, and Charles Taylor would have had to find different topics.

The suggestion that one might be anti-essentialist all the way is the suggestion that one might cease to see an interesting, Diltheyan, difference between the procedures of the physicist and the sociologist—or, more precisely, that one might find a context in which these differences became irrelevant, and then find advantages in staying within that context. It is a suggestion that Taylor once satirized by saying that Mary Hesse and I shared the "pleasing fancy" that "old-guard Diltheyans, their shoulders hunched from years-long resistance against the encroaching pressure of positivist natural science, suddenly pitch forward on their faces as all opposition ceases to the reign of universal hermeneutics."[14] I still share something like this fancy, but it is not exactly a fantasy of the reign of universal hermeneutics. It is, rather, the fantasy that the very idea of hermeneutics should disappear, in the way in which old general ideas do disappear when they lose polemical and contrastive force—when they begin to have universal applicability. My fantasy is of a culture so deeply anti-essentialist that it makes only a sociological distinction between sociologists and physicists, not a methodological or philosophical one.

In order to spell out my fantasy in detail, I shall, yet again, use the strategies suggested by my favorite contemporary anti-essentialist, Donald Davidson. Davidson seems to me to be doing the same job within the vocabulary of analytic philosophy (roughly, the vocabulary that has replaced "thoughts" by "sentences" and "ideas" by "words") that Dewey did within an earlier philosophical vocabulary. Both spend most of their time breaking down the Greek dualisms that, like Heidegger, they see essentialism as having built into the philosophical problematic. What Davidson is particularly good at is breaking down a distinction that his teacher, Quine, unfortunately left intact: that between the areas of culture in which there are "facts

[14]Taylor, "Understanding in Human Science," p. 26.

of the matter" (roughly, the physical sciences) and those in which there are not.

I begin with a Davidsonian topic about which Taylor is dubious—radical interpretation, the process by which Quine and Davidson think the anthropologist learns the native's hitherto unstudied language. Taylor says that Davidson's paper "Radical Interpretation" is inadequate for the same reason as are Quine's fables about occasions on which the native makes the sound "*gavagai.*""Like all naturalistic theories," he says, those of Quine and Davidson are "framed as theories elaborated by an observer about an object observed but not participated in."[15]Taylor admits that their theories may work for "the domain of middle-size dry goods, the ordinary material objects that surround us." But, he says, "when we come to our emotions, aspirations, goals, our social relations and practices, this cannot be. The reason is that these are already partly constituted by language, and you have to understand this language to understand them."[16]

I take the appropriate Davidsonian response to go as follows: the middle-sized dry goods are already as much or as little "constituted by language" as the emotions and the goals. For this notion that some things are "constituted by language" is just a way of saying that two groups are not talking about the same things if they talk about them very differently—if wildly different beliefs and desires are aroused in them by these things. It is not that nonlanguage constitutes some things and language others. It is, rather, that when the natives' and our behavior in response to certain situations is just the same, we think of both of us as simply recognizing the plain facts of how things are—the noncontroversial objects of common sense. But when these patterns of behavior differ wildly, we shall say that we have different *Weltanschauungen*, or cultures, or theories, or that "we carve up the world differently." But it would create fewer philosophical problems just to say that when these patterns differ, communication becomes harder and translation less helpful. Translation may become so awkwardly periphrastic, indeed, that it will save time simply to go bilingual.

Examples may help make this point. Davidson thinks that you should not translate *gavagai* as "rabbit" nor *Unheimlichkeit* as "homelessness" unless you are prepared to say that most of what the na-

[15]Taylor, "Theories of Meaning," *Philosophical Papers* (Cambridge: Cambridge University Press, 1985), 1:255.
[16]Ibid., p. 275.

tives say about rabbits and most of what the Germans about homelessness is true. You should also be prepared to say that most of their desires concerning these objects are reasonable ones. More simply, you should not make these translations unless you find the natives behaving toward *gavagais* pretty much as we behave toward rabbits, and the Germans toward *Unheimlichkeit* pretty much as we behave toward homelessness.

You will be led to revise your tentative translation of *Unheimlichkeit* by realizing that the Germans would have to be crazy to say *that* about *homelessness*, and to react in *that* way to the threat of it. You may be led to revise your translation of *gavagai* once you recognize the crucial role played by *gavagais* in the spiritual life of the tribe, and once you recall the occurrence of the root *gav* in various words which you have provisionally translated as specifically theological terms. It may turn out that Taylor will have to view *gavagais*, though not rabbits, as "constituted by language."

Conversely, it might turn out that the native word *boing*, though the name of an emotion, is easily and elegantly translated by "nostalgia," and indeed that all known languages have a word equally easily so translated. The temptation to say that nostalgia is constituted by language would then become as slight as the temptation to say that toothache was. This suggests that the interesting line is not between the human and the nonhuman, nor between material objects and emotions, but between the behavioral patterns that you and the natives share and the patterns that you do not. If all humans regret the passing of all and only the sorts of things we do, it is likely that all humankind will have a terse and unambiguous expression that English speakers can translate as "nostalgia." So we may complacently view *boing* as just a label for something as banally intercultural as toothache. But if the natives take *gavagais* as central to the structure of the universe, then it is reasonable that they should have no terse and unambiguous expression that we can translate as "rabbit." Under these circumstances, we conclude that rabbits are less banally intercultural than we had thought. We turn out to have made, initially, the same sort of mistake as was made by certain natives who rearranged, for ease of carrying, the baggage of the first Christian missionaries to arrive on their shores. These natives thought that objects consisting of short pieces of wood perpendicularly fastened a third of the way down the length of long pieces of wood—a sort of middle-sized dry good for which, as it happened, they had a terse term in their own tongue—were banally intercultural objects.

The claim I made a little way back—that we are not talking about the same thing if we say very different things about it—is both central to Davidson's view and a good illustration of anti-essentialism at work. This claim amounts, once again, to an implicit denial of Russell's Principle. This principle says, you recall, that *it is not possible to make a judgment about an object without knowing what object you are making a judgment about.*

Two ideas lie behind this principle: (*a*) the idea that you can be wrong only about what you are largely right about, and (*b*) the idea that you might be right only about *what something is* and wrong in everything else you believe about it. Davidson thinks that (*a*) is a good idea and (*b*) a bad one. For him, there is no such thing as "knowing what something is" as distinct from knowing that it stands in certain relations to certain other things.[17] His anti-essentialism here amounts to the claim that we cannot divide things up into what they are and what properties they have, nor (*pace* Bertrand Russell and C. I. Lewis) knowledge up into knowledge of "what" and knowledge that. To say that you can be wrong only about what you get mostly right is not to say that you can misdescribe only what you have previously identified. It is, rather, to say that you can misdescribe only what you are *also* able to describe quite well. If you accept the Russellian distinction between identifying and describing, you are likely to think of the world as presenting itself to the mind as divided up into objects, divisions detectable by some means that is prior to, and independent of, the process of forming beliefs. Or, at least, you may think this about the world of banally intercultural middle-sized dry goods. However, if you start reading the history of science, or ethnography, you may begin to wonder whether this principle applies to the strange things mentioned in these books. Then you may find yourself saying that Aristotle was talking about something that did not exist—(something initially identifiable only as "what Aristotle called *kinesis*")—and that Polynesians talk about something else that doesn't exist ("whatever it is they call *mana*").

But the same essentialist instincts that led you to accept Russell's Principle may lead you to accept Parmenides' Principle: you cannot talk about what does not exist. If so, you will look for some special kind of existence for the putatively nonexistent to have: subsistence, or notional existence, or representational existence, or mental exis-

---

[17]This is, of course, Wittgenstein's point when he says that it takes a lot of stage setting in the language to get the point of an ostensive definition.

tence. Or, perhaps, "linguistic existence"—the sort of existence that things "constituted by language" have. Cheered by this notion, you become a Diltheyan and divide the world up into the non-language-constituted domain of natural science and the linguistically constituted domain of the human sciences.[18]

But we anti-essentialists who believe neither Russell nor Parmenides, and who do not distinguish between objects found prior to the process of belief formation and objects made in the course of this process, can still cut at pretty much the same joints as does Taylor's Diltheyan distinction. We can draw a line between objects that cause you to have beliefs about them by fairly direct causal means and other objects. In the case of the latter, the relevant causal relations are either terribly indirect or simply nonexistent. Most middle-sized pieces of dry goods are of the former sort. These will be the objects whose names come up fairly quickly in the course of a causal explanation of how you acquired certain beliefs and desires—namely, the ones that you express in sentences that contain those same names. Tracing the causes that have led us all to have beliefs and desires about Gorbachev, for example, leads us back fairly quickly to Gorbachev himself. By contrast, the explanation of how we have been caused to have beliefs and desires about happiness, chastity, and the will of God will not lead you back to these objects. (Or, rather, they will do so only on the basis of theories of immaterial causality such as Plato's or Augustine's.) The same goes for beliefs and desires about neutrinos, the number pi, the round square, *mana*, and *kinesis.* Causal explanations of how we acquired the beliefs and desires that we express by sentences containing names of *such* things will *not* normally mention those things themselves.

We anti-essentialists do not think that this shows that the number pi and the virtue of chastity have another kind of ontological status than that possessed by Gorbachev and the rabbits. For, once we dump the idea that the aim of inquiry is to represent objects and substitute the view that inquiry aims at making beliefs and desires coherent, then the Parmenidean question of how we can represent

---

[18]The same Parmenidean considerations may move you to become a van Fraassen-style instrumentalist in the philosophy of natural science—letting atoms be "constituted" and "accepted," whereas tables are "found" and "believed in." Or they may lead you to postulate as many worlds *tout court* as there are *notional* worlds and thus to say, with Kuhn, that Aristotle and Galileo lived in different worlds. I discuss both Bas van Fraassen's and Kuhn's suggestions in "Is Natural Science a Natural Kind?", *Objectivity Relativism, and Truth* (Cambridge: Cambridge University Press, 1991), pp. 46–62.

accurately what does not exist is irrelevant, and the notion that there is truth only about what is *real* gets set aside. So the only notion of "object" we need is that of "intentional object." An intentional object is what a word or description refers to. You find out what it refers to by attaching a meaning to the linguistic expressions to that word or description. That, in turn, you do by either translating or, if necessary, becoming bilingual in, the language in which the word or description occurs. Whether that is a good language is as irrelevant to objecthood as the question of whether the object has any causal powers.

Anti-essentialists think of objects as what we find it useful to talk about in order to cope with the stimulations to which our bodies are subjected. *All* objects, including Quine's "stimulations," are what Quine calls "posits." If you are willing to give up the idea that you can identify some *non* posits and to agree that what precedes positing is just stimulation and not knowledge (not, for instance, "knowledge by acquaintance" or "perceptual knowledge" or "knowledge of your own experience"), then you can avoid the idea that some objects are constituted by language and others not. The difference between banally intercultural and controversial objects will be the difference between the objects you have to talk about to deal with the routine stimulations provided by your familiars and the objects required to deal with the novel stimulations provided by new acquaintances (for example, Aristotelians, Polynesians, avant-garde poets and painters, imaginative colligators of texts, and the like).

So far I have been making suggestions about how to capture some of Taylor's distinctions without talking about anything being "constituted by language." What about his distinction between observing the native culture and participating in it? More specifically, what about his claim that Davidson's truth-conditional account of radical interpretation will not work because "we cannot adequately grasp what some of the truth-conditions are without some grasp of the language"[19]—that is, without previously participating in the use of that language. This is a challenge Davidson meets fairly directly. He poses to himself the question "Can a theory of truth be verified by appeal to evidence available before interpetation has begun?"[20] and answers it by saying: Yes, if we (*a*) can identify certain native behav-

[19]Taylor, "Theories of Meaning," p. 275.
[20]Davidson, "Radical Interpretation," in *Inquiries into Truth and Interpretation* (Oxford: Oxford University Press, 1984). p. 133.

ior as the holding true of a sentence, and (b) apply the Principle of Charity. The latter condition amounts to saying that our form of life and the natives' already overlap to so great an extent that we are already, automatically, for free, participant-observers, not *mere* observers. Davidson thinks that this overlap in effect reduces the intercultural case to an intracultural one—it means that we learn to handle the weirder bits of native behavior (linguistic and other) in the same way that we learn about the weird behavior of atypical members of our own culture. Such members include quantum physicists, metaphysicians, religious fanatics, psychotics, Oscar Wilde, Mrs. Malaprop, and so on—all the people who express paradoxical beliefs and desires in (mostly) familiar words of our mother tongue.[21]

One can imagine Davidson asking Taylor: if you grant that we can learn to talk quantum mechanics, or learn how to understand Mrs. Malaprop, on the basis of the very considerable overlap between our linguistic behavior and Planck's or Malaprop's (plus a bit of curiosity and imagination), why should you think things are any harder or any different in, for instance, your imagined case of the barbarian in ancient Athens?[22] In the case of Planck, we figure out what he's going on about by asking him questions and listening to the answers, including questions about what he means by a given expression. We are satisfied that we understand him once we find ourselves bickering about quanta with him like a brother. In the case of Malaprop, as in

[21]On the analogies between malapropisms and metaphors, see Davidson, "What Metaphors Mean" in ibid., "A Nice Derangement of Epitaphs" in the Lepore collection *Truth and Interpretation,* and my "Unfamiliar Noises," in *Objectivity, Relativism, and Truth,* pp. 162–72.

[22]Taylor writes, immediately after the passage about truth conditions that I quoted above: "observers from some totally despotic culture, dropped into classical Athens, we keep hearing this word 'equal', and its companion 'like' (*isos, homoios*). We know how to apply these words to sticks, stones, perhaps also houses and ships; for there is a tolerably exact translation in our home language (Persian). And we also know *a* way of applying them to human beings, for instance physical likeness or equality of height. But there is a peculiar way these Hellenes have of using the words which baffles us."

Taylor continues: "Now our problem is not just that we have to grasp that this is a metaphorical use. Presumably this kind of thing is not unfamiliar to us . . . But what we have not yet got is the positive value of this mode of life. We do not grasp the ideal of a people of free agents . . . We do not see, in other words, the nobility of this kind of life. . . . Hence, to understand what these terms represent to grasp them in their representative function, we have to understand them in their articulating-constitutive function. We have to see how they can bring a horizon of concern to a certain articulation." (Taylor, "Theories of Meaning," pp. 275–77; my ellipses sometimes indicate omissions of a paragraph or more.)

that of someone with a weird foreign accent, we guess what she might be saying, check our guesses by responding to what we think she *ought* to have said, and so gradually pick up the knack of understanding her without conscious puzzlement or inference. Surely the Persians did the same sorts of thing when trying to cope with the Athenians? If doing this sort of thing counts as "participating" rather than "observing," then the idea of a "mere observer" is a straw man. Quine and Davidson never imagined that the radical interpeter could do his job without stimulating responsive native behavior, any more than the marine biologist could do hers without stimulating her squids. But both might deny that he need have any more empathy with his subjects than she does.

It seems to me that Taylor interprets Davidson as a kind of atomist, someone who not only, as he says, "sees meaning entirely in terms of representation"[23] but who assumes that one can represent a little hunk of reality without simultaneously representing lots and lots of reality. But this ignores the holism that Taylor and Davidson share, and the fact that both have equally little use for Russell's Principle. Davidson thinks that you can have one belief only if you have lots, and can interpret one bit of behavior only if you can interpret lots.[24] Nor is it the case that Davidson sees meaning in terms of representation, if this means that, as Taylor puts it, he "maps what is said on what is the case in such a way that along with plausible hypotheses about people's desires and intentions it issues in plausible ascriptions of propositional attitudes to speakers."[25] He does not map what is said on what is the case. Rather, he correlates what is the case with what is said (for example, that Kurt usually utters "Es regnet" only when it is raining, "Ich bin ein Esel" only when he looks sheepish, and so forth), and uses these correlations as evidence for hypotheses about truth conditions. This is no more a process of mapping, or of

[23]Ibid., p. 279. See also p. 255: "Seeing theory as observer's theory is another way of allowing the primacy of representation; for a theory also, on this view, should be representation of an independent reality." Davidson's subsequent writings have made his antirepresentationalism clearer than in the articles that Taylor was discussing.

[24]For a good statement of this holism, see the closing paragraphs of Davidson's "Reality without Reference" (in his *Inquiries into Truth and Interpretation*). There (p. 225) he rejects what he calls "building-block theories" for "trying to give a rich content to each sentence directly on the basis of non-semantic evidence" and ends by saying, "Reference, however, drops out. It plays no essential role in explaining the relation between language and reality." Neither, Davidson has subsequently argued, does "representation."

[25]Taylor, "Theories of Meaning," p. 253.

representing, than is the physical scientist's use of macrostructural correlations to inspire or confirm hypotheses about microstructure.

What I have been urging is that *holism takes the curse off naturalism,* and that one can be as naturalistic as Davidson as long as one is careful to be as holist as Taylor. To be a naturalist, in this sense, is to be the kind of anti-essentialist who, like Dewey, sees no breaks in the hierarchy of increasingly complex adjustments to novel stimulation—the hierarchy that has amoebae adjusting themselves to changed water temperature at the bottom, bees dancing and chess players checkmating in the middle, and people formenting scientific, artistic, and political revolutions at the top.

What is lost at this quasi-Skinnerian level of abstraction—this level where we view all inquiry as a matter of responding to the incoherence among beliefs produced by the production of new beliefs? Everything that makes it possible to draw a philosophically interesting distinction between explanation and understanding, or between explanation and interpetation. That is, of course, just the sort of thing we anti-essentialists *want* to lose.

What do we hope to gain? Oddly enough, it is pretty much the same thing Taylor wants to gain from deploying his Diltheyan dualisms: a safeguard against reductionism, against the idea that human beings are "nothing but" something subhuman. For notice that one consequence of giving up notions of truth as accuracy of representation, or correspondence to how things are in themselves, is that we pragmatists cannot divide up culture into the bits that do this job well and those that do not. So we are deaf to Skinnerian attacks on notions like "freedom" and "dignity," deaf to the appeal of "scientism." A Skinner-like, but holistic, naturalization of the theory of inquiry brings with it an inability to take seriously a Skinner-like reductionism. Viewing inquiry as recontextualization makes it impossible to take seriously the notion of some contexts being intrinsically privileged, as opposed to being useful for some particular purpose.

By getting rid of the idea of "different methods appropriate to the natures of different objects" (for example, one for language-constituted and another for non-language-constituted objects), one switches attention from "the demands of the object" to the demands of the purpose that a particular inquiry is supposed to serve. The effect is to modulate philosophical debate from a methodologico-ontological key into an ethico-political key. For now one is debating what purposes are worth bothering to fulfill, which are more worthwhile than others, rather than which purposes the nature of humanity or of reality obliges us to have. For anti-essentialists, all possible purposes compete with one another on equal terms, since none are more "essentially human" than any others.

One might insist that the "desire to know the truth," construed as the desire to recontextualize rather than (with Aristotle) as the desire to know essence, remains characteristically human. But this would be like saying that the desire to use a opposable thumb remains characteristically human. We have little choice but to use that thumb, and little more choice about using our ability to recontextualize. We are going to find ourselves doing both, whatever happens. From an ethico-political angle, however, one can say that what is characteristic, not of the human species but merely of its most advanced, sophisticated subspecies—the well-read, tolerant, conversable inhabitant of a free society—is the desire to dream up as many new contexts as possible. This is the desire to be as polymorphous in our adjustments as possible, to recontextualize (following such examples as Herodotus, Johann Gottfried von Herder, Laurence Sterne, James Joyce, Margaret Mead, and Derrida) for the hell of it. This desire is manifested in art and literature more than in the natural sciences, and so I find it tempting to think of our culture as an increasingly poeticized one, and to say that we are gradually emerging from the scientism that Taylor dislikes into something else, something better.[26] But, as a good anti-essentialist, I have no *deep* premises to draw on from which to infer that it is, in fact, better—nor to demonstrate our own superiority over the past, or the nonwestern present. All I can do is recontextualize various developments in philosophy and elsewhere so as to make them look like stages in a story of poeticizing and progress.[27]

[26]I read Taylor's "The Diversity of Goods" (included in his *Philosophical Papers*, vol. 2) as a splendid contribution to this poeticization. But there is a strain in Taylor's writing—one that I think of as unfortunately Aristotelian and as opposed to the laudable, dominant Hegelian strain—that leads him to want a theory of the self as *more* than a self-reweaving mechanism. It leads him to want something like metaphysical, as well as democratic, freedom.

[27]I try to spell out this notion of "the poeticization of culture" in more detail in chap. 3 of *Contingency, Irony and Solidarity* (Cambridge: Cambridge University Press, 1989).

CHAPTER 5

Pragmatism or Hermeneutics? Epistemology after Foundationalism

CHARLES B. GUIGNON

> They were offered the choice between becoming kings or couriers of kings. The way children would, they all wanted to be couriers. Therefore there are only couriers who hurry about the world, shouting to each other—since there are no kings—messages that have become meaningless.
>
> —Kafka

It has become common in certain circles lately to divide the world up into foundationalists and nonfoundationalists. Nonfoundationalists, who rally around Richard Rorty's new pragmatism, see the later writings of Ludwig Wittgenstein and Martin Heidegger as showing us that all justification and belief are matters of social practice. They describe foundationalists as Platonists or Cartesians who still cling to the discredited metaphysics of presence or to the dream of certainty. Behind this picture is the assumption that traditional epistemology, the principal backer of foundationalism, went to pieces somewhere during the second half of the nineteenth century, and that heroic measures to save it by positivists, phenomenologists, conceptual analysts, and scientific naturalists have all failed. The pragmatists recommend we lay the body to rest. And since, as Rorty says, dispensing with foundations "is in a fair way toward dispensing with philosophy,"[1] the demise of epistemology-centered philosophy should bring with it the end of philosophy in general.

A first version of this essay was presented at the April 1988 Oberlin College colloquium "The Social Dimension in Knowledge."
[1]Richard Rorty, "Epistemological Behaviorism and the De-Transcendentalization of Analytic Philosophy," in *Hermeneutics and Practice*, ed. Robert Hollinger (Notre Dame, Ind.: Notre Dame University Press, 1985), p. 102.

81

A different reading of the attack on epistemology is offered by a
hermeneutic writer like Charles Taylor, who takes the thought of
Wittgenstein and Heidegger as pointing to a new direction for philos-
ophizing. As Taylor sees it, the critique of epistemology has undermined the old representationalist picture of our human situation—
the view of ourselves as, at a basic level, minds striving to ground
our beliefs about objects in privileged representations. But this critique, far from killing off philosophy, reinvigorates "the tradition of
self-critical reason" by ridding us of the "distorted anthropological
beliefs" linked to epistemology. It leads us to a "deeper and more
valid" view of ourselves by revealing "something of our deep or
authentic nature as selves."[2] For Taylor, then, the interesting division
is between representationalist and nonrepresentationalist pictures of
humans. When we have fully grasped this truer insight into our
condition, he thinks, we will be able to reformulate traditional epistemological questions on a firmer basis.

Rorty, in contrast, is suspicious of this talk of a "better" and
"truer" understanding of who we are. In his view, intellectual history is not a matter of "progress" but of evolutionary drift, "new
forms of life constantly killing off old forms—not to accomplish a
higher purpose, but blindly."[3] It is the job of future intellectual historians to tell the story of what we are accomplishing; *we* have no idea
what rough beast is slouching toward the East Coast APA meetings
to be born. So Rorty recommends simply changing the subject: dropping all the bad old questions in the hope of bringing about a new
form of intellectual life. Since arguing against philosophical views
just gets us embroiled in their vocabulary, he suggests we simply
brush off the whole set of questions and say, " 'Try it this way,'
unsupplemented by an attempt to spell out what the 'it' refers to."[4]

In what follows, I try to focus the issues involved in this "struggle
over the corpse of epistemology."[5] I first sketch out the hermeneutic
picture of our human situation Taylor draws from Wittgenstein and
Heidegger and consider Rorty's criticisms. Then I briefly lay out Rorty's reading of the impact of Wittgenstein and Heidegger and identify

[2]Charles Taylor, "Overcoming Epistemology," in *After Philosophy: End or Transformation?* ed. K. Baynes, J. Bohman, and T. McCarthy (Cambridge: MIT Press, 1987), pp.
479, 482–83.
[3]Rorty, *Contingency, Irony, and Solidarity* (Cambridge: Cambridge University Press,
1989), p. 19.
[4]Rorty, "Beyond Realism and Anti-Realism," in *Wo Steht die Analytische Philosophie
Heute?* ed. L. Nagl and R. Heinrich (Vienna: R. Oldenbourg Verlag, 1986), p. 115.
[5]Taylor, "Overcoming Epistemology," p. 485.

some problems with his position. By showing the shortcomings of his pragmatism, I hope to show there are good reasons to follow out the hermeneutic project of recasting epistemological questions and our understanding of what is at stake in confronting them. From this hermeneutic standpoint, the distinction between foundationalism and nonfoundationalism just proves to be uninteresting.

Hermeneutics and Philosophical Anthropology

In Taylor's view, what Wittgenstein and Heidegger have given us is a new ontological understanding of ourselves, a new "philosophical anthropology" that displaces the representationalist picture we inherited from epistemology. Starting from descriptions of our everyday, pretheoretical practical lives, they proceed by what Taylor describes as a kind of "transcendental argument" to reveal the conditions that make possible our involvement in the world. For example, the early Heidegger's description of agency as being-in-the-world shows that we are for the most part caught up in practical activities, grappling with contexts of equipment that are "significant" in the sense that things show up as *counting* or *mattering* to us in relation to our undertakings. What is "given" at the most basic level in ordinary practical activity, for Heidegger, is not isolated objects with properties (present-at-hand things), but a holistic web of functional relations organized around our projects (the ready-to-hand). When I am busy working in my workshop, the hammer presents itself as hammering "in order to" fasten boards together, which is "for" building a bookcase, which is "for the sake of" my being a home craftsman. Moreover, my own identity as an agent here is defined by the familiar equipmental context in which I am absorbed: in this context I can be a home craftsman, but not a priest serving Mass. The possible stances I can take in my agency are themselves preformed by my enculturation into the social practices of the community in which I live.

In this description of our everyday practical lives there is no role to be played by the picture of an isolated subject confronting a world of present-at-hand objects and forming representations of them. Heidegger says that the idea that there is "'at first' only a thing [which] is present-at-hand . . . in a space in general" is an "illusion."[6] In an

---

[6] Martin Heidegger, *Being and Time*, trans. J. Macquarrie and E. Robinson (New York: Harper & Row, 1962), p. 421.

ingenious historical analysis, he tries to show how modern objectifying science and its handmaid, epistemology, arose as a specialized
way of dealing with the world for particular purposes. The naturalistic model of reality, which portrays the world as a universe of material
objects occupying positions in a space-time coordinate system, provides us with a way of construing the world that has certain advantages. But this "regional ontology" gives us no privileged access to
the way things really are independent of our practices and interests.
It follows that cases of formulating and justifying beliefs about objects
"in the external world"—of detached "knowing that"—are made
possible by a practically engaged "know-how" where we are, so to
speak, already up to our elbows in the midst of things. Hence being-
in-the-world is said to be "more primordial" than knowing in the
sense that (1) forming representations is derivative from and parasitic
on our prior participation in a practical life-world, whereas (2) our
everyday practical affairs cannot be accounted for solely in terms of
the picture of subjects representing meaningless objects. This kind
of primordiality claim can be thought of as transcendental, according
to Taylor, because it tries to show "the indispensable conditions of
there being anything like experience or awareness of the world in
the first place."[7]

In a similar way Taylor suggests that Wittgenstein shows how our
use of words and our grasp of things depends on our understanding
of intelligible situations and our participation in the practices, cus-
toms, and common ways of acting of our community. In this sense,
"we are aware of the world through a 'we' before we are through
an 'I'."[8] The shared background of socially attuned understanding
cannot be seen as built up from isolated bits of information about
brute facts, since our ability to discriminate what "facts" are *relevant*
presupposes a prior mastery of the meaningfulness of the public situations in which they first show up.

The lesson Taylor finds in Wittgenstein and later Heidegger is that
language is the medium which orients us within the shared life-
world. Our public language articulates the centers of significance of
our practical life-world and makes manifest what counts for us. From
the standpoint of this description of everyday agency, we find ourselves "always already thrown" into a communal background of intelligibility that preshapes how the world appears and who we *are* as

[7]Taylor, "Overcoming Epistemology," p. 473.
[8]Taylor, *Philosophy and the Human Sciences* (Cambridge: Cambridge University Press,
1985), p. 40.

agents. We are therefore unavoidably caught up in a hermeneutic circle to the extent that our grasp of the things around us is always preshaped by a general mastery of the meaning of the entire context. And so there is no way to drive in a wedge between "what things are really like in themselves" and the interpretations we bring with us to situations. Since there is no way to objectify this background of understanding in order to treat it as a web of beliefs, there is no way to accomplish the foundationalist project of grounding it in privileged representations.

Taylor thinks that the kind of transcendental arguments found in Wittgenstein and Heidegger can give us a deeper, truer grasp of who we are as agents because they formulate and make explicit what he calls our "agent's knowledge." The claim here is that we must always have a privileged access to our own agency because action (as opposed to inadvertent movement) is *directed* by the self-understanding of the person who acts. This is a consequence of the familiar point that action is identifiable only under a description, and that only certain descriptions capture the behavior *as* action. When my hand goes up at a meeting, for example, it is true of me that I am flexing my deltoids, displacing air molecules, and voting for the man I like. But you have correctly identified my *action* only if you grasp it under the description it bears for me. Of course, you may have a better insight into what I am really doing than I have; you may see, perhaps, that actually I am displaying my sexist attitudes by voting for the man rather than for the woman. But this sort of revisionary description must start out from, and be able to make sense of, the original explanandum, my own self-description. This is why Taylor says that "the very nature of human action requires that we understand it, at least initially, in its own terms; that means we understand the description it bears for the agent."[9]

Taylor also suggests that to have this grasp of our own actions is to have some understanding of the conditions that make the action possible. No matter how ignorant I am of the theory behind voting, I must have a tacit grasp of what voting is all about, since I can call "foul" when something contravenes the constitutive rules of the practice. More importantly, Taylor holds that, as agents, we must have some understanding of the conditions that make action in general possible: our understanding of ourselves as agents is constitutive

[9]Ibid., p. 140.

of our agency, and so is "essential to our acting."[10] With an air of paradox that is only apparent, Taylor claims that this understanding of our own agency is both unchallengeable and defeasible. It is unchallengeable because it captures the most basic conditions that make possible our own self-understanding as agents. Yet it is also defeasible because it tries to make explicit "what is most difficult for us to formulate"[11]—the all-pervasive background conditions for any agency whatsoever. This points to a new task for philosophy: the hermeneutic project of explicating the background of intelligibility that makes action possible. The hope is that we will gain insight into the structures of self-interpreting activity that underlie all interpretations.

But Taylor is also aware that our ordinary self-understanding often is shot through with distortions and deceptions mediated by popular theories and current fads. It is necessary, therefore, to make sense of how interpretations can be validated. His suggestion is that we abandon the old Cartesian ideal of certainty and try to clarify what goes on in the kinds of validation we actually find in everyday life. Consider, for example, how we explain personal transformations in our lives—the move from an initially inadequate view of things to a better, deeper understanding. Usually we proceed by telling a story about how we came to realize the inadequacy of the old view and how we came to adopt our present view. Because our actions are guided by our interpretations of things, a distorted interpretation will generate blocked, impeded, or self-defeating activity. When we improve our interpretations, the transformation is reflected in more coherent and effective action. In the stories we normally tell of such personal transitions, we explain how we came to realize that the original position was out of touch with our true aims, and how we came to see that the new interpretation helped us to achieve those aims. The new outlook "supersedes" the older one because it can explain the inadequacy of the older view in its own terms—that is, in terms of the aims it sought to realize but could not. For example, I might tell a story about my transformed views on childrearing that begins by saying, "I used to think that I should save my children trouble by doing things for them, but now I see it is better to let them try it themselves."

---

[10]Taylor, *Human Agency and Language* (Cambridge: Cambridge University Press, 1985), p. 206.

[11]Taylor, "The Validity of Transcendental Arguments," *Proceedings of the Aristotelian Society* 79 (1978–79): 165.

These stories of personal transitions, according to Taylor, provide a "practice criterion" for validating interpretations. They show how one outlook was found to be superior to another in the course of acting, and so they can make sense of epistemic advance in the flow of our practical lives. Of course, these examples of ordinary ways of validating views will fail to satisfy the foundationalist's longing for certainty and closure. But they suggest that there might be a way of reconciling the hermeneutic circle with the belief that we can gain greater "self-clarity about our nature as knowing agents, by adopting a better and more critically defensible notion of what this entails."[12]

Pragmatism and Playfulness

In Rorty's view, the hermeneutic attempt to find something for philosophy to do after the death of epistemology is simply a failure to carry the thought of Wittgenstein and Heidegger through to its inevitable conclusions. What these writers have shown us, he claims, is not a new direction for philosophy, but a way of trivializing the traditional problems of philosophy. "When Wittgenstein is at his best," Rorty says, "he resolutely avoids constructive criticism and sticks to pure satire; . . . he just makes fun of the whole idea that there is something here to be explained."[13] And the later Heidegger, who gave up on the idea of ontology, offers us only "the endless, repetitive, literary-historical 'deconstruction' of the 'Western meta-physics of presence'."[14] What Wittgenstein and Heidegger have taught us is that we are self-interpreting beings who draw our self-understanding from the language games circulating in our culture. Since there are no vocabulary-neutral facts or criteria that could give us a reason for adopting one vocabulary over another, we have no basis for claiming that one vocabulary gives us a "truer, better" insight into things than another. *Within* any vocabulary there will be "normal discourse" with its standardized criteria and rules that dictate "what society lets us say."[15] But there is no exit from the play of irreconcilable language games to a privileged vocabulary.

[12]Taylor, "Overcoming Epistemology," p. 479.
[13]Rorty, *Consequences of Pragmatism* (Minneapolis: University of Minnesota Press, 1982), p. 34.
[14]Ibid., p. xxii.
[15]Rorty, *Philosophy and the Mirror of Nature* (Princeton: Princeton University Press, 1979), p. 174.

The conclusion Rorty draws from Wittgenstein and Heidegger is that we should adopt the position he calls "textualism": the view "that all problems, topics, and distinctions are language-relative— the results of our having chosen to use a certain vocabulary, to play a certain language-game." From the textualist standpoint, science is not "less primordial" than everydayness; it is just one vocabulary among others, a "vocabulary which happens to be handy in predicting and controlling nature." Science may have grown up in the same neighborhood with epistemology, but it was never dependent on philosophical grounding and can get along without it. Rorty claims that "*real* theories"—actual first-order inquiries in the various special sciences—will go on as before after philosophy is disbanded. There is no "fundamental ontology" that could ground these regional inquiries. Although Rorty backs up his pragmatism with a barrage of Berkeleyan arguments designed to show that "we can never compare human thought or language with bare, unmediated reality," his claim is that the philosophical quest for essences and certainty never has made any actual difference and has not panned out anyway. Real, ongoing inquiry in the arts and sciences swings free of philosophical pretensions.[16]

Rorty is sharply critical of Taylor's attempt to use hermeneutics to formulate a new philosophical anthropology. First, he sees the belief that a phenomenology of agency will lead to a deeper knowledge of who we are as merely a vestige of essentialism. If we know reality only under descriptions made available by current language games, then the same is true of our knowledge of ourselves. We have no privileged access to our own nature as humans, no way of gaining self-knowledge by "reading our own program." The recognition that we are self-interpreting beings shows us that a human is "a self-changing being, *capable of remaking himself by remaking his own speech.*"[17] We are, in H. L. Dreyfus's words, "self-interpretation all the way down." Our "intuitions" into our own nature are either side-effects of current language games or the precipitates of traditions we would do well to discard. There are innumerable ways of describing human beings, and no reasons to accord any of these a special status. Hermeneutics is right to say that "there is nothing much to 'man' except one more animal, until culture . . . begin[s] to shape him into something else."[18] But it is wrong to think that reflecting

[16]Rorty, *Consequences of Pragmatism,* pp. 139–40.
[17]Rorty, "Epistemological Behaviorism," p. 104.
[18]Rorty, *Consequences of Pragmatism,* p. 208.

on our latest cultural self-descriptions will give us information about timeless structures of agency or about deep meanings built into the human condition as such. And if we lack privileged insight into our being as agents, then Taylor's types of transcendental argument cannot get off the ground. Rorty grants that certain sorts of ad hoc "parasitism arguments" may be useful in showing that particular views are unacceptable, but these arguments are purely negative and cannot establish any deeper necessities. The faith that attacking a philosophical view will lead us to a deeper, more fundamental truth about ourselves buys into the old grand metanarrative of progress that is no longer credible in our postmodern world.

Second, Taylor's attempt to show that there are postfoundationalist ways of validating beliefs also fails. We can always make our current views look good by cooking up some story about how those views supersede the older ones, but this fact shows us more about our skills at storytelling than about the validity of our beliefs. And the feeling that our new practices help us cope better—that our lives are running smoother or getting us in touch with what we really want—is no reason to think our current views are better than older ones. Certainly, *within* a particular language game with its inbuilt notions of "coping," "world," and "success," we can make sense of the idea of more successful ways of coping. But there is no way to see "language-as-a-whole in relation to something else for which it is a means to an end."[19] From where Rorty sits, the notions of coping or success, looked at outside of particular regional activities, are wheels in a machine that turn when nothing else is moving. Over time, vocabularies mutate into ways of talking we regard as "better in the sense that they come to *seem* clearly better than their predecessors."[20] But the *feeling* that they are better gives us no reason to think they *are* better in any absolute sense. The metaphors of "depth" and "primordiality" should be tossed aside with the old metaphors of mirroring and correspondence.

The upshot of Rorty's critique of epistemology-centered philosophy is a kind of linguistic perspectivism that regards our understanding as always preshaped by the language games currently in the air in our cultural world. We do best to think of ourselves as perpetually self-reweaving webs of beliefs and desires who play language games off one another to produce new language games to suit our current

[19]Ibid., p. xix.
[20]Ibid., p. xxxvii.

purposes. When we see that there is "no way to underwrite or criticize the ongoing, self-modifying know-how of the user of language" in terms of an account of human nature,[21] we will "become increasingly ironic, playful, free and inventive in our choice of self-descriptions."[22] The character-ideal Rorty proposes for our postmodern age is "self-enlargement": the Nietzschean experimentalist and aestheticist project of multiplying perspectives and playing with them in order to create one's life as a work of art. The ideal for the "syncretic, ironic, nominalist intellectual" is "to treat all vocabularies as tools rather than as mirrors,"[23] and to swing freely between alternative language games, knowing that none of them gives us any "primordial" insight into the truth about ourselves or our world.

At the same time, Rorty suggests that it is best for practical purposes to go along with the "normal discourse of the day" in dealing with our fellow inquirers in public life. The conception of a shared background of agreement about the results of normal inquiry in our social context is the basis for Rorty's "mild ethnocentrism": the view that we must always start from "what society allows us to get away with saying," or from "what inquiry for the moment is leaving alone." There is "nothing to be said about either truth or rationality apart from the familiar procedures of justification which a given society—*ours*—uses in one or another area of inquiry."[24] For Davidsonian reasons, there is no way to formulate the scheme-content distinction with respect to our normal discourse, and hence no way to make sense of the idea that the majority of our beliefs are false. What counts for us in our public lives, then, should be achieving greater solidarity by encouraging the uncoerced continuance of normal conversation, not discovering truths about objective reality.

Rorty proposes ways of demystifying the key concepts of traditional epistemology by translating them into an idiom that refers solely to features of our social practices. We should adopt "a sociological view of the distinction between knowledge and opinion," he suggests, treating "opinion" as belief for which deviance is compatible with membership in a community, and "knowledge" as belief

[21]Rorty, "From Logic to Language to Play," *Proceedings and Addresses of the American Philosophical Association* 59 (June 1986): 751.

[22]Rorty, "Freud and Moral Reflection," in *Pragmatism's Freud: The Moral Disposition of Psychoanalysis*, ed. Joseph H. Smith and William Kerrigan (Baltimore: Johns Hopkins University Press, 1986), p. 12.

[23]Ibid., p. 15.

[24]Rorty, "Solidarity or Objectivity?" in *Post-Analytic Philosophy*, ed. John Rajchman and Cornel West (New York: Columbia University Press, 1985), p. 6.

for which such deviance is not permitted.[25] We should regard "truth" as whatever is regarded as commendable in the way of belief by some group, and falsity as what runs against the grain. "Rationality" is defined by what is the normal outcome of normal inquiry in the regional sciences. In general, Rorty recommends " 'stepping back' in the historicist manner of Heidegger and Dewey, or in the quasi-anthropological manner of Foucault"[26] in order to regard our "intuitions" as countenanced moves in current language games rather than as insights into truths about our human nature. The goal of this "historicist understanding of social practices"[27] is to help us forget about pointless foundationalist worries and to redirect our energies to "the real problems of men." Philosophical reflections on "the big questions," like our religious views or our sexual preferences, are best kept to ourselves.

The Limits of Pragmatism

Rorty's pragmatism is woven together from two central but not always harmonious strands. On the one hand, there is his communitarian confidence that there is always a stable, all-pervasive background of normal discourse circulating in our culture that backs up our mundane reflections on truth, rationality, and justification in first-order "real" inquiry. This conception of a background of agreement in judgments underwrites the ethnocentric claim that, because we are always "insiders" within a particular historical and cultural group, we "have to start from where we are," and so "we must, in practice, privilege our own group."[28] As insiders, we should accept as true whatever is the outcome of normal discourse in our culture at the present time. There can be no deeper grounding for our beliefs and practices than the fact that we are participants in a community where these things are generally accepted.

On the other hand, however, this communitarian strand is coupled with an existentialist strand that follows from Rorty's textualism. Since all our beliefs are language-relative—"the result of our having

[25]Rorty, "The Historiography of Philosophy: Four Genres," in *Philosophy in History*, ed. Richard Rorty, J. B. Schneewind, and Quentin Skinner (Cambridge: Cambridge University Press, 1984), p. 66.
[26]Rorty, *Consequences of Pragmatism*, p. xxi.
[27]Rorty, "Epistemological Behaviorism," p. 115.
[28]Rorty, "Solidarity or Objectivity?" p. 12.

chosen to . . . play a certain language-game''[29]—and since there are
no pregiven criteria guiding our choice of a vocabulary, we should
recognize that all language games are ultimately optional, a matter
of free decision. As a result, we always have the freedom to step
outside normal discourse in order to create new forms of abnormal
discourse. In fact, since we are most human when we are creating
''ever more various and multicolored artifacts,''[30] we most fully realize our potential for freedom when we treat all vocabularies as tools
at our disposal and dedicate ourselves to playfully inventing new,
idiosyncratic metaphors in composing our own lives as ''poems of
existence.''

Rorty tries to combine these two strands by portraying the ideal
pragmatist's life as neatly compartmentalized into public and private
spheres. In our public lives we should adopt the insider's perspective
on our beliefs and practices and warmly embrace the normal results
of normal discourse. Rorty fully agrees with Joseph Schumpeter's
claim that ''what distinguishes a civilized man from a barbarian'' is
the ability ''to realize the relative validity of one's convictions and
yet stand for them unflinchingly.''[31] In our private lives, however,
we should recognize that current normal discourse is only ''an eva-
nescent moment in a continuing conversation''[32] with no binding
significance for us, and that we are therefore free to weave our own
personal webs of belief and desire in any way we like. This separation
of public and private leads to Rorty's vision of an ''ideal world order''
as an ''intricately-textured collage of private narcissism and public
pragmatism.''[33] On pain of inconsistency, Rorty must hold that the
only reason for accepting this picture of an ideal world is itself pragmatic: it *seems* clearly better in the light of our favorite practices and
institutions at this time.

The question here, however, is whether this vision of a segmented
life really can make sense of our beliefs and practices. It is not clear,
first of all, that the ideal pragmatist's life will realize either the kinds
of freedom or steadfast convictions we admire. Critics of Rorty have
pointed out that the pragmatist's ethnocentric solidarity in public life
would tend to breed an uncritical conformism to the status quo which

[29]Rorty, *Consequences of Pragmatism*, p. 140; my emphasis.
[30]Rorty, *Contingency, Irony, and Solidarity*, p. 54.
[31]Ibid., p. 46.
[32]Rorty, *Consequences of Pragmatism*, p. xlvii, n. 50.
[33] Rorty, ''On Ethnocentrism: A Reply to Clifford Geertz,'' *Michigan Quarterly Review*
25 (1986): 533–34.

would block out meaningful reflection on the worthiness of our community's convictions. Unflinching commitment here begins to look like closeminded pigheadedness.

But, less obviously, it does not seem likely that the image of the private individual weaving personal webs of abnormal discourse will ensure real freedom. This will become evident if we examine Rorty's picture of choice. Rorty suggests that we will realize our freedom when we recognize that there are no constraints on our self-interpretations other than personally chosen aesthetic standards, and when we take self-enlargement as our only goal in life. The question here, however, is whether this picture of our situation can make sense of real choice. The private spinner of webs of belief and desire is seen as set before an endless array of possibilities where all choices are equally optional, including preferred aesthetic standards. On this picture, the agent lacks any stable vocabulary for expressing the superiority of one course of action over another, and choice is portrayed as a matter of merely plunking for some particular option, of going with one's current inclinations. It could be argued, however, that an agent of this sort would be buffeted about by every passing whim and caprice, a slave to shifting desires and feelings, with no capacity for meaningful choice whatsoever. Freedom is indistinguishable from compulsion. Thus, there is no reason to accept Rorty's experimentalist faith that expanding our sense of the available options will lead to genuine freedom just by liberating us from a narrow and one-sided view of things. For where there is no pregiven moral map to help us identify the paths worth following, the endless multiplication of possibilities in the quest for "self-enlargement" seems to lead to the kind of distraction and dispersal that destroys genuine freedom.

Rorty's goal is to offer a description of our everyday lives which will undercut the assumptions that breed pointless epistemological puzzles. The ideal pragmatist is pictured as a sort of split personality who can swing back and forth between the insider's and outsider's perspectives, going with the flow of normal discourse in his or her public affairs and cooking up revolutionary forms of abnormal discourse in private. It is fair to ask, however, where Rorty himself stands when he formulates this description of our situation. For the most part, his claim is that he is merely engaging in normal discourse, making sociological and historical observations about where we currently stand in our postmodernist culture. Yet it might be argued that this sociological and historical stance of cool, detached reporting itself presupposes an outsider's perspective on our practices. For it is only when we look down on our community's forms of life from a platform of disengaged, quasi-scientific "objectivity" that we can see our own practices as the "play" of a particular group or our own history as a pageant of irreconcilable worldviews.

I want to suggest that this objectifying stance toward our practices in fact *creates* the new pragmatist picture of our identity as individuals who vacillate between absorption in normal discourse and invention of types of abnormal discourse. By adopting the point of view of the external observer, Rorty tacitly assumes that we get the clearest view of our lives when we are disengaged subjects who are not ourselves involved in any particular practices or historical events, but are merely observing the behavior of a group. Yet it may be that such an outlook fixes in advance how our own lives can show up for us. It is natural, from this standpoint, to see ourselves as individuals set before an array of language games and traditions we can take up or discard at will, and to see our ordinary acceptance of normal discourse as the result of a kind of stupefaction brought on by our immersion in public preoccupations. In other words, we can see our practices and history as items on hand for playful invention or unflinching conviction only if we first assume that we are, at a basic level, detached subjects set before a world that has no necessary connection to our own identity. But it should be obvious that this picture of our situation gets off the ground only because it buys into and reflects the very epistemological model that Rorty intends to reject. His critique of the epistemological tradition therefore must surreptitiously presuppose the initial validity of that very tradition as a basis for developing his pragmatist descriptions.

The tensions built into this picture become apparent in Rorty's inability to account for what actually goes on within the insider's perspective. The historicist and sociological view of our lives portrays us as a collection of individuals periodically sounding off in ways we label "true" or "false" relative to some grid of criteria we currently hold in common. The correct description of our epistemic practices, on this view, should be given in terms of what a group happens to find commendable in the way of belief at a given time. But this description fails to make sense of why we *care* about forming true beliefs or trying to be rational. Rorty suggests that we would do well to replace our ordinary ways of talking about what we do with what he calls "behaviorist" descriptions. Instead of saying "We have good reasons for believing such-and-such" or "This theory is better than that," we should say "Our peers currently let us get away with saying such-and-such" or "Our group currently takes this theory to be more commendable than that." Yet, because this way of leveling all epistemic discourse down to the monochromatic level of behaviorist descriptions makes it impossible to see why we should care whether theories are rational or true, it would probably undermine any meaningful talk of "reasons" or "better theories" whatsoever. At times, Rorty seems to suggest that this sort of detached behavioristic talk is appropriate only for second-order metadiscourse about first-order real theories, a discourse to be used by defrocked philosophers in a post-Philosophical age. But this distinction of levels threatens to generate a culture split into two groups: the suckers who keep trying, and an elite band of historicist intellectuals, hooting and jeering from the sidelines, who see it all as a transient game. Such a culture seems out of tune with Rorty's democratic sentiments.

Not only does Rorty fail to make sense of our own insider's experience of our practices; he cannot make sense of his own position in formulating his pragmatism. What motivates Rorty's adoption of the detached sociohistoricist stance toward our forms of life is a strong commitment to realizing the Enlightenment ideal of freedom. In other words, the stance of detached objectivity and ironic playfulness is driven by what Nietzsche calls the "ascetic ideal": the desire to cast off custom, tradition, and authority—to wear the world like a loose cloak—in order to be an autonomous, self-defining individual. But it is not clear that Rorty's account of our situation can make sense of the strong moral commitments that motivate his project. It is crucial to Rorty's postmodernist view of our situation that we see morality as nothing other than the practices a group happens to commend at a given time, and that we see all goods as internal to the practices of a group. Our commitment to realizing freedom, then, should be seen merely as the preference of a particular group—we affluent, leisured North Atlantic social democrats—and not as an intrinsic good. Instead of saying "Freedom is good," we should stick to the behaviorist description: "There is a group—ours—that thinks freedom is worth pursuing."

Now given this internalist reading of goods, Rorty does not seem to be able to make adequate sense of his own motivations in defending pragmatism. We have a reason to adopt the ascetic ideal and to take an outsider's perspective toward our own practices only if we believe that impartiality, objectivity, and disengagement will help us get something genuinely worth having. Yet the upshot of adopting this detached attitude is the realization that all strong commitments are ultimately optional matters of personal preference. What this implies is that Rorty must rely on certain deep commitments while simultaneously undercutting our ability to make sense of them. Or, to put this point differently, our ability to see everything we do as "play" undermines our ability to see why we would *want* to see things in this way.

Rorty's response to this sort of criticism is to shift ground back to his communitarian and ethnocentric stance, saying that we heirs of the Enlightenment just *do* value freedom and cannot, for the moment, question this commitment. But there are a number of problems with this way of brushing off the criticism. First, by insisting on a single, univocal set of values we all *must* hold, Rorty closes off meaningful discussion of alternative goods circulating in our pluralistic world. The call for ethnocentrism in just *this* way begins to look like a dogmatic imposition. Second, since it is not clear that Rorty's implied picture of freedom as unconstrained leaps of radical choice captures the actual notion of freedom we liberals have inherited from the Enlightenment, there is room for debate about what sort of freedom we *do* value. And, finally, it is hard to see how the pragmatist confidence that there is some particular set of convictions we must all hold can be made consistent with the picture of all belief as the result of choosing some optional language game. For where belief is regarded as just a transient choice, it loses the bindingness of a genuine conviction.

My claim is that Rorty's pragmatism looks plausible only because it buys into all the key assumptions of the epistemological tradition, and because it surreptitiously presupposes commitments that its own position makes unintelligible. This criticism might be construed as a transcendental argument of the type Rorty sanctions: as a "parasitism argument" designed to show the inadequacy of a position by showing that it cannot account for the background conditions that make our practices possible. We might grant that such arguments do not establish necessities and still hold that they help to eliminate contenders. If this is so, then we are justified in rejecting Rorty's new pragmatism.

Hermeneutics Reconsidered

Hermeneutics insists on holding fast to the insider's perspective as the source from which all reflection, including philosophy, ultimately originates. The awareness that we cannot escape the insider's perspective results from acknowledging our own "finitude"—our root-edness in a cultural, historical, and linguistic context we can never fully objectify or ground. This finitude is seen not as a constraint, however, but as an enabling condition that first gives us a window onto ourselves and our world. Recognizing our finitude points to an understanding of philosophy as necessarily starting from our best grasp of ourselves as agents in the world. Heidegger is driving at this conception of philosophy when he distinguishes his own method, "genuine philosophical 'empiricism,' " from the kinds of "constructivism" that operate with presuppositions about our condition as inquirers drawn from epistemology or from scientific methodology.[34] The goal of the description of everyday agency is to arrive at what Heidegger calls "transcendental generalizations" concerning the bases for alternative interpretations and worldviews,[35] findings that are confirmed or revised through an ongoing dialogue within our own tradition and with other cultures. Such a hermeneutic approach is unavoidably open-ended, but there is no reason to claim in advance that it is an exercise in futility.

From the hermeneutic standpoint, the untenability of Rorty's pragmatism can be diagnosed as a result of his clinging to ontological assumptions drawn from the epistemological model even while claiming that epistemology is dead. This dependence on the tradition becomes apparent when we reflect on how Rorty is led to his "textualism." The epistemological model had assumed that we are subjects set over against an independently existing world we want to know. When it becomes clear that we can have no direct access to "Nature as it is in itself" distinct from our interpretations, it seems natural to just drop the scheme-content distinction and to acknowledge that there is no exit from our socially conditioned beliefs and practices. The result of this textualist move, however, is a feeling of loss: where we had formerly looked for Reality, we now find only a gap or hole—an empty place nothing could fill. We begin to think of ourselves as entangled in perspectives, adrift on an endless sea of interpretations, cut off from solid ground.

Ever since the "linguistic turn," the shift to textualism has been made in terms of theories of reference. Language traditionally had been treated as a tool for representing a nonlinguistic domain of objects. In this picture of language, the traditional binary oppositions

---

[34]Heidegger, *Being and Time*, p. 490, n. x.
[35]Ibid., p. 244.

are recapitulated in the distinctions between sign and signified or between sentence and fact. When we find that there is no way to specify what a sign signifies without using other signs, or that there is no way to carve out facts without using sentences, we begin to cast around to find what it is that language refers to. The natural answer is that language hooks up with other language. Once again, there is the feeling of loss. The conclusions that "there is nothing outside the text" or that "signs refer only to other signs" capture the sense that there is no way to get out of language to make contact with the nonlinguistic reality language is supposed to designate.

What should be noted here is that this picture of our predicament as cut off from Reality makes sense only because of the way it contrasts with the binary opposition of self versus world it is supposed to replace. But that means that the textualist picture is parasitic on the scheme-content or sign-signified oppositions it initially set out to defeat. In other words, the critique of epistemology relies on the representationalist model in order to question the possibility of representation. Nietzsche saw that rejecting the reality pole of the subject-object opposition would lead initially to feelings of disappointment and to nihilism: "Where we had sought Reality, there is now only nothingness." Rorty's recommendation for a new stance of playful irony is supposed to provide a more upbeat response to this situation. Instead of nostalgically longing for a world we could never have anyway, we should simply give up the notions of "objective truth," "reference," and "reality," and join together in keeping the conversation going with no pretense of getting in touch with something beyond ourselves. Conversation now appears as a one-dimensional play of signifiers which either occludes genuine distinctions of better and worse or regiments such distinctions into a sociological vocabulary dealing with how a group behaves. As Taylor has pointed out, what often motivates the latter sort of "communitarian" conclusion is a metaphysics of individual will run mad: "the license it offers to subjectivity, unfettered by anything in the nature of a correct interpretation or an irrecusable meaning of either life or text, to effect its own transformations, to invent meaning."[36] Given this postmodernist picture, it takes fancy footwork to try to avoid charges of pernicious relativism and irrationalism.

Hermeneutics avoids these consequences of pragmatism by simply

---

[36]Taylor, "Overcoming Epistemology," p. 482.

discarding the ontological assumptions built into the epistemological model. When we start from a description of our everyday agency before theorizing, we see that our own identity as agents is bound up with concrete situations and a practical life-world that we *find* rather than create. In this respect Heidegger and Wittgenstein propose a sort of Ptolemaic reaction to Kant's Copernican revolution: although our practices preshape how things show up in our lives, we are nevertheless dependent on the world around us in order to *be* practical agents. There is no way to sever ourselves from our ties to the world without undercutting our ability to be human at all. In Heidegger's vocabulary, our being-in-the-world—our involvement in contexts of significance—is the bedrock for all theorizing. And, to the extent that there is no external vantage point from which we can describe this all-pervasive background of everydayness, there is no way to make it explicit once and for all. But the fact that our quest for insight into our being as situated agents is open-ended does not imply that everything is up in the air, a matter of mere "play." This seems to be Wittgenstein's point when he says, "The difficult thing is not to dig down to the ground; no, it is to recognize the ground that lies before us as the ground."[37] A hardy hermeneutic realism can insist on the "primordiality" of the ready-to-hand while acknowledging that the project of interpreting the significance of the everyday life-world may be interminable.

The hermeneutic characterization of everyday existence leads to a transformed understanding of the role of language in our lives. Heidegger suggests that, instead of seeing language as a tool on hand for designating an independently existing world of objects, we think of it as primarily the medium through which the world is "made manifest" to us. On this view, the fundamental role of language is not representing things by means of assertions, but rather *presenting* things—disclosing how they are present—in our attuned dealings with them. To use Taylor's example, when I get on a crowded bus on a hot day and say to a fellow passenger, "Hot, isn't it?" my utterance neither conveys information nor poses a question. Instead, its role is to make manifest a shared sense of how things stand with us, to get something out into the open between us, or to body forth our attuned ways of being together in public space.[38] Here the distinc-

---

[37]Ludwig Wittgenstein, *Remarks on the Foundations of Mathematics*, rev. ed., trans. G. E. M. Anscombe (Cambridge: MIT Press, 1978), 6: 31.
[38]See "Theories of Meaning," in Taylor's *Human Agency and Language*.

tion between linguistic sign and object signified has no purchase. The world just *is* what emerges into presence in our discourse, and discourse relies on the disclosedness of the world for its sense. The picture of the disengaged subject trying to correlate signs either with objects or with other signs cannot capture fully what goes on in using language. For if mastery of a language requires being in on a form of life—being able to participate, to some extent at least, in a public life-world—the pure disengaged observer could never speak a language. When we see our assertions as bound up with our involvement in the familiar world, there is no longer any toehold for the picture of ourselves as playing with language games and cut off from a nonlinguistic reality.

On the hermeneutic view, traditional epistemological questions about truth, rationality, justification, and relativity should be reformulated and addressed only after we have worked out a general account of our situation as being-in-the-world. Old notions of correct representation and Cartesian certainty, along with the inner-outer and subject-object distinctions, will probably prove unhelpful except when discussing certain regional activities. The project of clarifying our being as agents will proceed by a series of skirmishes in discussing particular problems rather than by knockdown arguments based on global advance assumptions about our epistemic predicament. Of course, a central part of this investigation will consist of making sense of the actual kinds of delusion, deception, and distortion that arise in different areas of our lives. But there is no a priori reason to think that delusion is so endemic that we can *never* arrive at deeper insights into ourselves and our world.

Current writings of hermeneutic thinkers show how this project of working out a post-Epistemological epistemology might go. These include attempts to clarify the role of practical reason and narrative historiography in justifying knowledge claims, reflections on rationality as the ability to adopt multiple partially disengaged perspectives rather than a totally disengaged stance of pure "objectivity," and descriptions of the experience of gaining insight through literature and works of art. Heidegger's characterization of truth as a disclosedness that lets things show up, and Wittgenstein's therapies aimed at debunking the idea that a uniform pattern of explanation must be applicable to all areas of life, are also examples of this project of reinscribing epistemological questions within a nonrepresentationalist picture of our lives as agents. For hermeneutics, the important thing is not to pour new wine into old bottles—not to impose the theoretical requirements of the old representationalist model onto the genuine epistemological questions that arise in the course of our lives.[39]

[39]I am deeply indebted to David Hiley for feedback during every stage of thinking through this paper, and to Paul Roth for careful criticisms of an earlier version.

CHAPTER 6

Beneath Interpretation

RICHARD SHUSTERMAN

I

Kohelet, that ancient postmodern who already remarked that all is
vanity and there is nothing new under the sun, also insisted that
there is a time for everything: a time to be born and a time to die, a
time to break down and a time to build up, a time to embrace and a
time to refrain from embracing. There is no mention of a time for
interpretation, but surely there is one; and just as surely that time is
now. Our age is even more hermeneutic than it is postmodern, and
the only meaningful question to be raised at this stage is whether
there is ever a time when we refrain from interpreting. To answer
affirmatively by citing dreamless sleep is to dodge the real issue,
which is whether we can ever refrain from interpreting without
thereby refraining from intelligent activity altogether. There is a host
of universal hermeneuts who answer this firmly in the negative,
maintaining that simply to perceive, read, understand, or behave
intelligently at all is already, and must always be, to interpret. They
hold that whenever we experience anything with meaning, such
meaningful experience must always be a case and product of interpretation.

This position of hermeneutic universalism[1] dominates most current

---

[1] In an earlier version of this paper I was tempted, by alliteration, to describe this
position as ''hermeneutic holism'' (see Richard Shusterman, ''Beneath Interpretation,
Against Hermeneutic Holism,'' *Monist* 73 (1990): 181–204). Though the term ''hermeneutic universalism'' is longer and more plodding, it has the advantage of more clearly
distinguishing the position I attack from another position that the term ''hermeneutic
holism'' might suggest. This second view maintains that the meaning of a word or

interpretive theory. Loss of faith in foundationalist and realist objectivity has made it the current dogma. Having abandoned the ideal of reaching a naked, rock-bottom, unmediated God's-eye view of reality, we seem impelled to embrace the opposite position—that we see everything through an interpretive veil or from an interpretive angle. Indeed, on a pragmatist account of meaning, one might further assert that since the terms "veil" and "angle" inappropriately suggest that we can even make sense of the idea of a naked, perspectiveless reality, we do not merely *see* everything through interpretation, but everything *is* in fact constituted by interpretation. In other words, there is nothing real (and certainly nothing real for us) that is not interpreted. This theory can, of course be traced back to Nietzsche's famous remark that "facts are precisely what there is not, only interpretations,"[2] and it is not surprising that today's heremeneutic universalists have turned to him as a major philosophical inspiration. Alexander Nehamas's fine book on Nietzsche is in large part a contemporary defense of Nietzschean perspectivism and universal heremeneutics.[3] Nehamas in fact identifies the two positions by defining Nietzsche's perspectivism as "the thesis that every view is an interpretation," and he goes on to assert that not only all views but "all practices are interpretive," since "all our activity is partial and perspectival" (*N*, pp. 66, 70, 72).

Pragmatists, like Nietzcheans, insist on rejecting the very idea of any foundational, mind-independent, and permanently fixed reality that could be grasped or even sensibly thought of without the mediation of human structuring. Such structuring or shaping of perception is today typically considered to be interpretation, and so we find contemporary pragmatists like Stanley Fish repeatedly insisting that interpretation comprises all of our meaningful and intelligent human

---

statement, or the justification of a knowledge claim, is not an affair of simple atomistic reference to foundational objects or atomistic correspondence to privileged representations, but instead always depends on a larger context of words, statements, beliefs, and so forth—a whole background of social practice, and one that is not immune to change. As will be clear from the nonfoundationalist pragmatism of my paper, I am not at all opposed to this sense of interpretive holism; what I challenge is the idea that interpretation constitutes the whole of understanding and meaningful experience. Since several readers found the term "hermeneutic holism" confusingly ambiguous with respect to these issues, it is here replaced by "hermeneutic universalism" or (occasionally) "universal hermeneutics."

[2]Friedrich Nietzsche, *The Will to Power* (New York: Vintage, 1968), para. 481.

[3]See Alexander Nehamas, *Nietzsche: Life as Literature* (Cambridge: Harvard University Press, 1985); hereafter abbreviated in text as *N*.

activity, that "interpretation is the only game in town."[4] All perception and understanding must be interpretation, since "information only comes in an interpreted form." Thus, even in our most primitive and initial seeing of an object, "interpretation has already done its work."[5] Moreover, quite apart from such radical Nietzschean and pragmatist perspectives, we find hermeneutic universalism firmly endorsed by a traditionalist like Hans-Georg Gadamer, who baldy asserts that "all understanding is interpretation."[6]

In short, the various camps of the ever-growing antifoundationalist front seem united by the belief that interpretation subsumes all meaningful experience and reality. This was brought home to me, gently but relentlessly, by my friends from the NEH institute on interpretation held at Santa Cruz.[7] These independent thinkers from divergent philosophical perspectives and professional disciplines converged almost unanimously on the motto that "interpretation goes all the way down," that there is nothing beneath interpretation which serves as the object of interpretation, since anything alleged to be such is itself an interpretive product.

Perhaps a perverse nonconformity (or still worse the posture thereof) made me begin to suspect such a widely held philosophical view, one that I myself had initially found so convincing. Though I remain deeply impressed with the pervasive role of interpretation in human life, I have come to think it may best be understood and sustained by more modest pretensions than hermeneutic universalism. I think interpretation is best served by letting it leave room for something else (beneath or before it); by slimming it down from a bloated state that courts coronary arrest; by saving it from an ultimately self-destructive imperialist expansion.

In this paper then, and in a Nietzschean spirit of affirming by negating, I wish to question the faith in hermeneutic universalism by critically examining what appear to be its best arguments. Having

---

[4]Stanley Fish, *Is There a Text in This Class?* (Cambridge: Harvard University Press, 1980), pp. 350, 352.

[5]Stanley Fish, "Working on the Chain Gang: Interpretation in the Law and in Literary Criticism," *Critical Inquiry* 8 (1982): 204.

[6]Hans-Georg Gadamer, *Truth and Method* (New York: Crossroad, 1982), p. 350; hereafter abbreviated in text as *TM*.

[7]This paper is dedicated to the spirit of that Santa Cruz encounter, and to the most inspiring spirits there: my fellow NEH participants, the moon-loving dreamers, those few Gaiea-respecting dowsers, the playfully surging surf (just as alive and enlivening), and the unforgettably fragrant and sheltering pines and redwoods that shade the Chinquapin jogging trail at UCSC.

shown that those arguments need not compel belief in hermeneutic universalism, I shall go on to suggest why such a belief is more dangerous and unprofitable than the contrary idea that our intelligent and meaningful intercourse with the world includes noninterpretational experience, activity, and understanding, so that we should not think interpretation is the only game in town. Finally, I shall try to determine what distinguishes interpretation from those uninterpreted understandings and experiences that hermeneutic universalists, however, regard as fully subsumable under the concept of interpretation. In drawing this distinction I am not claiming it is a rigid ontological one, where interpretation and understanding are different natural kinds that can never share the same objects. But I hope to show that some functional distinction between them is pragmatically helpful and illuminating, and can itself be helpfully illuminated.

II

Before undertaking these tasks, however, I need to distance my challenge of interpretation from an earlier and influential critique advanced by Susan Sontag in "Against Interpretation."[8] Sontag's attack is directed not at interpretation per se but at the global claims of interpretation over *art*. Indeed, she explicitly endorses hermeneutic universalism's notion of "interpretation in the broadest sense, the sense in which Nietzsche (rightly) says, 'There are no facts, only interpretations' " (*AI*, p. 5). But what *are* the claims of interpretation's dominion over art? Arthur Danto and others have argued that a work of art is ontologically constituted by interpretation. Since physically identical things can be different works if they have different interpretations, "interpretations are what constitutes works, there are no works without them"; without them, works would be the "mere things" of their material substance.[9] This view that the art object is not a physical or foundational fact but must itself be constituted by an interpretive perspective is essentially an application of the Nietzschean view of objects that Danto here confines to the domain of art, elsewhere remaining a realist. Such *constitutive* interpretation of

[8]Susan Sontag, "Against Interpretation," in *Against Interpretation and Other Essays* (New York: Dell, 1966); hereafter abbreviated in text as *AI*.
[9]Arthur Danto, *The Philosophical Disenfranchisement of Art* (New York: Columbia University Press, 1986), p. 45.

art, as Danto notes, should not be the target of Sontag's attack, though its alleged omnipresent ineliminability—that art cannot be meaningfully experienced without being interpreted—will be a target of mine.

The interpretation she instead impugns is the deliberate act of explaining, disclosing, or decoding the content or meaning of the object (interpretively) constituted. Such interpretation of content is indicted as a corruptive act "of translation. . . . The interpreter, without actually erasing or rewriting the text, *is* altering it," making it "into something else," distracting us from "experiencing the luminousness of the thing in itself" by putting us on a false quest for its meaning (*AI*, pp. 5, 6, 8, 13). Rather than opening us up to the powerful sensuous experience of art's surface form, which is the essence of art's liberational challenge to the primacy of the cognitive and discursive, interpretation "poisons our sensibilities" and represents "the revenge of the intellect upon art" at the expense of our "sensual capability" (*AI*, p. 7). Sontag therefore urges, "In place of a hermeneutics we need an erotics of art," and she conceives this erotics in terms of a criticism that gives "more attention to form in art," "that dissolves considerations of content into those of form," and that "would supply a really accurate, sharp, loving description of the appearance of a work of art," "to show *how it is what it is*"(*AI*, pp. 12–14).

Though I support Sontag's protest against hermeneutics' imperialist conquest of all artistic understanding and share her insistence on greater recognition of sensuous immediacy in aesthetic experience, I cannot accept her critique of interpretation. This is not because its repudiation of content for pure form and eros seems to reflect and legitimate what is arguably the worst of American culture—meaningless sex, empty formalism, and contempt of intellect. Such deep ideological complaints we can leave to students of Adorno and to our own moments of alienated discontent. What I instead wish to show is that whatever our verdict on its ideological stance, Sontag's critique is severely crippled by deep confusions and unwarranted assumptions.

First, in claiming that all interpretation "sustains the fancy that there really is such a thing as the content of a work of art" and in subsequently demanding that criticism instead confine itself to form, which is contrastingly real, Sontag relies on a naively rigid content-form distinction which suggests that form itself has no content and which she herself later wishes to deny (*AI*, pp. 5, 11–12). Second, Sontag betrays a naive realism about the work of art's identity and form which is not only unconvincing but totally at odds with the Nietzschean interpretive position she claims to endorse. Her attack on interpretation for necessarily "altering" or "translating" the work "into something else" rather than describing the work as "just what it is," "the thing in itself," presumes first that there is some foundational identity of the work "just as it is" apart from our constitutive and perspectival grasping of it, and second that we can transparently grasp that identity (*AI*, pp. 6, 8, 11, 13). "Transparence", which Sontag claims as the highest value in art and criticism, "means experiencing the luminousness of the thing in itself" (*AI*, p. 13). But the Nietzschean notion of constitutive identity not only rejects such nonperspectival transparency; it repudiates the very idea of the uninterpreted "thing in itself" as a dogmatic notion.[10]

Sontag's third confusion is her presumption that while interpretive content represents "the revenge of the intellect on art" by taming art's sensuous liberational power into something "manageable, conformable" (*AI*, p. 8), form, on the other hand, is neither intellectual nor constraining but simply liberationally erotic. This is obviously false, as the very morphology of the word "conformable" makes clear. Indeed, since the time of Plato and Aristotle, who essentially formed our notion of form, we regard form as something paradigmatically intellectual and constraining. Moreover, as has been emphasized since Kant, the formalistic appreciation of aesthetic objects demands much more intellectual power and repressive austerity than appreciation based on content, which can simply rely on our ordinary feelings associated with and immediately evoked by the content. Formalists like Kant and Clive Bell condemn the more natural, less intellectualized appreciation of content as philistine barbarism.[11] Sontag similarly condemns interpretation of content as philistinism and privileges the appreciation of form. But she mistakenly confuses formal analysis with unintellectual "sensuous immediacy" (*AI*, p. 9), when it instead requires no less (and usually much more) intellectual mediation than the interpretation of content.

[10]See Nietzsche, *The Will to Power*, paras. 556, 557, 559, 560. I examine Nietzsche's alternative account of objects (viz., as interpreted unities) in "Nietzsche and Nehamas on Organic Unity," *Southern Journal of Philosophy* 26 (1988): 379–92.

[11]I discuss the intellectual demands and social preconditions of formalist appreciation in "Of the Scandal of Taste: Social Privilege as Nature in the Aesthetic Theories of Hume and Kant," *Philosophical Forum* 20 (1989): 211–29. But see especially Pierre Bourdieu's systematic and empirical treatment of this topic in his *Distinction: A Social Critique of the Judgement of Taste* (Cambridge: Harvard University Press, 1984), a most illuminating study to which my own work is deeply indebted.

This leads to the fourth crucial error in Sontag's position—her failure to recognize that she is not really sustaining a global rejection of interpretation; for the formalistic analysis she advocates is itself a recognized form of interpretation. It is simply a mistake to think all interpretation is governed by the depth metaphor of uncovering hidden layers or kernels of meaning. Interpretation is also practiced and theorized in terms of formal structure with the aim not so much of exposing hidden meanings but of connecting unconcealed features and surfaces so as to see and present the work as a well-related whole. Recognition of this formalist interpretive mode which aims "to grasp the whole design" of the work is what swayed an earlier rejector of interpretation, T. S. Eliot, from his view that "the work of art cannot be interpreted" to an acceptance of interpretation's ineliminable role and value.[12]

Sontag should similarly recognize that her apparent critique of all interpretation is but a privileging legitimation of one interpretive form above and against all others. She provides no argument that we ever should or could do without interpretation altogether, or that in fact we ever do do without it in at least its Nietzschean constitutive sense. Indeed, she does not even consider hermeneutic universalism's arguments for holding that interpretation is ineliminably and necessarily present in any meaningful or valuable experience of art, or of anything. In short, Sontag's critique is simply normative, that we should not interpret for content. She does not even address the logical issue of whether in fact it is possible not to interpret at all; and her Nietzscheanism and formalism contradictorily suggest it is not. My critique, in contrast, is not primarily normative, since I think that interpretation *should* and *must* be practiced on innumerable occasions. What I wish to contest is the view that, logically and necessarily, we are always interpreting whenever we meaningfully experience or understand anything, the view expressed in Gadamer's dictum that "all understanding is interpretation." I must therefore address hermeneutic universalism's powerful arguments for this view.

III

Since our current hermeneutic turn derives in large part from the rejection of foundationalism, it is not surprising that the central argu-

[12]T. S. Eliot, "Hamlet," in *Selected Essays* (London: Faber, 1976), p. 142; and his

ments for hermeneutic universalism turn on rejecting foundationalist ideas of transparent fact, absolute and univocal truth, and mind-independent objectivity. For such ideas underwrite the possibility of attaining some perfect God's-eye grasp of things as they really are, independent of how we differently perceive them, a seeing or understanding that is free from the corrigibility and perspectival pluralities and prejudices that we willingly recognize as intrinsic to all interpretation.

I think the universalists are right to reject such foundational understanding, but wrong to conclude from this that all understanding is interpretation. Their mistake, a grave but simple one, is to equate the nonfoundational with the interpretive. In other words, what the universalists are sucessfully arguing is that all understanding is non-foundational; that it is always corrigible, perspectival, and somehow prejudiced or prestructured; that no meaningful experience is passively neutral and disinterestedly nonselective. But since, in the traditional foundationalist framework, interpretation is contrasted and designated as *the* form of nonfoundational understanding, the inferior foster home of all corrigible, perspectival perception, it is easy to confuse the view that no understanding is foundational with the view that all understanding is interpretive. Yet this confusion of hermeneutic universalism betrays an unseemly residual bond to the foundationalist framework, in the assumption that what is not foundational must be interpretive. It thus prevents the universalists from adopting a more liberating pragmatist perspective which (I shall argue) can profitably distinguish between understanding and interpretation without thereby endorsing foundationalism. Such pragmatism more radically recognizes uninterpreted realities, experiences, and understandings as already perspectival, prejudiced, and corrigible; in short, as nonfoundationally given.

So much for a general overview of the universalist arguments. I now want to itemize and consider six of them in detail. Though there is some overlap, we can roughly divide them into three groups, respectively based on three ineliminable features of all understanding: (a) corrigibility, (b) perspectival plurality and prejudice, and (c) mental activity and process.

"Introduction" to G. W. Knight, *The Wheel of Fire* (London: Methuen, 1962), p. xix. For a detailed account of the arguments motivating Eliot's hermeneutic turn and for a critical analysis of his mature theory of interpretation, see Richard Shusterman, *T. S. Eliot and the Philosophy of Criticism* (New York: Columbia University Press, 1988), pp. 107–55.

(1) What we understand, what we grasp as truth or fact, frequently turns out to be wrong, to require correction, revision, and replacement by a different understanding. Moreover, this new understanding is typically achieved by reinterpreting the former understanding, and can itself be replaced and shown to be not fact but "mere interpretation" by a subsequent understanding reached through interpretive thought. Since any putative fact or true understanding can be revised or replaced by interpretation, it cannot enjoy an epistemological status higher than interpretation; and interpretation is paradigmatically corrigible and inexhaustive. This is sometimes what is meant by the claim that there are no facts or truths but only interpretations.

The inference, then, is that since understanding is epistemologically no better than interpretation, it is altogether no different from interpretation (as if all meaningful differences had to be differences of apodicticness!). The conclusion is reinforced by the further inference that since all interpretation is corrigible, and all understanding is corrigible, then all understanding is interpretation. Once formulated, the inferences are obviously, indeed pathetically, fallacious. But we tend to accept their conclusion, since we assimilate all corrigible and partial understanding to interpretation, as if genuine understanding itself could never be revised or enlarged, as if understanding had to be interpretive to be corrigible. But why make this rigidly demanding assumption? Traditionally and foundationally, the reason was that understanding (like its cognates truth and fact) was itself defined in contrast to "mere interpretation" as that which *is* incorrigible. But if we abandon foundationalism by denying that any understanding is incorrigible, the idea of corrigible understanding becomes possible and indeed necessary; and once we recognize this idea, there is no need to infer that all understanding must be interpretation simply because it is corrigible. When hermeneutic universalists make this inference, they show an unintended and unbecoming reliance on the foundationalist linkage of uninterpreted understanding with incorrigible, foundational truth.

(2) The second argument for hermeneutic universalism derives from understanding's ineliminable perspectival character and the inevitable plurality of perspectives. We already noted how Nehamas builds his argument that all understanding is interpretive on the premise that all understanding, indeed "all our activity is partial and perspectival." I think the premise is perfectly acceptable and can be established by an argument that Nehamas does not supply. All understanding must be perspectival or aspectual, since all thought

and perception exhibit intentionality (in the phenomenological sense of being about something), and all intentionality is aspectual, in grasping its object in a certain way. But the very idea of perspective or aspect implies that there are other possible perspectives or aspects, which lie (in Gadamer's words) outside "the horizon" of a particular perspectival standpoint and thus outside its "range of vision" (*TM*, p. 269). If all understanding is aspectual and admits of other possible and legitimate perspectives, there can be no univocal and exclusive understanding of any thing, but rather many partial or perspectival ways of seeing it, none of which is wholly and exclusively true.

So much for the premise, but how does it follow that all understanding is interpretive? Again, in the traditional foundationalist framework, interpretation marks the realm of partial, perspectival, and plural ways of human understanding in essential contrast to some ideal understanding that grasps things as they really are univocally, exhaustively, and absolutely. Rejecting the very possiblity and intelligibility of such univocal and complete understanding (as Nehamas and Gadamer rightly do), the universalists infer that all understanding is thereby reduced to interpretation—the foundationalist category for understanding which is not necessarily false and illegitimate (not a *mis*understanding) but which cannot represent true understanding since it is perspectivally plural and not necessarily and wholly true. However, again we should realize that once we are free of foundationalism's doctrines, there is no need to accept its categorizations. There is thus no need to deny that true understanding can itself be perspectivally partial and plural, and consequently no reason to conclude that since all understanding must be perspectival, it must also be interpretation.[13]

(3) In speaking of understanding as perspectival and hence partial, we have so far meant it cannot exclude different perspectives and can in principle always be supplemented. But partiality also has the

[13]I have elsewhere argued that in pragmatic terms we can indeed have complete (albeit perspectival) understanding, and that only in pragmatic, contextual terms is the idea of complete understanding at all intelligible. The idea of completeness always presupposes a particular and limited context or purpose of fulfillment, so the foundationalist idea of completeness in and for itself, without aspects or horizons or purpose, is simply a meaningless notion, not a regrettably unreachable ideal. For more on this see my *T. S. Eliot and the Philosophy of Criticism*, pp. 126–28.

I should also suggest that a radical break with foundationalism allows us to regard things themselves (in the nonfoundational sense of objects we experience) as perspectival. The keyboard I press *is* (and is not simply interpreted as) a writing tool, though I can also treat it as a paperweight or a book prop.

central sense of bias and prejudice. The third argument why understanding must always be interpretation is that it is always prejudiced and never neutrally transparent. This is a key point in the Nietzschean, Gadamerian, and even pragmatist attacks on foundationalist understanding. Any understanding involves the human element that prestructures understanding in terms (and in service) of our interests, drives, and needs, which significantly overlap but also frequently diverge among different societies and individuals. Moreover, for Nietzsche, Gadamer, and the pragmatists the fact that understanding is always motivated and prejudiced by our needs and values is a very good thing; it is what allows us to thrive and survive so that we can understand anything at all.

From the premise that "all understanding necessarily involves some prejudice" (*TM*, p. 239), "that every view depends on and manifests specific values" and "antecedent commitments" (*N*, pp. 67–68), it is but a short step to the view that all understanding and perception is interpretation. But it is a step where the more canny pragmatist fears to tread, and where she parts company from grand continental hermeneuts like Nietzsche and Gadamer. In rejecting the foundationalist idea and ideal of transparent mirroring perception, she recognizes that understanding is always motivated and prejudiced, just like interpretation. But she wonders why this makes understanding always interpretive. It just does not follow, unless we presume that *only* interpretation could be prejudiced, while (preinterpretive) understanding or experience simply could not be. But to her, this inference is as strange and offensive as a sexist argument that all humans are really women because they all are influenced by emotions, while presumably real men are not.

(4) The fourth argument for hermeneutic universalism inhabits the overlap between understanding's perspectival partiality and its active process. The argument is basically that since all understanding is selective—focused on some things and features but not others—all understanding must therefore be interpretive. We find an analogous argument in the philosophy of art criticism, where it is held that we cannot distinguish between describing and interpreting the work; since any description of the work already constitutes an interpretation by its selection of certain features to describe rather than others, such selection representing an interpretive decision about what is important and meaningful in the work. Moreover, hermeneutic universalists like Fish go on to say that not only every description but every reading or perception of the work is similarly selective, and

thus already an interpretation of it. Hence, "interpretation is the only game in town."[14]

The fact that understanding is perspectivally partial (in both senses of incompleteness and purposive bias) implies it is always selective. It always grasps some things rather than others, and what it grasps depends in part on its antecedent purposes. This much seems uncontestable. What I challenge is the inference that since understanding (or indeed any intelligent activity) is always selective, it is therefore always interpretive. Such a conclusion needs the further premise that all purposive selection must be the product of interpretive thinking and decision. But this premise is false, an instance of the philosophical fallacy John Dewey dubbed "intellectualism."[15] For most of the selection involved in our ordinary acts of perception and understanding is done automatically and unconsciously (yet still intelligently and not mechanically) on the basis of intelligent habits, without any reflection or deliberation at all.[16] Interpretation, in its standard ordinary usage, certainly implies conscious thought and deliberate reflection; but not all intelligent and purposive selection is conscious or deliberate. Walking down the stairs requires selecting how and where to place one's feet and body, but such selection involves interpreting only in cases of abnormal conditions when descent of the staircase presents a problem (as with an unusually dark or narrow winding staircase, a sprained ankle, or a fit of vertigo).

Just as it wrong to confuse all purposive intelligent choice (some of which may be prereflective) with interpretive decisions requiring ratiocination, so we need not confuse perceptions and understandings that are immediately given to us (albeit only corrigibly and mediated by prior experience) from understandings reached only by interpretive deliberation on the meaning of what is immediately given. When I awake on the beach at Santa Cruz with my eyes pierced by sunlight, I immediately perceive or understand it is daytime; only when I instead awake to a darkish gloom do I need to interpret that it is no longer night but merely another dreary morning in Philadelphia.

---

[14]For more detailed discussion of the problematic (but still functional) distinction between description and interpretation in literary criticism, see Richard Shusterman, "Interpretation, Intention, and Truth," *Journal of Aesthetics and Art Criticism* 46 (1988): 399–411.

[15]John Dewey, *Experience and Nature* (LaSalle, Ill.: Open Court, 1929), pp. 21–24.

[16]See Dewey's remark that "primary non-reflectional experience . . . has its own organization of a direct, non-logical character"; in John Dewey, *Essays in Experimental Logic* (Chicago: University of Chicago Press, 1916), p. 6.

In short, I am arguing that though all understanding is selective, not all selective understanding is interpretive. If understanding's selection is neither conscious nor deliberate but prereflective and immediate, we have no reason to regard that selection or the resultant understanding as interpretation, since interpretation standardly implies some deliberate or at least conscious thinking, whereas understanding does not.[17] We can understand something without thinking about it at all; but to interpret something, we need to think about it. This distinction may recall a conclusion from Wittgenstein's famous discussion of seeing-as, where he distinguishes seeing from interpreting: "To interpret is to think, to do something; seeing is a state."[18]

(5) Though insightful, Wittgenstein's remark is also problematic. For it suspiciously suggests that we could see or understand without doing anything; and this suspicion suggests the fifth argument for hermeneutic universalism. Understanding or perceiving, as Nietzscheans, pragmatists, and even Gadamerians insist, is active. It is not a passive mirroring, but an active structuring of what it encounters. To hear or see anything, before we even attempt to interpret it, involves the activity of our bodies, certain motor responses and tensions in the muscles and nerves of our organs of sensation. To characterize seeing or understanding in sharp contrast to interpretation as an achieved "state" rather than as "doing something" suggests that understanding is static rather than active; and if passively static, then it should be neutral rather than selective and structuring. The fifth argument for hermeneutic universalism therefore rejects this distinction between understanding as passively neutral and interpretation as actively structuring, and infers that since all understanding is active, all understanding must be interpretive.

My response to this argument should already be clear. As a pragmatist, I fully assent to the premise that all perception and under-

---

[17]Of course, the hermeneutic universalists would contest such a view of standard usage and insist that even unconscious actions and immediate perceptions are and must be interpretive, and indeed that they may be so described without gross violation of diction. My point is that the universalists give no compelling reason to extend the use of interpretation this way, and that in recommending linguistic revision or the denial of a useful distinction, the burden of proof lies heavily with them. As should already be clear, the appeal of their case derives from the hasty presumption that uninterpreted understanding is impossible because it must be conceived foundationally.

[18]Ludwig Wittgenstein, *Philosophical Investigations* (Oxford: Basil Blackwell, 1968), p. 212. Wittgenstein quickly goes on to specify the sort of thinking we do in interpretation: "When we interpret we form hypotheses, which may prove false" (ibid.).

standing involve doing something; but I deny this entails that they always involve interpretation. The inference relies on an implicit premise that all "doings" that are cognitively valuable or significant for thought are themselves already cases of thinking. Hence any active selection and structuring of perception must already be a thoughtful, deliberate selection, one involving an interpretive decision. This is the premise I contest, the assimilating conflation of all active, selective, and structuring intelligence with the active, selective, and structuring of the interpreting intellect. Understanding can actively structure and select without engaging in interpretation, just as action can be intelligent without engaging thought or the intellect. When, on my way to the beach, I am told that the surf is up, I immediately understand what is said, prereflectively selecting and structuring the sounds and meanings I respond to. I do not need to interpret what is said or meant. Only if I were unfamiliar with idiomatic English, or unable to hear the words, or in a situation where the utterance would seem out of place, would I have to interpret it. Only if there were some problem in understanding, some puzzle or doubt or incongruity, would I have to thematize the utterance as something that needed interpretation, something to think about and clarify or resolve.

(6) But this assertion is precisely what is challenged by the sixth argument for hermeneutic holism, an argument that highlights the intimate link between the hermeneutic turn and the linguistic turn in both Continental and Anglo-American philosophy. Briefly and roughly, the argument goes as follows. All understanding is linguistic, because all understanding (as indeed all experience) involves concepts that require language. But linguistic understanding is essentially a matter of decoding or interpreting signs that are arbitrary rather than natural and whose translation into meaningful propositions thus requires interpetation. To understand the meaning of a sentence, we need, on the Quinean-Davidsonian model, to supply a translation or interpretation of it in terms already familiar to us (whether those terms be in the interpreted language itself or in another more familiar "home" language). So Davidson baldly asserts that "all understanding of the speech of another involves radical interpretation" and firmly equates "the power of thought" with "speaking a language."[19] And from the Continental tradition, Ga-

[19]Donald Davidson, "Radical Interpretation" and "The Very Idea of a Conceptual Scheme," in *Inquiries into Truth and Interpretation* (Oxford: Oxford University Press, 1984), pp. 125, 184.

damer concurs by basing the universal scope of hermeneutics on "the essential linguisticality of all human experience of the world" and on a view of language as "itself the game of interpretation that we are all engaged in every day."[20] Hence, not only all understanding but all experience is interpretive, since both are ineliminably linguistic— a conclusion endorsed by Richard Rorty, Jacques Derrida, and a legion of hermeneutic universalists.

Though the consensus for this position is powerful, the argument strikes me as less than persuasive. It warrants challenging on two points at least. First, we can question the idea that linguistic understanding is always the decoding, translation, or interpretation of arbitrary signs in terms of specific rules of meaning and syntax. This is, I think, an overly formalistic and intellectualized picture of linguistic understanding. Certainly, it is not apparent that we always (or ever) interpret, decode, or translate the uncoded and unproblematic utterances we hear in our native tongue simply in order to understand them. That is precisely why ordinary language distinguishes such direct and simple understandings from decodings, translations, and interpretations.

But, the hermeneutic universalists will persist: Mustn't we be interpreting even when we don't know it, since no other model can account for our understanding? No, because an alternative model *is* available in Wittgenstein, where linguistic understanding is a matter of being able to make the right responses or moves in the relevant language game, and where such ability or language acquisition is first gained by brute training or drill.[21] Language mastery is (at least in part) the mastery of intelligent habits of gesture and response for engaging effectively in a form of life, rather than the mastery of a system of semiotic rules for interpreting signs.

So I think a case can be made for some distinction between under-

[20]Hans-Georg Gadamer, "On the Scope and Function of Hermeneutical Reflection," in *Philosophical Hermeneutics* (Berkeley: University of California Press, 1989), pp. 19, 32. Gadamer, however, does not always seem perfectly consistent on this last matter. At one point in *Truth and Method* he speaks of "an understanding of language," which "is not yet of itself a real understanding and does not include an interpretive process but it is an accomplishment of life. For you understand a language by living in it" (p. 346). Could Gadamer here be acknowledging, albeit in a rather odd and contorted manner, the point I wish to make that interpretation does not go all the way down, but always relies on some more primitive linguistic understanding? This alternative (and hardly typical) view of Gadamer was suggested to me by John Connolly, one of the Santa Cruz posse, who made helpful comments on an earlier draft of this paper.

[21]See, for example, L. Wittgenstein, *Zettel* (Oxford: Basil Blackwell, 1967), para. 419; and *Philosophical Investigations*, pp. 4–7, 40.

standing and interpreting language, between an unreflective but intelligent trained habit of response and a thoughtful decision about how to understand or respond. I have to interpret or translate most utterances I hear in German in order to understand them, but I understand most sentences I hear in English without interpreting them; I interpret only those that seem unclear or insufficiently understood. To defend the conflation of understanding and interpretation by arguing that in simply understanding those alleged uninterpreted utterances, I am in fact already interpreting sounds as words, or perhaps further that my nervous system is busy interpreting vibrations into sounds, is not only to stretch the meaning of "interpretation" for no productive purpose; it also misrepresents our actual experience. Certainly we can make a distinction between the words and the sounds, and between the sounds and the vibrations that cause them. But this does not mean they are really distinct or distinguishable in experience and that I therefore must interpret the sounds in order to understand them as words. On the contrary, when I hear a language I understand, I typically do not hear the sounds at all but only the understood words or message. If any interpretive effort is needed, it is to hear the words as sounds or vibrations, not vice versa.

There is, then, good reason to reject the view that linguistic understanding is always and necessarily interpretation. But even granting it, we still need not grant the conclusion that all understanding is interpretive. For that requires the further premise that all understanding and meaningful experience is indeed linguistic. And such a premise, though it be the deepest dogma of the linguistic turn in both analytic philosophy and Continental hermeneutics, is neither self-evident nor immune to challenge. Certainly, there seem to be forms of bodily awareness or understanding that are not linguistic in nature and in fact defy adequate linguistic characterization, though they can be somehow referred to through language. As dancers, we understand the sense and rightness of a movement or posture proprioceptively, by feeling it in our spine and muscles, without translating it into conceptual linguistic terms. We can neither learn nor properly understand the movement simply by being talked through it.[22]

Moreover, apart from the nonlinguistic understandings and experiences of which we are aware, there are more basic experiences or

[22]This point was tangibly impressed on me through the help of Jaime Stover, who gracefully guided my exploratory steps in dance and somatic awareness. I gratefully acknowledge her gentle gifts.

understandings of which we are not even conscious, but whose successful transaction provides the necessary background selection and organization of our field which enables consciousness to have a focus and emerge as a foreground. We typically experience our verticality and direction of gaze without being aware of them, but without our experiencing them we could not be conscious of or focused on what we are in fact aware of; our perceptual field would be very different. As Dewey insisted, there is a difference between not knowing an experience and not having it. "Consciousness . . . is only a very small and shifting part of experience" and relies on "a context which is non-cognitive," a "universe of non-reflectional experience."[23]

To all such talk of nonlinguistic experience or understanding the hermeneutic universalists have a ready and seemingly irresistible response. How can I claim any experience is nonlinguistic, when in that very claim I have had to talk about it, refer to it by language? Any attempt to characterize something as nonlinguistic or describe it as linguistically inexpressible self-refutingly renders it linguistic and linguistically expressed. Therefore, whatever can be said to exist, or even is explicitly thought to exist (since explicit thinking can be seen as conceptual and language dependent), is and must be linguistic. Hence Gadamer, for example, concludes, "Being that can be understood is language" (TM, p. 432), and the likes of Derrida and Rorty similarly deny any "hors-texte."

This argument has, I admit, considerable suasive power, and it has long swayed me. But recently it has come to seem more like a sophistic paradox about talking without language than a deep truth about human experience and the world. Surely, once we have to talk about something, even merely to affirm or deny its existence, we must bring it into the game of language, give it a linguistic visa or some conceptual-textual identity; even if the visa be one of alien or inferior linguistic status, like "inexpressible tingle" or "nondiscursive image." But this only means that we can never talk (or explicitly think) about things existing without their being somehow linguistically mediated; it does not mean that we can never experience them nonlinguistically or that they cannot exist for us meaningfully but not in language.

We philosophers fail to see this because, disembodied talking heads that we are, the only form of experience we recognize and legitimate is linguistic: thinking, talking, writing. But neither we nor

---

[23]See Dewey, *Essays in Experimental Logic*, pp. 4, 6, 9.

the language that admittedly helps shape us could survive without the unarticulated background of prereflective, nonlinguistic experience and understanding.[24] Hermeneutic universalism thus fails in its argument that intepretation is the only game in town because language is the only game in town. For there is both uninterpreted linguistic understanding and meaningful experience that is nonlinguistic. We can find them in those darkly somatic and illiterate neighborhoods of town that we philosophers and literary theorists are occupationally accustomed to avoid and ignore, but on which we rely for our nonprofessional sustenance and satisfactions. After the conference papers are over, we go slumming in their bars.[25]

IV

Thus far I have resisted the universalists' arguments that understanding and interpretation cannot possibly be distinguished since all understanding is and must be interpretation. What remains, for the final sections of this essay, is to show why the distinction is worth making and how it should be made and understood. There are three reasons why I think it important to preserve some distinction between understanding and interpretation.

First and most simply, it provides interpretation with a "contrast-class" to help delimit and thus shape its meaning. Without an activity to contrast to interpretation, what can interpretation really mean? The possibility of alternatives is a necessary condition of meaningfulness. This principle of choice, endorsed not only in structuralist semantics but in analytic information theory, recognizes that the meaning of a term or proposition is a function of those terms or propositions it opposes or excludes.[26] Notions of unlimited extension,

---

[24]Moreover, recent work in linguistics and philosophy of language shows how many of our linguistic structures and meanings (including some of our more abstract logical principles) reflect and seem constrained by more basic preconceptual and prelinguistic patterns of bodily experience See Mark Johnson, *The Body in the Mind* (Chicago: University of Chicago Press, 1987).

[25]But such uninterpreted experiences and understandings can, of course, also be found in our professional activities, as underlying more deliberative, reflective thought.

[26]See John Lyons, *Semantics* (Cambridge: Cambridge University Press, 1977), 1:33–50.

like tautologies that are universally true, tend to evaporate into semantic emptiness. If everything we do or experience is always and must always be interpretation, the notion of interpretation becomes synonymous with all human life and activity, and thus loses any real meaning or specific role of its own. Uninterpreted understandings and experiences provide a relevant contrast-class for interpretations, enabling interpretation to be distinguishable as having some definite meaning of its own, since its meaning is in some way defined and limited by what falls outside it and is contrasted to it.

Second, understanding provides interpretation not only with a meaning-giving contrast, but with a meaning-giving ground. It supplies something on which to base and guide our interpretations, and represents something by which we can distinguish between different levels or sequential acts of interpretation. How does understanding ground and guide interpretation? We can find the makings of an answer in Heidegger and Wittgenstein, two revered progenitors of hermeneutic universalism who I think wisely resisted that doctrine. The complexly reciprocal and leveled relationship between understanding and interpretation is suggested in the second dimension of the hermeneutic circle, which Heidegger calls to our attention in his famous remark that "any interpretation which is to contribute understanding must already have understood what is to be interpreted."[27]

Elucidating this idea with respect to a literary text, we can say that before and while we try to interpret its meaning, we must be struck and directed by some sense of what it is we are trying to interpret. At the very least, we need some primitive understanding of what we are individuating as the textual object of interpretation, simply to identify it as such. Moreover, it is our initial understanding or experience of the text as something meaningful and perhaps worth understanding more fully that generates our desire to interpret it. We do not interpret every text we encounter. But our attempt to interpret the given text is not only motivated but guided by this prior understanding, though it be inchoate, vague, and corrigible. For we form our interpretive hypotheses about the text (and accept or reject alternative interpretations) on the basis of what we already understand as properly belonging to the text rather than falsely foisted onto it.

But how do we determine whether our initial guiding understanding is valid and not a misunderstanding? We cannot appeal to the apodicticness or incorrigibility of understanding, because we have

<hr>

[27]Martin Heidegger, *Being and Time* (New York: Harper & Row, 1962), p. 194.

rejected all foundationalist accounts of understanding. Nor can we simply test the validity of our initial understanding by measuring it against the meaning of the text. For since the text's meaning is not self-evidently given but is precisely what is in question, we would first have to determine more clearly what this meaning is. Yet to do this we must interpret, and thus we can only test our prior understanding by subsequent interpretation. In other words, though interpretation of the text must be based on some prior understanding of it, this understanding itself requires interpretation of the text for its own clarification and justification, if indeed we wish to pursue this. But that clarificatory and justificatory interpretation depends again on the very understanding it has to sharpen or validate. And so the hermeneutic circle revolves in a cycle of understanding and interpretation.

Considerations of this sort have led Gadamer and other hermeneutic universalists to the radical claim that "all understanding is interpretation" (TM, p. 350). But this claim, I have argued, is not only uncompelling but misleading in suggesting that we can never understand anything without interpreting it. For in many cases we are simply satisfied with our initial understanding and do not go on to interpret; there are always other and usually better things to do.

Moreover, if we could never understand anything without interpreting it, how could we ever understand the interpretation itself? It, too, would have to be interpreted, and so would its interpretation, and so on ad infinitum. As Wittgenstein notes, "Any interpretation still hangs in the air along with what it interprets." Interpretation must ultimately depend on some prior understanding, some "way of grasping . . . which is *not* an interpretation."[28] This is just a point of philosophical grammar about how these notions are related: understanding grounds and guides interpretation, while interpretation enlarges, validates, or corrects understanding. We must remember that the distinction is functional or relational, not ontological.[29] The prior and grounding understanding "which is not an interpretation" may have been the product of prior interpretations, though now it is

---

[28]Wittgenstein, *Philosophical Investigations*, pp. 80, 81.

[29]The same can be said for another problematic distinction that much contemporary philosophy seems bent on confusing and then denying—the conventional versus the natural. Convention is always more superficial than the natural which grounds it; but what we regard in one context as conventional in contrast to its more natural background can itself be regarded as natural in relation to something still more superficial or artificial. For more detailed argument of this thesis, see Richard Shusterman, "Convention: Variations on a Theme," *Philosophical Investigations* 9 (1986): 36–55.

immediately grasped. Moreover, it need not be an explicitly formulated or conscious understanding, and the ground it provides is not
an *incorrigible* ground.[30]

Though the universalists are wrong to deny that a helpful distinction can be drawn between simply understanding something and
interpreting that which was understood, their attempts to deny it
have not been unhelpful. For they showed that there is no rigid or
absolute dichotomy, but rather an essential continuity and degree of
interdependence, between understanding and interpretation. What
is now immediately understood may once have been the product of
a labored interpretation and may form the basis for further interpretation. Words of a French song I once labored to interpret are now
immediately understood, and this understanding affords me the
ground for an interpretation of their deeper poetic meaning. Though
frequently what we encounter neither demands nor receives interpretation, many things are felt to be insufficiently understood until they

[30]This is one reason why my rehabilitation of uninterpreted understanding should
not be seen as simply resurrecting what Sellars called "the myth of the given." See
Wilfrid Sellars, "Empiricism and the Philosophy of Mind," in *Science, Perception, and
Reality* (London: Routledge & Kegan Paul, 1963); and Richard Rorty's supportive elaboration in *Philosophy and the Mirror of Nature* (Princeton: Princeton University Press,
1979), pp. 182–92. I agree with Rorty and Sellars that any understanding that functions
as epistemological grounding for another understanding must always exist within "the
logical space of reasons" and hence must be conceptual. But I maintain, first, that
such conceptual understandings can still be immediately (though not apodictically)
given; they need not be interpretations. Moreover, I would hold that nonconceptual
(e.g., kinesthetic) experiences, though they be beneath the logical space of reasons,
may nonetheless be meaningful and constitute a form of understanding. Finally,
though I agree with Rorty and Sellars that such experiences cannot provide epistemological grounding or justification for further understanding unless they get conceptual-
ized, they can still provide the practical ground and orienting background for such
understanding.

   In other words, I am here urging recognition of a category of embodied, experienced
practice that grounds and guides intelligent activity but that is neither at the discursive
and epistemological level of the logical space of reasons nor simply reducible to the
physical conditions and causes described by natural science. Nor should this category
be seen as *epistemologically* grounding the categories of reasons and physical causes.
Sellars and Rorty would no doubt retort that all forms of grounding necessarily fall
into the logical space of reasons or otherwise enter the physical space of causes, spaces
that must not be confused and whose dichotomy exhausts the ways of understanding
human experience. They are surely right not to confuse logical reasons with physical
causes, and also right to criticize traditional epistemological notions of "the given" for
such confusion. But to regard these two categories as an exhaustive dichotomy seems
an unnecessary limitation on understanding human being-in-the-world and an unfortunate vestige of Cartesiansism, with its rigid and exhaustive dualism of mind and
body, thought and physical extension.

are interpreted by us or for us. We seek an interpretation because we are not satisfied with the understanding we already have—feeling it partial, obscure, shallow, fragmented, or simply dull—and we want to make it fuller or more adequate. Yet the superior interpretation sought must be guided by that prior inadequate understanding. We no longer feel the need to interpret further when the new, fuller understanding that interpretation has supplied is felt to be satisfactory. Criteria of what is satisfactory obviously will vary with context and will depend on the sort of understanding sought. Wittgenstein effectively puts this pragmatic point: "What happens is not that this symbol cannot be further interpreted, but: I do no interpreting. I do not interpret, because I feel at home in the present picture."[31]

The third reason I think it worth distinguishing between understanding and interpretation is to defend the ordinary: not only ordinary usage, which itself draws and endorses the distinction, but ordinary experiences of understanding whose legitimacy and value tend to get discredited by hermeneutic universalism's assimilation of all experience into interpretation. In commonplace discourse not all understanding is interpretation. There are countless contexts where one might justifiably reply to a query of how one interpreted something by denying that one actually interpreted it at all: "I didn't bother interpreting what he said; I just took it at face value." "I didn't pause to interpret her command (question); I immediately complied with it (ignored it)."

Even if these direct or immediate understandings are always based on the funded habits and capacities of prior efforts of interpretation, there is still a difference between such effortless, unthinking acts of understanding (or experiences of meaning) and acts of interpretation, which call for deliberate, focused thought. In marking a difference between interpretation and the more direct experiences or understandings on which it is based, ordinary language respects the role of the unformulable, prereflective, and nondiscursive background from which the foreground of conscious thinking emerges and without which it could never arise. In rejecting this distinction by asserting

---

[31]Wittgenstein, *Zettel*, para. 234. The imagery of this remark makes me hazard the suggestion that we are today so preoccupied with interpretation largely because we so rarely feel comfortably at home in the often conflicting worlds of our understanding, that our age is an age of interpretation because it is one of alienation and fragmentation. However, this is not so much to be mourned nostalgically as the loss of unity and smug certainty, but rather recognized as the price of our greater freedom and pluralistic possibilities.

that all experience is interpretation, hermeneutic universalists deny this very ordinary but very crucial *unthinking* dimension of our lives and indeed of our thinking.

We can see a variation of this discrediting denial of the ordinary and unreflective in Stanley Fish's account of reading. As hermeneutic universalist, he asserts that all our activity is essentially interpretive. We cannot simply read or even recognize a text without interpreting it, since the text can only be constituted as such by an act of interpretation. Now since interpretation implies active thinking and discourse, it cannot be a merely mirroring representation of the text, but must in some way supplement, shape, or reconstruct it. Hence all our apparent practices of reading are really "not for reading but for writing texts."[32] Having conflated reading with interpretation, Fish further conflates interpretation with the institutionalized interpretation of professional academic criticism, where an interpretation must not only be discursively formulated but must provide "something different" or significantly new in order to be legitimate and "be given a hearing." Hence he concludes that all reading of a text must not only be interpreting it but also "changing it" in some professionally meaningful way.[33]

The result is that ordinary, unreflective, nonprofessional modes of reading are discredited and dismissed as foundationalist myth. Yet precisely these unreflective unoriginal readings, which anticipate the attempt to interpret, are what in fact provides the basis for professional transformative interpretations by supplying some shared background of meaning which enables us to identify what we agree to call "the same text" so that we can then proceed to interpret it differently. Fish himself must and does appeal to this unformulated "core of agreement" or "general purpose," which prestructures and constrains interpretive strategies. But he simply ascribes it to "the literary institution" or "interpretive community" (another dangerous conflation) and fails to realize that such a community exists only as embodied in the concrete experiences and understandings of readers, just as its most basic constraints are embodied in the prereflective,

---

[32]Fish, *Is There a Text in This Class?* p. 14.

[33]See Stanley Fish, "No Bias, No Merit: The Case Against Blind Submission," *PMLA* 103 (1988): 739; "Working on the Chain Gang," p. 211; "Profession Despise Thyself: Fear and Self-Loathing in Literary Studies," *Critical Inquiry* 10 (1983); and most recently, "Change," *South Atlantic Quarterly* 86 (1987).

uncritical habits of reading, habits that precede the attempt to interpret what is read.[34]

Here, as elsewhere, universal hermeneutics' dismissal of the preinterpretive reflects an intellectualist blindness to the unreflective, nondiscursive dimension of ordinary experience, a bias at once haughtily
elitist and parochially uncritical. To defend this ordinary, unassum-
ing, and typically silent dimension, we need to preserve something
distinct from interpretive activity, even if it cannot and perhaps
should not be immune from interpretation and may indeed rest on
what was once interpretation.

V

I have argued that we can eschew foundationalism without maintaining that all experience and understanding must be interpretation.
We can do so by insisting that understanding should itself be understood nonfoundationally, that is, as corrigible, perspectival, pluralistic, prejudiced, and engaged in active process. I have further argued
that there are at least a few good reasons for admitting some meaningful activity or experience other than interpretation, and thus for
allowing or indeed making some distinction between interpretation
and understanding. What remains is to suggest how this distinction
might best be drawn or understood, largely by recollecting and recasting some of the central points already made in our discussion.

First, the distinction between understanding and interpretation is
not a rigid ontological one, where the two categories cannot share
the same objects. Second, they cannot be distinguished by epistemological reliablity, where understanding implies univocal truth while
interpretation connotes pluralistic error. Nonetheless, understanding
and interpretation are epistemologically different in terms of their
functional relations: understanding initially grounds and guides interpretation, while the latter explores, validates, or modifies that initial ground of meaning.

---

[34]Fish, *Is There a Text in This Class?*, p. 342; and "Change," p. 432. The multiple
confusions of Fish's theory of interpretation and its totalizing professionalism are
treated in much greater detail in chapter 4 of my *Pragmatist Aesthetics: Living Beauty,
Rethinking Art*, forthcoming from Basil Blackwell in 1992.

Other differences to be drawn between understanding and interpretation are probably more debatable. While understanding, even intelligent understanding, is often unreflective, unthinking, indeed unconscious (even if always purposive), interpretation proper involves conscious, deliberate thought: a clarification of something obscure or ambiguous, a deciphering of a symbol, an unraveling of a paradox, an articulation of previously unstated formal or semantic relations between elements. While understanding is frequently a matter of smoothly coordinated, unproblematic handling of what we encounter,[35] interpretation characteristically involves a problem-situation. We only stop to interpret in order to resolve a problem—some obscurity, ambiguity, contradiction, or, more recently, the professional academic problem of *generating* an interpretive problem. The intrinsic problem-solving character of interpretation explains why it involves conscious, deliberate inquiry. Solving a problem demands thinking, seeing the obvious does not.

On this question of consciousness, our ordinary linguistic usage (to which I earlier appealed) does not give unchallengeable support. Although it sounds strange to speak of someone's unconsciously interpreting some remark or event, it is not a blatant contradiction or solecism. But that is simply because language aims more at loose flexibility than precision, and because hermeneutic universalism has accustomed us to think loosely of interpretation as subsuming all construals, understandings, or meaningful experiences, some of which are obviously unconscious. If our ordinary speech does not always draw a distinction between interpreting and understanding, it more often makes it and never implies that it is not worth making.

The conscious and problem-solving character of interpretation suggests yet another feature that might help distinguish it from understanding. Though both are inevitably perspectival, interpretive activity seems intrinsically aware that alternative interpretations may be given to resolve a problem, while understanding can be unreflectively blind to the existence or possibility of alternative understand-

---

[35]Bert Dreyfus, in glossing Heidegger's notions of "circumspection" and the "ready-to-hand," aptly describes this smoothly coordinated understanding as "everyday skillful coping" or "absorbed coping." See Hubert Dreyfus, *Being-in-the-World: A Commentary on Being and Time, Division I* (Cambridge: MIT Press, 1991), chapter 4. The idea is also central to Dewey's concept of unreflective intelligent behavior versus conscious inquiry. See, for example, John Dewey, "The Practical Character of Reality" and "The Unit of Behavior," in *Philosophy and Civilization* (New York: Minton, Balch, 1931), pp. 36–55, 233–48.

ings, since it can be unaware of any problem of understanding that might present alternative solutions.

I conclude with one last suggestion for distinguishing interpretation from more primitive or basic understandings and experiences, one that reaffirms the link I established between hermeneutic universalism and the linguisitic turn. Interpretation is characteristically aimed at linguistic formulation, at translating one meaningful expression into another one. A criterion for having an interpretation of some utterance or event would be an ability to express in some explicit, articulated form what that interpretation is. To interpret a text is thus to produce a text.[36] Understanding, on the other hand, does not require linguistic articulation. A proper reaction, a shudder or tingle, may be enough to indicate one has understood. Some of the things we experience and understand are never captured by language, not only because their particular feel defies adequate linguistic expression but because we are not even aware of them as "things" to describe.[37] They are the felt background we presuppose when we start to articulate or to interpret.

"There are, indeed, things that cannot be put into words. They *show* themselves. They are the mystical."[38] So said the greatest twentieth-century philosopher of language in his first philosophical masterpiece. What Wittgenstein fails to emphasize here is that the

[36]It might seem that artistic interpretation, i.e., interpretive performance, would constitute a refutation of this claim, since Rubinstein's interpretation of Beethoven's *Moonlight Sonata* is not a linguistic text. One need not meet this objection by arguing that "interpretation" is used here in a different, derivative sense. For again we have the translation of one articulated text (the score) into another articulated form (the actual sonic performance); and the criterion for having an artistic interpretation is expressing it in such an articulated performance or in explicit instructions for one.

[37]Rorty's most recent and inspiring advocacy of aestheticism occasionally comes very close to recognizing the deep value of the sublinguistic, as when he suggests it is better "to produce tingles than truth." See Richard Rorty, *Contingency, Irony, and Solidarity* (Cambridge: Cambridge University Press, 1989), p. 152. But he remains more faithful to hermeneutic universalism than to Deweyan pragmatism by asserting that the subsentential is always dependent on the sentential (p. 153n.) and by essentially equating human experience with linguistic experience (e.g., people are "nothing more than sentential attitudes," p. 88). For more detailed critique of the residual linguistic essentialism that sadly eviscerates Rorty's very welcome and promising "aesthetic turn," see Richard Shusterman, "Postmodernism and the Aesthetic Turn," *Poetics Today* 10 (1989): 605–22; and chapter 9 of *Pragmatist Aesthetics.*

[38]Ludwig Wittgenstein, *Tractatus Logico-Philosophicus* (London: Routledge & Kegan Paul, 1961), 6.522 (I depart from the translation of Pears and McGuinness by more simply rendering *zeigt* as "show" rather than "make manifest" and *das Mystiche* as "the mystical" rather than "what is mystical").

ineffable but manifest is as much ordinary as mystical, and it is only mystifying to those disembodied philosophical minds who recognize no understanding other than interpretation, and no form of meaning and experience beyond or beneath the web of language.

CHAPTER 7

Holism without Skepticism: Contextualism and the Limits of Interpretation

JAMES F. BOHMAN

A variety of interpretive acts pervades both everyday life and more formal, scientific settings. Intentional actions must be interpreted as much as verbal expressions: a passerby who raises her hand may be giving a greeting, stretching, dancing, or signaling the car to halt. Interpreting texts may require explicit reformulation: in performing a composition, musicians often must weigh the differences among the variants of the written score as well as various unwritten performance traditions. Encounters with the expressions and activities of other cultures cannot occur without interpretation. Often things may not be as they seem to "us," as when bets on cockfights in Bali are not just games but "deep play," a dramatic form of social commentary on status.[1] Ordinarily, it is expected that such matters can be settled. To do so, interpreters appeal to circumstances and context, to authorial intention and textual coherence, or to the details of a practice and its relation to other practices. When called into question, interpretations must be supported by reasons, and it is a philosophical question when such claims are justified and if such issues can be settled rationally.

[1] Clifford Geertz, "Deep Play: Notes on the Balinese Cockfight," in *The Interpretation of Cultures* (New York: Basic Books, 1973), pp. 412–54. Geertz's interpretation of the cockfight distinguishes between what appears to be going on "for us" and what is really going on for the Balinese: "For it is only apparently cocks that are fighting there. Actually it is men" (p. 417). This essay is arguably a paradigm case of interpretive social science, as Paul Rabinow and William Sullivan use it in the introduction to their reader, *Interpretive Social Science* (Berkeley: University of California Press, 1979).

Many theorists of interpretation today express doubts about the possibility of answering the question of the rational justification or "correctness" of interpretations, and even argue that correctness may not be the proper goal of interpretive procedures at all. Such skepticism is supported by some version of the thesis commonly called "universal hermeneutics"; it is captured well in Stanley Fish's colloquial slogan that "interpretation is the only game in town" or Hans-Georg Gadamer's more formal assertion that "all understanding is interpretation."[2] The universality of interpretation, they argue, is a direct consequence of the fact that no cognitive activity can privilege a particular content as "given" or "self-verifying" apart from the context of all other contents and activities. If this is true, then it follows that all such activities are interpretive and that any belief or practice can be understood only in light of all other beliefs and practices. Hence, skeptical contextualism is a two-step thesis: first, that interpretation is universal and hence ubiquitous in every cognitive activity; and second, that it is holistic and hence takes place only against the background of all of our beliefs and practices. Together these two theses imply that no interpretation can be singled out as uniquely correct, since the assertion that it is so would itself be an interpretation within a particular context. Thus, this conclusion is but one way of expressing the famous "hermeneutic circle": everything is interpretation, and interpretation is itself indeterminate, contextual, and circular.

My contention is that holistic indeterminacy and circularity are indeed epistemologically inevitable aspects of interpretation. But from these warranted assumptions some contextualists, whom I shall call "strong holists," draw the unwarranted skeptical conclusion that valid interpretations do not constitute knowledge based on evidence.[3] For example, the perspectival and contextual character of in-

---

[2] Stanley Fish, *Is There a Text in This Class?* (Cambridge: Harvard University Press, 1980), p. 352; Hans-Georg Gadamer, *Truth and Method* (New York: Seabury Press, 1982), p. 350. For a conceptual criticism of these claims, see Richard M. Shusterman, "Beneath Interpretation," in this volume. Shusterman, however, takes his aim primarily at universalism, whereas my target is contextualism, an overly strong version of holism. As I see it, the problem has more to do with how to understand the holistic epistemology of interpretation itself. Shusterman's epistemological point is to argue that interpretations are based on prior, preinterpretational evidence. My argument is that it is not necessary to make an appeal to such evidence to show that interpretations are based on evidential warrants. It is necessary only to understand the epistemological implications of the hermeneutic circle correctly.

[3] Alexander Rosenberg puts it this way for an empiricist holism like W. V. O. Quine's: "If meanings are ultimately underdetermined by the evidence, the appeal to them

terpretation leads to the most common form of skepticism about interpretation: since we can interpret things only from "our" point of view, our interpretations are inevitably ethnocentric. It is impossible to understand others as they understand themselves: we understand them only according to "our own lights."[4] My aim here is to dispute the common philosophical basis for all such views that assert that there are such inherent, contextual limits on how we interpret others.

Various arguments have been given to support this type of skeptical conclusion, including considerations of the theory of meaning for natural languages. However, as Gadamer and others have done, I present a reading of such arguments as being transcendental in form, that is, as dealing with holistic conditions for the possibility of interpretation. Although some contextualists may dispute this reading, I want to show that the analogy illuminates fundamental problems in the argument—in particular, its unwarranted skepticism. Indeed, the skeptical conclusion, I argue, is established through something like a transcendental argument from conditions of possibility that are also limits on acts of interpretation, limits that would disallow any epistemic clarification of "correct" interpretations or "true" meanings. It is precisely this transcendental limit argument that I want to challenge,

---

cannot constitute knowledge of any kind empiricism would sanction." Rosenberg, *Philosophy of Social Science* (Boulder, Colo.: Westview Press, 1980), p. 110. Paul A. Roth makes similar arguments in his paper in this volume and in his *Meaning and Method in the Social Sciences* (Ithaca: Cornell University Press, 1987). More hermeneutically oriented philosophers like Charles Taylor and Hubert Dreyfus make a similar point when they argue that interpretation cannot produce knowledge of the sort the natural sciences would sanction. Though many holists do formulate their own account of interpretation as a distinct form of knowledge, it is often by denying that it is "theoretical" knowledge, or by claiming that it must be based on insight and not evidence.

[4]This position sketched here is adopted by Rorty in his arguments for "frank ethnocentrism"; see Richard Rorty, "Solidarity or Objectivity?" in *Post-Analytic Philosophy*, ed. J. Rajchman and C. West (New York: Columbia University Press, 1984). Rorty argues that we must be "frank" about our inevitable ethnocentrism, because Donald Davidson's holism teaches us that there is no distinction between understanding and imposition. This argument for ethnocentrism is a good example of the ambiguities of holism: Davidson makes a weaker, nonskeptical argument, from which Rorty draws a stronger, more skeptical conclusion. Clifford Geertz provides the weak holist response to Rorty as well as to James Clifford in his Tanner Lecture, "The Uses of Diversity," *Michigan Quarterly Review* 23 (1988): 105–23. Geertz condemns Rorty's position for allowing "the easy comforts of merely being ourselves." Moreover, he challenges Rorty's empirical assumptions: "The social world does not divide at its joints into perspicuous we-s with whom we can empathize, however much we differ with them, and enigmatical they-s, with whom we cannot" (p. 112).

while invoking neither determinate meanings (and hence avoiding semantic objections) nor a noncircular process of interpretation (and hence recognizing what is true about holism).

In what follows I focus primarily on the more extreme skeptical inferences drawn from the holistic features of interpretation, since they reveal the structure of the inference that can be found in much more modest and weaker forms as well. Against the interpretive skeptics, I will argue that there is evidence within the "hermeneutic circle" to underwrite fallibilistic claims to knowledge that are inter-subjectively valid and capable of public adjudication. I shall call such contextualist skeptics "strong holists" in order to contrast them with "weak holists" who accept the same holistic premises but not their contextualist and skeptical conclusions.

It is important to challenge this implicitly transcendental argument because it is as widespread as it is unacknowledged, commonly found among hermeneutic, empiricist, and postmodern philosophers and social scientists alike. Strong holists come in two common varieties. On the one hand, there are strong holists per se. Among those who turn universal hermeneutics into an explicitly skeptical position are Derridean literary theorists, so-called anthropologists of science like Bruno Latour and Steve Woolgar, and James Clifford and post-modern ethnographers. Members of this group make their skeptical purposes quite clear. In his analysis of science as an interpretive and practical activity, Woolgar argues that the impossibility of objective, representational knowledge of facts shows that "science itself is not scientific."[5] Deconstructionists argue that, because "there is nothing outside the text" to warrant claims to true meanings or the manifest content of texts, interpreters can only proliferate alternative readings.[6] In the social sciences, self-proclaimed "postmodernists" challenge interpretive ethnography on epistemological grounds, pointing out the various textual ruses anthropologists use to establish "ethnographic authority."[7] On the other hand, strong holists of the second variety do not make anything like such sweeping pronouncements of skepticism about knowledge as such. Instead, they draw specific skeptical inferences based on holism in order to cast doubt upon

[5]See Steve Woolgar, *Science: The Very Idea* (London: Tavistock, 1988), p. 107.

[6]See Jonathan Culler, *On Deconstruction* (Ithaca: Cornell University Press, 1982), p. 102. A version of this same holistic argument informs such Derridean and deconstructive notions as "dissemination" and "the logic of the supplement."

[7]James Clifford, "On Ethnographic Authority," in *The Predicament of Culture* (Cambridge: Harvard University Press, 1988), pp. 21–54.

the possibility of various particular theories or to criticize specific knowledge claims. Such specific skeptical claims might include Taylor's assertion that prediction in the human sciences is "radically impossible";[8] Dreyfus's arguments against theories of artificial intelligence, decision theory, and formal theories of rule-following;[9] and Gadamer's criticism of the Marxist theory of ideology.[10] Because both groups draw the same faulty inference from the same premises, the specific conclusions of the more modest second group of strong holists are no more warranted than the more general skepticism of the first group.

This brief but easily amplified list of various recent claims in philos-

[8]Charles Taylor, "Interpretation and the Sciences of Man," *Collected Papers*, vol. 1 (Cambridge: Cambridge University Press, 1985), p. 55. In this essay Taylor argues that because interpretation cannot appeal to "brute data" as evidence, but only to other interpretations, "a hermeneutic science cannot but rely on insight" (p. 55). Such a science requires not publicly accessible evidence, as in the natural sciences, but "the sensibility and understanding necessary to make and comprehend the readings by which we can explain the reality concerned." Insight is "unformalizable" and the only possible form of verification, since Taylor asserts that the limits on interpretation mean that evidence must eventually fail to resolve disputes. I want to show that if this is the case, it is not because of the holistic character of interpretation. Indeed, there is evidence enough within the hermeneutic circle.

[9]Dreyfus argues repeatedly that one of the central insights of Heideggerian "practical holism" is to show why social science cannot have theories like the natural sciences. Citing Pierre Bourdieu, he criticizes Claude Lévi-Strauss's formal theory of gift giving by claiming that such formal rules cannot replace the practical grasp of a whole social background in which agents act. All these related arguments are brought together in "Why Current Studies of Human Capacities Can Never Be Made Scientific," *Berkeley Cognitive Science Report* 11 (1984): 1–17. What Dreyfus calls "practical holism" is not necessarily skeptical in the philosophical sense, but rather an ambitious redescription of human knowledge in terms of skills and capacities. As his specific skeptical arguments show, not all theoretical knowledge can be redescribed in this way and must be shown to be "impossible" (such as theories of artificial intelligence). Joseph Rouse's "practical holism" developed in *Knowledge and Power* (Ithaca: Cornell University Press, 1987) is ambiguous with regard to skepticism, although his intentions are not skeptical. After his description of natural science in holistic terms, he judiciously suggests that his view "does not mean that science should be rejected, abandoned, or even necessarily modified in significant ways" (p. 208). Yet, he argues that we should not understand the transfer of scientific knowledge outside the laboratory as "an instantiation of universally valid knowledge claims" (p. 72); instead, the understanding that science produces is to be understood as "local knowledge." This claim does not follow from holism and does modify how science and theoretical knowledge is understood.

[10]See Gadamer's debate with Jürgen Habermas in *Hermeneutik oder Ideologiekritik?* (Frankfurt: Suhrkamp Verlag, 1975). Habermas's initial volley in the debate is reprinted in *Understanding and Social Inquiry*, ed. F. Dallmayr and T. McCarthy (Notre Dame, Ind.: Notre Dame University Press, 1977), pp. 335–83. My argument here is close to Habermas's in this debate.

ophy of science, literary theory, and anthropology show both how common global and specific arguments for skepticism are and how often they are based on arguments about the role of interpretation in knowledge. Often this interpretive skepticism serves quite good purposes, as when it rids ethnography of residual Romantic exoticism and colonialism or disabuses the philosophy and sociology of science of an overly idealized picture of actual scientific practice. But this critical work can be done better by other means, and a proper analysis of how interpretation works in these various fields supports, rather than undermines, public claims to knowledge. I leave a positive account of such knowledge for another occasion.[11] My arguments here are primarily negative: I show only that the skepticism about interpretive knowledge is not warranted by any proper inference from the main premises of holism, which I here accept as true.

The Transcendental Argument for Holism: Limits or Constraints

The most widespread skeptical argument about interpretation and the limits of knowledge employs two main premises; although each one could form the basis for a separate argument for holism, they are usually united as the twin supports of an overall, anti-epistemological, skeptical position. Both premises can be read as presenting fundamental conditions for the possibility of interpretation: its circularity and hence its necessary reference to other interpretations; and its assumption of an unanalyzable background, or the necessary presupposition of an indefinite set of other beliefs and practices. If these two premises hold as conditions for any interpretation, then it is easy, or so strong holists think, to construct an argument for contextualism: the skeptical conclusions that there are no uniquely correct interpretations and that the validity of interpretations are limited to

[11]See my *New Philosophy of Social Science: Problems of Indeterminacy* (London: Polity Press, 1991), chap. 3. Here I argue that the issue for the social sciences is how to resolve problems of the indeterminacy of interpreting the actions and expressions of knowledgeable social agents who can reflect upon and transform their circumstances; problems resulting from holistic conditions of possibility of interpretation are not that central. I hold that there are as many different forms of interpretive adequacy as there are types of interpretation. My account of interpretive adequacy in the social sciences emphasizes the *epistemological* presuppositions of entering into dialogue with others and the *moral* responsibility in them to interpret others correctly. Social scientific interpretations should be judged on such a dialogical model, including cross-cultural interpretations.

their context. After discussing the premises upon which these views are based, I argue against the conclusions of the "strong holists"[12] and show the superiority of a nonskeptical argument from similar premises favored by "weak holists."[13] Strong holism is skeptical about whether the scope of claims made in interpretations qualify them as knowledge, limited as they are to particular contexts. Weak holism uses these same premises to establish a transcendental analysis of interpretation and its own public warrants for correctness.

The Transcendental Argument for Strong Holism

(1) Interpretation is circular, indeterminate, and perspectival (the thesis of the "hermeneutic circle").

(2) Interpretation occurs only against a "background," a network of unspecifiable beliefs and practices (the thesis of the "background").

(3) The background is a condition for the possibility of interpretation,

---

[12]A list of strong holists might include Jacques Derrida, Stanley Fish, James Clifford, Steve Woolgar, and Bruno Latour, and other postmodernists in various disciplines. A list of holist philosophers who make specific strong holistic inferences include Richard Rorty, Hubert Dreyfus, Charles Taylor, Joseph Rouse, Hans-Georg Gadamer, and, more generally, many neo-Heideggerians and neo-Aristotelians. True to the second variety, these philosophers are not generally skeptical and often take "weak holist" positions on other issues. Besides Latour's notion of a "network" as the limits of an activity's validity, Pierre Bourdieu's concept of a habitus, a set of unreflective dispositions that we are socialized into and become "variants" of, is certainly a strong holist concept of Heideggerian inspiration; see Bourdieu, *Outline of a Theory of Practice* (Cambridge: Cambridge University Press, 1977), pp. 85–87; it is also an example of how, when strong holist concepts are employed empirically, they become highly dubious. Here holism is employed as part of an empirical theory of cultural reproduction. As in Latour's case, it is had only by impoverishing sociological explanation of social practice and agency.

[13]Weak holists include John Searle, Donald Davidson, Jürgen Habermas, Clifford Geertz, and Alasdair MacIntyre. An example of the resistance to skeptical inferences from antifoundationalist, holistic premises comes at the end of Davidson's "The Very Idea of a Conceptual Scheme," where he denies that holism requires giving up truth claims: "In giving up dependence on the concept of an uninterpreted reality, something outside of all schemes and science, we do not relinquish the notion of objective truth." See Donald Davidson, *Inquiries into Truth and Interpretation* (Oxford: Oxford University Press, 1985), p. 198. Like Rouse, MacIntyre is an ambiguous case: his notion of resolving cultural and epistemic crises by strong cross-contextual claims established in "the better argument" is a criterion typical of weak holism; however, his neo-Aristotelian insistence on submission to the authority of a practice reflects strong holism. For MacIntyre as "weak holist," see his essay in *After Philosophy*, ed. K. Baynes, J. Bohman, and T. McCarthy (Cambridge: MIT Press, 1987), pp. 381–411, and my introduction to it.

which limits its possibilities for epistemic justification (the thesis of contextual limits).

(4) All cognitive activities take place against a background and are interpretive and hence circular, indeterminate, and perspectival (the thesis of the universality of interpretation). *Therefore,* the conditions of interpretation are such that no "true" or "correct" interpretations are possible (interpretive skepticism).

In my analysis of this argument I defend premises 1 and 2. Properly interpreted, they form the core of a more defensible "weak holism." Premises 3 and 4 do not follow from them, and hence the inference to interpretive skepticism is unwarranted.

The thesis of the "hermeneutic circle" (premise 1) has formed the core of almost every holistic theory of interpretation since Friedrich Schleiermacher, both as an explication of the relation of parts to wholes in interpretation and as a denial of the possibility of a separate metalanguage to discuss interpretations (because interpretation is circular, every treatment of an interpretation is itself an interpretation).[14] If correct, it also means that interpretations cannot be independent of the standpoint of the interpreter, in that interpreters are embedded in their situation and hence their understanding remains partial and incomplete. The language of the interpreter is not some metalanguage outside the circle, but a fallible and partial understanding within it.

The thesis of the "background" (premise 2) is also a statement of the practical and conditioned character of interpretations. Any attempt to explicate the intention or meaning of an action or utterance requires the assumption of an indefinite number of other beliefs and purposes, as Searle tries to show by attempting to specify all the presuppositions of a single, simple sentence.[15] Far from being contingent facts, these indeterminate and holistic constraints are part of what makes communication possible, since we may understand the assertions of the true beliefs of others only by reference to publicly shared beliefs.[16] But in its most radical form, the background thesis

[14]See Gadamer, *Truth and Method,* pp. 147-50.

[15]John Searle, *Intentionality* (Cambridge: Cambridge University Press, 1983), p. 158.

[16]Donald Davidson makes this weak holist argument in discussing Carl Hempel's antiholist explanations of intentional action when he argues that rational explanations cannot work for single actions but can work for identifying coherent patterns of actions; hence, they involve interpretation. See Davidson, "Hempel on Explaining Action," in *Essays on Action and Events* (Oxford: Oxford University Press, 1980), pp. 261-78.

makes all actions, theories, and expressions context dependent. Taken together, circularity and reference to a background exclude the possibility of reducing interpretations to semantic explication or to some other procedure for fixing determinate meanings without reference to holistic constraints.

These two premises alone are insufficient to warrant skepticism about interpretation. It is commonplace in hermeneutics to argue that circularity need not be vicious. As Gadamer argues, it can be an ever-enriching process of relating parts and whole, with an "anticipation of completeness." Similarly, Heidegger argues that "positive possibilities for knowing" emerge in the hermeneutic circle when we overcome our "fancies and popular conceptions" and work through "these fore-structures in terms of the things themselves."[17] But skepticism begins when this circularity applies reflexively to the standards of correctness themselves: what is "completeness" but itself something to be interpreted? What are "things in themselves," and how do we gain access to them as evidence against which we modify the preconceptions that make up the background to our interpretive acts? Even if such norms of "completeness" or the evidence of "things themselves" exist, circularity at least makes it indeterminate how they should be applied in any given case: "correct" interpretations are not produced by some standardized method, algorithm, or semantic theory. Even so, circularity still might support only fallibilism, not skepticism, in that interpretations are put forward in a public process and subject to constant revision. It is the addition of the third and fourth premises that transforms the holistic conditions into finitistic limits on the capacity of interpretations to support knowledge claims. After examining the conceptual and empirical cogency of these next two premises, I will test the validity of the inference as a whole.

Quite apart from a close examination of the argument as a transcendental fallacy, a good case can be made that both the core premises of contextualism (3 and 4) fall prey to conceptual confusions, particularly with regard to the thesis of interpretive universality (premise 4). This thesis makes an overly quick identification of all forms of indeterminacy with interpretation. There are any number of other, distinct forms of indeterminacy. First, observational indeterminacy may result from the unavoidable involvement of the observer in certain social and physical processes; this involvement may be due to

[17]Martin Heidegger, *Being and Time* (New York: Harper and Row, 1962), p. 195.

contingent facts about certain processes, such as the nature of light or the interaction between particles. Second, causal indeterminacy may be found in the case of identifying whether or not a particular intention "really" brought about an action; here such problems emerge when we compare an interpretive account of an action with one based on some mechanism such as psychic repression. Third, following a rule is indeterminate, insofar as a rule does not strictly determine what sort of action may or may not be construed as following it: as any game like chess shows, the variety of possible moves may have more to do with differences in judgments and strategies than with different interpretations of the rules. Since none of these forms of indeterminacy can be assumed to be identical with hermeneutic circularity, on closer examination "the reign of universal hermeneutics" is often mere decree and stipulation. From a methodological perspective, "universal hermeneutics" also suffers from the problems of all reductionistic and overextended programs: if it is to fit all the variety of human cognition and action into its interpretive framework, its categories must become more and more vague and less and less informative.

But even when conceptual distinctions among different forms of indeterminacy are made, circularity still might undermine the truth claims made in interpretations, if the presupposed background supplies a finite limit on validity or correctness (premise 3). If this premise is also true, the universality thesis would then make these limits general and hence would warrant skepticism about the valid application of any epistemic norms to interpretations: as always against a background, they might be inevitably subject to ethnocentrism and other inaccessible limitations. For this reason, the limit thesis as an interpretation of background constraints does all the work in this argument for skepticism and is therefore the real defining premise of a strong holist position. Such a limit thesis can be found not only in Clifford and Woolgar but also in Taylor's claim that interpretations rely on "unformalizable" insight rather than public evidence.

Such holism is, I believe, open to two different objections, one weaker and empirical and the other stricter and logical. I will make the first objection quickly to cast doubt on the empirical plausibility of such limits. It involves conceiving such limits as really operative: what would the cognitive capacities of actual interpreters have to be like if they were so limited? Second, I shall turn to the core of.my criticism of strong holism, its interpretation of background constraints. How must the background function in interpretation to act as a determinate limit? The argument about limits involves a fallacy of "amphiboly" (confusions of the empirical and the transcendental concepts, as well as determinate and reflective judgments) in the use of the background as a condition of possibility.

My first objection is that the limit thesis is empirically implausible: it implies that the involvements in the shared practices and beliefs that make up any particular "background" or culture are so strong that we cannot take any distance from them. Strong holists argue that the reference to a background means that our involvements in our shared language establish "a way of living and grasping the world that has us";[18] they are, in other words, interpretive orientations that cannot be brought under our reflective control all at once and that we incorporate by being socialized into a set of interpretive practices and acquiring its context-specific, prethematic skills.

It is certainly empirically correct that socialization involves acquiring a number of prereflective orientations to the world, and that as a whole they are not reflectively accessible all at once. But it is unlikely that our involvement in them, both individually and as a whole, is always so strong or immediate that they act as determinate limits; nor does their prereflective immediacy preclude the possibility of thematizing them reflectively, of freeing them from their local context, and thus of revising any one of them. Not only is it possible to thematize and change such orientations, but being conditioned by social constraints in no way precludes the possibility of valid knowledge emerging within them, any more than the organic constraints on the human eye's ability to see color implies limits about what we may know about the spectrum, or, similarly, the fact that we see within a horizon limits the knowledge gained by visual perception. More modest strong holists might reply that some beliefs or skills can be brought under reflective control, but not all. If that is true, the strong holist has lost the argument. None of our practical involvements then sanction skepticism about any specific knowledge claim, since it may be one that has already been taken out of its practical context and submitted to public scrutiny, as in the sciences, or to explicit formal interpretation, as in the law. Indeed, in many complex societies there is already a social division of labor for formally testing

[18] As put by a practical holist, Joseph Rouse, as a gloss on Heidegger's notion of the hermeneutic circle; see *Knowledge and Power*, p. 67. What is most striking about this locution is the way it reifies our own interpretations and shared understandings. This view of our prereflective orientations explains why Rouse thinks that theoretical knowledge is "local" and context dependent.

and validating our prethematic orientations in different institutional settings, from Talmudic discussion to legal review.

In general, this thesis transforms what can only be an empirical question into one of principle. Not all involvements and backgrounds are the same. Although the holist is correct in pointing out that the interpreter is never a Cartesian ego, various forms of socialization into practices permit greater or lesser degrees of autonomy and prereflective involvement. "Backgrounds" are always empirically specific, and nothing apart from some very formal properties (like their holistic character) can be settled a priori. Certainly, on the basis of the existence of specific backgrounds for specific practices, it cannot be established that scientific knowledge acquired in them is "local" or "contingent,"[19] unless there are independent reasons for thinking so. A more empirical strategy is needed here to avoid empty conceptual claims. Feminist analyses of science show just how such empirical limits operate in community-wide gender biases that are a matter of social fact.

The same is true of the supposed unavoidability of "prejudice" in interpretation.[20] Although the appeal to some unexamined assumptions is a formal requirement of interpretation, it remains an empirical question the degree to which the prejudices of a specific interpreter with the background of a specific culture distort his or her interpretations. As the ethnomethodologists put it, being socialized into a culture or background does not turn us into "judgmental dopes" who passively and unreflectively assimilate roles, norms, and skills.[21] The necessity of the background establishes nothing about the status of any particular belief or skill, any particular interpretation or practice. Despite these remarks about socialization and reflection, however, this empirical objection does not yet show definitively that there are no such limits on interpretation, especially if "everything is interpre-

---

[19]These claims are made by Rouse and Woolgar, respectively.

[20]Gadamer makes this argument in *Truth and Method*, pp. 238–40.

[21]See Harold Garfinkel's criticism of Talcott Parsons's holistic concept of "internalization," in *Studies in Ethnomethodology* (Englewood Cliffs, N.J.: Prentice-Hall, 1967). When used by strong holists and even some ethnomethodologists who talk of everyday practical knowledge, the skill metaphor, like all overly specific models of the variety of acts that make up interpretation, is seriously misleading as a general model of interpretation. At best, it generalizes one type of interpretation to all; at worst, it leads to the confusion of prereflective orientations and interpretations. Even if we are skillful at an activity, we could still be a "dope" about its conditions and constraints. Reflection has to have more epistemic content than "practical holism" sometimes seems to allow.

tation.'' In eliminating all empirical differences, we are left, as Hegel put it, in a skeptical night where all cows are gray.

The more fundamental challenge to strong holism is its error in transcendental logic. It is certainly true that something like a "background" makes up the public conditions for the possibility of interpretation; it is also true that we cannot detach ourselves completely from our involvements or leap out of our skins. Although some deeply interested interpretations are for that reason limited, these conditions are no cause for a general skepticism about epistemic and critical reflection on interpretation. They warrant skepticism only when various conditions of possibility are confused in its transcendental argument: the main problem with strong holism is that it confuses constraints with limits, or more precisely, enabling conditions with limiting conditions.

The strong holists' inference works only if one ignores the many differences between these two types of conditions. Whereas limiting conditions are determinate and fixed, enabling conditions are variable and alterable. Certainly, all conditions act as constraints on that which they condition. However, the variability of enabling conditions makes them formal: any number of different beliefs and skills can function as a background. A limiting condition is specific and material in character: it is *this* belief or *this* set of skills within which the actor operates, whether she knows it or not. Enabling conditions also have quite different epistemic properties: they are reflectively accessible and alterable. Most importantly, each has different functional properties and hence works differently. As opposed to limiting conditions, enabling conditions are open-ended and permit different degrees of knowledge; as determinate, limiting conditions permit only specific things within its field. Different aspects and levels of the ability to speak a language illustrate this nested set of contrasts. Though it is a formal property of my linguistic ability that I can speak some language, it is a material property of my linguistic competence that I specifically speak English. This material condition is not necessarily limiting, since I can always learn another language. Now compare two nonnative speakers of a foreign language, one using a phrase book and the other fluent. The phrase book speaker's expressions and interpretations do have determinate limits (the number of sentences in the book), whereas the fluent speaker's do not: she can form and understand an indeterminate number of sentences, constrained only by what native speakers find acceptable and by the contingent occasions of language use.

In order to untangle this confusion further and to show its relation to skepticism, I will use an analogy to transcendental argumentation. This analogy shows that the thesis of the background, or of context dependence, does not justify epistemological skepticism about correct interpretations any more than Kant's thesis that concepts require sensation is meant to limit the objectivity of knowledge: Kant's formal conditions on cognition and the holistic conditions on interpretation are both epistemologically neutral in exactly the same way. Contextualists deny purely formal and hence universal conditions that enable interpretation, putting in their place particular material and ontological conditions that limit interpretations: the possession of the prereflective stances and background knowledge necessary to participate in one's own particular culture or in one of its practices. In order to engage in scientific practices, for example, we must have acquired an unspecifiable but still finite set of presuppositions and orientations appropriate to the science of our age. However, the reflective and prereflective aspects of the background function quite differently in this example. Although the acquisition of specific orientations makes it possible for our statements and activities to be recognized as "scientific," it has nothing to do with whether or not they are well warranted. Such ontological conditions by themselves only make it possible for a claim to be part of meaningful scientific practice; it does not guarantee or deny its truth or objectivity. With regard to any particular content, whether it be a statement, theory, or text, the transcendental presuppositions of interpretation do not determine the extent of the capacity to know or judge what something means, nor do they determine how we reflectively judge the adequacy of such an account.

With regard to the content of judgments, Kant makes a similar point in his analysis of the subjective conditions for the possibility of experience. Kant saw that these conditions have two sides: they are enabling conditions with regard to objective knowledge of phenomena, and limiting conditions only with regard to knowledge of noumena or things in themselves. Despite the constraints on human knowing such as the unity of consciousness or the spatial-temporal character of intuitions, knowledge claims produced in judgments are not merely subjective. While the formal conditions for the possibility of knowing make it impossible to know all the determinations of an object, this conditioned character does not imply that what we do know does not have objective status.[22] The antiskeptical requirements

---

[22]Kant, *Critique of Pure Reason*, A572. Kant does have limiting concepts, although

for interpretation are much more minimal: they need not be objective, but only capable of being intersubjectively warranted and publicly adjudicated. Because what makes a set of assumptions and stances a background is the fact that it is shared, the conditions of interpretation also make possible a process of testing that is governed by epistemic norms of publicity and employs the same skills that made the interpretations themselves possible in the first place.[23]

Such confusions between formal and empirical concepts common to contextualism are the skeptical counterpoint to the metaphysical error that Kant calls "the amphiboly of concepts of reflection."[24] Whereas Kant saw metaphysicians like Leibniz as making illicit inferences from formal concepts to determinate judgments about empirical truths, skeptical strong holists infer determinate and empirical limits on knowledge from the holistic but enabling conditions of interpretation. The confusion begins in the universality thesis, since the

---

they are inferred dialectically and not arrived at as a result of transcendental analysis: the concept of the noumena, which has no content whatsoever. As Kant puts it, "The concept of the noumena is thus a merely limiting concept, the function of which is to curb the pretensions of sensibility; it is therefore only of negative employment" (B310). Strong holists are guilty not only of an amphiboly but also of confusing the positive and negative employment of limit concepts, which leads to skepticism.

[23]Strong holists dispute this view of reflective adjudication. When replacing epistemic accounts, they often appeal to practical forms of knowledge within interpretive limits, such as Gadamer's analysis of "phronesis" and Dreyfus's arguments for the superiority of "practical" over "theoretical" holism. See Hubert Dreyfus, "Holism and Hermeneutics," in *Hermeneutics and Praxis*, ed. R. Hollinger (Notre Dame, Ind.: Notre Dame University Press, 1984), pp. 227–47. Practical holists see interpretation as "practical" in the sense of a skill and take Wilhelm Dilthey to be their main opponent, the founder of misleading theoretical and epistemological approaches to hermeneutics. I will defend Dilthey's approach at the end of this essay, but not his specific theory of interpretation. In his essay in this volume Dreyfus goes beyond this discussion of practical holism and argues that the background enables some beliefs to be "decontextualized"; this is sufficient to establish the possibility of theoretical knowledge and a notion of truth not simply relative to social purposes.

[24]Kant, *Critique of Pure Reason*, B316. Some have argued that interpretive realists like Charles Taylor commit a paralogism, a false inference from the nature of the concepts describing a thing (interpretations) to the things themselves (interpreters). See Mark Okrent, "Hermeneutics, Transcendental Philosophy, and Social Science," *Inquiry* 27 (1984): 23–49; and Joseph Rouse, *Knowledge and Power*, esp. chap. 6. In any case, weak holists that accept the possibility of "correct" interpretations do not reify meanings in entities. It does not require anything of interpreters as metaphysical objects, but just agents with certain capacities to whom we stand in dialogical relationships. Further, it commits no paralogism, since its main point is not about an essentialistic human nature but about methodology and verification: interpretation requires at least considering as evidence what meanings actions or expressions have for those who perform them, even if they are not ultimately accepted. Weak holists do not therefore privilege self-knowledge, but consider it to be part of the evidence grounding an interpretation.

holist loses sight of the fact that holism is itself a formal theory resulting from transcendental reflection on the general conditions of interpretation and not an interpretation itself. If holistic concepts like the
background are formal, reflective, and interpretive, then the premises
of the holistic argument violate its own antitheoretical account of
interpretation as always contingent and context dependent.

Once the formal and reflective character of transcendental concepts
like the background is clarified, it should also be clear that the background describes an enabling and not a limiting condition that enables interpretation. This is precisely the way that Searle uses the
concept: the background refers to a whole set of nonrepresentational
presuppositions that enable intentionality. As he puts it, the background is not any particular set of beliefs or practices but a set of
presupposed practices and stances that "provide the enabling conditions for the operation of intentional states."[25] Thus, the second amphiboly of strong holism is the confusion of enabling conditions with
limiting conditions that is equivalent in Kantian terms to confusing
the enabling conditions for objectivity in the constraints on sensibility
with the limiting conditions of transcendental notions like the noumena. Or, to return to our example: speaking a particular language
is an enabling condition of communication. It is not a fixed limit on
our capacity to communicate with others, since it may be expanded
to incorporate new contexts and possibilities of understanding, as
well as novel, never heard or uttered sentences. Thus, like speaking
a particular language, interpreting within a certain background is best
understood as presenting a set of loose constraints, rather than strict
limits, upon activities of interpretation and understanding. Certainly,
even limiting conditions have two sides as well. They may enable a
certain type of performance: the traveler can read from the determinate list of sentences in the phrase book and order her meal. This
capacity does not require much reflective access to the structure of
the activity of speaking this particular language. Such determinately
limited knowledge is indeed local and contingent. In order to interpret the sciences, for example, as "locally, materially and socially
situated skills and practices," similar limits must be instrumentally
and socially enabling conditions for the things science does. If these
conditions are seen as limiting ones, then it follows that these local
limits enable only a nonuniversal theoretical knowledge that is "indexical" and "contingent," a description that seems difficult to un-

[25]Searle, *Intentionality*, p. 158.

derstand without resorting to some form of skepticism.[26] As opposed to the material limiting conditions on skills and power, the social enabling conditions of science do not necessarily say anything about the epistemic status of theories: they could be universal and transcend the context that produced them. That they are not universal has to be established independently from the mere fact that they are socially conditioned. Thus, the skeptical argument from enabling, rather than disabling, conditions that are also determinate limits also fails to establish any skeptical conclusions.

Restating the Argument: The Case for a Nonskeptical Holism

The failure to establish the skeptical conclusion of strong holism suggests that a revised version of the same transcendental argument could establish a nonskeptical conclusion. The theses of the hermeneutic circle and of the background were accepted as part of a transcendental analysis of the conditions for the possibility of interpretation, and it remains only to recast the offending premises into enabling transcendental conditions of possibility for fallible and revisable claims to interpretive correctness. Here the analogy to good transcendental argumentation serves us well again. Although Kant defended the objectivity of knowledge within formal conditions, he did not provide a transcendental justification that supported the overly strong claims of a metaphysical realism. So, too, with interpretation: weak holism will have to modify overly strong criteria of correctness, as in the case of a semantic realist notion of fixing "true meanings." However, such conditions enable interpreters to engage in publicly shared epistemic practices like the sciences, in which revisable, well-warranted interpretive claims may be put forward and criticized. Here interpreters are guided by epistemic considerations of evidence to warrant their specific claims, in the same way that scientists revise their theories in light of new social experiences.

[26]As Rouse claims in *Power and Knowledge*, esp. in chap. 4, which is entitled "Local Knowledge." It is hard not to see epistemic qualifiers like "local" as anything but skeptical; if they are not, Rouse needs to distinguish what he means by them more clearly from the obviously skeptical meanings they have for Woolgar and Latour, whom he quotes approvingly and without criticism throughout this chapter of his book.

Thus, hermeneutic circularity and indeterminacy point in the direction of fallibilism, not skepticism.

The Transcendental Argument for Weak Holism

(1) Interpretation is circular, indeterminate, and perspectival (the thesis of the hermeneutic circle).
(2) Its circularity may be defined by the necessity of a "background," a set of shared and accessible conditions of possibility (the background as a reflective-transcendental concept).
(3) As a formal condition of possibility, the background acts as an enabling condition and not a limiting condition for interpretation (the distinction between "enabling" and "limiting" conditions).
(4) The conditions of interpretation are neutral with regard to the warrants of knowledge claims, including claims about interpretations (the denial of hermeneutic universality). *Therefore*, interpretations can produce revisable, public knowledge based on evidence.

This weak holistic argument tries to show that there is no reason for skepticism in properly understood interpretive circularity. Rather, it argues not only that this circularity is nonvicious but also that it is based on enabling conditions analyzed as shared background constraints. Like other public and constrained epistemic activities, such as Rawlsian reflection, the constraints are not strong enough to act as a fixed limit or to make it impossible to decide normatively between interpretations on the basis of evidence. Indeed, such evaluation will always be comparative, fallibilistic, and revisable, in that yet a better interpretation could come along, encompassing the strengths and overcoming the weaknesses of previous interpretations.[27] Strong holism cannot really make sense of a process of evaluating interpretations comparatively, for a number of reasons. First, it excludes a priori the weighing of public evidence to settle interpretive disputes and conflicts. Second, it makes any process of reflection and evaluation limited by its contingent background. Its version of the background thesis entails that few conflicts are manageable except within

[27] Alasdair MacIntyre uses this type of epistemological, weak holistic argument in his recent work *Whose Justice? Whose Rationality?* (Notre Dame, Ind.: Notre Dame University Press, 1988) but undercuts it with his historicism.

the limits of more or less identical implicit assumptions. If my criticisms of the assumptions of this argument are correct, such unreflective consensus is not necessary for adjudicating interpretive claims. Background constraints on reflective evaluation only eliminate the possibility of uniquely true interpretations; they imply nothing determinate about how better or worse interpretations can be established. Questions involving the comparison of conflicting interpretations emerge on the basis of shared understandings, no matter how minimal, and can be answered by closely examining the reflective practices in which interpretive claims are publicly warranted and adjudicated.

As opposed to strong holism's nonreflective account of the background, weak holism sees one aspect of interpretation as explicitly evaluative and critical. As in Neurath's boat, interpreters may modify their assumptions and thematize their constraints, although not all at once. Holistic constraints and circularity do not limit in advance what the critical assessment and evaluation of interpretations can achieve in changing whole interpretive patterns that may be deeply embedded in a culture. For example, in evaluating the strengths of two interpretations, one can show different parts of a scene or text to be problematic on the pattern suggested by one interpretation and less problematic and fragmentary on the pattern suggested by another. Thus, interpretation is better understood as including critical appropriation, a process that, though circular and fallibilistic, is also governed by epistemic norms like coherence and correctness. This is not to say that some epistemic value like coherence may not be overemphasized in some interpretations; but when it is, that very exaggeration can be shown by public adjudication in light of supporting evidence.

The basic thrust and usefulness of this argument against contextualist skepticism can be illustrated by briefly examining two recent debates in the philosophy of social science: first, Steve Woolgar's challenge to "the ideology of representation" and standard sociologies of science; and second, recent discussions of the falsifications of interpretive ethnography, in particular the exchange between Clifford Geertz and James Clifford.[28] In both cases holistic assumptions

---

[28]See Steve Woolgar, *Science: The Very Idea* (London: Tavistock, 1988), esp. chaps. 2 and 6. An actual debate as such did not occur between Clifford and Geertz; however, they do explicitly criticize each other's views. See James Clifford, *Predicament of Culture*; Clifford Geertz's response in *Works and Lives: The Anthropologist as Author* (Stanford: Stanford University Press, 1988), esp. the concluding chapter.

about interpretation lead to an unwarranted skepticism about knowledge claims in various disciplines. At least in the social sciences, concerned as they are with the social conditions of activities, strong holism is alive and well. It comprises a common philosophical mistake that leads many contemporary analyses of knowledge and interpretation to exaggerate their conclusions.

As its title suggests, Woolgar's *Science: The Very Idea* is a skeptical work, offering a "reflexive ethnography of the practice of representation."[29] The critical purpose of this ethnography and its detailed descriptions of what scientists actually do is to cast doubt upon the idealized picture of science as objective knowledge of an independent world of facts. Woolgar's skeptical strategy is to show that if science is a social practice like any other, then "objective, representational knowledge is not possible." The mythologies of representation are justified by what Woolgar calls a false objectivist epistemology: its main contention is that science is able to "capture some feature independent of the activity itself."[30] For example, objectivism asserts that the inscriptions on a meter are said to register "voltage," a feature of the world independent of scientific activity of measuring and not produced by it. The contrary, nonobjectivistic account of this scientific activity is "constructivist": voltage is defined by the background context of the practices and instruments that produce it, and truth claims about it are confined to the social networks that produce and reproduce the beliefs in them. In order to establish these strong claims, Woolgar repeatedly argues against "objectivism" and for "constructivism" by employing a version of the usual two-step argument of strong holism: the indeterminate, indexical, and context-dependent character of science as interpretive practice is supposed to establish determinate and contextual limits on the knowledge so gained. Apart from the first premise, Woolgar's argument should now seem familiar:

(1) Science is a social practice.
(2) As a practice, science always takes place within the assumptions of a larger context and social network (the thesis of the background as contextual limit).

[29]Woolgar, *Science: The Very Idea*, p. 92.
[30]Ibid., p. 30. Besides my argument for public as opposed to objective validity, Dreyfus's essay in this volume shows that the commitment to holism is entirely consistent with a belief in the context- and purpose-independent status of scientific claims, even a form of realism.

(3) As socially and contextually bound, science and scientific facts are as perspectival and indeterminate as any other interpretation (the thesis of interpretive circularity). *Therefore*, science cannot attain objective, representational knowledge.

Leaving empirical questions aside, the conclusion simply does not follow from premises 2 and 3. Woolgar simply never considers that both premises could just as well be enabling social conditions for scientific knowledge. To return to my analogy: there is no reason to suppose that the inscriptions of the experiment that measure voltage are like the sentences in the phrase book, limited to the context in which they appear. Thus, the skeptical conclusions about representation and public evidence do not follow, nor do the conclusions that the objects of knowledge are "constructed" or have truth value "only" in certain social networks, or that scientific theories are like indexical utterances. What does follow from a weak holistic interpretation of premises 2 and 3 is only a reflexive awareness of the socially constrained character of scientific knowing as an interpretive practice, constraints that may or may not enable particular publicly warranted and context-independent truth claims.

Woolgar draws an explicit comparison between his conclusions about the social study of science and Clifford's reflexive ethnography of western anthropology. Just as Woolgar wants to show that the "very idea of science" is radically impossible in order to attack the "authority of science," he interprets Clifford as demonstrating that in light of interpretive limits the very idea of achieving an "adequate understanding" across cultures "involves a relatively uncritical reliance upon conventional forms of representation."[31] The comparison is more telling than Woolgar imagines. Both Woolgar and Clifford are led to skepticism through false inferences from well-warranted reflexive criticisms of naive knowledge claims, properly showing that they are not independent of interpretive and social constraints. Just as Woolgar correctly challenges the nonreflexive character of past sociology of science, Clifford and other "postmodernists" rightly challenge the falsifying aspects of much traditional ethnography, its Romantic exoticism and overly unifying claim to represent other cultures as discrete, meaningful worlds.[32] So far, so good: Clifford is

[31]Ibid., p. 93.
[32]This analysis is made particularly well in Clifford's essay, "On Ethnographic Authority," *Predicament of Culture*, p. 38. Although "authority" could be taken as an epistemological term, Clifford never analyzes it as such, concerning himself only with

offering a quite valid, epistemically informed, and reflective criticism of the methods and politics of ethnographic interpretation. But he quickly transforms such criticisms into a postmodern, skeptical doubt about the textual authority of interpretation as such. By presenting the Nuer or Balinese as a unified whole subject, Clifford claims skeptically, "the ethnographer transforms the research situation's ambiguity and diversity of meaning into an integrated portrait,"[33] and necessarily occludes the dialogical and situational limits to ethnographic interpretation and authority. Geertz's response to postmodern criticisms that he ignores the limits on interpretation is quite in the spirit of what I have been calling "weak holism": though he grants the discursive and moral constraints on ethnographic interpretation, he finds in them only " the end to certain pretensions" rather than a cause for skepticism. As he puts it, "The moral asymmetries across which ethnography works and the discursive complexity within which it works make any attempt to portray it as anything more than the representation of one sort of life in the categories of another impossible to defend."[34] Apart from some transcendental illusions, interpretation needs no more than that: such public constraints do not necessarily limit the interpretive activity of the ethnographer but enable it to take place, particularly if the interpreter is

---

how such claims are established in writing and the rhetoric of "being there," as a participant observer. But the problem is more interesting from an epistemological point of view, since first-person authority and witnessing of events do not guarantee the veracity of accounts of them.

[33]Ibid., p. 44. Clifford argues that ethnography must become "mutual construction" instead of the attempt to interpret the other's point of view. The latter is inherently falsifying. "Thus, for example, the ethnographer of the Trobriand Islands does not openly concoct a version of reality in collaboration with his informants but rather interprets the 'Trobriand point of view' " (p. 43). One wonders, however, how this mutuality would be created except by each person's interpreting the other's beliefs and utterances, or by each person's expanding the horizon of discourse to incorporate the other's point of view. Though a desirable practical ideal, mutual collaboration does not avoid the problems of interpreting different points of view. Such dialogue is just where intercultural problems begin.

[34]Geertz, Works and Lives, p. 144. This is not a concession to his postmodern critics, nor a new view of the nature and limits of ethnographic interpretation. Already in his essay "Thick Description" Geertz describes such interpretation as "our formulations of other people's symbol systems." In good weak-holist fashion, Geertz argues that we must therefore "begin with our own interpretations," with the reflective awareness of how they come into play when we try to understand the expressions of other cultures. This reflection is only the first step. To achieve such understanding often requires that we expand our "universe of discourse." See Geertz, The Interpretation of Cultures, pp. 14–15.

critically and reflectively aware of them. Such an awareness is the cognitive condition of possibility of responsible, cross-cultural dialogue that is guided by the ideal of the public and mutual correction of each other's misunderstandings.

The debate between Clifford and Geertz is that between strong and weak holism, between whether interpretation is subject to enabling or limiting conditions, between an interpretive skepticism and an epistemic fallibilism. The problem with Clifford's argument and the case for Geertz's weak holism can be seen by an analogy: it is no more true that we should doubt ethnographic interpretation than that we should doubt the representational and artistic potentials of black-and-white photography. In the hands of an artist aware of its constraints, black and white may be the preferred medium, as it was for Diane Arbus's attempt to "interpret" social outcasts so as to represent the ordinary in the strange. Geertz, too, is arguing that good ethnography will have to be aware of the difficulties imposed by the moral, discursive, and interpretive constraints on cross-cultural writing. How does one, then, responsibly and accurately portray another form of life in the categories of one's own? As correctly as possible, constantly revising and judging the adequacy of interpretation in light of an openness to new and broader evidence, discovered in this case by free and open dialogue with other interpreters and with the participants in that form of life. When faced with these constraints, ethnography should not, with Clifford, produce "multiple interpretations," but rather, with Geertz, produce better, epistemically and morally justified ones, the evidence for which is an increased space for dialogue and mutual criticism. Weak holists like Geertz reflect upon the ways in which interpretations of other cultures may be justified within those constraints: he claims only to be able to know something about what others are saying and doing, but not to be able to jump into their skin. As for interpretive responsibility, the postmodern proliferation of interpretations is as much a moral as it is an epistemological dodge of the deeper issues of interpretive knowledge across boundaries that do not disappear behind uncommitted and ultimately apolitical and aesthetic multiplicity.

Conclusion

For all their claims to give a new "practical" and sometimes "political" view of interpretation, these contextualists do not get us much beyond skeptical doubts about interpretive validity. The practical tasks of interpretation are better served by a good transcendental theory, one that supplies a proper understanding of the normative epistemology of interpretation. For all the weaknesses of his particular views on empathy and his historicism, Dilthey already saw that a normative epistemology was one of the important tasks of the theory of interpretation. Such a theory is necessary, he argues, to counteract "the constant irruption of Romantic whim and skeptical subjectivity" in the human sciences.[35] Postmodern skepticism certainly properly criticizes the Romantic whims of earlier hermeneutic theories, as well as the idealizing excesses of past epistemology. But, by denying the possibility of any appeal to evidence or epistemic norms, it takes away all of the resources necessary for overcoming

[35]Wilhelm Dilthey, *Gesammelte Schriften*, vol. 5 (Stuttgart: Teubner Verlag, 1958), p. 337. In *Being and Time* Heidegger also sees reflection on whim and prejudice as a way out of the vicious hermeneutic circle: What is decisive, he writes, is "to get out of the circle in the right way." Circularity is never a determinate limit for Heidegger, since "our first, last and constant task is never to allow our . . . [prior understandings] to be presented by fancies and popular conceptions" (p. 195). This goal did not lead Heidegger to examine the many popular misconceptions and Romantic whims contained in his writings, particularly his more egregiously Eurocentric statements, including ones in *Being and Time* about "primitive peoples" as "less concealed and less complicated by extensive self-interpretation" (p. 78). The question is, of course, whether Heidegger's account of this epistemic possibility of getting out of the vicious circle is adequate to all the tasks of interpretation, particularly in the social sciences. A positive Heideggerian account sees true interpretations as disclosures of other possibilities of being. In *Heidegger's Pragmatism* (Ithaca: Cornell University Press, 1988), Mark Okrent interprets Heidegger's conception of truth not as correspondence but as pragmatic in the following sense: "the truth of an interpretation rests on the success of that interpretation for the ends from which it is carried out, whatever they happen to be. . . . The significant whole that must be understood is always the significant whole of the interpreter's own community" (p. 163). Regardless of whether or not this is Heidegger's view, I cannot agree with either part of this gloss as offering a way out of the viciousness of the hermeneutic circle: many interpretations are dialogical and not merely relative to the purposes of my community; true interpretation requires that the interpreter take up a moral responsibility toward others, such that the rendering of their beliefs will be as correct and accurate as possible. True interpretations require this moral responsibility, if others are to be disclosed for their own possibilities, not for their possibilities relative to my purposes. Dreyfus's essay in this volume suggests why Heidegger's notion of truth may not be pragmatic, if truth is really disclosure. I am suggesting here that moral responsibility demands that interpretive dialogue with others be disclosures of their point of view, not the imposition of purposes or norms upon them. Like decontextualized knowledge of nature, dialogue with others cannot be achieved if our interpretations of them are simply regarded as "true" relative to our purposes. Interpreting others requires the possibility of placing "our" purposes and norms in question, and interpretations are irresponsible and inaccurate to the extent that they do not do so.

equally problematic skeptical subjectivity. If my criticisms are correct, no transcendental holistic argument warrants such skepticism about the validity or correctness of interpretation. Rather, properly understood, the opposite is true: shared, weak holistic constraints provide a possible basis for the possibility of the public validity of interpretation, much as Kant saw that the very constraints on our knowing apparatus could make objective knowledge possible.

But as the name that I gave to nonskeptical holism suggests, the claim made here is the result of a "weak" transcendental argument. It is certainly true that the positive argument sketched above does not supply the definitive criteria to settle all interpretive disputes, nor to identify any particular interpretation as uniquely correct or even definitively superior. That was not its purpose. Like the circular relation between theory and observation, the holistic character of interpretation entails that evaluative considerations are themselves revisable and fallible. Too often, however, this feature of interpretation is taken to mean that validity is impossible. This objection again misunderstands the transcendental response to skepticism. Just as a theory of truth does not establish which sentences are true, so, too, a theory of validity does not pick out which interpretations are correct. In either case, skepticism lives off an all-or-nothing appeal. Once we see that the argument for such a conclusion is based on errors similar to well-known errors in transcendental reasoning, interpretive contexts become no different than other epistemic contexts; they, too, are governed by evidence and normative warrants of their own. Once the illusions of contextualism are seen through, interpretation again becomes part of our attempt to know the world and others in it. It is neither Romantic whim nor skeptical subjectivity, but a distinct way to establish a claim to knowledge about what others are doing or saying. Although the contemporary skeptics counsel that all we can do is proliferate and multiply interpretations, I hope that I have shown that their assertion is a matter of taste and not of transcendental necessity.

A further issue about validity remains: the multiplicity of types of interpretation and interpretive contexts. There are indeed many types of interpretations, each engaging the different ideals that we bring to the interpretive enterprise—whether they be aesthetic, moral, explanatory, or critical. But this multiplicity merely reflects the many purposes to which interpretation can be put, not its conditions of possibility. Thus, the distinction of types is a pragmatic affair. Even so, more has to be said about interpreting other human beings, perhaps the most common form of interpretation. Besides having its own distinctive purposes, interpreting others also brings with it stronger cognitive and moral requirements: the norms of interpretation are further structured by the social and political situation of dialogue, demanding of the interpreter the moral and cognitive responsibility of correctly interpreting others' beliefs and desires. Here interpretive correctness and moral responsibility are intertwined: false interpretations of others are not only incorrect but irresponsible. In order to understand others, it is necessary that we engage them in dialogue, and to do so often demands a self-conscious broadening of the constraints on our capacities and purposes. We may interpret others correctly, only if we are open to having them place our beliefs and purposes in question. Even within these other activities and contexts, the weak holist transcendental argument demonstrates that interpretation has its own public exigencies and demands, reflected in its normative epistemology.

CHAPTER 8

Is Hermeneutics Ethnocentric?

DAVID COUZENS HOY

Hans-Georg Gadamer's hermeneutical philosophy is preeminent in this century in that it represents a radical break with Cartesian and Kantian theories of knowledge. Here I start from the assumption that Gadamer is correct to criticize traditional epistemological models that posit the ideal of context-free knowledge, and that he is right to insist instead on the context-bound character of interpretive understanding. My specific concern here is whether his program can be defended against those who infer from the hermeneutical insistence on context-boundedness that hermeneutics necessarily condones ethnocentrism. Of course, I have to distinguish between those who think ethnocentrism is wrong and those who think that it is inevitable and perhaps even desirable. So the task is complex, and the outcome will have implications for larger questions such as whether philosophy is not itself ethnocentric, being a product of the West. Should philosophy be suspicious of its own aspirations to universality? Does it deceive itself by concealing from itself the thought that its belief in its own rationality is simply a veiled desire to universalize western culture?

The debate about ethnocentrism has been lively of late. Gadamer's position has been attacked for being ethnocentric by Jürgen Habermas, but it has been defended from the charge of ethnocentrism by Charles Taylor. In contrast to Habermas and Taylor, who oppose ethnocentrism, Richard Rorty accepts and defends ethnocentrism. Rorty believes that a degree of ethnocentrism is inevitable in any interpretation, and on his reading it was Gadamer's contribution to see this. In contrast, the anthropologist Clifford Geertz has objected to Rorty's defense of ethnocentrism because Geertz believes that ethnocentrism in any form leads to a monolithic misconstrual of one's own culture. Anthropology is currently a crucial case, with Habermas arguing that Gadamer cannot explain the need for anthropologists to criticize other societies, and Geertz maintaining that anthropologists must become more aware of the intrusion of their own cultural beliefs in their readings of other cultures. Allan Bloom has added a twist to this controversy by maintaining that a primary virtue of western culture is that it is *not* ethnocentric, whereas other cultures are the ones that are ethnocentric. The danger of Bloom's claim is that it sounds suspiciously ethnocentric itself. Ethnocentrism is not easy to avoid, and it can return to corrupt even the most well-intentioned theories. The question is whether it also corrupts hermeneutical philosophy.

What is lacking in this many-sided debate is a clear account of exactly what is meant by ethnocentrism. I will try to explain how hermeneutics can preserve its belief in the context-bound character of understanding without falling into a pernicious ethnocentrism. To make this last point, I will identify the specific features of ethnocentrism that are pernicious, arguing that they should not be confused with the tenets of hermeneutics. In particular, I claim that it is not insidiously ethnocentric to maintain, as hermeneutics does, that it is inevitable that interpreters see the world through their own self-understandings. What is misguided is instead the further expectation that every other understanding of the world *converge* on one's own. I do not see the hermeneutical claim of the context-bound character of understanding and interpretation as pernicious, so long as interpreters remain open to differences between their own understanding and that of others. Only the requirement of convergence is oppressive, precisely because it obstructs this awareness of difference. Thus, only the addition of the requirement of convergence would make hermeneutics insidiously ethnocentric.

I maintain that if the expectation of convergence can be found in some contemporary theorists influenced by Gadamer (such as Habermas and Taylor, although for different reasons), it is not essential to a philosophy that desires to be hermeneutical. My contention is that hermeneutics is best formulated, not by presupposing the eventual convergence of every other understanding with one's own self-understanding, but, on the contrary, by resisting the invidious consequences of this presupposition.

Consistent with this claim, however, I must admit that I would not expect every other interpreter of Gadamer, or perhaps even Gadamer himself, to agree with my reconstruction of his theory. My interpretation is underdetermined by Gadamer's texts, which do not address this issue specifically. However, that Gadamer's hermeneutical philosophy can evolve through the history of its reception, a history with allegations such as that it is relativistic, nihilistic, and ethnocentric, is, I believe, testimony to its soundness and viability.

Monism, Pluralism, and Ethnocentrism

The goal of this first part of my essay is to explore why Gadamer's hermeneutical theory raises the problem of the inevitable ethnocentrism of interpretation. The current preoccupation with this problem could not have been foreseen when *Truth and Method* was being written. The difficulty emerges, however, when later positions such as Habermas's theory of communicative action, Jacques Derrida's deconstructive disseminations, or Rorty's pragmatism force us to raise questions about whether Gadamer's hermeneutics is consistent or inconsistent with them. I am therefore not simply repeating what Gadamer has said, but I am interpreting him in a specific way that other readers of *Truth and Method* may resist. I first need to suggest a framework in which different possible positions stand in contrast to one another. Interpreters of Gadamer will probably vary on which of these positions to attribute to Gadamer, and I have to argue for what I think is the most advantageous reconstruction of hermeneutics in the light of these possibilities.

Monism versus Pluralism, Critical versus Metaphysical

First, I think that we need to distinguish monist from pluralist theories of understanding and interpretation. Monism insists that all the possible questions about all the features of an object of interpretation (paradigmatically, but not necessarily, a text) must be resolvable, at least at the ideal limit. More generally, monists have the intuition that there must be only one right interpretation of a text, problem, or subject matter. They may think that the ideal of the completely correct interpretation lies somewhere in the distant future, but they think that we need this ideal to believe that conflicts of interpretation in the present are rationally adjudicable. Pluralists, in contrast, do not share the monists' intuition that there is a single right interpretation. Pluralists believe that there can be rational disagreements that do not presuppose ideal convergence or consensus as the final arbiter of the dispute. Monists will find pluralism inadequate because they think that interpreters necessarily believe that their own interpretations are correct even if there are competing interpretations. Monists also fear that pluralism will be uncritical in principle because of its failure to appeal to a single set of standards.

These characterizations of the positions are only approximate, however, since monism and pluralism can be further distinguished into metaphysical and critical versions.[1] Metaphysical monism thus posits a unity of the object, whereas critical monism would not require the object (for example, a text) to be unified, but only an understanding of the text. (So a unified understanding of a given text could be that the text was not unified.) Critical pluralism can accept this insistence that the understanding be internally consistent, but it thinks that critical monism draws a stronger conclusion from this thought than is warranted. That is to say, critical monism contrasts with critical pluralism on the question of whether there can be more than one interpretation. Critical monism insists that there is necessarily only one best understanding. In contrast, critical pluralism resists this claimed necessity by holding that there can be more than one equally acceptable interpretation according to the best available standards.

Let me illustrate these distinctions by pointing to one case, the critique of hermeneutics by deconstructionists, as a currently topical place where the four-way framework can come into play and clarify a controversy. Deconstructionists construe hermeneutics as a version of metaphysical monism, but I see hermeneutics as critical pluralism. I am not analyzing deconstruction in this essay, but let me simply note that deconstruction is itself sometimes formulated as a metaphysical pluralism. This at least seems to be the position entailed by any claim that the object (whether the text or what Gadamer calls the

---

[1]The contrast can be stated in other terms and is not intended to be either technical or mysterious. Instead of "critical" I could have said "interpretive," and instead of "metaphysical" I could have said "transcendental." This four-way distinction is of course reminiscent of Kant's distinctions between realism and idealism in their transcendental and empirical versions. I have chosen the terms I have because Hilary Putnam has used the term "metaphysical realism" in place of Kant's "transcendental realism" (since the realism in question is really transcendent and not transcendental, at least in Kant's stricter usage of these terms). The term "critical" already means "interpretive," but it also suggests that interpretation can have an element of criticism in it. Kant sometimes spoke of his philosophy as critical philosophy, and the first *Critique* is a critique of metaphysics. But Kant also had definite metaphysical commitments, as his moral philosophy makes clear.

Sache, or subject matter) is divided against itself, and necessarily so (because of the nature of language, for instance). The difficulty with the metaphysical pluralist's construal of deconstruction, however, is that one can be a metaphysical pluralist and still slip back into critical monism against one's intentions. Deconstruction would seem to be a version of critical pluralism, yet if the deconstructionist method claims metaphysical pluralism for every text, then it has to avoid falling back into critical monism, which it would do if it claimed that its discovery of this pluralism in any particular text were the only possible reading of that text.

On my understanding of these distinctions, there is no reason to think that the only way to oppose critical monism is to adopt the position of *metaphysical* pluralism. Hermeneutics has no metaphysical commitments of the sort described here, but instead, it seeks to avoid both metaphysical monism and metaphysical pluralism. As a form of critical pluralism, hermeneutics would lead to the recognition that interpretations are always derived from a particular cultural context. Given this claim, ethnocentrism seems to follow necessarily, if by ethnocentrism one means that we always start from our own historical and social context. But this claim may be benign if it asserts merely that although we *start* from a context, we can nevertheless *transcend* that context. Certainly an invidious sense of ethnocentrism would follow either if we could never understand another culture or time in its own terms, or if we could understand that other culture or time only in our own terms exclusively. Saying that we can never understand the other culture at all raises the problem of objectivity and leads to the problem of epistemological relativism. I have addressed that problem in other places and am here worried more about the second claim, which is that understanding does take place but is invariably in *our* language and from our point of view.

This claim needs to be thought through carefully, since understanding it as a claim raises questions. One question is, Who are "we"? To say that the understanding is "ours" requires an ability to distinguish "our" understanding from another understanding, for instance, "theirs." But then how do we know that there is such a thing as "their" understanding at all? Any construction of "their" understanding would invariably seem to be "our" activity and, therefore, "ours" instead of "theirs."

Something seems to be going wrong in this chain of reasoning. The mistake is that the process of understanding is being reified into a count noun. By this I mean that understanding is turned into a hardened object, or (to use another image) a closed horizon, so that one can then start *counting* different understandings (for example, ours, theirs, and so on). Although "understanding" can function as a verb and a noun, the mistake here is to take it as a count noun. Similarly, the "we" gets reified into a self, which is then construed as a fixed object. The antidote to this reification of the "we" will be a more hermeneutical conception of the self, as I suggest below.

The further problem here is that these reifications result from sliding from critical pluralism into either metaphysical monism or metaphysical pluralism. The mistake is to think that the position of critical pluralism needs to be *grounded* in a metaphysical position. This mistake gets made, for instance, in the attempt to adjudicate the conflict between monism and pluralism. So critical monists slide into metaphysical-monist claims when they say things like "the text is self-identical and remains the same throughout its different readings and interpretations." Even constructing the author's intention as the single thing that the text must be meaning is a move toward a metaphysical grounding of the monist reading. Pluralists make the same mistake when they enter the dispute by saying that every text is "really" a disunified plurality because language always doubles back on itself, undermining the writer's intention to produce a single, unified whole. Metaphysical pluralism can also result from speaking of a *Sprachwelt* and then assuming a plurality of these worlds that can be totally individuated from one another.

The positions that I am calling metaphysical monism and metaphysical pluralism are two different versions of metaphysical realism, and, on my account, critical pluralism is philosophically the attempt to avoid or to undermine metaphysical realism. Critical pluralism holds that what counts as real is determined *internally* within an interpretation and is not something external to the interpretation that the interpretation is *about*. (Critical pluralism is not redefining reality, when so construed, but it may be conceiving of *interpretation* differently than realists normally do.) So another way of putting the point that I wish to make here is that metaphysical pluralism is a form of (metaphysical) realism and thus should not be adopted as a defense or "grounding" of the arguments of critical pluralism. Although I have in mind Hilary Putnam's general distinction between metaphysical realism and internal realism,[2] I am confining my remarks to the

---

[2]See Hilary Putnam, *Reason, Truth and History* (Cambridge: Cambridge University Press, 1981).

more specific question of what might be called "meaning realism" or "meaning nonrealism," where the question is whether certain kinds of things (for instance, texts, but also mental states, actions, lives, cultures) have a determinate meaning independently of any interpretation of them.[3]

Drawing all these distinctions may seem scholastic and empty, but I think that ethnocentrism provides a good way to test these differences to see whether they make a genuine difference, that is, whether they are conceptually distinct enough to make for viable philosophical confrontation and clarification. If the pernicious sense of ethnocentrism follows from the positions of critical monism, metaphysical monism, *and* metaphysical pluralism, but *not* from critical pluralism, which I think implies only the *benign* sense of ethnocentrism, then some indirect evidence is gained for the advantages of reading hermeneutical philosophy as itself a form of critical pluralism.

Critical Pluralism and the Danger of Ethnocentrism

In a short essay I obviously cannot reason through the complexities of these positions as systematically as I would like. Let me therefore proceed more interpretatively than systematically by at least showing how this framework functions in reading Gadamer in the light of the more recent debates about ethnocentrism. The worry about ethnocentrism arises from the hermeneutical insistence, which Gadamer inherits from Martin Heidegger,[4] that our understanding of a text is

---

[3]I am grateful to the participants at the 1988 Santa Cruz–NEH Summer Institute on Interpretation for discussion of the distinctions I present in this section.

[4]According to Heidegger in *Being and Time*, understanding is always conditioned by prior factors that cannot be made fully explicit in our attempts to articulate and justify the way we understand a text, the context in which we interpret it, and the situation and purposes that generate our interest in interpreting it. Heidegger lays out three dimensions in which we already relate to what we interpret *in advance* of our explicit articulation of our understanding. We have beforehand a network of involvements (the *Vorhabe*) in which what is being interpreted already has some role. There is always already a point of view within this network from which we see whatever is being interpreted in advance (the *Vorsicht*). The concepts we will then use to articulate these prior ways of seeing the significance of what is at stake are themselves already prefigured (in the *Vorgriff* or fore-conception). Heidegger thinks that for the most part we are not aware of all these factors, and that they usually become problematic for us when there is a breakdown in some part of the network. We usually are forced to the explicit task of interpretation when something has become problematic. Although we are interpreting all the time, we are forced to articulate and justify our interpretations as a result of specific conditions, such as the disruption that raises specific questions and problems.

conditioned by our preunderstanding of what Gadamer refers to as the *Sache*. This preunderstanding includes background assumptions and everyday practices, which Gadamer refers to as *Vorurteile* and which can be translated as either "prejudgments" or "prejudices." The question is, then, whether the validity of interpretation is undermined by the admitted inability of any given interpretation to articulate fully all the background assumptions and conditions that are generally understood as what goes without saying. More briefly, do different background contexts produce different interpretations? Since backgrounds are cultural, is an interpretation limited by its cultural background such that ethnocentrism is inevitable?

This belief in the cultural conditionedness of interpretation is generally a major reason for thinking that hermeneutics should be pluralistic, since monism tends to restrict interpretation to a single one that will presumably be the product of only one cultural background, which will most likely be the monist's own. But in this very attempt to avoid the ethnocentrism inherent in critical monism by insisting on cultural variance, critical pluralism would seem to be forced to admit that its own interpretations are inevitably ethnocentric. Critical pluralism claims to go beyond critical monism's blindness to its own cultural background by arguing that interpretations are always relative to their cultural backgrounds. But this claim apparently entails that a given interpretation is unable ever to transcend its particular cultural background.

What is the critical pluralists' best line of response? Most likely

---

The philosophical significance of Heidegger's conception of understanding is best summed up by Heidegger's own claim that "an interpretation is never a presuppositionless apprehending of something presented to us" (*Being and Time*, trans. John Macquarrie and Edward Robinson [New York: Harper & Row, 1962], pp. 191–92; German, p. 150). We no longer need to think of knowledge in the Cartesian fashion as grounded in a presuppositionless starting point, and available to a Cartesian or a Kantian ego that is either epistemologically or transcendentally independent of the world in which it finds itself. Understanding is only ever acquired in a context, and there is no contextless viewpoint that represents the only proper grasp of anything and everything. If philosophy gives up the ideal of the single starting point for knowledge, it must also give up the goal of the end of knowledge. We do not have to believe that unless we have fully systematized all our beliefs, we do not have genuine understanding. We do understand the world and how to comport ourselves in it because we are already in a world, and that world is itself at once a condition of and conditioned by our preunderstanding of ourselves in our situations.

Gadamer's theory goes beyond Heidegger's account, which is presented initially as an account of everyday contexts such as the practical use of a tool, and extends it to complex objects such as texts, cultures, or historical periods.

they will argue that although it is true that the cultural backgrounds can never be *entirely* transcended, this limitation need not entail that the cultural background can never be transcended *at all*. There may be specific features of the cultural background that become manifest as being unduly biased and that therefore need to be transcended. Consistent with Heidegger's analysis, this need might become apparent only after an interpretative breakdown, for instance, where a cultural bias shows itself to have pernicious consequences.[5] This breakdown, as well as the emergence of a need to transcend a particular bias, does not entail that the entire background should be called into question. Nor *could* the entire background be questioned all at once, according to the hermeneutical account, since such a global questioning would only be abstract and empty.

Gadamer: Monist or Pluralist?

Now that I have constructed the pluralist line of response, the next question is whether this response is compatible with Gadamer's own

[5]At this point one move that could be made to avoid the problem would be to draw a further distinction between *critical* pluralism and *cultural* pluralism. The latter would be the doctrine that there are *substantive* cultural differences. In contrast, critical pluralism would be a *procedural* or metaconception of interpretation that would not be bound to only one culture, but would presumably apply whenever there is an act of interpretation.

I see no reason to try to avoid the problem in this way but prefer to confront the problem more directly. For one thing, I see no empirical reason to believe that the hermeneutical account of interpretation is not culture bound. It certainly would not have been possible except as a product of the tradition of western, and more particularly, German philosophy. I do not know how there even could be empirical confirmation of such a metaposition. Hermeneutical points are much like the claim that observation is always theory laden, which is an observation that itself is theory laden and cannot be confirmed in a theory-independent way. (At most, the historian of science like Thomas Kuhn can give some examples that seem better explained by the theory-ladenness assumption than by theory-neutral explanation.)

In addition to the unlikeliness of the de facto claim that critical pluralism is not culturally dependent itself, I see no reason to make the de jure claim that it is true necessarily of any and every act of interpretation. One could try to make the de jure case by advancing transcendental arguments to the effect that if experience is such-and-such, it must also be so-and-so. But these arguments do not prove that experience *is* such-and-such, and they can often be extended in such a way as to make the inferential connections seem more and more problematic until finally the initial assumption is not confirmed so much as reduced to an absurdity. So for these reasons I do not want to invoke the distinction between substantive and procedural claims, and I do not claim that hermeneutics offers any more than *one* conception of interpretation, although I know of no better conception to date.

language.[6] Is Gadamer best construed as a critical monist or a critical pluralist, and will either of these constructions save his theory from the charge of ethnocentrism? There are three central Gadamerian concepts that may be principally responsible for the charge of ethnocentrism. These are: (1) the "fusion of horizons"; (2) the idea of prejudice; and (3) the emphasis on *Vollkommenheit*, or the completeness and perfection of interpretation.

In explicating these points, I must stress that some confusion may result if these points are understood as models of perception instead of as an account of *linguistic* understanding. Unlike physical objects that could be said to persist independently of any perception of them, texts come to be only in acts of reading (with writing always also involving reading). Gadamer's most general statement of this point is his claim that "Sein, das verstanden werden kann, ist Sprache."[7] Both Heidegger and Gadamer work with a model in which language as such is not different from and in a representational relation to an independent reality, but where it would not make sense to speak of reality or Being. In other words, the terms "reality" and "being" would not refer except within a language.

That understanding is a linguistic phenomenon can be lost from sight if one gets misled by the quasi-perceptual metaphor of the fusion of horizons. Gadamer uses the phenomenological notion of a horizon and then asks the apparently epistemological question how it is possible for us to represent within our horizon the horizon of the other time or culture that we find speaking to us from a text. He then characterizes his solution as a *Horizontverschmelzung*. The question Gadamer poses is a classic one in traditional hermeneutics: if the understanding is *ours*, how do we discover differences between the text (or the tribe, or the culture) and ourselves?

His immediate answer consists of two phenomenological observations. The first is that meanings simply cannot be understood arbitrarily.[8] Thus, we cannot avoid hearing sentences as making sense in particular ways, and we cannot simply will to hear them differently than we do. The second is that we often do find that the text either

---

[6] This section is excerpted and modified from my forthcoming book with Thomas McCarthy, *Critical Theory* (Oxford and New York: Basil Blackwell), where it serves in a different construction of the contrast between monism and pluralism.

[7] Hans-Georg Gadamer, *Wahrheit und Methode*, 2d ed. (Tübingen: J. C. B. Mohr, 1965), p. xxi.

[8] See Hans-Georg Gadamer, *Truth and Method*, 2d ed. p. 268. Further references will be to this second, revised translation of *Wahrheit und Methode* by Joel Weinsheimer and Donald G. Marshall (New York: Crossroad, 1989), and will be cited in the text as *TM*.

does not make sense or seems to be saying something that strikes us as false. Gadamer cites the experience of the text's giving us a shock or even an offense (*Anstoss*).[9]

Taken together, these points suggest that in general some of what we read, hear, and encounter will seem familiar, and some particular things will strike us as being strange and unlike what we expected. The point is not, then, to translate the strangeness into something with which we are already familiar. Instead, the *Anstoss* may force us to question whether what seemed familiar may instead be hiding further strangeness. So although understanding is always "our" understanding (where "our" designates whatever is the historical present), we can recognize differences between "other" understandings and "our" understanding.

But we should not fall into the historicist illusion that we can entirely recreate that past understanding and contrast it totally to our own. Though Gadamer uses the notion of horizons, he does not want us to think of the past and present as separate horizons that are closed off from one another. When we understand the past, with its many differences, we are expanding our horizon, not stepping out of our horizon into the other horizon. Unfortunately, the idea of a *fusion* or *melting* of horizons (*Horizontverschmelzung*) has misled some readers to project the image of two countable horizons flowing into one another. If the past horizon were totally reconstructible, then there would be a historical *Gegenstand an sich* that the historical sciences could aim to recover. But this picture is precisely the one that Gadamer intends to destroy with his insistence on the circularity of understanding and the multifariousness of possible historical voices instead of a single privileged one.

The notion of the multifariousness (*Vielfachheit*) of possible historical voices is a point that Gadamer raises to describe the difference between the natural and the human sciences. But I would like to bring it up now more to show that Gadamer does recognize diversity and plurality. His critics read him as saying that our understanding is always conditioned by our tradition, and they accuse him of thinking that the tradition is always a single thing, or a unified whole. In contrast, they insist that a tradition or a culture is often divided against itself, or even many-sided and diverse to such an extent that it becomes impossible to know that there is *a* tradition or culture behind our understanding.

[9]See Gadamer, *Wahrheit und Methode*, p. 252.

These critics would thus find the notion of a "fusion" of horizons to be insidiously hegemonic. But I think that hermeneutics can recognize that complexity and tensions are always to be found in a tradition or culture. Gadamer's point that the difference between the natural and the human sciences is the multifariousness (*Vielfachheit*) of possible historical voices suggests to me that he would not accept a belief in the unidirectional, developmental, or hegemonic character of *history*. The mistake that Gadamer's critics make may be to turn the horizon into an object. Gadamer wants to distinguish between human and natural science because if history is the object (*Sache*) of the human science, it is not the sort of object (*Gegenstand*) that scientific research can posit as its telos. There is no thing-in-itself (*Gegenstand an sich*) for historical research, unlike the physical sciences' research into nature. Thus, a difference between the natural and the human sciences is that "whereas the object [*Gegenstand*] of the natural sciences can be described *idealiter* as what would be known in the perfect, complete [*vollendeten*] knowledge of nature, it is senseless to speak of a perfect or complete knowledge of history [*einer vollendeten Geschichtserkenntnis*], and for this reason it is not possible to speak of an 'object in itself' [*Gegenstand an sich*] toward which its research is directed."[10]

This notion of the circularity of understanding underscores the contextuality of understanding. Gadamer says that he often prefers to read the great old historians (for example, Theodor Mommsen and Johann Gustav Droysen) instead of the latest accounts. His reason is that since there is no historical thing-in-itself, and no ideal knowledge of history, what each historian's voice reflects is a particular grasp of tradition. These different ways of grasping the tradition form the complex tradition in which our own understanding emerges. Let me express this point by speaking of background contexts. While our context conditions our understanding, for example, of the past, that understanding also conditions the context. There is a circular or feedback relation between the background out of which a particular interpretation emerges, such that the interpretation also changes the background.

Another point of Gadamer's that has misled his critics is his notion that the Enlightenment belief that prejudice must be eliminated is itself a prejudice. Gadamer's account of prejudice suggests that understanding consists exclusively of judgments, most of which remain

---

[10]Ibid., p. 269; *TM*, 285.

tacit *Vorurteile,* prejudgments or prejudices. Our understanding would then be a belief system, which we do not give up as a whole even if we abandon or revise particular beliefs. Any particular prejudgment *could* be examined on this model, but our finitude keeps us from examining them all. Hubert Dreyfus therefore concludes that Gadamer's view is nihilistic in the long run, since "it bases its claims that pervasive 'prejudices' are unchallengeable simply on their inaccessibility to the people who hold them, which runs the risk of making a virtue of obscure, pervasive obsessions and compulsions."[11]

There are two central features of Gadamer's hermeneutics that seem incompatible with the label of *theoretical* holism that Dreyfus therefore attaches to Gadamer, in contrast to the practical holism that Dreyfus prefers. The first is Gadamer's account of understanding as *phronesis,* and the second is his claim that understanding is always already *application.* These concepts are closely connected, since by application Gadamer does not mean applying something (like a general principle) to something (for instance, a specific situation). Instead, by application he means that we see a text or a situation as already significant, that is, there are already meanings, issues, or principles at stake in ways presenting us with or even forcing on us "live" options (even if the text is from a remote past). Similarly, Gadamer draws on Aristotle's notion of *phronesis* to argue that understanding is more like practical everyday reasoning (or what Aristotle calls deliberation) than like theoretical reasoning (or at least a certain picture of theoretical reasoning as deducing conclusions from general principles, rules, or laws).

Although it might seem that Gadamer's account of the correction of prejudice leads him to a model in which understanding ourselves involves examining our prejudices one by one and therefore working toward (but never achieving) total self-knowledge, that is not what he projects. That would be the Enlightenment picture. However, Gadamer gives his account of prejudice as part of his characterization of the historical conflict between the Enlightenment and its Romanticist critics, a conflict that he wants to get beyond by rejecting both positions. So the account that Dreyfus criticizes is really an account that Gadamer is criticizing as well, and not finally his own. Gadamer himself echoes Heidegger's critique of modern "theory," which Gadamer describes as "the will to dominate what exists" (*TM,* p. 454).

---

[11]Hubert L. Dreyfus, "Holism and Hermeneutics," *Review of Metaphysics* 34 (1980): 21.

Returning to a different notion of theory he finds in the ancient Greeks, Gadamer also has a different account of what we learn from experience, that is, from the process of questioning our assumptions. What we acquire is not more "justified beliefs," but, instead, what Gadamer calls "openness to experience" (*TM*, p. 355). He illustrates this with a reference to Aeschylus and "learning through suffering," where what we learn is not definitive knowledge. Instead, we learn more vaguely that we are finite, that nothing returns, and what reality is (where reality is defined, following Leopold von Ranke, as "what cannot be destroyed" [*TM*, p. 357]).

My way of reading Gadamer's notions of the "fusion of horizons" and prejudice is deliberately intended to make him seem more of a pluralist than a monist. But I must acknowledge that there are moments when he does sound like a monist, and these are connected to his claim that there is an expectation (*Vorgriff*) of completeness (*Vollkommenheit*) in every interpretation. Some places where he sounds like a monist include the following. In a gloss on Heidegger he affirms that there is no pure knowledge of *vorhanden* facts in which the totality of understanding is not also functioning (*TM*, p. 262). In explicating the hermeneutic circle as movement back and forth between part and whole, Gadamer suggests that the "criterion of correct understanding" is "the harmony of all the details with the whole" (*TM*, p. 291). Of course, the whole here is not the metaphysical whole ("everything"), but only the whole of a given text. However, theorists like Derrida and Roland Barthes have suggested that even the belief that a work is a whole and has a unity or harmony is a vestige of metaphysics. So even this limited "textual holism" may be problematic. Gadamer seems to build monism into his model of understanding through his notion that understanding must always anticipate the completeness of the text through the *Vorgriff der Vollkommenheit*, in which we anticipate the truth of what the text says (*TM*, p. 293). In a later essay he underlines the term *Vorgriff*, insisting that we only ever anticipate the final harmony and never grasp it fully. So his textual monism seems at best a regulative principle that guides our interpretive activity but that we never achieve.

Gadamer does seem to think that language and meaning form a whole that is invoked with any particular use of language. But he qualifies this view by saying that language is not an *existing* whole, but an "infinity of discourse" opened up with any single utterance (*TM*, p. 549). So his picture is not of the whole existing prior to the part in some way, but of its being projected out of particular instances. Thus, he does claim for hermeneutics, as a "speculative" activity in his special sense, "the task of revealing a totality of meaning in all its relations" (*TM*, p. 471). (The speculative activity, of which both poetry and philosophical hermeneutics are examples, tries to envision the whole of being instead of particular beings [*TM*, p. 469].) But this totality cannot be captured in only one way, since the task arises in specific ways and differently at different times. So unlike the ideal of pure, theoretical inquiry, interpretation is always motivated by a particular need, and the results of interpretation will always be configured by the special need that motivated the interpretation: "Only because the text calls for it does interpretation take place, and only in the way called for" (*TM*, p. 472).

Thus, he insists that we are always in a situation and therefore can never have objective knowledge of it. As a result *total, complete* self-knowledge is never really possible (*TM*, p. 301). He does speak of "our whole being" (or more precisely, "unser im Ganzen unsrer Geschicke gewirktes Sein"),[12] but only to insist that our knowledge of ourselves is never adequate. Perhaps he does not even project a historical whole, since he objects to Droysen and Dilthey for trying to read all history as a single book. "The concept of the whole," he asserts, "is itself to be understood only relatively. The whole of meaning that has to be understood in history or tradition is never the meaning of the whole of history" (*TM*, p. xxxv). This passage makes the important point that it is *meaning* realism that is at stake, and thus that we need the metaphysical-critical distinction.

If I am right in how I interpret these central hermeneutic notions, there is no reason to think that hermeneutics is hiding deep within itself a *metaphysical* yearning for monism. However, I do see that someone might wish reasonably to attribute to hermeneutics a version of critical monism. This attribution might follow, for instance, if there is a regulative ideal of unity or completeness built into every act of understanding. I myself find the insistence on such regulative ideals empty and prefer to push hermeneutics toward critical pluralism. The emptiness can be seen from the failure of such a regulative ideal to undercut deconstructionist readings, for instance, which do have a unity of approach, method, or style even if their point is that the text is not itself a unity. So the ideal should not be invoked to distinguish (contentiously and incorrectly, in my view) two different kinds of interpretations, "deconstructive" versus "hermeneutical"

---

[12]Gadamer, *Wahrheit und Methode*, p. xx.

ones. On my understanding, deconstruction as an approach can be explained with the tenets of hermeneutics and need not be a practical rival to hermeneutics.

Ever since Kant we have learned that what makes an ideal regulative rather than constitutive is that there could never be proof that the ideal had been empirically obtained. So the expectation of completeness or *Vollkommenheit* would simply amount to the recommendation that interpreters avoid inconsistency and keep testing their interpretations against other interpretations with more readings that take more aspects of the text into account. But there is no reason to think that there is a final end to this process, or that critical monism is the only rational stance.

Convergence versus Contextuality

Avoiding critical monism does not mean, however, that a critical pluralist version of hermeneutics escapes the suspicion of ethnocentrism. Critical monism tries to solve the problem of ethnocentrism by assuming that the one right interpretation will be one that any rational being would have to accept, whatever cultural context is presupposed. The danger of this solution is that when interpreters believe that they have a correct interpretation, they also seem obliged to believe that their interpretation is context independent and culturally neutral.

Hermeneutical philosophy suggests that such neutrality is really a *blindness* to context dependence, and thus to the way the interpreter's standpoint is conditioning the interpretation. Furthermore, since what is being interpreted are cultural and historical products, cultural neutrality in a strict sense seems more likely to be undesirable than desirable. An interpretation should speak to the needs of a specific cultural and historical conjuncture. Interpretations aiming at eternal verities may turn out to be abstract, empty of content for the present's self-understanding, and therefore simply uninteresting.

In more hermeneutical terms, embracing critical monism tends to deemphasize the development of the interpretation's *wirkungsgeschichtliches Bewusstsein*, which is more likely to be fostered by embracing critical pluralism. The problem that then arises, however, is that the pluralistic insistence on the contextuality of understanding implies that if the understanding is always *our* understanding, we may not be able to escape ethnocentrism. Among hermeneutic theorists there are those like Rorty and perhaps Gadamer who seem to think that we have to live with our own ethnocentrism, and those like Habermas and Taylor who deny that we are unavoidably ethnocentric. So the issue becomes whether ethnocentrism is always an evil that any rational communicator should want to overcome, as Habermas and Taylor might maintain, or whether there is a more benign ethnocentrism. A benign ethnocentrism might be benevolent in its intentions and would do all it could to keep from imposing its own views on the "other." But it would not be doing this with the intention of overcoming ethnocentrism altogether. Instead, it might grant that differences are sometimes rational and that one might finally prefer one's own practices to those of other people. While there may be limits to how much difference can be tolerated,[13] the pluralists do not think that the final goal of interpretation must be to adjudicate and transcend difference altogether.

Both sides in the debate between pluralism and monism can find support in Gadamer's texts. Gadamer's insistence on situatedness and finitude provides pluralists with some means for thinking that his view does not imprison us in ethnocentrism narrowly construed as blindness to one's own context. For one thing, he does commend interpreters for becoming more aware of the extent to which their own readings are conditioned by the intervening *Wirkungsgeschichte*. So he commends those interpretations that develop *wirkungsgeschichtliches Bewusstsein*, that is, awareness of the extent to which our present standpoint differs from and conditions our readings of other texts, times, or cultures. He speaks specifically about the capacity for language to expand to include ideas that had not previously been expressed in it. So although there are different historical worlds, because each world is linguistic, it is *open* to every possible insight. Each world or language is thus open to expansion by others as well as being itself available to others (*TM*, p. 447).

This linguistic rephrasing of the phenomenon of the "fusion of horizons" has the advantage of making ethnocentrism less of a psy-

---

[13]Richard Rorty says, for instance, that we are inevitably ethnocentric, since we just do prefer our own democratic, liberal discourse but have no way to justify our preference. This admission might seem to put us in a difficult position vis-à-vis others whom we perceive as being ethnocentric in different ways that we resent and believe to be dangerous and thus even less justifiable. His point is not that we should give up defending ourselves against fanatics, but only that we should give up the stronger rationalist assumption that we could not justifiably defend ourselves unless we could first *prove* that only we and not the fanatics could inhabit an ideal, universal community.

chological phenomenon. Charles Taylor has developed Gadamer's point in much more detail in his essay "Understanding and Ethnocentricity," so I should like to examine the claims made there. I cite this essay in particular, however, because I think that Taylor renders Gadamer's notion of the fusion of horizons more in a monist than a pluralist way. So I shall want to identify and isolate what the crucial assumption is that Taylor imports into Gadamer's notion to push it in the direction of monism.

Taylor thinks ethnocentrism can and should be avoided. He insists, however, that the solution is not to be found in the natural scientific model of constructing a neutral language that is outside all cultures, since he thinks such a language remains unwittingly ethnocentric. But he also resists the "mind-numbing" relativism that he finds in those who think other cultures are "incorrigible," that is to say, uncriticizable. Like Habermas, Taylor thinks that criticism must be possible. To explain how it is possible, Taylor rephrases Gadamer's fusion of horizons, speaking instead of a "language of perspicuous contrast," formed in the effort of understanding another culture: "This would be a language in which we could formulate both their way of life and ours as alternative possibilities in relation to some human constants at work in both. It would be a language in which the possible human variations would be so formulated that both our form of life and theirs could be perspicuously described as alternative such variations."[14] Much as Gadamer argues that understanding is always self-understanding, Taylor insists that we thereby come to understand our own practices better. We do not remain ethnocentric to the extent that this new self-understanding moves us to criticize ourselves: "while challenging their language of self-understanding, we may also be challenging ours. Indeed, what I want to argue is that there are times where we cannot question the one properly without also questioning the other. . . . Understanding is inseparable from criticism, but this in turn is inseparable from self-criticism."[15]

Although these points are well taken, I have at least two doubts about the solution through the model of the "language of perspicuous contrast." The first doubt comes from reflecting on who speaks the language of perspicuous contrast. Using the terms "us" and "them" advisedly, I say that the answer is that *we* do. So there is still a sense in which ethnocentrism has not been avoided.

---

[14]Charles Taylor, *Philosophy and the Human Sciences: Philosophical Papers 2* (Cambridge: Cambridge University Press, 1985), p. 125.

[15]Ibid., pp. 125 and 131.

Also, is Taylor saying that we (for example, "we" the anthropologists versus "they" the "natives") speak the language of perspicuous contrast, whereas the tribe members do not and are stuck in "their" language? Taylor's account seems to suggest that "we" must now describe "their" language as "unperspicuous." This suggestion is also implied in Habermas's criticism of Gadamer for failing to explain how the interpreter, for instance, the anthropologist, must sometimes criticize that which is being interpreted. This complaint suggests that anthropology should be concerned with criticism of the other, but many contemporary anthropologists would find the suggestion that they be critical in this way either irrelevant or deeply problematic. The conception of anthropology Habermas seems to be using is probably a myth left by earlier anthropologists that has been dispelled by more recent anthropologists or historians of anthropology (including Clifford Geertz, but also Renato Rosaldo or James Clifford, for instance). Clearly the tribe being studied is also studying the tribe that believes it alone is doing the studying. So perhaps *two* languages of perspicuous contrast are developed. Moreover, I see no reason to believe that these converge into a single language of perspicuous contrast that everybody could speak.

Indeed, the tacit assumption in Taylor's and Habermas's account that I find and question is that the different languages would converge ideally into a single language. The assumption of such convergence is thus my second doubt. I suspect that the tendency to assume convergence results from a vestigial commitment to monism.

There is, however, a crucial difference between the way that convergence is posited in Taylor and in Habermas. In brief, Habermas's consensus theory suggests that the convergence is on *us*, whereas Taylor suggests that convergence is on *the truth*.[16] That is to say, Habermas's consensus theory implies that what we would all agree to in the long run would be true, so what we aim at is reaching agreement. Taylor, in contrast, posits a language that transcends our present agreements and thus one that is better because it is a more perspicuous (that is, "truer") description both of ourselves and others than we now have.

Both theorists posit convergence on what is thus said to be a "better" language. Gadamer, however, has demurred from saying that we understand authors "better" than they understood themselves, and he has suggested instead that the most we can say is that we

---

[16]This formulation was suggested to me by Hubert Dreyfus.

understand them differently. I would infer that he might also resist the normative convergence assumed by Taylor and Habermas, claiming instead only that a language will capture the central insights of other languages differently.

Of course, Taylor's account can be traced to Gadamer's statement that any language can formulate every possible insight. But I see two reasons for refusing to infer from this claim to the critical-monist conclusion that hermeneutics must be tacitly assuming the possibility of convergence on a single language. First, I do not really believe that we can talk intelligibly about "every possible insight." We could never know that a language had stated every possible insight, and in any case, "insight" is often not used as a count noun but more as a mass noun, expressing a person's unusual grasp of a subject matter. Second, despite much that is shared, natural languages strike me as being interestingly different, and although translatable, not *univocally* translatable (since translations are relative to a given translation manual, and different manuals give different translations).

Talking about horizons or translations may finally be the cause of the problem because such talk may always invoke monism. So let me shift to an example and ask whether we would need or be able to formulate a contrast that could be resolved perspicuously. Why could we not rest content with *our* tendency to say such things as, "society X was wrong in setting too low a value on human life (although we of society Y now *understand* why society X did so, given frequent famines, plagues, wars, and a high child mortality rate)"? We could say this while recognizing that we do not set a high enough value on life in our own practices (given the low level of response to such problems as the medical needs of the poor, world hunger, or the unnecessary slaughter of animals). So we could be critical, and even self-critical. At the same time, we could consistently hold that there is no perspicuous language to adjudicate between, for instance, the claim of Jerusalem-based religions that there can be undeserved suffering or the Hindu's belief in the opposite claim that suffering is necessary, deserved, and not to be regretted.[17] Who is to say which belief and the related practice of resisting evil or not resisting it is more perspicuous or clear-sighted?

The doubt that I am raising here calls into question the very idea of "understanding ourselves better." Perhaps to be consistent, her-

[17]The example is from Alan Donagan, *The Theory of Morality* (Chicago: University of Chicago Press, 1977), p. 34.

meneutics should just say that we understand ourselves differently as a result of encountering others who have a different self-understanding themselves. Clifford Geertz's recent conclusions about his return to the field, as reported in the *New York Times,* suggest this rephrasing to me. He seems reluctant to say that he understands either the people he studied or himself better or even at all. Although this may seem like a despairing admission for an anthropologist, perhaps the despair could be avoided both by substituting "different" for "better," as Gadamer suggested about Kant, and by adopting a more hermeneutical and less reified conception of the self. Then we could admit that our understanding both of ourselves and others changes, so that new problems emerge. These new problems do not imply that we understand ourselves less well, but only that we are different as a result of now having these particular problems to face. The self-understanding would be "better" only to the extent that we see through our earlier myths about what we were doing when we thought we were observing others.

In conclusion, let me stress that the difficulty with ethnocentrism is not so much that we see the world through our own self-understanding, but instead that we expect every other self-understanding to converge with ours. I do not see the former as necessarily an evil, as long as we remain open to differences and are willing to exercise our imaginations when we encounter otherness. But the latter (the expectation of convergence) does seem oppressive, Whiggish, and colonialistic. Since the label "ethnocentric" is pejorative, I propose that it be attributed not to hermeneutics, but only to the monistic theories that add to the analysis of understanding and interpretation the additional requirement of convergence.

PART THREE

INTERPRETATION

CHAPTER 9

Interpretation as Explanation

PAUL A. ROTH

> By turning the Platonic parts of the soul into conversational part-
> ners for one another, Freud did for the variety of interpretations
> of each person's past what the Baconian approach to science and
> philosophy did for the variety of descriptions of the universe
> as a whole. He let us see alternative narratives and alternative
> vocabularies as instruments for change, rather than as candidates
> for a correct depiction of how things are in themselves.
> —Richard Rorty, "Freud and Moral Reflection"

A concern to distinguish between explanation and understanding
harks back to a time when, some thought, humanistic inquiry needed
to be made safe from positivism. The distinction is one between analyses conforming to the terms and laws of a causal-mechanistic idiom
and analyses couched in the language of intentions and human significance. Explanations explain by subsuming specific cases under
laws; understanding proceeds by making plain the rules and relations
in which activities are embedded, and which give them their significance qua human actions.

An explanation of a particular car radiator's cracking might consist
of citing the water in the radiator, a drop in ambient temperature,
how water so confined reacts in such conditions, and so forth. An
understanding of the cracked radiator might plausibly involve, inter
alia, an appreciation of inconveniences caused, acceptance of an excuse for lateness, or tolerance of a bad mood.

This way of framing the distinction between explanation and understanding has, as an important consequence, that reasons *cannot*
count as explanations of action. They cannot because reasons do not
constitute the appropriate sort of causal antecedents. Reasons seem

too tied to specific contextual concerns and to the intentional idiom; they lack the law-like relations to actions demanded by explanation. Yet, to acquiesce to an exclusion of reasons from the realm of explanations leaves mysterious our practice of citing reasons as causes.[1]

Psychoanalysis provides, I argue, an important test case against which to evaluate the viability of the explanation-understanding distinction. For, if the *Naturwissenschaften* are to provide explanations and the *Geisteswissenschaften* are to generate understanding, then psychoanalytic practice, for one, belongs to both while fitting neither.[2] The distinction between explanation and understanding—between causal-nomological analyses and those that promote comprehension—is challenged by any discipline, such as psychoanalysis, that promises both understanding and change.

There is a further important respect in which psychoanalysis resists classification within the traditional dichotomy. On the one hand, psychoanalysis is charged with being unscientific by virtue of failing to satisfy criteria for scientific explanations. On the other hand, although some theorists emphasize psychoanalysis as an interpretative strategy, this characterization is seriously incomplete. For a chief goal of this practice is the change, and not just (or even primarily) the understanding of behavior.

What is important is that psychoanalytic practice traffics primarily in interpretations. Conventional wisdom links interpretation with the understanding of behavior—the reasons and rules, articulated or not, that provide behavior with its meaning for ourselves and others.[3] As a result, I maintain, any linking of interpretations of behavior to

[1]Unlike the way in which debate has developed in, e.g., action theory in analytic philosophy, philosophical debate in the philosophy of history and the philosophy of social science characteristically contrasts the giving of reasons and the giving of causes. For reviews of recent debates in this area, see David Braybrooke, *Philosophy of Social Science* (Englewood Cliffs, N.J.: Prentice-Hall, 1987) and Alexander Rosenberg, *Philosophy of Social Science* (Boulder, Colo.: Westview, 1988). Rosenberg has a particularly good discussion of why "folk psychology" fails to satisfy demands for explanation. Jürgen Habermas, *On the Logic of the Social Sciences* (Cambridge: MIT Press, 1988), and K.-O. Apel, *Understanding and Explanation: A Transcendental-Pragmatic Perspective* (Cambridge: MIT Press, 1984) offer good overviews of this debate.

[2]Similar points apply, I would argue, to the practice of most social sciences. However, it is particularly acute in the case of psychoanalysis, and that is my focus here.

[3]The assimilation of interpretation to understanding, and so as a notion that contrasts with that of explanation, animates Charles Taylor's well-known essay "Interpretation and the Sciences of Man," in *Interpretive Social Science: A Second Look*, ed. Paul Rabinow and William Sullivan (Berkeley: University of California Press, 1987). Indeed, that anthology celebrates the contrast I wish to call into question.

changes of behavior undercuts the either-or of explanation-understanding.

In opposition not only to the explanation-understanding distinction but also to many standard explications of explanation, I term
psychoanalytic explanations "narrative explanations."[4] My suggestion, building on the work of Roy Schafer, Donald Spence, and others, construes psychoanalytic explanations as a type of historical
narrative. Specifically, they are *reconstructions* by reemplotment of an
analysand's narrative, tellings and retellings of a particular tale.[5]

By identifying three components of the psychoanalytic process—
the self-understanding of an analysand, the reemplotment offered by
a psychotherapist, and the implications of an analysand's acceptance
of such a reemplotment—I suggest how psychoanalytic explanations
enable change. What is novel about explanation so conceived is that
it involves no relation of specific cases to general rules; it is not explanation by subsumption. The therapeutic process melds explanation,
interpretation, and change, on the account I outline, in fundamentally the same way that Thomas Kuhn's well-known account of
theory-change in science involves a rejection of law-governed explanations of such changes.[6]

In the first part of this essay I develop a conception of psychoanalytic explanation as a type of historical narrative. The second part
examines how this model links interpretation with behavioral
change.

[4]In a series of papers I have attempted to defend this notion as appropriate in,
at least, history, anthropology, and psychoanalysis. See Paul A. Roth, "Narrative
Explanation: The Case of History," *History and Theory* 27 (1988):1–13, "How Narratives
Explain," *Social Research* 56 (1989):449–78, and "Truth in Interpretation: The Case
of Psychoanalysis," *Philosophy of the Social Sciences* 21 (1991):175–95. I am extremely
sympathetic to the views on causality, and much of his account of theory in psychoanalysis, expressed in Richard Miller's *Fact and Method* (Princeton: Princeton University
Press, 1987). There is much I find congenial in Ronald Giere's *Explaining Science* (Chicago: University of Chicago Press, 1988), as well, though I share neither Miller's nor
Giere's realist proclivities.

[5]See Hayden White, *Tropics of Discourse: Essays in Cultural Criticism* (Baltimore: Johns
Hopkins University Press, 1978), and his *Content of the Form* (Baltimore: Johns Hopkins
University Press, 1987); Donald Spence, *Narrative Truth and Historical Truth* (New York:
Norton, 1982); Michael Roth, *Psycho-Analysis as History* (Ithaca: Cornell University
Press, 1987); P. A. Roth, "Truth in Interpretation."

[6]I want to emphasize that what follows represents only a partial explication of the
psychoanalytic process. A fuller account would need to examine factors relating to the
interaction between analysand and analyst. In addition, I ignore throughout the vexed
issues of the therapeutic efficacy of psychoanalysis and its status vis-à-vis other forms
of therapy.

I

Psychoanalysis, though conceived by Freud as an incipient science, faces at least two challenges to this self-conception. One challenge is to the scientific aspirations of the discipline. The specifics of this challenge vary, but common to the otherwise divergent critics, for example, Karl Popper and Adolf Grünbaum, is the complaint that psychoanalytic procedure fails to satisfy an acceptable model of scientific explanation. That is, these critics accede to Freud's assimilation of psychoanalysis to a natural science model. The problem here, the complaint runs, is that those employing psychoanalytic methods either do not formulate explanations that actually are scientific (Popper), or do form explanations, but ones that the available data invariably do not sustain (Grünbaum). In either case, all claims of psychoanalysis to scientific legitimacy are held to be without warrant.

A second, seemingly sympathetic, attempt to examine the practice of psychoanalysis poses a different challenge. On this account, psychoanalysis constitutes a "depth hermeneutics," a method for interpreting human action. The aim of psychoanalysis qua hermeneutics is to uncover unacknowledged but intentional contents of actions of an agent. Psychoanalytic explanations so construed reveal the meaning of action—its intentional content—and so contributes to an understanding of action, not to its explanation.

But this account, as Paul Ricoeur and Habermas acknowledge, ill accounts for the presumed therapeutic efficacy of psychoanalysis. Habermas, for example, although he argues that psychoanalysis is misunderstood if given a mechanistic model, can do no more than ascribe the therapeutic efficacy of such explanations to the powers of self-reflection. "Depth hemeneutic understanding takes over the function of explanation. It proves its explanatory powers in self-reflection, in which an objectivation that is both understood and explained is also overcome."[7] But left undeveloped are why the Habermasian conditions of "self-reflection" manage to function as conditions of change.

Ricoeur insists that any satisfactory account of psychoanalytic explanation must include an account of the mechanism of change; however, he has no such account to offer.[8] The hermeneutic stress on

[7]Jürgen Habermas, *Knowledge and Human Interests* (Boston: Beacon, 1968), p. 272.
[8]Paul Ricoeur, "The Question of Proof in Freud's Psychoanalytic Writings," in *The Philosophy of Paul Ricoeur*, ed. Charles Reagan and David Stewart (Boston: Beacon, 1978), p. 201.

the narrative features of psychoanalytic explanation aggravates rather than resolves the question of how such narrations influence behavior (on the assumption that they sometimes do).

Some theorists respond to the charge that psychoanalytic explanations are not scientific by suggesting a different, and specifically historical, model for such inquiry. The comparison between psychoanalytic practice and history has been suggested by a number of writers.[9] What distinguishes Roy Schafer's work, in this regard, is his systematic reworking of Freud's mechanistic terminology into an idiom better suited for other, more history-like, explanations.

Indeed, his "translations" from conventional psychological accounts into his "action language" terminology emphasizes the parallels between psychoanalytic practice and humanistic inquiry.

> The discipline of psychoanalysis faces problems that are much more like those of the humanities than those of the natural sciences. These are the problems of perspective, subjective evidence and inference, and the reliability and validity of interpretation. Specifically, the discipline must develop an ordered account of the doings of human beings in a special kind of relationship into which only language-using, historically oriented human beings can enter—the psychoanalytic.[10]

> The project . . . is one by means of which psychoanalysts may hope to speak simply, systematically, and nonmechanistically of human activities in general and of the psychoanalytic relationship and its therapeutic effects in particular. (p. 7)

For Schafer, psychoanalytic explanations offer reasons for the analysand's behavior which reveal the analysand as agent, that is, a purposive actor. The problem is learning why analysands typically disown responsibility for their desires and behavior.

But the suggested assimilation of psychoanalysis to history is odd in at least one major respect. On the one hand, Schafer claims that

---

[9]See, e.g., discussions in Habermas, *Knowledge and Human Interests*; Samuel Novey, *The Second Look: The Reconstruction of Personal History in Psychiatry and Psychoanalysis* (Baltimore: Johns Hopkins University Press, 1968); Ricoeur, "The Question of Proof"; Michael Sherwood, *The Logic of Explanation in Psychoanalysis* (New York: Academic Press, 1969); and Spence, *Narrative Truth*. Roy Schafer also belongs in this group; I discuss his work in detail below. Miller, in *Fact and Method*, sketches a suggestive account of how theory functions to guide research in history and in psychoanalysis.

[10]Roy Schafer, *Language and Insight* (New Haven: Yale University Press, 1978), p. 7. Further references to this work are given by page citations in text.

the psychoanalytic case history is a more comprehensive, a better integrated account of biographical data than the account that an analysand offers (p. 57). Yet, on the other hand, Schafer insists that psychoanalytic inquiry is fundamentally a particular type of *retelling*. *"Every psychological theory is a narrative development. It is a narrative development, not of theory-free or prenarrational events, but of events that have already and necessarily been rendered in the terms of one or another theory or narrative strategy, even if only incompletely and inconsistently."*[11] But if the key to a psychoanalytic retelling is not in the acquisition of new or additional facts, or even a checking of alleged events, in what respect is it a more consistent and complete history?

The contribution is thematic. A psychoanalytic retelling interprets analysands as responsible for their lives in ways in which they have not previously acknowledged. Scattered happenings in life are united by their interpretation as choices on the part of the patient. Gain is achieved by *reemplotting* a life story.[12]

Thus, in the course of personal transformation, analysands discover, acknowledge, and transcend their infantile categories and their defects as life-historians and world-makers. They see that they have been not the vehicles of a blind repetition compulsion, but the perpetrators of repetition at all costs. They reclaim their disclaimed actions, including their so-called mechanisms of defense, and in so doing, they revise them and are in a position to limit their use of them or in some instances to discontinue using them altogether. (p. 23)

The emphasis in Schafer's account falls not on the facts cited in a narration, but on the categories by which the narrative is formed. What counts is how significance is assigned and how connections are depicted; the documenting of events is not (characteristically, anyway) at issue.

Schafer contends that an analytic encounter is "second-order history" that has as its events, its data, the initial analytic dialogue.[13] The psychoanalytic enterprise seeks integration of the first-order his-

[11]Roy Schafer, *Narrative Actions in Psychoanalysis* (Worcester, Mass.: Clark University Press, 1981), p. 24.
[12]Although I do not discuss the point in this essay, I do not assume that all aspects of one's life are *equally* open to reemplotment or interpretation. How evidence and other factors function to constrain interpretations is an issue I hope to address in later work.
[13]Roy Schafer, "Narration in the Psychoanalytic Dialogue," in *On Narrative*, ed. W. J. T. Mitchell (Chicago: University of Chicago Press, 1980), p. 49.

tory—the story told by the analysand—by second-order reflection, that is, considering the categories by which that history is initially told.

In this regard, Schafer distinguishes between the primary and the "second" reality constituted in the analytic situations. The first or primary reality is the life history as an analysand tells it. In the second reality, however, "events or phenomena are viewed from the standpoint of repetitive recreation of infantile, family-centered situations bearing on sex, aggression, and other such matters."[14] This is a narrative that invokes the distinctively psychoanalytic categories for retelling the analysand's reports. Schafer also refers to this as the patient's "psychic reality." " 'Psychic reality' refers to subjective meaning, especially unconscious meaning. Its usefulness resides in its reminding us that psychoanalytic explanation depends on our knowing what an event, action or object means to the subject; it is the specifically psychoanalytic alternative to descriptive classification by a behavioristic observer."[15] It claims to be "more coherent and inclusive" and by its use "one achieves a narrative redescription of reality."[16] Indeed, Schafer, insists, "each narrative establishes a reality of its own."[17]

Speaking of a narrative establishing "a reality of its own" involves no recherché sense of "reality." As I argue below, a person instantiates his or her own sense of their history in everyday actions. For example, possessing particular anxieties or fears might cause a person to flee or avoid certain situations or involvements. Relief from these anxieties, in turn, opens new possibilities for action. One cannot undertake to reach the Indies by sailing west from Spain until one has certain beliefs about the shape of the earth, and so forth. Similar considerations apply, I suggest, to much more mundane actions and beliefs.

Since events are emplotted relative to developmental and affective states, their genuineness is not a function of some simple correspondence to fact, but of faithfulness to the second reality, to the experience of the patient. As Novey emphasizes, genuineness is determined by what may be called "affective correspondence."[18] What

[14]Ibid., p. 46.
[15]Roy Schafer, A New Language for Psychoanalysis (New Haven: Yale University Press, 1976), p. 89.
[16]Schafer, "Narration in the Psychoanalytic Dialogue," p. 46.
[17]Schafer, Narrative Actions, p. 15.
[18]Novey, The Second Look, p. 148.

makes an interpretation compelling and convincing is critically dependent on how events are emplotted in the analysand's emotional life.

Psychoanalytic explanations, construed as historical narratives, are characterized not by fact finding but by a deliberate choice of narrative strategy. The point is not that interpretations are indifferent to the events of one's life, but that interpretations are not determined by them. Indeed, Schafer contends that "from the analytic point of view, there is, strictly speaking, no independent biographical material that counts."[19] Biographical material counts not "independently," but dependently, that is, in the context of answering some question, some problem confronted in analysis.

Interpretations are retellings fashioned by altering the categories for organizing and relating events. If one imagines the moments of a life arranged chronicle-like, there is no assignment of significance to these events apart from first learning how some of them are bound into the story one tells of this life. A missed appointment may be a lost opportunity, or it may be a successful avoidance of unwanted scrutiny. In addition, each characterization has its own attendant reasons, and so leads to yet other stories.

The "data" for the reconstruction of a history of one's emotional life is just the tale told by analysand. "To the extent that the debate over therapeutic action is carried on in terms of 'evidence', to that extent is it meaningless. The debate should be conducted in terms of the advantages of one narrative strategy over another."[20] In this sense, the history of an analysis is a record of successive retellings of events.

This emphasis on the way the story is told, and not the verification of statements, underlines elements common to historical, psychoanalytic, and fictional narratives. Schafer's views here follow Hayden White's discussion of the "emplotment" of historical narratives. White argues that how a historical happening is to be depicted—emplotted—is not itself a question of fact. What happened to Napoleon at Waterloo has no intrinsic valence as, for example, tragic. White maintains that it is in the writing of a narrative that the facts become part of a particular scheme of development that is, for example, tragic or comic. The choice of narrative form is the historian's

[19]Roy Schafer, "The Appreciative Analytic Attitude and the Construction of Multiple Histories," *Psychoanalysis and Contemporary Thought* 2 (1979): 3–24, quoted from p. 23.
[20]Schafer, *Narrative Actions*, p. 40.

doing. This choice of emplotment is the fictive element in an historical narrative.

> But historical situations do not have built into them intrinsic meanings in the way that literary texts do. Historical situations are not *inherently* tragic, comic, or romantic. . . . *How* a given historical situation is to be configured depends on the historian's subtlety in matching up a specific plot structure with the set of historical events he wishes to endow with a meaning of a particular kind. This is essentially a literary, that is to say fiction-making, operation.[21]

White's thesis more generally is that it is by use of culturally familiar modes of emplotment that historical narratives explain changes. The different literary forms are just matrices for ordering and structuring events.[22]

Emplotment involves a point of view. Each point of view defines a set of relevant events and their relation. "But transference and resistance themselves may be viewed as narrative structures. Like all other narrative structures, they prescribe a point of view from which to tell about the events of analysis in a regulated and therefore coherent fashion. The events themselves are constituted only through one or another systematic account of them."[23] The analysis of transference is thus conceived not as "a window on the past"[24] but as a story jointly made.

White characterizes the challenge to psychoanalytic practice, conceived in this way, as one of convincing "the patient to 'reemplot' his whole life history in such a way as to change the *meaning* of those events for him and their *significance* for the economy of the whole set of events that make up his life."[25] Both Schafer and White maintain that the vision of reality that results from a choice of plot type is neither factual nor fictional.[26] It is not factual because there is no essential nature that events have. It is tragic or not on some telling of it. But the telling of it as tragedy is not a mere fiction; there is nothing false about events so represented.[27]

A chronicle of events is not a history of them, and it surely is no

---

[21]White, *Tropics*, p. 85.
[22]Ibid., pp. 95–99.
[23]Schafer, "Narration in the Psychoanalytic Dialogue," p. 32.
[24]Novey, *The Second Look*, p. 144.
[25]White, *Tropics*, p. 87.
[26]Schafer, *A New Language*, p. 56.
[27]See, esp., the first two essays in White, *Content of the Form*.

explanation. If all histories are emplotments of events, then, as odd as it may sound, the chief basis for accepting explanations is not their truth. There is no life of someone to be told *wie es eigentlich gewesen;* hence, histories of that life may be better or worse, relative to some purposes, but no history is *the* true one.[28]

Those who have studied the logic of psychoanalytic explanation reluctantly concede that interpretations need not be *true* in order to have beneficial effects.[29]

What is crucial, it appears, is the reconceptualization of the analysand's experience that the interpretation permits. Sherwood offers an interesting characterization of this point.

> There seems to be a definite and very basic "rationalizing drive" in human experience, a need to see one's own behavior as forming a reasonable and coherent pattern. The adequate psychoanalytic narrative, by providing such a pattern, by giving reason for 'unreasonable' behavior, satisfies this need and thereby allays anxiety—a therapeutically valuable consequence. . . . The psychoanalytic explanation provides that patient with a handle, a lever by which behavioral change may be effected. Both these obvious therapeutic benefits—diminished anxiety and more realistic behavior—will result from a patient's acceptance of a psychoanalytic narrative, whether or not that narrative does in fact outline the true cause of the patient's neurotic behavior. Therapeutic efficacy, then, may be entirely unrelated to the truth of such narratives. It will depend solely upon the ability of the analyst to persuade the patient . . . to accept his narrative as being true; if this occurs, then the therapeutic benefits outlined above will be achieved.[30]

Sherwood puzzles why there need be no fundamental correspondence between events in a patient's life and the interpretation that has therapeutic effects. One part of this puzzle is how *any* interpretation leads to change; that I address below. A second part, the one most troubling to Sherwood, is how therapeutic efficacy of interpretations is disassociated from truth. One answer here is that no history offers the correspondence he seeks. Modes of emplotment are fictive in the sense that the significance given events, and the way of relating

---

[28]I argue this view in detail regarding historical and psychoanalytic interpretations in P. A. Roth, "Narrative Explanation," and "Truth in Interpretation."

[29]See, e.g., Sherwood, *The Logic of Explanation,* pp. 250–51; Novey, *The Second Look,* pp. 148–49.

[30]Sherwood, *The Logic of Explanation,* pp. 250–51.

them, is a consequence of the mode of telling. *All* histories are, to this extent, fictive.[31]

Moreover, if verisimilitude is not to be had for historical narratives, then a response is available as well to some critics of the scientific status of psychoanalytic explanations. In particular, one of Grünbaum's most devastating criticisms of psychoanalytic explanation is based on Freud's claim that only veridical interpretations will have therapeutic efficacy. Freud held, as well, that a mark of veridicality is an analysand's acknowledgment of the verisimilitude of an interpretation. Grünbaum points out that this claim for veridicality as a necessary condition for therapeutic efficacy is simply unsubstantiated by any argument. There is no distinguishing between the claim that an interpretation has therapeutic effect because veridical and, for instance, the suggestion that a therapeutically beneficial intervention is merely an instance of the placebo effect.[32]

However, if the notion of "truth as correspondence" is not, for the reasons rehearsed above, germane to the therapeutic point, then criticisms such as Grünbaum's become irrelevant. That is, if psychoanalytic explanations constitute a type of history, a history providing, inter alia, an etiology of why one feels and does what one feels and does, then the bases for assessing such a history are going to have to be other than those on which Grünbaum, and Freud, insist. For the evaluating of a history is not like the evaluation of hypotheses in the natural sciences, and questions of verisimilitude do not always apply.

An analyst's judgment regarding the reality basis of an analysand's narration will doubtless influence the retelling that the analyst offers. "The history of psychic reality amounts to a special kind of narrative—what may be called *the psychoanalytic life history* . . . I emphasize that for psychoanalysis, one *tells* a history; one does not *have* a history. It is a history of something, however, a fabrication won't do" (pp. 181–82). But significance remains defined by what a person took to happen. (pp. 14–15)

What is of concern is how actions (including, for example, fantasies

---

[31]Given the sort of antirealism that is now commonplace in the philosophy of science, and given that interpretation is no less theory driven than explanation in science, there is nothing especially radical about my claims. I defend this type of antirealism regarding the interpretation of behavior in *Meaning and Method in the Social Sciences* (Ithaca: Cornell University Press, 1987).

[32]For a concise summary of Grünbaum's criticisms in his characteristically vigorous style, see his "Epistemological Liabilities of the Clinical Appraisal of Psychoanalytic Theory," *Noûs* 14 (1980): 307–85, esp. 352–54.

and dreams) that at first seem puzzling, dissociated, or just happenings become part of a more complete and integrated history that reveals the analysand as agent, and so a locus of control and change.

> The function of the therapeutic process is to resolve this tension between the past and the present and future. . . . The intent of the historian is not simply to assign cause and responsibility for events in the past but also to place them in a perspective which invites action in the present and the future. The intent is fully to accept responsibility and freedom to choose.[33]

The analyst qua historian is committed, from the outset, to creating a "revisionist" history of the analysand's life.

Psychoanalytic interpretation, on the account I am advocating, is a "reading" of the tale one tells about one's own life. This historicized view of the process of constructing one's biography is in keeping with the pragmatist maxim that anything real in its effects is to be counted as real.

Yet, Schafer misses the force of his own insight by concluding just that psychoanalysis, as a second-order history, is compatible with a number of different retellings of an analysand's first-order account. For, given that indefinitely many reconstructions may be possible, he sidesteps the issue of which account to favor. He does claim a special comprehensiveness for the psychoanalytic account. But why should comprehensiveness be persuasive to someone, indeed, so persuasive that an analysand makes the story his or her own? But by sketching what might constitute a reason for accepting a psychoanalytic explanation, I suggest as well how reemplotment causes change.

II

Motivation to construe psychoanalysis as a physics of the unconscious arises from the desire to depict the process ultimately in mechanistic terms. Schafer, among others, understandably rails against the sort of hypostatization of the mental that this approach countenances. But if there is no physics of the mental such as Freud (and many of the heirs to his theory) imagined, then how is it possible for

---

[33]Novey, *The Second Look*, p. 13.

some redescription of a life to effect change? In sketching a theory below that answers this question, I suggest that such an account makes a general or principled distinction between explanation and understanding irrelevant. For, if my account is plausible, it indicates how a change in the story one tells of oneself enables changes in actions—makes different behavior possible.

Schafer, in this regard, stresses the redescription as a reconceptualization of an analysand as agent rather than victim, as a doer and not as bystander. The life story so recast depicts the individual as responsible for what previously appeared to be happenings beyond the individual's control.

> In another form, this question asks how any of this is changed, or changed for the better, by the construction of a Freudian life history and present subjective world.
>   . . . Under the influence of the psychoanalytic perspective, the analysand not only begins to live in another world but learns how to go on constructing it. It is a transformed world, a world with systematically interrelated vantage points or rules of understanding. It is a world of greater personal authority and acknowledged responsibility. (pp. 24–25)

Change is possible, Schafer asserts, because the analysand learns to "live in another world" and to "go on constructing" such a world. But, as noted before, Schafer gives no explanation for why a narrative offering "interrelated vantage points" or a tale of a world where one must acknowledge one's own responsibility should be attractive or persuasive. What requires identification is those advantages that might accrue to someone from a self-understanding of the sort Schafer proposes.

One way of specifying what advantages this approach offers is to attend to Schafer's remarks regarding "living in another world." These statements echo Thomas Kuhn's description of a paradigm shift. I propose to exploit this parallel in the following way. It is as an account of paradigms that I read Freud's famous discussion of psychoanalytic types, for instance, the "exception" and "criminality from a sense of guilt."[34] The "exception " is someone who suffers from some problem, for example, a congenital deformity, for which they are blameless, but by which they rationalize claims for special privileges, as if owed compensation for an injury.

---

[34]These are discussed in Freud's "Some Character-Types Met with in Psychoanalytic Work." Citations are from Philip Rieff, ed., *Character and Culture* (New York: Collier, 1963).

The young man who believed himself watched over by a special providence had been in infancy the victim of an accidental infection from his
wet-nurse, and had lived his whole later life on the "insurance-dole,"
as it were, of his claims to compensation, without having any idea on
what he based those claims.[35]

Likewise, there is the person who commits criminal acts and so creates an actual criminal history in order to accommodate a prior sense
of guilt.[36] It is in terms of a particular event or basic relation, for
instance, unresolved feelings about an early injury or guilt related to
the Oedipus complex (in classical Freudian theory, anyway), that
subsequent understanding of oneself and one's relations to others
are constructed or emplotted.

These are paradigms in the most straightforward sense of that ambiguous term, that is, models that serve as a problem-solving basis,
as a model for normal interactions, in an individual's life. Psychoanalysis qua therapy seeks to identify what the details of an individual's
paradigm happen to be, details that the individual is assumed to
have repressed. "The practice of psychoanalysis is to replace etio-
lated derivatives by the original and fundamental."[37] This part of
therapy constitutes a type of phenomenology.

But phenomenology is only descriptive. How does one move beyond "mere description" to change? My suggestion is that therapy,
if successful, induces a paradigm shift, a shift to a different model
for self-understanding. Schafer et al. prefer talk of reemplotting the
significance of events in one's life. What this misses is the functional,
the pragmatic role self-understanding has in guiding ongoing actions,
one's ongoing interpretation of events. Difficulties arise not primarily
in recollection, but when guiding assumptions engender too many
anomalies, that is, experiences that cannot be reconciled with or accommodated to the story one lives by.

Novey remarks that "reconceptualizing his world, including his
self percept, will eventuate in different modes of experiencing and
feeling on the patient's part."[38] Schafer, in a related vein, views an
interpretation of transference as an attempt to convince an analysand
to abandon an unconsciously held paradigm.

[35]Rieff, *Character and Culture*, pp. 159–60.
[36]Ibid., pp. 179–81.
[37]Ibid., p. 158.
[38]Novey, *The Second Look*, p. 149.

The transference interpretation is an attempt to correct certain beliefs about self and others that the analysand has been holding fast against all evidence. The analysand has been holding these beliefs so fast that he or she gives every appearance of using them as methodological principles or principles of knowing. This is to say that, for the analysand, these beliefs must be taken as true if he or she is to be able to make judgments of claims about anything else, for nothing is more certain than they are. They serve as tests of what is true.[39]

In steadfastly and perspicaciously making transference interpretations, the analyst helps constitute new modes of experience and new experiences. This newness characterizes the experience of analytic transferences themselves. Unlike extraanalytic transferences, they can no longer be sheerly repetitive or merely new editions. Instead, they become repetitive new editions understood as such because defined as such by the simplifying and steadfast transference interpretations.[40]

Schafer imagines the cognitive change as effected by a metaphor, that is, by changed associations. But the key is that the Schaferian metaphors function by taking previous experiences and "organizing and implicitly rendering these constituents" in a new, less emotionally debilitating way.[41] "Thus, when one says, 'That's it exactly!' one is implicitly recognizing and announcing that one has found and accepted a new mode of experiencing one's self and one's world, which is to say, asserting a transformation of one's own subjectivity."[42] The transformation, I would like to say, is of the terms in which problems are posed. By reorganizing experiences, one discerns new patterns, and so different solutions become available.

Personal development recapitulates, on this scheme, Kuhn's account of revolutionary developments in natural science, and to much the same effect. For just as adopting a new scientific paradigm creates new options for engaging with the world, so too, I hypothesize, with a change of personal paradigm. Actions one could not previously undertake, or would not have thought to do, now appear as possibilities. One "lives in another world" if that world is free of, say, fears that dictated, in the world previously inhabited, how one needed to live.

[39]Roy Schafer, "The Interpretation of Transference and the Conditions for Loving," *Journal of the American Psychoanalytic Association* 25 (1977): 335–62, quoted from p. 350.
[40]Ibid., p. 356.
[41]Ibid., p. 353.
[42]Ibid., p. 354.

It is Kuhn who taught us how to link *redescription* and change. By developing the analogy between a gestalt-switch and a change of paradigm, Kuhn insists that "though the world does not change with a change of paradigm, the scientist afterward works in a different world."[43] The world has changed because, in the case of Kuhnian revolutionary science, what is introduced is a new set of problems, new criteria for what counts as a solution to a problem, and new categories with which to describe and perceive the world.

> Through the theories they embody, paradigms prove to be constitutive of the research activity. They are also, however, constitutive of science in other respects, and that is now the point. In particular, our most recent examples show that paradigms provide scientists not only with a map but also with some of the directions essential for map-making. In learning a paradigm the scientist acquires theory, methods, and standards together, usually in an inextricable mixture. Therefore, when paradigms change, there are usually significant shifts in the criteria determining the legitimacy both of problems and of proposed solutions.[44]

The changed categories are not, and this is the revolutionary point of Kuhn's own analysis, mere extensions of or developments from what came before. Scientific change is coming up with a different story to tell about things already known.

Scientific revolutions are precipitated, on Kuhn's analysis, when an accepted theory becomes overburdened by anomalous events, that is, occurrences that it cannot explain. There is no algorithm of theory change, however, no set formula that announces when the time has come to abandon a theory. Moreover, history suggests that a necessary condition for a scientific revolution is the existence of an alternative problem-solving model. Paradigms, on this view, are satisfactory insofar as they promote and guide the usual business of puzzle solving. It is their practical utility that leads to conceptual reorganization.

Of the two paradigms of personality mentioned above, Freud provides a relatively clear and straightforward account of how to reemplot the "exception." Such people must renounce the sort of gratification obtainable by constantly demanding compensation for their injury. Instead, as Freud remarks, they "must make that ad-

---

[43]Thomas Kuhn, *The Structure of Scientific Revolutions*, 2d ed., enlarged (Chicago: University of Chicago Press, 1970), p. 121.
[44]Ibid., p. 109.

vance from the pleasure-principle to the reality principle by which the mature human being is distinguished from the child."[45] The man who imagined himself watched over by a special providence because of his childhood injury was letting a wish substitute for the practical need to take care of himself. Freud's discussion here is of particular interest, I suggest, for Freud makes clear that the reemplotment is not a matter of finding new facts about the patient's background, but of factors present in the analytic relationship. "By the side of the necessities of existence, love is the great teacher; and it is by his love for those nearest him that the incomplete human being is induced to respect the decrees of necessity and to spare himself the punishment attendant on any infringement of it."[46]

Retellings become a patient's own, for the reemplotted life history solves at least some of the anomalies, the failures an analysand recognizes in his or her own current configuration of the world. An analysand must come to see the value of the new paradigm, but the same process is true of changes of allegiance in the case of natural scientific theories. Kuhn stresses that science education is a matter of indoctrination; students are taught to see the world in a certain way. If paradigms are acquired through education, this might explain the length of time and some other processes characteristic of psychotherapy.

What is required of a paradigm qua problem-solving model is that it be a guide to understanding past experience and to successfully integrating new experiences on the basis of this prior understanding. In this respect the paradigm commands interest for its pragmatic functions, and not because it satisfies some logical schema.

My goal has been to unify, using a conceptually familiar model, seemingly disparate methods, and their respective idioms, for accounting for human behavior. Much more needs to be said regarding what makes one paradigm more satisfactory than another. However, the conceptual problem of how any therapy might alter behavior is not obviously different from understanding the logical, psychological, and sociological factors that prompt major scientific change.

Psychotherapy is based on a certain paradigm, Freud's "talking cure." Psychoanalytic technique, and the process of constructing psychoanalytic explanations of an individual's actions, is tantamount to attempting to reeducate a person to a certain way of thinking about

[45]Rieff, *Character and Culture*, p. 158.
[46]Ibid.

his or her relation to others. The model outlined here is nonmechanistic. In the context of psychoanalytic practice, explanation and understanding occur without reducing one to the other. It was the belief that they could not so coexist that led to forced attempts to establish each as sui generis. However, attention to the case of psychoanalysis suggests that the explanation-understanding distinction is a fabrication that goes when positivism does; it is a distinction that marks no necessary difference.[47]

[47]John Connolly, Larry Davis, Bob Gordon, Charles Guignon, and Roy Schafer provided valuable critical readings of earlier drafts of this essay.

True Figures: Metaphor, Social Relations, and the Sorites

SAMUEL C. WHEELER III

"What then is truth? A mobile army of metaphors, metonyms, and anthropomorphisms—in short, a sum of human relations, which have been enhanced, transposed, and embellished poetically and rhetorically, and which after long use seem firm, canonical, and obligatory to a people: truths are illusions about which one has forgotten that this is what they are; metaphors which are worn out and without sensuous power; coins which have lost their pictures and now matter only as metal, no longer as coins."[1]

What is the criticism in this passage? Truth, the set of true sentences of a human language, is or uses a mobile (changing, shifting, inconstant) array of figures of speech. These figures, metaphors, metonyms, and anthropomorphisms are defective on many counts: they are enhanced, transposed, and embellished to produce an *appearance*. They seem to be something they are not really. A figure is thus a kind of lie. A metaphor transfers a meaning from one thing to which it properly belongs to another to which that meaning does not properly apply. A metonym names an associated item in place of the proper item itself. Anthropomorphism humanizes objects by giving clocks faces, tables legs, and hurricanes eyes. More generally, anthropomorphism conceives things in human terms, relative to human interests and considerations.

So, how are words, the foot soldiers of the mobile armies, lies? The words of a human language are pretenses of being something

[1]Friedrich Nietzsche, "On Truth and Lies in an Extra-Moral Sense," in *The Portable Nietzsche*, ed. Walter Kaufmann (New York: Viking Press, 1954), p. 42.

else because they are *mere* words. "Red" has nothing in its nature
that connects it with or makes it be red. "Red" is not an authentic
name, not a term that really means red. Friedrich Nietzsche's denun-
ciation of truth despairs of the sorts of connections that, according
to his deluded predecessors, could make words authentic. Words
were supposed to gain a kind of magical connection with the things
by a connection with "ideas," something authentically referring.
Nietzsche realizes that no such ideas "before the mind" or "before
the brain" would be better than words. Marks on neurons, brain-
tissue lesions, or ghost-tokens would have all of the distance from
genuine naming that words have.

But then, Nietzsche has given us a very odd derogation of metaphor and the "truth" of human speech! Consider the criticism of
metaphors that they are like worn coins, without the pictures. What
would freshly minted coins be like? To speak of an empty or washed-
out metaphor presupposes a contrast with the sensory fullness of
things, or the sensory fullness of a kind of thought uncorrupted by
the language-like, a kind of thought where terms directly and transparently meant the sense experiences or realities that they meant.

Alas, Nietzsche says, nothing attaches words or thoughts to things
except human relations, and human relations, as referential equipment, are necessarily deceptive and defective. But Nietzsche has no-
ticed that, in principle, nothing better than word-like marks could
exist. This bewailing of deficiency that is a necessary deficiency of
every case, and so a deficiency only relative to an impossible dream,
can be termed "nostalgia," the longing for what is past and so inaccessible. So, what is Nietzsche (perhaps pretending to be) nostalgic
about?

He is nostalgic for some version of Plato's vision of Souls and
Forms. The Forms can be present to the Soul, according to Plato. The
Form then functions as a word that can have only one interpretation.
Thus Forms would constitute a kind of magic language of items that
were their own meanings and so, by their very nature, determined
which objects fall into their extension. Other versions of this model
are the ideas of the British Empiricists, sense-data, and intensions.
Regular human words, which are all we have, according to Nietzsche, fall short of this authentic grip on the real and on meaning.
But what exactly must be the relation between a spirit blip and an
extension? And how could metaphors, our empty words, fail to live
up to the literal without the possibility of something to live up to?
That is, without the possibility of Platonic or Cartesian spirit tokening
to be the full-fledged "literal"?

What would a theory of language be that was Nietzschean, but without the nostalgia? This essay is an attempt to sketch an account of truth and meaning that is not nostalgic, that recognizes that words are nothing but a sum of human relations, and that they could be nothing better in principle.

This essay is midrash on Donald Davidson and W. V. O. Quine, with supplementation by Jacques Derrida, Paul de Man, and Michel Foucault. The general account of language, which will be described but not really argued for, is Davidson's and Quine's. The main additions to Davidson's sophistication of Quine's picture of language are two:

First, I try to incorporate some account of how power relations affect what is true. I do not pretend that this essay is a full account of how "power" affects language and reality. Nor do I suppose that there is nothing going on but politics. What we say is affected by aesthetics, by laziness, and by other considerations than power and interest.

Second, I argue that the *unanimous* "cultures," "(scientific) communities," and "forms of life" that analytic philosophy has assumed are deceptive fictions. Thus "community" does not support the philosophers' notion of language as a unified system of rules. Cultures and communities are more or less disunified coalitions of more or less disunified groups of more or less disunified individuals.

In the last sections I show how metaphor and the infamous sorites are accommodated on this modified Davidsonian-Quinean account. Important metaphors show the relevance of power in an especially transparent way. Sorites arguments show the necessity for an account of truth that lets truth be adjudicated rather than pre-fixed. A struggle over literal truth illustrates how persuasion and power affect truth values, in an especially transparent way.

What Language Is Not: Some Premises for a Nietzsche without Nostalgia

There are two possible sources for the Platonist picture of language and truth: First, there might be a "magic language" as described below. Second, even lacking a magic language, there might be a natural segmentation of the world so naturally well founded that any plausible language would have to have terms whose extensions matched that natural segmentation. The fundamental premises of a

Davidsonian Nietzscheanism are the denial of the magic language and the denial of natural segmentation.

Magic Languages and Magic Arrows

To deny the possibility of a magic language is to say that no representing tokens have natural semantic natures. Nothing intrinsic to g-u-i-n-e-a-p-i-g gives that sequence of types an extension that includes my late pet Celeste. But thoughts and their components are no better than words. There is no "magic language of the mind" whose terms, by their very nature, fix an extension. A magic language is one whose terms directly and necessarily express Fregean senses. Fregean senses themselves, as objects before the mind, would constitute a magic language.

An alternative magical connection of terms and things is Ludwig Wittgenstein's *Tractatus*'s magical arrows. On a *Tractatus*-like account, there are no mental terms that by their own nature attach to an extension, but the mind can "intend" extensions for its thought terms. Theories that call on such magical apparatus need to explain how a term can have magical bonds of affinity with items in its extension. There are too many relations among thoughts and objects, even if we restrict attention to causal relations, so a theory must privilege this spiritual intentional grasp as a *magic* bond.

A magic language or arrow would allow a clear notion of literal truth independent of culture and convention. With a magic language of interior meanings, truths could be formulated privately, in thought, whether or not there were an external language.

The relevance of "politics," broadly construed, to extensions of terms follows from the denial of the separability of fact and value and the denial of the analytic-synthetic distinction. These denials in turn follow from the absence of a magic language and from the consequent absence of an epistemological given.

The absence of a magic language means that there is nothing more purely meaningful than words; there is no kind of representation that can carry the pure fact component of a word and keep it separate from the "value" part of a word. That is, if facts and values were genuinely theoretically separable, there would have to be representations that were purely factual and representations that were purely valuational. But, since all radical interpretation is *action* interpretation, and since action reflects belief and desire, all intentional tokenings express belief and desire. So there is no "purely factual" meaning.

The lack of an epistemological given follows from all representations' being word-like and nonmagic. As Davidson has often pointed out, without a magic language whose terms carry meanings by their very nature, the determination of what sentences mean and what is true, that is, what the facts are, rest on a single kind of data, what people say when.[2] Thus, without a magic language, there is no separating learning a language from learning about the world, and so no principled separation of the analytic and the synthetic. If this is true, then there is likewise no difference between "contingencies" of what we say and might have said and contingencies about what the world is or could have been.

So, changing language is continuous with changing the facts; and changing the facts is continuous with reevaluation.

Natural Fixation

A sort of Platonist truth that will sustain an invidious distinction between genuine truth and conventional construction can be constructed from the hypothesis that, although there are no "magic terms" whose very nature determines what they mean, there is a privileged "partition" of the world relative to which "labeling behavior" can be matched to natural kinds. Such a partition would be either a naturally given set of properties or a naturally determined array of "real essences." So although there is nothing about "dog" that connects it to dogs, charity of translation dictates that the term fit the only candidate kind. With a naturally selected "partition," supposing that "partition" can be made sense of, there are only a limited number of extensions, so nature will supply enough purchase to get reference and truth and falsity.

I have argued against the possibility that objects whose natures were fixed by natural necessity could provide a determinate interpretation of terms. If there is an objective segmentation, it does not divide the world into people, medium-sized physical objects, or personal relations. In several discussions of sorites arguments I have argued that, since it is arbitrary where we draw a line between a tall man and a man who is not tall, "tall" is not a genuine natural property.[3] That is, "the nature of things" does not select the extension of

<hr/>

[2]See for instance Donald Davidson, "Radical Interpretation," in *Inquiries into Truth and Interpretation* (New York: Oxford University Press, 1984), pp. 125–40.

[3]See my articles "Reference and Vagueness," *Synthese* 30 (1975): 367–79; "On That Which Is Not," *Synthese* 41 (1979): 155–73; "Persons and Their Micro-Particles," *Noûs*

"tall." The presumption of such arguments is that, for objects whose essences are fixed by natural necessities, every thing will either be one of those objects or not, and this determination is made in advance. Thus, the combination of the intuition that, for instance, if one hair is removed from a nonbald man's head, the man is still nonbald, conflicts with the supposition that baldness is a feature that is determined naturally, by the combination of nature and the meaning of the predicate "is bald." Exactly what we must say about such predications must wait until we have discussed metaphor, in the last section.

Similar arguments to the ones constructible for "tall" can be constructed for such predicates as "is a person," "is a table," "is alive," and virtually every other term for things and properties of the lived world. Only mathematical objects and perhaps micro-particles have "essences" in the sense required to give nature a chance to genuinely determine a segmentation into preferred objects and preferred groups.[4]

So, for instance, there is no *set* of entities determined by "is a person." There is no matter of fact about whether a given entity is a person or not in every case. If there were, then there would be one-second intervals separating nonpersons from persons. Most importantly, we know that there is no "hidden fact" about whether a given entity is or is not tall. The inability to apply the predicate is not a lack of information.[5]

So, even if there were a privileged "segmentation" into properties and objects, persons, tables, and tall men could be neither parts of that segmentation nor definable in terms of parts of that segmentation. If medium-sized objects were so definable, there would be answers in the nature of things about exactly which objects were

20 (September 1986): 333–49; and "Indeterminacy of Radical Interpretation and the Causal Theory of Reference," in *Meaning and Translation,* ed. F. Guenthner and M. Guenthner-Reutter (London: Duckworth, 1978), pp. 83–94.

[4]An electron can have only this precise charge. Such kinds of objects would satisfy the condition that any item is either an electron or not. No medium-sized object-kinds satisfy the concept of object that requires that any object is of a kind and that whether a given object is of that kind is fixed by nature.

[5]Notice that in a sense there *is* a well-defined extension of "person." The class of persons is the extension of "person." The sorites rests on constitutive dimensions. Just as being tall is nothing but a question of height, and we cannot find a line in terms of millimeters, so being a person is nothing over and above certain capacities and conditions, and we cannot find a line in terms of those capacities and conditions.

persons, tables, and tall men. But there are no such general answers, and all such borderlines drawn in other terms are arbitrary.

I do not conclude that, since there is no sharp line between dogs and nondogs, that there are no dogs. The only conclusion justified is that there are no dogs if being a dog is determined by natural necessities. The sorites arguments show, not that there are no dogs, but that dogs are not a natural kind, not a kind of object fixed by an array of natural necessities such that whether an object is or is not a dog is determined by the nature of things. What to say about border-line dogs must wait for the last section, after we have seen how metaphors can become true.

Sorites arguments show that, in the sense of "natural object" in which to be an object is fixed in advance by natural necessities, there are no medium-sized natural objects. Tables, heat, justice, persons, and reason have an existence and essence that rests in part on who says and does what when. These contingencies about what we say are not "merely verbal" but also "substantive decisions."[6]

Part of what it is to be a person is determined by culture, not by natural necessities. Though nature has a lot to do with whether persons exist, there is no systematizable relation between what is really happening, as a configuration of micro-particles, and persons and other familiar objects.[7] Natural kinds and natural laws are relevant to the language of social existence and medium-sized objects, but their influence on what's what is mediated and diffuse.

"Social constitution" is not a simple derivation from a "cluster theory of reference" that makes the reference of a term a function of the beliefs associated with the term.[8] There are more activities involved in cultural constitution than just the cognitive. A concept is a

[6]The contrast between the "verbal" and the "substantive" is not sustainable as a principled distinction, but is, rather, a dimension that allows more or less. Nothing purely factual or purely linguistic is required for some kinds of change to be more "merely verbal" than others.

[7]Sorites arguments also bear on the possibility of magic-language terms, if the terms of the magic language of thought are supposed to fix extensions. Reference is a function of sense, and terms of the magic language have their sense in virtue of their nature. If the contents of such terms are available to introspection, then we could have no doubt about whether an arbitrary object was in the extension of a magic language term or not. Given our assurance that there are only arbitrary answers in borderline cases of persons and tall men, persons and tall men cannot be extensions of magic-language terms.

[8]Crawford Elder has shown that such "social objects" are not just what people think they are. See his "Realism, Naturalism, and Culturally Generated Kinds," *Philosophical Quarterly* 39, no. 157 (1989): 425–44.

complex of desires, actions, beliefs, things known, and every other social phenomenon that involves "propositional attitudes."

Such "socially constituted" entities cannot be "artifacts" of the culture, even though they are things whose reality and nature depend at least in part on contingencies about us and what we do. "Artifacts" are objects made from something. But the only objects not subject to sorites desecration are objects that could not supply the material for a construction. Only micro-particles and mathematical objects could have sharply defined "good essences" that would provide well-defined sets as extensions. So, whether or not there is or could be an ontologically privileged partition of the world, there is nothing *from* which the objects of the lived world are constructed.

For the languages in which we think and speak, as opposed to the mathematical constructs we might fantasize, the very items that are to be elements of sets are not given by the nature of things. There is no truth value-bearing or reference-bearing manifold prior to conceptualization, that is, prior to language or the language-like. So there are no items of any kind waiting to be grouped into sets. Without a manifold of epistemologically given objects, there are no alternative "conceptual schemes" to be formulated as "constructions" or "artifacts."

If what we are to say when is not fixed by nature, then by what? We also do not want to say that what is the case is fixed by our wishes or by our mere decisions about what is to be called what. Let me begin to deal with this by two examples:

(1) Suppose our mothers and fathers had all applied the same term to both cats and dogs. Would they *be* the same kind of animal? It seems that nonnostalgic Nietzscheanism must say "yes," since what a thing is depends on this sort of training. But how do we construe the counterfactual? We should not construe this as a question of what we would judge if *our* parents had done this. We describe what is going on in the imagined situation in *our* terms. And in our terms, surely, cats and dogs are two kinds of animal, not one. We, after all, believe that what we say is true. However, we can recognize that nothing much hangs on what we say about cats and dogs being two kinds or one kind. (Of course, a lot depends on what else these people say, whether this is part of a system or part of massive error.)

(2) "If there had been no cultures, would there have been dogs?" Of course. If there were no people, there might well still be dogs. Once again, *we* are describing the situation. Now, would the statement "There are dogs" be true? No, if by that we mean that, for

instance, if the sequence of shapes T-H-E-R-E A-R-E D-O-G-S occurred in a situation with no culture, then it would express a truth. On the other hand, our statement "There are dogs in that eventuality" is true of that way things could have been.

So, finally, what is the dependence on us? Even though we are trained as we are, we have to recognize that that particular training is contingent: We could have been trained otherwise, and then other things would have been true.[9] Apart from other stage setting, we are imagining that a single change in what we say has occurred, while everything else stays the same. Such alternative training is like learning French rather than learning English as babies, it might be "merely linguistic." But there is no principled distinction between that kind of "different training" and substantive differences of opinion.

So, how do our terms end up being "fixed by the culture?" As a first, vague, and familiar approximation, the extensions of terms are fixed by "practices in a culture."

A Practicing Culture

Joke: Well-armed hostile native Americans have surrounded the Lone Ranger and Tonto.
LR: "It looks like we're in deep trouble."
T: "What do you mean 'WE,' white man?"

Suppose we start with the following: What we mean depends on what we say, do, and write when, and how what we say when fits in with our lives and relations.[10] But how does this work, and what are these "practices?" Well, practices involve, among other things, norms. Norms are what we do, as in "We don't bite other children, do we?"

Now, for a pattern to be a practice rather than a natural necessity, the practice must be "unnatural." The practice might not exist, and there is a tendency to fall away from it. So the practice continues to exist only in virtue of activities that keep the practice in existence.

[9]The application of "contingent" as a way of saying that things could have been different without supposing "alternative conceptual schemes" is borrowed from the first of Richard Rorty's series of articles in the London Review of Books, "The Contingency of Language," 8 (April 17, 1986): 3–6.
[10]Some of the theses in this section were proposed in "Truth and Training," an unpublished manuscript by John Troyer and Samuel Wheeler from 1973.

That is, norms and thus practices are enforced against some opposition. Since norms are enforced, and enforcement involves some kind of forcing, power relations are essential to the existence of practices, and so of cultures.

Anything cultural, then, requires at least token resistance on the part of at least the draftees to the culture, the babies. By the very unnatural nature of norms, then, there is always resistance to authority, and so nonunanimity in any culture. In this minimal sense, then, a culture is necessarily built on power and coercion. There is no pure unanimous culture. The only question about coercion and repression in a culture is how much there is of it and who gets to coerce whom, not whether the culture is repressive and coercive.

So, why do we call these objects "dogs"? Well, because they are dogs. There is a temptation here to divide the question: What we call the dogs is up to us, we might say; but which things are really dogs is fixed by nature. The dogs are already there, waiting to be called something. But this is to suppose that something like "choice of language" or "stipulation" is up to us. But this stipulation requires both that what is merely linguistic can be separated from the factual, and that there is a magic ur-language in which stipulations can be formulated. So what the dogs are is set by what we say in what circumstances. As Davidson has shown the "circumstances" are not a world that we "organize." There are no preconceptual neutral terms in which we contemplate choices that this is a dog and this is not. Both the world "as artifact" and as "given" presuppose a given.

But who says which the dogs are? Some want to call things dogs when they are not, and vice versa. Practices and norms prevent or inhibit such deviation. Now, the practices that constitute language can be matters of contention. There are speakers who resist practices. Such speakers go along with practices because they must think and talk, even though their language serves those who say what is what. Resisters and reluctant collaborators are, as it were, trapped in alien practices of thought and speech. With no magic language, there is no private language, so people learn language by finding out what to say when and where. But this learning, like learning table manners, can require more or less punishment. Also, habits of applying terms can fit or fail to fit something that could be called interests, whether of classes or of genders.

Linguistic norms can serve or disserve interests. Here are two ways this can happen: First, entrenched connections of terms may serve or disserve interests, given an application to a case. An obvious case:

If fetuses are properly called persons, then, given what we are inclined to say about persons, other practices are brought to bear. If
these fetuses are persons, then you women must not dispose of
them. What are they really?[11]

Second, the underdetermination of what we say in a new case by
previous practices guarantees the continued occurrence of opportunities to be pragmatic (by our ruling lights). Given a new borderline
case, such as a fertilized egg in a divorce settlement, whether it is a
property issue or a custody issue is a matter of moment. The issue
turns on who is in charge. Of whose lives are these practices forms?
Who gets to decide which forms of life there shall be?[12]

I want to assert two theses about interest and language: (1) The
language in which the underlings formulate beliefs and desires can
be against their interests, and (2) they can be aware of this. Both of
these theses are difficult to construe, given that we think and desire
in a language. The underlings cannot have any clear idea of alternatives, since all clear ideas are formulated in a language, and the underlings have learned to think by learning to speak and think in the
"masters' language." So, the underling cannot formulate the exact
better pattern of what is said when before a change has been made,
since that is a position from which they must think within "the language of the oppressor." (The oppressor has a similar problem of
thinking his way out of his situation.)

In order to proceed, we need to purify ourselves from two nostalgic
prejudices: We need to avoid thinking of language and interests as
premeditated. By the premises above, such meditation supposes that
we would already have a language in which to contemplate how to
talk in various situations. Also, we should be post-Romantic about
power relations and the fact that someone says what is what. Mom,
after all, is our authority on many topics. Language, culture, and
therefore thought disappear if everybody gets to decide for themselves (so to speak) what to say and do. A culture is essentially differ-
ential relations of authority and power.

A culture is, just by the nature of norms, not a unified "we." This

[11]How does "you women" come to exist as a group? Such a group is not just
preculturally there, and it is a mistake to think that *this very group* lost out in an initial
world-historical defeat.

[12]What we resolve to say may not work out even for us. Sometimes things we have
decided on force us to say things we would prefer not to. So, keeping both "all men
are equal" and "blacks are not equal" in our collection of truisms will require that
some extensions we are inclined to assign be modified.

does not mean that some class or group must dominate others on all topics at all times, but just that some class or group has to be authoritative on each occasion where something comes up. So, "what do you mean 'WE'?" I think "culture" has to be construed holistically, in much the way we would construe "language." That is, given both the social nature of language and the fact that no two people have exactly the same pattern of what they say when, "same language" must be construed holistically, with nothing guaranteed to be the same from speaker to speaker. If languages are artifacts of cultures, the same will hold true of "is in the same culture."

What happens when a coalition of groups has more than its fair share of power? "We" can serve the interests of those who have authority or who may be able to appropriate authority. "We" sometimes implicitly recruits the hearer, getting me to acquiesce in what we say and do. "We" sometimes innocently undermines the illusion that the hearer is included.[13] "We" is often a coercive or self-deceptive "we," a fiction that supposes a unanimity of interest and decision, that projects an hegemony into a unanimity.

What is hidden by our use of this term "culture"? I am in my culture along with people who watch the Cosby show and care about the Red Sox. "Culture," especially in what some wishfully call "late capitalism," hides a diversity of incompatible groups. Has there ever been a culture that fits the "philosophical" notion of a culture? Or is this always a masking term, referring to a loose assortment of coexisting, overlapping, and interacting groups and individuals? Just as Davidson has suggested that the philosophical notion of a language does not fit anything real, so, given that language is a function of culture, the same applies to "culture."[14]

The important question, for those who want to rearrange or preserve the power distribution and the degree to which various interests are served, is how much those games cohere, both internally and among themselves? The picture of a typical "culture" now is both more hopeful, since the culture is too loose and diffuse to really keep the alienated in line, and more ambiguous, because the alien-

[13]Compare H. D. F. Kitto, *The Greeks* (Baltimore: Penguin, 1963), p. 234: "*We* find perfectly good evidence that women went to the theatre—often to see plays which *we* would not allow *our* women to see"—in a passage pointing out that although English women are equal in every way, equality is an unreasonable standard to apply to ancient Athens. (My emphasis.)

[14]Donald Davidson, "A Nice Derangement of Epitaphs," in *Truth and Interpretation*, ed. Ernest LePore (New York: Basil Blackwell, 1986), pp. 445–46.

ated are also products of and thinkers within the culture from which they imagine themselves alienated.

Thus, a disunified concept of culture shows how "we"s that are not heard with authority, who do not get to decide what gets said when, still get to be heard, sort of.[15] This is a tricky notion, given that there is no language helpfully more transparent in meaning than the one we speak, think, and write in. The various "we"s themselves exist only in virtue of a somewhat ineffectively constituting culture. That is, the groups in a culture are constituted as groups by that culture, not by natural divisions alone.[16]

Why can't a hegemonic discourse, typically, keep people in line? On the one hand, we have something like reality interfering with a construction imposed by the dominant. The dominant ideology is supposed to be cognitive, a theory. But just as importantly, such a cultural "theory" is an organization of pleasure and pain, of what is valuable and despicable. But the "data" in this case, though they are not independent of the hegemonic conceptual scheme, yet resist it. Things just are not working out very well for the underclasses. Pleasure and pain, in practices, are something like "observation" in science. There is no "pure data" but the world troubles "theory" nonetheless. Such accounts, in this broad sense of "account," can run afoul of the others who are subordinated.

So this hegemonic discourse is analogous to a kind of theory and fails to fit the world of the underlings in the very way that Kuhn describes the Aristotelian physical concepts as not fitting the world.[17] It is not that any general views are exactly mistaken in their own terms, by not applying or fitting, but rather that the system as a whole gives bad results.

In the same way, if we think now of a culture's "theory" as always at every level of representation a mix of value and fact, the "theory" does not contain any "mistaken values" but gives bad results. "Bad" to the underlings, but not in the sense that there is an alternative

[15]But they, as part of this culture, come to see themselves, *as* outside and *as* oppressed. How can a group (constituted by the culture) have interests *as* a group that are different from the interests that the oppressors would assign to the group (cooperation in their appropriate role, with all doing their bits)?

[16]Alleged "hegemonies" are themselves incoherent, and so less than totally determining of what we say. Maybe there can exist simple enough collections of people so that no discontented underlings arise (i.e., where no one disputes the dominant discussions). This would be like a perfectly simple being.

[17]Thomas Kuhn, *The Structure of Scientific Revolutions*, 2d ed. (Chicago: University of Chicago Press, 1970).

ready to be articulated. This is more or less like the way Albert Michelson and Edward Morley were faced with a bad result in the measurement of the earth's speed through the ether. There was no indication what exactly was wrong—things just were not working out. When "theory" is generalized to be adequate to practices, a very analogous "incommensurability" still must allow that there are differences in "success," defined, now, truly pragmatically.

In a sense, the interests of everyone are being served, since no thinkable alternative to the dominant conception of "true interests" yet exists. In the same way, on a Kuhnian account, Newtonian principles were not being *ignored* in the Aristotelian physics. The alleged would-be "interests" that are excluded from language games are thereby excluded from clear thought, as well.

But the very incoherence of the "culture" and of the "hegemony" leaves room for discontent. There is not a single discourse, but a variety of competing attempts to say what is what. As it were, many regions of "what is to be said when" are up for grabs, or, more politely, under discussion. That "culture" is an oversimplification does not necessarily mean that no interests are in charge, just that the charge cannot be total. There is a kind of hegemonic "we," even though it is not a single totally coherent "it." But not all of us are in it, although most of us are on a subcommittee. (I mean "us professors.") The powers that be do get to say what is what, and this is not a bad thing, really. At least from our point of view.

Metaphors, Dogs, and Truth: Extending Terms to the Limits of Their Extensions

Metaphor

The application of figural speech is especially clearly underdetermined by either practices or nature. The periphery called "metaphor" is a particularly revealing illustration of the Nietzschean-Davidsonian position on truth. Nietzsche's assimilation of predication to figuration is justified in this section.

What happens when one of us says something such as "Celeste is a real eggplant?" In particular, is what we have said true? "True" means, we might start by saying, that the facts fit the rules of what is to be said. Now, the facts are the truth conditions of true sentences. By the rules of the language, "Celeste is an eggplant" is true if and only if Celeste is an eggplant. Notice that without a magic language, there are no facts as mediators fitting our language to the world.[18]

Any "conversational" or "rhetorical" rules of what is to be said are equally unhelpful. In appropriate circumstances, the rules would tell us to say "Celeste is an eggplant" if and only if Celeste is an eggplant. The "rules" that get enforced in determining what we say in what circumstances cannot be *linguistic* rules. The question of what the proper application of a term is must come down to: Who's in charge here?

When a term is being contested, as "human being" is now, "true" is out of place, as is "false." "Language," we might say, is being challenged. But there is no principled distinction between challenging language and challenging an account of what is the case, since without a magic language there is no principled distinction between the analytic and the synthetic.

The philosophers' notion of "true" and "false" seem to (almost) fit when the practices are (almost) completely fixed, so that it is already (almost) laid out in advance, for every possible object and kind of object, whether that object is in the extension of the term. A full-blown philosophers' language would have determinate extensions for its terms. Each term would determine a class, whatever happened and whatever the world turned out to be.[19] We could expect good application of "true" and "false" in the case of totalities that we can figure out in advance, like the numbers and the sets of grammatical sentences in first-order quantification theory. There, we can prepare for every eventuality, in those terms. But the objects in this case are given in advance, and a language already exists for stating the possibilities.

But in natural languages, the very items that are to be elements of sets are not given by the nature of things. There is no manifold prior to conceptualization, that is, prior to language. Without a manifold of given objects, there are no alternative "conceptual schemes" to be formulated as "constructions" or "artifacts."

So, what about metaphor? Davidson is almost right, as always.[20]

---

[18]The scripture on which this is midrash is Donald Davidson's "True to the Facts," *Journal of Philosophy* 66 (1969): 748–64.

[19]"Possible kind of object" is itself a mysterious construct—are we supposed to be able now to imagine or conceive of every possible kind of object? What kind of god-like language is it that would distinguish every possible way of thinking about mana, snow, honor, or micro-particles?

[20]Donald Davidson, "What Metaphors Mean," in *Inquiries into Truth and Interpretation* (New York: Oxford University Press, 1984), pp. 245–64.

But he retains the redundant term "literal," by which the claim that Celeste is an eggplant is "literally" false. His analysis is that "Celeste is an eggplant" is proposed for other reasons than saying what is the case—it functions, rather, as a device to get us to see Celeste in a certain light, as an eggplant. And this analysis is right about many metaphorical uses of terms.

But Davidson has no basis deeper than thinking that Celeste is *not* an eggplant for rejecting the claim that Celeste is really an eggplant, or for in general rejecting metaphors as literally true. In theory, there is no problem whatsoever with truth definitions and true metaphors: The consequence that "Celeste is an eggplant" is true if and only if Celeste is an eggplant certainly goes through. Notice that "true" here functions solely as a kind of semantic linking concept between sentences and their truth conditions. And the truth conditions of "Celeste is an eggplant" are quite clear.

Davidson denies that Celeste is an eggplant because of such prior commitments as that all eggplants are vegetables. But this new case is not in principle different from the dispositions people used to have to say that all swans are white. Besides, guinea pigs are vegetables, in their way. Adjustments in other things we say have to be made in any case where we find unusual cases in which a predicate applies.

Davidson is surely right about many metaphorical speech acts. In this case, in fact, I called Celeste an eggplant not to inform anyone but to tease her. But sometimes our intention in saying such things as "Criminals are victims of their environment," "Fetuses are persons," or "Wildernesses have rights" is to *urge* that the statement be true. This urging, especially when the topic matters, is not just observing the obvious, but it is not really distinguishable from literal predication, either.

Davidson's view gives no account of the drift from live to dead to literal. Most importantly, Davidson's view gives no account of political struggle to make live metaphors literally true. What happens when ideas become literally thought objects, or when thought can become literally clear? A theory that has abandoned culture as monolithic and coherent must account for the figural becoming literal.

Davidson notices that with no magic language, and so nothing better than words, there is no room for "metaphorical meaning" and so nothing to be the literal meaning. So any difference between the literal and metaphorical has to be difference in "force," in "how" rather than "what" is said. So, "Celeste is an eggplant." True or false? False, but amusing. How about "victim" in "Jones is a victim of AIDS'' or "Martha is a victim of a sexist society's pattern of female childrearing"? "Victim" is clearly being extended metaphorically, at least at this very moment (except that "merely metaphorical" is, in this context, itself a political move of derogation), but the metaphor may soon die. The point of the struggle is that a lot hangs on this categorization. If you are a victim, you have been attacked unjustly, there is an attacker, and compensation is owed. In the same way, if alcoholism is an illness rather than a character defect, then treatment rather than condemnation is in order. Likewise, if a periodically recurring desire to have sexual activity is an addiction, then we should try to end it. What are the "facts" of literally correct application versus mere metaphor?

If truth is a matter of what the norms are, and what "we" say when, and there is a struggle about what is to be said, truth is loose. We should not think that somehow the truth is already there, waiting to be discovered. "Is true" is like "is a turning point," "is the winning run," or "is a decisive play." Such concepts can be applied only retrospectively. Whether respect could be literally deep had to wait for the outcome of a cultural development. Remember that apart from "this is what we say here," nothing *makes* our application of "table" to a new case fit the literal meaning. Metaphorical application is continuous with "regular" application of predicates.[21] Exactly analogous remarks apply to metonymy and other figures.

This is not to say that there is no difference between the figural and the literal; just that the difference is not a principled distinction of two kinds of use of language. We can still say that "Fred is a heroin addict" is more literal than "Fred is addicted to sexual activity." That a particular theoretical division is not supportable does not mean that the distinction, as a normal part of a natural language, and so vague and loose, is not valuable.

Where a term or a region of discourse is being struggled over, or perhaps just quarreled over, there is nothing close enough to the "real language" to give us a concept of preexisting truth, if the sides are well matched. No future god-like presence, no Moira, has determined a winner already. As language is used and things are meant, there is no secret fix in. At the moment, and at every moment, whether a controversial figural utterance is true or not depends on what happens. So, for now, it is neither true nor false. In an impor-

[21]I argue that there is no "natural" basis for applying predicates to new cases in "Metaphor According to Davidson and de Man," in *Redrawing the Lines*, ed. Reed Way Dasenbrock (Minneapolis: Minnesota University Press, 1989), pp. 116–39.

tant way, "logic" does not apply to natural languages. No natural language has a *natural* interpretation that assigns truth values to all of its sentences.

The Solution to Sorites Problems

So what should a Nietzschean-Davidsonian say about borderline dogs? Such cases are undetermined, neither dogs nor nondogs. "Borderline" dogs have much the same status as metaphorical applications of terms. Before such cases are in dispute, nothing is true about them. When such cases come under discussion or dispute, then they get decided one way or another.

The solution to the "logical" paradox of sorites arguments is equally simple. Given the above account of the extension of predicates to new cases, the crucial premise is that if a is a dog, and b differs from a by only c, then b is a dog. But this premise is false, when we are applying predicates on borderlines. In disputed or disputable areas, the principle would be read as: If it were adjudicated that a is a dog, and b differs only by c from a, then it would be adjudicated that b is a dog.

But this is false of human adjudication. The next case may have different contestants, and the other side may have more persuasive arguments. "Precedent" is always subject to interpretation and so is only an unpredictable constraint on new cases. Besides, the adjudicators may change, and "good reason" may subtly shift in its application. The important point, as I argue below, is that the unpredictability of adjudication does not mean that application of "dog" in borderline cases is "unobjective."

There is no answer now as to what exactly the dogs are. Those borderline cases are not yet discussed, so their status must await actual adjudication. Also, there are no items that *must* be borderline, or that are guaranteed by the nature of the case always to be borderline.

In cases where our practices do not already strongly predispose us to make certain predications, there is no guarantee that we will decide one way or another. For most uncontested cases, we don't care, and so they are left undecided. Briefly, natural languages are not systems in the way philosophers have often imagined. In some ways, "logic" does not apply to a real language.

Borderline cases are different from metaphorical extensions of terms in that they seem to require something like continuous variation. But some extensions of terms may strike us as both metaphorical and borderline.[22] The "borders" in "borderline cases" are not natural boundaries, except in the rather limited paradigm range of tall and heavy. There are numerous considerations here that must be glossed over: With a predicate such as "tall," exactly one feature is going to be relevant.[23] We are convinced that, even if it is important to be tall for tax purposes, there is nothing "objective" about the line between the tall and the nontall. Such distinctions are always "merely verbal."

For predicates that are unlike "tall" in being determined by more than one "dimension," several differences obtain: First, more than one kind of case can be "marginal." A "borderline" of a case of personhood, for instance, may well be a metaphorical extension of "person." Certainly we could describe the extension of "addiction" to sexual desire equally as metaphor or as the extension of a vague borderline. Second, a predicate such as "person" or "bald" does not yield an ordering such that for all x and y, either x is more F than y, or y is more F than x, or x and y are equally F. Third, a multidimensional concept is subject to "factual changes" and "reevaluations" in many more ways than a one-dimensional term, since a dimension may itself have disputed borderline cases.

Multidimensional concepts are concepts with many connections in our webs of belief and desire. For the same reason that a statement like "Bachelors are unmarried" seems merely verbal, so a decision that only those six feet and up are tall seems purely verbal. For richer concepts, there is nothing "merely verbal" about an unpredetermined application of a predicate.

Since facts and values are always together in any predication, an adjudication can be "objective," even though competent speakers could disagree. Without "unanimous culture" there is no single standard of the rational or the objective. Nothing more fundamental than "this is what we do" governs adjudication. So, the apparent "irrationality" of deciding that a is a person and b is not, even though a

[22]I have proposed such sorites arguments in a paper that "justifies" property rights by a borderline-case argument moving from rights to control bodies to rights to unlimited property. Samuel Wheeler, "Natural Property Rights as Body Rights," Noûs 24 (May 1980): 171–94. In that article, pieces of property such as cars were entitled to treatment as parts of bodies because there were no ethically significant lines along the continuum between "real" bodies and the "extended bodies" that consisted of cars and houses.
[23]If the application of "tall" approached that of "lean," then we might have genuine disagreements that did not seem arbitrary.

differs on dimension D by only g, need not be "unobjective." So an actual adjudication we agree on is a result that is more than "merely verbal."

For some predicates, the single-dimension ones, decisions are more arbitrary. For others, the decision is more substantive. For multidimensional predicates, predicates connected to many other determinations and judgments, a judgment that this is a dog can be objectively correct. That truth, though, is not already there in the position—it must await the outcome of a struggle or discussion. So, the borderline dogs are not already one or the other. Retrospectively, they will always have been dogs, if they are judged to be dogs. (Those future language-users are speaking from their position, using their language.)

Consider two stories about a borderline dog: Suppose that there is a special tax on dogs but not on any other kind of animal. A ruling must be sought. Now, if nothing but the tax hangs on it, we may say the outcome is "merely verbal." That is all right, if "merely verbal" is not taken to have a principled contrast with the "genuinely factual." Because only a bit more involvement of "dogs" is needed to make this substantive:

If dogs have rights, and dog ownership brings on special obligations to care and train and nurture, then there will be a more serious battle about a given borderline dog, with lawyers and scientific testimony. With more connections to belief and desire, the issue is what the real dogs are, not merely verbal, even though last year's clear nondog can be today's clear dog.

Truth

So, what is truth? At every point in these sequences of changes, the homophonic truth definition holds, while disagreements about surrounding sentences continue. However, nothing about the truth of individual statements follows from the truth of the biconditionals. That is, we can continue our discussion of whether "Celeste is an eggplant" is true while agreeing that "Celeste is an eggplant" is true iff Celeste is an eggplant. In the same way, once baldness becomes punishable by death, we can discuss whether Fred is bald while agreeing that "Fred is bald" is true if and only if Fred is bald. As liberal men, we would be eager to limit applications of "bald," of course.

A sequence of symbols is not just true tout court, but "true in L"

and our whole question can be put as "What is it to have an *L*?" The slightest reflection shows that any *L* is only as good as its explicating language that states what is what—so we can expect nothing much from application to our own case.

In a real language the *L* is under dispute. That dispute is not about which meanings to attach to which words, but rather about what is to be said when.[24] All such disputes about what is to be said take place in a particular concrete situation that makes some predications suitable. That is, the particular pattern of interconnections that more or less is taken as fixed determines which further determinations of the not-yet-fixed serve which concerns.[25] Truth is "a mobile army of metaphors, . . . metaphors which are worn out and without sensuous power." More exactly, truth is the momentary balance of power in a many-sided war among various guerrilla bands.[26]

[24]Sometimes the issue is the meta-issue about who gets to decide, rather than the particular ramifications of a kind of application. A lot of discussions "on principle" do not matter except that they keep the determiners determining. Look how unhappy we get when "metaphysics" comes to mean the occult.

[25]For instance, whether it suits interests to be a "real Marxist" depends on the political and social surroundings, which are essentially connected to what else is being said and done.

[26]Versions of this paper were read at Wesleyan and Brandeis. It was in conversation with Eli Hirsch that the necessity of treating sorites arguments and metaphors in the same way dawned on me. John Troyer provided helpful, if unpersuaded, commentary.

CHAPTER 11

Rhetoric in Postmodern Feminism:
Put-Offs, Put-Ons, and Political Plays

ELOISE A. BUKER

Feminist theories in general can be thought of as interpretive turns that give both modern and postmodern philosophical frameworks a new and decidedly different spin. By beginning with the simple assumption that women are as central to cultural life as men are, and by seeking to articulate just gender relationships, one modifies philosophical foundations such as liberalism, marxism, psychoanalysis, existentialism, and socialism to such an extent that one seems almost compelled to turn them into adjectives that describe the noun "feminism"—liberal feminism, marxist feminism, psychoanalytical feminism, existential feminism, socialist feminism, postmodern feminism. In this sense, feminist theories perform a radical hermeneutics that appropriates other philosophies in order to reflect on issues arising from women's confrontations with injustices.

Some feminists have been bothered by this appropriation. Western feminism seems to depend upon philosophical frameworks developed within western patriarchy. Radical feminists especially have endeavored to move outside of this philosophical tradition to develop feminist models that come more directly from women's experiences. However, even this work appears to depend upon patriarchy in that women articulate their experiences through a patriarchal language, so that even "raw" experience is shaped by the patriarchal foundations of society. Escape seems not possible. Yet, feminism does transform the philosophies it appropriates.

Nonetheless, the radical hermeneutics that engages feminists not only makes explicit the ways in which feminist theories involve quests for the good and just life (for both men and women) but also benefits from the critical reflections embodied in a variety of social theories. Because the present status of feminist theory is ambiguous— both accepted as philosophy and criticized as a controversial field touched by politics—feminist theorists and others who challenge present value systems have the opportunity to become more reflective about the political dimensions of their work than do those whose work primarily supports prevailing belief systems. This is so much the case that Michelle Rosaldo suggests that central to feminist work is questioning the questions.[1] Postmodern feminists as well as other feminists demonstrate that feminist work not only questions patriarchal questions but questions feminist questions as well. Postmodern feminists emphasize that their feminist theory is a process of critical inquiry impelled by their desire to move toward justice but at the same time making no claim to have the one right answer for all people in all cultures or historical periods. Postmodern feminist theory acknowledges its connections to a particular historical cultural society and finds in those connections the conditions that make it possible for its work to be useful to that society.[2]

An Interpretive Strategy

This essay examines three themes that can be found in current postmodern feminist conversations in the United States.[3] The first theme examines some of the issues raised by those who are critical of incorporating postmodernism into feminism; they are *put off* by it

---

[1]Michelle Z. Rosaldo, "Moral/Analytic Dilemmas Posed by the Intersection of Feminism and Social Science," in *Interpretive Social Science: A Second Look*, ed. Paul Rabinow and William M. Sullivan (Berkeley: University of California Press, 1987), pp. 280–301, esp. pp. 286–89.

[2]For an analysis of the importance of this limit to cultural historical context within philosophical hermeneutics, see Hans-Georg Gadamer, *Reason in the Age of Science*, trans. Frederick G. Lawrence (Cambridge: MIT Press, 1981), and for an analysis of the epistemological connections between philosophical hermeneutics and feminist social science, see Eloise A. Buker, "Feminist Social Theory and Hermeneutics: An Empowering Dialectic?" *Social Epistemology* 4 (1990): 23–39.

[3]Even though French feminists have made central contributions to postmodern feminism, I am not including them because my emphasis here is on the American political context. For commentaries on French feminist theory, see Elizabeth Grosz, *Sexual Subversions: Three French Feminists* (Boston: Allen & Unwin, 1989); Toril Moi, *Sexual/Textual Politics: Feminist Literary Theory* (New York: Methuen, 1985); and Chris Weedon, *Feminist Practice and Poststructuralist Theory* (London: Basil Blackwell, 1987).

and think that feminists should *put it off*. The second theme examines three images that postmodern feminists use to expose how we have constructed our identities—how we have *put them on*. Central to these identities are the tensions that we have embraced between the mind and the body and the ways in which we have constructed the body as a message system driven by a sex-gender dichotomy. The third theme explores the ways in which postmodern feminists use "play" to offer a new politics based upon the "play of difference."

Put-Offs

Three charges leveled at the politics of postmodern thought require careful reflection by feminist theorists who are drawn to such thought. First, postmodernism has been charged with a failure of communication. The generous charge it with a lack of clarity; the less generous, or perhaps merely more blunt, charge it with being deliberately incomprehensible—"jargon." The second charge is that postmodernism promotes relativism and thereby supports status quo politics and inhibits political change. The third charge is that postmodernism decenters the subject and eliminates human agency from its analysis.

American feminists have been suspicious of linguistic mystifications—"jargon." In addition, they are often committed to reflecting on the injustice in our present system and to offering transformative political models; they are critical of the status quo and press for social change. Furthermore, feminists are particularly interested in articulating how women have been subjects of their own actions. How then do postmodern feminists reconcile these three charges with their feminist commitments? How are postmodern feminists able not to be put off by these charges?

Putting People Off: Jargon or Political Challenge

The word "postmodern" puts people off. The "post" part of "postmodernism" might seem to be an easy place to begin to look at this problem. One wonders if it is better to be a post-something, an afterthought, than to claim to *be* something. Is it a lack of courage in the postmoderns that they will not name the thing they are? Or is it that what they are is the issue? Of course, this latter question catches the attention of feminists who raise questions about women's identities and find their own feminist identities the subject of controversy. It may be strategic not to propose a fixed identity if one wishes to elicit a multiplicity of identities. The third part of this essay examines this issue through the metaphor of play.

A second problem feminists raise is, Why turn—or one might even say turn *once again*—to theories of "man" which exclude women or at best lament the lack of women's presence in western philosophy?[4] Can't feminist theory be more independent? But can it? If we take Jacques Derrida seriously and see the ways in which we are caught in the web of language and meaning, then as long as we speak English and are reared in a culture shaped by patriarchy, our feminist theories will be mixed genre.[5] Even radical feminist theory, which comes closest in its attempt to establish a separate discourse, echoes patriarchal language patterns, symbols, and styles of argumentation. A pure feminist theory purged of patriarchy exists as an essentialist[6] feminist dream, but this may well be a utopian dream that fears politics and wishes to avoid political struggle.[7] As such it seeks to homogenize us all, hoping to make us so identical that we will not disagree or differ. Poststructuralism suggests that such a dream itself is a nightmare that would demand rigid political controls to maintain such commonalities.

Poststructuralism[8] shows how communication itself is an interactive process that depends upon differences which generate a language system that takes place through the interaction of two persons who share some similarities, making communication possible, and

[4]Postmodernism is in some respects less likely to offer a theory of *man* than it is to offer a theory of absence that articulates "woman" as the symbolic representation of absence. For critical commentary on the politics of how this constitutes women, see Robert Scholes, "Éperon Strings," *differences* 1 (Summer 1989): 93–104 (esp. pp. 103–4).

[5]The ways in which language limits even radical philosophers is a theme in Jacques Derrida, *Writing and Difference*, trans. Alan Bass (Chicago: University of Chicago Press, 1978).

[6]Essentialist feminism argues that the essence of women, their minds and bodies, offers a concrete material form that provides them with special talents and capabilities that make them well suited, even better suited, for political work than men, whose bodies and minds differ. It is woman as woman, her essential being, that makes the difference count in this way—i.e., women are born as well as made.

[7]For this argument, see Gayatri Chakravorty Spivak with Ellen Rooney, "In a Word. Interview," *differences* 1 (Summer 1989): 125–28.

[8]I refer to poststructuralism as a more narrow focused field within postmodernism. Poststructuralism emphasizes semiotics and develops from structuralist linguistics, as is manifest, for example, in the work of Roland Barthes. For a feminist analysis of poststructuralism, see Weedon, *Feminist Practice and Poststructuralist Theory*.

who differ, making misunderstandings both common and even creative. Developing from a semiotic explanation of language, poststructuralism emphasizes that meaning depends as much upon the listener as upon the speaker—as much on the reader as on the author.[9] Meaning takes place within a circuit of communication established between a speaker and a listener. This emphasis upon communication as interaction at the basic level of speech illuminates the interdependent nature of communication and shows that communication depends upon a "community of speakers" to stabilize its meaning system.[10] Hence, poststructuralism emphasizes both the static qualities of communication, which depend upon a given system of meanings, and the dynamic, creative aspects of speech by which new phrases, terms, and meanings are continually invented. These interacting dynamic and static qualities of communication give it both a stable code system and an innovative, transformative quality. As persons interact through speech, they both use and in some measure invent speech and language. Poststructuralism shows how communication takes place in the context of various systems or networks of meanings and languages. Not only are there various languages, of which English is one, but there are within those languages various discourses such as medical discourse, philosophical discourse, legal discourse, and so forth. The interactive nature of meaning suggests that to understand a discourse, one enters into that system in order to decode it and communicate with persons who utilize it.

To understand a different perspective may well require one to change to a different network of meanings. One might have to change the self to understand another, and such change is often accomplished only through struggle. Just as anthropologists find that they must change themselves in order to understand the cultures that they inhabit—to understand new points of view—readers must

[9]This is a point made from within a semiotic language theory that argues that communication depends on a circuit of communication created by an interaction between a speaker and a listener. The listener decodes the speaker's message through the language system. This theory develops from Ferdinand de Saussure's analysis of communication. For an analysis of the politics of this communication process, see Eloise A. Buker, *Politics through a Looking-Glass: Understanding Political Culture through a Structuralist Interpretation of Narratives* (Westport, Conn.: Greenwood Press, 1987), pp. 1–51.

[10]For an explanation of how community stabilizes meanings and interpretations, see Stanley Fish, "Normal Circumstances, Literal Language, Direct Speech Acts, the Ordinary, the Everyday, the Obvious, What Goes without Saying, and Other Special Cases," in *Interpretive Social Science: A Reader*, ed. Paul Rabinow and William M. Sullivan (Berkeley: University of California Press, 1979), pp. 243–66.

be ready to change themselves to understand a new cultural insight. The "jargon" label is often affixed to a text as an excuse for not struggling to understand a point of view that differs from one's own. The use of this label may represent an unwillingness to engage in a dialogue with those who talk that way. On the other hand, genuinely interested persons may be willing to forgo the jargon label and simply ask, What is meant? The claim that a discourse is "jargon"-filled is a general political claim designed to discredit it. It does not encourage a conversation.

But what can postmodernism say to such a challenge? How can it explain its difficult language? Does it refuse established ways of talking? Is it unable to speak in terms that are readily understood? Or is it simply delighted by its own strange new small-club talk? Because postmodernists locate political change in language, a new way of talking, a new language, seems required for a recontextualized politics. What they desire is unfolding possibilities. What they think possible is resistance[11] to the present order of things, the way things are, the reality, the BIG IS.[12] That resistance takes place in the form of linguistic changes that open up new ways of doing politics. Poststructuralism reminds us that the terms of the conversation are political and that to give way to another's discourse, whether it be legal, medical, religious, empirical, marxist, or whatever, is already to have conceded much of the argument. Hence, poststructuralists want to contend over definitions[13] and to contest verbal characterizations— even their own. These are not prepolitical struggles but struggles that are in themselves political.

Talking about talking is always difficult because one problematizes everything one is saying. Because we are used to taking language for granted and using it as a supposedly neutral tool, politicizing language and speech is unsettling. But language is both a vehicle for

[11]For an argument that supports feminism as a resistance strategy, see Teresa de Lauretis, *Technologies of Gender: Essays on Theory, Film, and Fiction* (Bloomington: Indiana University Press, 1987), and for a feminist critique of resistance strategy, see Laurel Richardson, "Resisting Resistance Narratives: A Representation for Communication," paper delivered at the Midwestern Sociological Society Meetings, Chicago, April 1990.

[12]The phrase the "BIG IS" is from Robert S. Cahill, who uses it to point out the political significance of taking our present ways of doing things and our present situations as the only way it ever could be. Lectures in Honolulu, Hawaii, University of Hawaii, 1977–1980, and discussions in Spokane, Washington, 1984–1990.

[13]For an argument about the importance of contesting definitions as a central political issue, see William E. Connolly, "The Politics of Discourse," in *Language and Politics,* ed. Michael J. Shapiro (New York: New York University Press, 1984), pp. 139–67.

communication and a medium for establishing political gains. If these political gains are realized, others may be lost, obliterated, forgotten, forced underground, silenced, killed. A contest over words is a political contest with severe consequences.[14] Once this premise is understood, the struggle that poststructuralism takes on is simultaneously being aware of its desire to communicate and acknowledging its own will to power and the violence that its own speech will do as it silences other discourses—other ways of talking, other ways of being. Such recognition is difficult and unpleasant.

For the most part those in power often find it easiest to dismiss their out-of-power opponents by dismissing the way they talk. The jargon label can function as the attempt of an established discourse to silence opposition to it by refusing to "listen" to a point of view differently articulated or formulated. This is politics at the basic linguistic level.

Relativism and Putting-Off Action

Postmodernism appears to put off or defer action because it tells us that we cannot rely upon reasoned knowledge as the basis for decisions; knowledge cannot tell us what to do. Critics reviewing the politics of this continuous deferment and its supporting epistemology—"relativism"—find encouragement in charges that characterize Michel Foucault and Jacques Derrida as young conservatives.[15] Jürgen Habermas suggests that postmodernism and premodernism form an alliance for a neoconservative politics.[16] The charge is political conservatism.

The emphasis upon discourse and the problem of interpretation includes an epistemological struggle with the issue of relativism. Sandra Harding articulates this charge from a feminist scientific point of

[14]For commentaries on the violence of language, see Jacques Derrida, "Violence and Metaphysics: An Essay on the Thought of Emmanuel Levinas," pp. 79–153, and "The Theater of Cruelty and the Closure of Representation," pp. 232–50, both in *Writing and Difference*. For a feminist examination of the violence of language, see Dale Spender, *Man Made Language*, 2d ed. (Boston: Routledge & Kegan Paul, 1985).

[15]For a summary of this argument as it relates to postmodern philosophy, see Andreas Huyssen, "Mapping the Postmodern," in *Feminism/Postmodernism*, ed. Linda J. Nicholson (New York: Routledge, 1990), pp. 252–55.

[16]Jürgen Habermas, "Modernity—An Incomplete Project," originally delivered as a lecture in Frankfurt, September 1980, when Habermas was awarded the Theodor W. Adorno prize, trans. Seyla Ben-Habib; reprinted in *Interpretive Social Science: A Second Look*, ed. Rabinow and Sullivan, pp. 141–56 (see esp. p. 156).

view by reminding her readers that women are especially vulnerable to the political effects of charges connected with relativism: "When women appeal to their interpretations of evidence,instead of this appeal having the meaning 'this is a good (or plausible, justifiable, reasonable) interpretation,' it asserts only that 'this is just my interpretation.'"[17] Women have been too often accused of constructing intellectual arguments on the basis of their feelings or intuition. Harding is hesitant to give up the rhetoric of objectivity and to accept the postmodern feminist position that places so much emphasis upon the partiality of its view, the limits of its vision, and the politics of its foundation, even though she acknowledges the partiality of all viewpoints.[18] She desires a nonviolent, fair, inclusive new science and hopes that feminist scientists will help move us in that direction. She holds onto the insights of empiricism and the possibility of an objectivity that can confront the problem of relativism.[19] And she is unwilling to give up falsification even though she rejects the ideological construct of science as the one true story. She uses Thomas Kuhn to fortify her commitment to falsification as an epistemological anchor.[20]

Donna Haraway, a biologist, is willing to embrace a postmodern epistemology. In *Primate Visions,* using the story metaphor especially in terms of science fiction, she affirms partiality and exclusivity as constitutive elements of the new evolving postmodern science but acknowledges that its motivating energy is political:

> My contention is that the intersection—coupled with other aspects of the "decolonization of nature" that have restructured the discourses of biology and anthropology, as well as other practices of international politics—destabilizes the narrative fields that gave rise to both primatology and feminism, thereby generating the possibility of new stories not strangled by the same logics of appropriation and domination, but also not innocent of the workings of power and desire, including new exclusions.[21]

[17]Sandra Harding, "Feminism, Science and the Anti-Enlightenment Critiques," *Feminism/Postmodernism,* ed. Nicholson, p. 88.

[18]Sandra Harding, *The Science Question in Feminism* (Ithaca: Cornell University Press, 1986).

[19]Ibid., pp. 137–38.

[20]Harding, "Feminism, Science and the Anti-Enlightenment Critiques," pp. 99–100. Her rejection of science as one true story is a theme in Harding, *The Science Question in Feminism.*

[21]Donna Haraway, *Primate Visions: Gender, Race, and Nature in the World of Modern Science* (New York: Routledge, 1989), p. 288.

For her a contextualized notion of truth which abandons absolute subjectivity and absolute objectivity is in some sense relative; it is relative to a particular historical, cultural, linguistic context that sets the human imagination into motion. In this sense it cannot claim to tell the grand narrative that captures all other stories.[22]

Claiming that truth is contextualized does not mean that truth is arbitrary and that anything goes. Our historical, cultural, and even biological and natural environmental contexts limit our interpretations and meaning systems; the context, though variable, constrains them; anything does not go. Certain stories *make* "sense" and produce meaningful commentaries—certain stories convey meanings that matter. Others do not, and they are cast aside; we do not give them much of a hearing, or we may sanction the storyteller. It is the task of each reader and community of readers to sort out the differences between the two, a judgment that is itself one of the most political ones we make. This requires an openness to other points of view so as not to disregard stories simply because they are irritating, and it requires us to accept the fact that we may disregard some important, maybe even vital, stories.

Haraway considers her work "simultaneously political theory, science fiction, and sound scholarship."[23] Her goal is not to displace one story with a better one; it is to hear the stories that we are currently telling one another—those that do make sense to us—especially in terms that focus on race and gender as they are constructed through discussions of nature and culture. She hopes that by retelling these stories, she might help develop "new possibilities for the meanings of difference, reproduction, and survival for specifically located members of the primate order—on both sides of the bio-political and cultural divide between human and animal."[24] She claims not to be "policing the boundaries" but instead to be creating traffic between them.[25]

What her story tells us minimally is that she can write 383 pages of very convincing prose while holding to her position as a relativist. It has not paralyzed her, nor has it kept her from making decisions

---

[22]For a feminist critique of the "metanarrative" and "grand social theories," see Nancy Fraser and Linda Nicholson, "Social Criticism without Philosophy: An Encounter between Feminism and Postmodernism," in *Feminism/Postmodernism*, ed. Nicholson, pp. 19–38.

[23]Donna Haraway, "Primatology Is Politics by Other Means," in *Feminist Approaches to Science*, ed. Ruth Bleier (New York: Pergamon Press, 1988), pp. 81–82.

[24]Haraway, *Primate Visions*, p. 377.

[25]Ibid.

about what she will say. Embracing contradictions has not depoliticized her; she is not prevented from making choices; nor has she become unreflective about her choices. What one can see upon reflection is that, just possibly, the world is so arranged that one can and must act. We are intricately woven into the social political fabric of life even if we do not chose to be there. Hence, even inaction constitutes a political act that has consequences.

It is only when we place ourselves in the position of requiring that universal reason rule us and that certainty serve as the foundation for political action that we find contextualized truth paralyzing. Those who charge postmodernism with relativism may be searching for a position in which reason would rescue us from uncertainty and provide us with clear unambiguous paths toward the good and just society. Such certainty would avoid politics, technicalize problems, and remove us from social struggles and negotiations. It would provide us with one aspect of the liberal dream—a world that maximizes our private lives and relieves us from civic responsibilities. By contextualizing truth, we remind ourselves that our communities must continually figure out what to do by struggling to understand situations; we cannot simply turn ourself over to Reason.

If we are able to reflect upon the ways in which all our actions involve some knowledge in the face of a great deal of ignorance, then we will no longer dream of certainty, and maybe we can bear the postmodern tale of contextualized knowledge. In fact, we may well find it liberating because we do not have to find our security in the pretense that we have found *THE* universal laws. We can figure out what we think best in our own limited worlds. We will not defer our decisions until we know for sure what to do since we will understand that we always act in the midst of both our knowledge and our ignorance. Putting-off politics is not possible. Politics is in what we do here and now and what we do *not* do here and now. In this sense deferral is not possible, for deferring action itself articulates a position on the truth of a situation.

Lost Subjects and the Politics of the Center

Deconstructing identity, postmodernism threatens to erase the self as the speaker, the author as the writer, and the individual as an autonomous integrated person. Postmodernists ask us to cease thinking of ourselves as having identities and to begin understanding ourselves as sites for competing cultural interpretations. Our utterances are not our own; instead, our language speaks us, and we are merely mouthing the grammars that we have learned. Our actions are set up for us by a culture that shapes us. In this sense, postmoderns decenter the subject and appear to erase the individual as an agent of his or her action. The grammar makes us speak in a certain way and our cultural habits design "our" actions. The charge is decentering the subject and obliterating human agency.

Not only does postmodernism see fit to emphasize the contingent nature of our understandings of our social situations, whose complexities are subject to a variety of interpretations, but it emphasizes the contingent dimensions of our very selves—our identities are not totally the product of our own invention. The categories that we use to describe ourselves—male, female, black, middle-class, marxist, Irish, perverse, kind, teacher, attorney—all are the social constructs of a particular historical culture. They are not things that we are by nature or that we create through our own raw uncontextualized imagination; we are those things because they are among the things that one can be within a given culture. Some identities have been historically made to disappear, and it is likely that those very identities that we put on or that are put on us will someday be gone, although we will probably always be obliged to find near cultural-historical equivalents.

Beginning with the deemphasis of the author as author(ity) over the text, the postmoderns have moved to the argument that the very subject of ourselves is a cultural product. There is no essence that we are, but instead our identity is a cultural complex whose stability depends upon the politics of its environment. Another time, another place, we will "be" something else. Nancy Hartsock points out that it seems quite curious that just at the time when women are finding themselves and becoming subjects, that "subject" itself is under attack.[26] This decentering of the subject is obviously a problem for feminists. Chris Weedon argues that although the time for the deconstruction of the male subject may be at hand, the time for decentering the female subject may not be. What Weedon does not say is that it may not be possible to decenter the female subject because she has not yet been fully centered.[27]

Weedon argues that feminists need to emphasize a different aspect of postmodernism from that emphasized by men in order to success-

[26]Nancy Hartsock, "Foucault on Power: A Theory for Women?" in *Feminism/Postmodernism*, ed. Nicholson, pp. 157-75.
[27]For this critical comment I thank Mary Jo Bona.

fully use postmodernism for feminist political projects.[28] Gayatri Chakravorty Spivak makes an important point in relationship to the political limits of deconstruction, and perhaps it will prove to hold true more generally for postmodernism. As she puts it:

> You cannot *decide* to *be* decentered and inaugurate a politically correct deconstructive politics. What deconstruction looks at is the limits of this centering, and points at the fact that these boundaries of the centering of the subject are indeterminate and that the subject (being always centered) is obliged to describe them as determinate. Politically, all this does is not allow for fundamentalisms and totalitarianisms of various kinds, however seemingly benevolent.[29]

She goes on to say that if deconstruction were to be used as a foundation for politics, it would be either "wishy-washy" pluralism or hedonism.[30] Politics requires a different basis. For American postmodern feminists, politics begins with struggles to deconstruct racism and sexism in order to construct just practices that enable a polity to grant full citizenship to women and people of color. An important site for that struggle is in our linguistic practices—stories, films, philosophies, news accounts, social theories, research reports, conversations. Postmodern feminists are activists engaged in politics, scholars engaged in analysis, and the subjects of their own self-critical reflections. To the degree that they are able to engage all three of these activities, they find themselves involved in a politics that goes beyond wishy-washy pluralism and self-centered hedonism.

Other post modern feminists give a different turn to the problem of the decentered self.[31] Judith Butler offers this explanation of the decentered subject: "The deconstruction of identity is not the deconstruction of politics; rather, it establishes as political the very terms through which identity is articulated."[32] Butler wants her reader to

---

[28]Weedon, *Feminist Practice and Poststructuralist Theory*, p. 173.

[29]Gayatri Chakravorty Spivak, *The Post-Colonial Critic: Interviews, Strategies, Dialogues*, ed. Sarah Harasym (New York: Routledge, 1990), p. 104.

[30]Ibid.

[31]Susan Hekman, wishing to move feminists toward the postmodern position, argues that the postmoderns do not simply replace the subject with the culturally determined "dupe." She explains that the postmodern position challenges "the subject-centeredness of modernist epistemology." Susan Hekman, "Reconstituting the Subject: Feminism, Modernism and Postmodernism," paper delivered at the American Political Science Association Meeting, Atlanta, 1989, p. 7.

[32]Judith Butler, *Gender Trouble: Feminism and the Subversion of Identity* (New York: Routledge, 1990), p. 148.

understand that identities can be constructed in and through the work of coalition politics rather than simply established as a condition for beginning such work. In her analysis, *fixed* identities—established as *essential* characteristics of persons—cripple political processes and unnecessarily limit the activities of what we refer to as political coalitions. She argues that we acquire our identities through our actions, our deeds: "My argument is that there need not be a 'doer behind the deed,' but that the 'doer' is variably constructed in and through the deed."[33] In her analysis it is not that postmodernism eliminates subjects and agency, but rather that it makes way for us to develop ourselves continually as various subjects and agents depending upon the actions in which we involve ourselves. But it is important to note that this is not a return to the old liberal romantic view that we are "self-made men" or even "self-made women." The subject is not solely the product of her or his own doing but is a part of the collective action of a community whose members recognize a certain aspect of themselves that emerges in the process of acting politically. Identity, subjecthood, being, emerges in action. A different sort of action constitutes a different "subject"—or more precisely, a different collection of subjects to "be."

Put-Ons

Feminist postmodern writers offer some surprising metaphors for us to try on in order to construct political understandings.

Hybrid Selves: Cyborgs, Animals, and Genders in Drag

Donna Haraway claims the cyborg[34] as her/our personal identity myth. She explains that her evocation of the cyborg myth is to speak about "transgressed boundaries, potent fusions, and dangerous possibilities"[35] as political work:

Cyborg imagery can suggest a way out of the maze of dualisms in which we have explained our bodies and our tools to ourselves. This is a dream not of a common language, but of a powerful infidel heteroglossia. It is

[33]Ibid., p. 142.
[34]A cyborg is a being who is both human and machine.
[35]Donna Haraway, "A Manifesto for Cyborgs: Science, Technology, and Socialist Feminism in the 1980s," in *Feminism/Postmodernism*, ed. Nicholson, p. 196.

an imagination of a feminist speaking in tongues to strike fear into the circuits of the super savers of the New Right. It means both building and destroying machines, identities, categories, relationships, spaces, stories. Although both are bound in the spiral dance, I would rather be a cyborg than a goddess.[36]

The human/machine boundary is crossed.

In another context a different but perhaps equally strange dream emerges from Haraway's text:

Indeed, I have always preferred the prospect of pregnancy with the embryo of another species; and I read this "gender"-transgressing desire in primatology's text, from the Teddy Bear Patriarchs' labor to be the father of the game, through *Primate Societies'* developmental-evolutionary narrative fragment about a heterogeneous sibling group of "almost minds."[37]

The animal/human boundary is violated.

Judith Butler, too, offers feminists a surprising new image as she explains how the power of parody and irony evoked by such images as drag or cross-dressing subverts domination politics: "I would suggest as well that drag fully subverts the distinction between inner and outer psychic space and effectively mocks both the expressive model of gender and the notion of a true gender identity."[38] The inner/outer distinction is subverted and genders are confused.

These passages go beyond reminding us that our identities are a result of the social construction of a political order. They point out that the language and cultural practices of our societies constrain the choices that serve as the basis for that construction work; they move toward deconstructing the distinctions that undergird those constraints.

At this point a central constraint that postmodern feminists illuminate is the construction of "woman" and "gender." The postmoderns bring a new interpretation to Simone de Beauvoir's insightful phrase, "One is not born, but rather becomes, a woman."[39] Moving on from this phrase to the general issue of how it may be that we

[36]Ibid., p. 223.
[37]Haraway, *Primate Visions*, p. 377.
[38]Butler, *Gender Trouble*, p. 137.
[39]Simone de Beauvoir, *The Second Sex* (New York: Vintage Press, 1973), p. 301.

choose to become a "woman," Judith Butler explores the intersection between cultural codes and individual choice.[40]

In *Gender Trouble* Butler shows how costly it is not to inhabit a gender classification; but more important, she shows the politics that have been created by the way in which feminists have constructed the sex/gender system as a distinction between biology (sex) and culture (gender). She wants us to see how the figure in drag mocks this distinction between culturally gendered subjects and anatomically sexed persons, the male anatomy dressed up in the culture of the female. At the same time she wants us to realize that the person in drag may well be a feminine person "masquerading" in a male body. Thus Butler questions the fixed order of things created by liberal feminists' faith in their ability to use anatomy or, even more narrowly, genital configuration to determine sex. Retelling Foucault's story of the hermaphrodite Herculine Barbin, Butler illuminates the serious problems that occur when a person's gender/sex cannot be designated within our dichotomous system.[41] Male/female ambiguity is difficult for us to tolerate. Only the comic fool, the drag figure, can get away with it.[42]

Does this taboo shed some light on the nasty comments made by both men and women to feminists—such as "They look like men; they act like men; they must be unsexed women; they advocate unisex (or merely unisex bathrooms) or they have butch haircuts"? Is this policing the sex-gender boundary done to protect male political privilege? Or is it an insecure man who fears that his male existence will be wiped out if he is not constantly participating in a performance in which he plays the male role to his female counterpart's feminine role? Is it likewise an insecure woman who needs a masculine counter. Or do women fear men's reprisal if they should even hint at cross-dressing or crossing over?

Would our world be politically different if we considered sex/gender a continuum, with the macho male at one end and the ultrafeminine woman at the other? In what ways do we make choices to dress

[40]Judith Butler, "Variations on Sex and Gender: Beauvoir, Wittig, and Foucault," *Praxis International* 5 (January 1986): 505–16.

[41]Butler, *Gender Trouble*, pp. 96–111.

[42]An important political aspect of this is the point made by Robert S. Cahill, who explains that the fool gets away with it because she or he agrees to eschew power. Discussion: Existentialism, Phenomenology, and Hermeneutics Conference, North Bend, Washington, Spring 1987.

ourselves up each day as male or female,[43] to perform as males or females? Have we as men learned how to be professional males; have we as women learned to be professional females? What happens when we cross over, and what counts as a cross-over? What does it mean to us to break this boundary, and what does this tell us about our political choices and how we have constructed and constrained ourselves through them?

Postmodern feminists not only raise questions about the way in which we have constructed "woman" in feminist as well as other discourses, but they enable us to see the ways in which our bodies serve both as sites for political performances[44] and as the medium through which we create political performances. For an interpretation of the body as the site for political performance one can turn to Michel Foucault, who, in *Discipline and Punish*, traces the history of the body as a site for cultural practices that focus on mechanisms for control.[45] While professional stage actors are used to talking about their bodies as part of their tool kit, perhaps we might all see our own bodies as a medium for action.[46] Judith Butler puts this succinctly:

> The choice to assume a certain kind of body, to live or wear one's body a certain way, implies a world of already established corporeal styles. To choose a gender is to interpret received gender norms in a way that reproduces and organizes them anew. Less a radical act of creation, gender is a tacit project to renew a cultural history in one's own corporeal terms.[47]

An insightful feminist analysis of the link between the female body

[43]This image of dressing ourselves each day as male or female comes from Phyllis Turnbull, Lecture and discussion, Honolulu, 1979.

[44]In this sense, the body is an object with which various political points are made. It is a staging ground. For example, decapitation during the French Revolution emphasized the central role of reason in governing the body and reminded citizens that if they did not govern their bodies well, then they would find themselves forever fragmented.

[45]Michel Foucault, *Discipline and Punish*, trans. A. Sheridan (New York: Vintage Press, 1977).

[46]At this point it is important to note that I am not talking about stage acting as a pretense at being something one is not. Rather, I am talking about stage acting as a performance in which the individual actor brings before the audience an interpretation of his or her individual everyday self as it merges with the self that the actor has been assigned to play in the story line of the drama. Always present on stage are at minimum both selves, the role in the play and the everyday person of the actor. It is the tension between these two selves that makes a play work. This observation about drama is articulated especially well in the work of director Eugene Lion in Montreal.

[47]Butler, "Variations on Sex and Gender," p. 508.

and communication symbols in western culture is provided by Susan Rubin Suleiman in "(Re)Writing the Body: The Politics and Poetics of Female Eroticism."[48] Examination of the ways in which the body is the object of our gaze as well as a medium of communication can be found in feminist semiotic analyses.[49]

Everyday experiences suggest some of the ways this works politically. Women often experience the fact that the presence of their bodies in a room makes a difference in the conversation—changing the postures of other bodies in the room, the ways in which hostility and friendship are expressed, the pronouns in use, and so forth. This is also true for male bodies, but because we have accepted the male body as normative and within that standard there has been a focus on mind over body, we have often failed to take note of the ways in which the body serves as both a metaphor for life and as an image for constructing a political language that serves as a subtext in many discourses. The male body of the warrior and his political stance suggests one way in which male bodies have changed the general conversations we have about courage, valor, and patriotism. The talking heads of the three national television evening news anchors serve as another in that they emphasize "man" as the "head" of the family among other things he heads. This head shot emphasizes the ways in which "he" is rational and belongs at the head of the flow of information that comes into our family homes.

The Body as Message

The body is a billboard on which we write messages about who we are as a culture as well as who we are as individuals. If those messages are critical of dominant norms, we take note—and approve or disapprove of the long hair, jeans, or buttons. If the messages are more ordinary, we may fail to notice how they, too, serve as billboards, selling particular cultural values. Business suits, ties, oxfords can go unnoticed unless they appear in an unusual context (such as at the beach) or on a differently gendered body (such as a female). It is important to realize that we do not totally make up the message

[48]Susan Rubin Suleiman, "(Re)Writing the Body: The Politics and Poetics of Female Eroticism," in *The Female Body in Western Culture: Contemporary Perspectives*, ed. Susan Rubin Suleiman (Cambridge: Harvard University Press, 1985), pp. 7-29.

[49]See, e.g., Laura Mulvey, *Visual and Other Pleasures* (Bloomington: Indiana University Press, 1989); and Mary Ann Doane, *The Desire to Desire: The Woman's Film of the 1940s* (Bloomington: Indiana University Press, 1987).

code; the codes are already given to us through cultural practices. Although we can innovate to some small degree, we rely upon a set of styles that we can mix and match to compose ourselves.[50]

There are clear limits in this code, and a central limitation is the dichotomous male/female sex-gender system that presents itself as a set of taboos. Males and females each have their own code; they cannot use the other's code. Catalogs, sizing, department store space arrangements—all carefully separate male things from female things so we will not become "con-fused." Although a few items are unisex, they are identified as such and serve only as an infrequent reminder that we need primarily to stay in our correct category—male or female. However, what we sometimes like to do when we take delight in doing politics is to test the boundaries to see how we can bend the styles to our own imaginations. What we fear is that, taking it too far, we will be seen as "far out" and suffer political, social, and economic consequences for challenging the taboo, breaking the rules. Our sex-gender identities are deeply held and yet fragilely constructed. We fear any infraction of the rules will break up our sex-gender system.

Breaking the Taboo of "Two Genders Only"

What postmodern feminist texts do is ask us to reflect on our gender-sex boundary—our distinctions between men and women, male and female, masculine and feminine—and consider in what ways those distinctions are silly, tenuous, fragile, permeable, harmful, helpful, or limiting. This does not mean that what postmodern feminists really want is to eliminate the distinction between males and females; it would be more accurate to say that what postmodern feminists want to do is multiply the number of genders available to us. But this in turn does not mean that we will find ourselves one day in a utopian society freed of such gender-sex limitations, for even to speak is to articulate a boundary. Words are based on divisions among things; we cannot speak all things at once; or even all words at once; every utterance is the utterance of a boundary that for the moment we have taken as given—as part of the BIG IS. What these

---

[50]Roland Barthes used fashion as a way of studying codes and exploring semiotics, as a form of cultural analysis. See Roland Barthes, *The Fashion System*, trans. Matthew Ward and Richard Howard (New York: Hill and Wang, 1983). For commentary on composing the self and politics, see the work of Henry S. Kariel.

feminists offer us is a strategy that will liberate us from a worshipful orientation toward our socially constructed sex-gender identities so that we might inhabit them more contingently and look upon others who break these boundaries with interest rather than with horror.[51]

This playing with boundaries is reminiscent of Robert Frost's ironic poem "Mending Wall," in which the naive neighbor says to the poet, "Good fences make good neighbors."[52] Of course, without some sort of boundary, fence, we have no such thing as a neighbor; we would all be considered one. But if we're going to "get through it," then our fences need to have occasional holes in them. And we need to see our fences as both problem and solution; walling things out, we wall ourselves in.

A central part of the postmodern feminist's task is to help us reexamine who and what we have fenced in and who and what we have fenced out. In American politics the ways in which we have used race, gender, sexual orientation, and class, among other categories, have created severe problems in which "we" have become fractured and injustices have been perpetrated. We need to reexamine these race and gender boundaries in particular, not to obliterate distinctions—which usually results in our all trying to fit into the white male model—but to embrace the diversities that "we" are. We need to be ready to put on new categories, new identities, as our political work opens up new possibilities for our selves to embody.

Political Plays and Stories

In three different ways the image of play is helpful for considering the politics of postmodern feminism. First, the drama analogy helps us to gain new insight into how we are all actors in our social political situations. Second, it helps us develop images of ourselves as persons engaged in serious play—spontaneously responding and re-creating our environment, not by building eternal structures, but by constructing temporary ones to solve immediate local difficulties. The play analogy can help us to become more aware of our own contingent

---

[51]Please note that although feminist arguments have made a distinction between "sex," which refers to biological phenomena, and "gender," which refers to sociological phenomena, postmodern feminists challenge this distinction inasmuch as our understanding of biology itself is constructed within a particular language-culture matrix.

[52]Robert Frost, "Mending Wall," in *The Poetry of Robert Frost*, ed. Edward Connery Lathem (New York: Holt, Rinehart and Winston, 1975), pp. 33–34.

existence by reminding us how delightful it is to interact with others who are able to surprise us into new ways of being. Third, if we become more aware of the play of difference that constructs our world, we may be able to resist reducing ourselves and others to a single unitary being; we may be better equipped to value the differences that we ourselves embody as individuals as well as the differences that others present to us. A politics built upon this play of difference promises to free us from our mean-spirited "tolerance" of others.[53]

Actors on Stage

The image of play reminds us of the ways in which all of us are in a story—players on a stage, acting out our various parts as we interpret the drama. By calling upon the play metaphor for politics to displace the game metaphor, we can deemphasize the ways in which we as individuals struggle against each other to gain our ends and emphasize the ways in which we cooperate to produce a life world; it is not one free of tension but it is one that presents a collective unified action. Plays work only when all the players work together. However, this does not mean that this life world is mere fantasy, the product of only our imagination. The play we are in counts; it is our life. We cannot take the story line and turn it anyway we choose, because others are present—including those who told the story before we came on stage. And we need to be mindful that the play goes on after our exit. Other actors will shape the tale; they are partially beyond our control. If we do not respect the limits this presents to us, it will not work.

This contingent nature of our existence might be articulated in the postmodern moral: We are not ever all that we can be, but we are always already something. Parts are in some degree assigned and fixed. The moment of our being, whenever that might be, is filled with cultural norms, articulated through a web of symbols. There are some freedoms and inventive features in our own parts; there are some restrictions and limitations. Not all stunts are do-able; our bodies and other bodies limit us. Not all stages are as technologically

---

[53]For an example of such a politics, see Iris Marion Young, "The Ideal of Community and the Politics of Difference," in *Feminism/Postmodernism*, ed. Nicholson, pp. 300–323, and Iris Marion Young, *Justice and the Politics of Difference* (Princeton: Princeton University Press, 1990).

equipped as we would like. Some of us may even be forced to revise our scripts without benefit of word processors.

Thinking as Serious Play

The play image is also helpful in understanding the politics of postmodern feminism insofar as it emphasizes the ways in which we are trying out new ideas and spontaneously responding to our environment. There is an innocence—even ignorance—involved in our experiments, and there is a way in which we are not in control of them. Work has come to represent such a serious and controlled endeavor. Perhaps our work is like play in that it is not predetermined; it is often the surprises that enable us to move ahead or take a delightful turn.

Haraway argues that our politics needs to make more use of irony and humor—"serious play."[54] Haraway cautions that we should not take our stories so seriously as to think that they are the very best ones—the only stories worth hearing.[55] The feminist critique of the canon has also included a feminist self-critique; there are to be no sacred tales for all persons for all cultures, even if for a time we are nearly totally enchanted by certain tales. Our attitude toward our philosophical work might be enriched by seeing ourselves as more involved in comedy than in tragedy. Maybe Shakespeare's tragic-comedies, for example *The Winter's Tale* or *The Tempest,* and ntozake shange's choreopoem, *for colored girls who have considered suicide/when the rainbow is enuf,*[56] articulate the spirit of this serious play. Postmodern feminists neither enthusiastically celebrate a prepatriarchal society nor look toward a postgender society. Rejecting the radical dream of an earlier matriarchal society, rejecting the liberal dream of continuous progress, rejecting the Marxist hope for the classless totally egalitarian society, and setting aside Adrienne Rich's "dream of a common language," postmodern feminists focus on local strategies.[57]

Reminding us that anthropologists have recently extended their local cultural focus to include urban areas of the United States, they point out that we are always already in a field. This is true in both

[54]Haraway, "Manifesto for Cyborgs," p. 190.

[55]Haraway, *Primate Visions,* pp. 303, 377–83.

[56]ntozake shange, *for colored girls who have considered suicide/when the rainbow is enuf* (New York: Macmillan, 1977).

[57]Butler, *Gender Trouble,* p. 149, and Elspeth Probyn, "Travels in the Postmodern: Making Sense of the Local," in *Feminism/Postmodernism,* ed. Nicholson, pp. 176–89.

senses of the word—in the sense of a particular disciplined way of thinking and in the sense that we are located in some particular geographic and cultural area.[58]

For example, Trinh T. Minh-ha illustrates the power of locale, place. She shows how our local native place travels with us even as we travel to new locales. She tells her life story, presenting it in written postmodern philosophical form in her book, *Woman, Native, Other,*[59] and in cinematic form in *Surname Viet Given Name Nam.*[60] We inhabit places as they inhabit us. The differences between the informant and the native is a difference within each of us. Depending on context, we play both native and informant.

The Play of Difference

The phrase "play of difference" and its multiplicity of meanings in our contemporary conversations have been brought to our attention in part through the work of Jacques Derrida.[61] The play of difference suggests the way in which words take on meanings through their similarities and differences within a language. The system of associations within a language is a web that prevents us from fixing a single meaning and avoiding ambiguity. In addition, it reminds us that every word we speak presents some difference that we want to speak about. At a philosophical level it explains how western thought has connected difference and deference. It suggests that when we are politically confronted with persons who differ from us, our choices involve strategies of deferring—*putting off action* (delay), *putting others down* (forcing them to defer to us), or *putting up with others* (deferring to them in some measure while holding on to our own arrogant toleration). In this case the language of difference introduces a win-lose game in which politics is a set of temporary compromises and coalitions built upon necessity rather than on community.

[58]For this field metaphor and its multiple meanings, see Haraway, "Primatology Is Politics by Other Means," pp. 81–89, and Haraway, *Primate Visions,* pp. 13–15, 279–303, 382.

[59]Trinh T. Minh-ha, *Woman, Native, Other: Writing Postcoloniality and Feminism* (Bloomington: Indian University Press, 1989).

[60]Trinh T. Minh-ha, *Surname Viet Given Name Nam,* produced, written, edited, and directed by Trinh T. Minh-ha, 1989.

[61]Jacques Derrida, *Margins of Philosophy,* trans. Alan Bass (Chicago: University of Chicago Press, 1982), pp. 1–28, and *Positions,* trans. Alan Bass (Chicago: University of Chicago Press, 1981), pp. 39–49; for commentary on Derrida's use of the term, see Jonathan Culler, *On Deconstruction: Theory and Criticism after Structuralism* (Ithaca: Cornell University Press, 1982), pp. 97–102.

If read more bluntly in the American feminist context, the phrase "play of difference" tells us something about the politics of the word "woman." "Woman" is a word constituted in terms of how it differs from "man," who turns out to be the standard human. The story often told about our work in western philosophy is that it is the study of "man," and the tales we tell about politics include an emphasis on political man. We put off studying women; we defer to the "normal" view and study men, male persons. Deferring and difference go together in ways that have important political consequences in liberal democratic societies because of their historic emphasis on unity and their allocation of secondary status to multiplicity. While pluralism is important, a strong central single organizing energy field has been even more important. We appear to "need" a state with a strong central power force; we "need" a "Supreme" Court; we label some rebellions "civil" wars and celebrate the victory of the union as a "national" event for all citizens, even those who lost the "civil" war. We appear to want an ideology that emphasizes the "melting pot" as the primary metaphor for our national response to immigrants since 1776.[62] What postmodernism offers, among other things, is recognition of the contradiction involved in our commitments to pluralism and to unity—a nationalism built upon a single unitary culture. That culture becomes so normative that it loses its cultural character and becomes *the* norm, the preferred or even only way of being fully human.[63]

This emphasis on difference requires either a new understanding of pluralism within liberalism or a transformation of liberalism into a new political theory that takes account of difference differently. First of all, from a feminist perspective liberalism has not yet been able to articulate a politics that is genuinely plural. It depends upon women's lack of participation and dedication to the private realm. Under

[62]For a discussion of this metaphor as a symbol of regeneration in the U.S. context, see Werner Sollers, *Beyond Ethnicity: Consent and Descent in America* (New York: Oxford University Press, 1986), pp. 66–101; and for an analysis of the politics of violence that regeneration elicits in the U.S. mythic story, see Richard Slotkin, *Regeneration through Violence: The Mythology of the American Frontier, 1600–1860* (Middletown, Conn.: Wesleyan University Press, 1973).

[63]Attempts to enforce a single English-language system within the United States are attempts to create this single culture out of the multiplicity of cultures that we are. Comments that "white" Americans make about themselves as well as the comments made about them often indicate a lack of awareness of the fact that white America represents a Euro-American culture. Americans often fail to notice that hamburgers, pot roast, pasta, and french fries *are* ethnic foods.

liberalism in the United States women have been excluded from politics. Only within the past seventy years have they won even the right to vote, so before 1920, in effect, the majority of U.S. citizens could not vote. That is hardly a case of pluralist politics. Furthermore, a politics of difference developed from postmodernism would not treat difference as a problem but as part of the promise for a continually changing politics. Liberalism fears difference and drives us toward unity, but that unity is based on the notion that our differences will be protected in the private sphere where we make the moral choices that count. An account of difference based upon postmodern thought would suggest that difference enables us to make public our differences without relegating some persons and some differences to positions of inferiority. It suggests that when one confronts another who is different, it is not so much as an opportunity for debate and deliberation as it is an opportunity for opening oneself up to play that promises transformation of the very self that we are. This fundamental transformation is very different from the model of compromise that is privileged in present interpretations of liberalism. This new account of difference argues that encounters with others are opportunities for consciousness transformation. In such situations, both individually and collectively, we can play out new parts of ourselves.

One political turn we might take is to celebrate some of those differences—cultural differences, gender-sex differences—rather than attempt to subvert, deny, annihilate or, as the saying goes, assimilate them. What this suggests is that ethnic differences, gender differences (however many there may be) strengthen societies. But they strengthen us as we allow them continually to change, to reorganize their cultural significances and to evolve. For example, our native American artists do not need to limit themselves to bead work or to themes that whites associate with eighteenth- and nineteenth-century Indian experiences. This focus on difference permits us to foreground multiplicity and to background unity.[64] Butler argues that if we are better able to see ourselves as developing our identities (however temporary they may be) in the process of doing politics, we would find coalition politics more open and enriching.[65]

Second, postmodern feminism suggests that we need not find a single unitary, homogeneous (homogenized) thing to be. For exam-

[64]It is important to note that unity, in this case, would not be obliterated. This is a matter of emphasis, not a matter of making dichotomous and mutually exclusive choices.

[65]Butler, *Gender Trouble*, pp. 15–16, 142–49.

ple, a black woman does not have to choose to present herself as either a black, a woman, or as a black woman; she can simultaneously present herself as all three and more. We might not have to choose even among apparently mutually exclusive categories such as male/ female. The quest for a single unified self might be a dangerous quest because it asks us to submerge possible identities in ourselves and deny contradictions that we embody. A view toward the construction of a multiplicity of identities might liberate parts of ourselves that we dared not voice.

This is not to argue that all selves should come forward. Some aspects of ourselves should be controlled, limited, subverted, and even perhaps eradicated; certainly the racist, sexist, homophobic aspects of ourselves as well as of our culture need to be undone. There are judgments to be made about the ethics of the parts we choose to bring forth. What is being suggested here is not a loose and free play of difference without restraints, but more recognition of the play of difference as a vitalizing force for political work, especially feminist political work.[66]

Postmodern feminists have let go of the old images of "grounding" and "foundation" as central images for theory "building." Buildings appear to us as fixed and static objects; they do not move and they take up a single space. Within this image our theories appear to be at odds with each other, overlapping, contending for spaces, and toppling one another. So the story metaphor appears now to be more able to articulate what most concerns feminist theorists. Postmodern feminists explain that they are telling a story about the world[67] in hopes of opening us up to the play of difference.[68]

After-Thoughts

Postmodern feminist thought draws attention to the politics of language, speech, and symbol-making. Western culture has certainly

[66]For an application of this play of difference in feminist political theory, see Young, "The Ideal of Community and the Politics of Difference," and Young, *Justice and the Politics of Difference.*

[67]Storytelling as a key image for theorizing can be found in Harding, *The Science Question in Feminism;* Carole Pateman, *The Sexual Contract* (Stanford: Stanford University Press, 1988); Haraway, *Primate Visions,* as well as in other feminist works.

[68]This is a theme in Haraway, *Primate Visions,* and Iris Young repeats this phrase from Fred Dallmayr in discussing the ways by which we might speak about a radical political theory that avoids the racism, sexism, xenophobia, homophobia, and other negative practices that prevent us from forming a just polity. "The Ideal of Community and the Politics of Difference," p. 320.

created political injustices for women through its symbolic realities. Postmodern feminist thought problematizes even how feminists constitute "woman" and critically examines theories of identity that endeavor to turn "us" into the "one true being." It invites citizens to find multiple identities in themselves and through actions with others, including a multiplicity of genders—not just two.

In doing this it argues for a praxis model that shows how genuine knowledge emerges only after we act upon our theories. This attention to language and the accompanying emphasis on how language is political may put us off because it politicizes our everyday discourse. However, it reveals that we have plentiful opportunities for political action in the everyday interactions that compose our lives. There is no need to wait for new national laws or new economic structures before we act politically. We do not have to defer action. We can do it here and now in the words we speak or fail to speak.

At the same time, postmodern feminists emphasize that our choices are limited by our cultural situations and the identities that those situations invent. An advantage for feminists is that, unlike their nonfeminist counterparts, they have already realized how much their "subjecthood" is invisible, denigrated, and culturally constrained.

Nevertheless, postmodern feminism does recognize human agency. Persons are capable of exercising power precisely because their own self-understanding does not depend upon a reified self-image—built with impermeable ego boundaries. Identities, both individual and communal, are formed, informed, and reformed through politics.

The interpretation of postmodern feminism which I have presented contains two ethical commitments. First, it affirms that women are as important as men. This means that postmodern feminists deconstruct the symbols and language practices within western patriarchy to reconstruct politics in a way that treats women as full citizens. While speech and language do not alone determine political life, they are powerful factors in shaping politics. Second, it affirms that genuine understanding does not take place until we have acted upon our theories and that through such actions we will reform our theories and reform ourselves. To do this, postmodern feminists invite us to put on various identities. Even our bodies can be used to say new things as we compose ourselves.

Most important, postmodern feminists invite us to see ourselves playing parts that enact our feminist political theories. Coalition politics brings out new selves in us as individuals and as communities when we are willing to engage in the back-and-forth, interactive, even spontaneous qualities of play. Such play enables us to put off a quest for final universal answers and to take on civic responsibilities as continuous struggles for justice. Thus we can turn to putting forth questions. Asking questions is a way of engaging in politics that urges citizens to negotiate with each other to formulate agendas that respond to issues refocused by the questions.

What philosophies, habits, symbols can we put on that will enable us to reconstruct our male/female identities? Are there some good feminist parts that have not yet come on stage? What genders will play them? Can we invent more genders in our sex/gender scheme? What political possibilities do we open up by recognizing the play of difference in gender and class, gender and race, gender and sexuality, class and gender, race and gender, sexuality and gender, and in any of the other categories we in-habit?[69]

[69]For comments on an earlier draft I wish to thank Robert Cahill, Henry S. Kariel, Laurel Richardson, Jane Rinehart, Tom Rukavina, and the Postmodern Faculty Feminist Seminar at Ohio State University.

CHAPTER 12

Constitutional Hermeneutics

JOHN T. VALAURI

This essay presents a practical hermeneutic approach to some chronic problems in American constitutional law—the framers' intent dispute, the search for consensus in method in constitutional interpretation, and the anxiety over underlying jurisprudence. In doing this, it highlights three important interpretive themes—the historicity of the understanding, the hermeneutic critique of method, and the antireductive emphasis on context and practice in understanding.

This conjunction of topics should come as no surprise to hermeneuts. Hans-Georg Gadamer has noted the exemplary status of legal interpretation for hermeneutics.[1] American constitutional law presents striking instances of some major hermeneutic problems. Authorial intent, the search for method, and the role of practice and context in meaning are interpretive and legal chestnuts.

The section of this essay on hermeneutics and framers' intent thematizes the historicity of the understanding and the ways in which most constitutional critics overlook this background aspect of interpretation. There are two main groups in contemporary constitutional theory. Originalists base constitutional interpretation on framers' intent; nonoriginalists reject a dominant role for framers' intent and usually rely instead on morality.[2] Although they disagree on how to

[1] Hans-Georg Gadamer, *Truth and Method*, trans. Garrett Barden and John Cumming (New York: Crossroad, 1975), pp. 289–305.
[2] Two quite different versions of originalism are presented by Raoul Berger in *Government by Judiciary* (Cambridge: Harvard University Press, 1977), and Ronald Dworkin in "The Forum of Principle," *New York University Law Review* 56 (1981): 469–518. A nonoriginalist alternative is presented by Paul Brest in "The Misconceived Quest for the Original Understanding," *Boston University Law Review* 60 (1980): 204–38. The whole distinction is undermined by David Hoy in "A Hermeneutical Critique of the

decide constitutional cases, both originalists and nonoriginalists are united in the assumption that there are discoverable right answers here that provide broad, sweeping, timeless principles or rules of law that can then be applied relatively mechanically to later cases in a top-down manner. But the search for these foundational facts is in vain. And the singleminded concentration on discovering them causes both sorts of theorists to miss the historical dimension of constitutional interpretation and adjudication.

According to originalists and nonoriginalists, these clear results are generated through the use of favored methods of interpretation. But there is no consensus over methodology. The most prominent methods have well-known defects and are based on questionable assumptions. Methodological debate in constitutional theory has a strong component of déjà vu. Yet, the most important case in modern constitutional individual rights litigation, *Brown v. Board of Education*,[3] would provide a more consciously hermeneutic approach to the resolution of these questions. Because it is a paradigm, not a method, *Brown* presents an exemplar and disciplinary matrix for constitutional adjudication, rather than a set of criteria or a mechanical decision procedure. It brings in the narrative, historical elements of interpretation left out of both originalist and nonoriginalist methodologies.

Theories based on commands, rules, and principles vie for hegemony as underlying jurisprudential theories to support constitutional practice. Yet, each is distorted and incomplete in its own way. Rather than propose another monolithic view of jurisprudence, I will antireductively suggest the nested relation of commands, rules and principle as well as of narratives and practices. Each is a limiting case of the next, which in turn provides a context or background against which the former shows up as what it is. This pluralistic configuration undercuts the deductive, top-down nature of master-concept jurisprudential theories.

A hermeneutic account of interpretation is not normative, but descriptive. It sets out not what constitutional adjudicators ought to do, but what they will inevitably do. This is the ontological claim of hermeneutics.[4] But unlike Ludwig Wittgenstein and Stanley Fish, I do not say that hermeneutic understanding leaves things as they

---

Originalism/Nonoriginalism Distinction," *Northern Kentucky Law Review* 15 (1988): 479–98.

[3]347 U.S. 483 (1954).

[4]Gadamer, *Truth and Method*, pp. 228–34.

are. On the contrary, self-reflection and self-understanding may well change and improve practice.

This hermeneutic critique of constitutional law has many affinities with American legal pragmatism. The hermeneutic-pragmatic relation is an important theme of much contemporary interpretive philosophy. Many of the hermeneutic points presented below find anticipations in the pragmatic philosophy of thinkers like Charles S. Peirce and Justice Oliver Wendell Holmes, Jr. Forgive me, then, if I use "hermeneutics" and "pragmatism" as near synonyms for purposes of this essay.

Let me add also a note on the practical hermeneutic orientation of this approach. Hermeneutic emphases on historicity and holism find resonances in the philosophical work of nonhermeneuts like Donald Davidson and W. V. O. Quine and even in the legal writing of Ronald Dworkin and Fish. But practical hermeneutics, taking its lead from pragmatism and Martin Heidegger, also breaks with the two-thousand-year-old theoretical orientation of philosophy and concentrates instead on the practical configurations on which theory rests. Its practical themes include antireductivism, local knowledge, and the importance of context.

Hermeneutics and Framers' Intent

Historicity should be a prime consideration for legal interpretation because courts are usually applying old laws and other legal texts to later, different, and often unanticipated cases. This is especially true of constitutional law since the text is in large part more than two hundred years old and frequently amended, and the area regulated is quite broad. Yet the main defect of both contemporary approaches to constitutional theory is that they do not take historicity seriously. Originalists insist that judges should scrupulously apply the specific intent of the framers to contemporary cases. Their opponents, the nonoriginalists, decry both the desirability and possibility of doing this, instead insisting on the application of moral principles to constitutional adjudication.

Let me summarize some assumptions typically made (although not explicitly) by originalists here.

(1) Framers' intent is a specific matter of historically discoverable fact.

(2) These facts can be determined from the writings, statements, and actions of particular historical actors.

(3) Somehow these specific statements and acts give rise to general, sweeping constitutional rules and principles that underlie the more ambiguous constitutional text.

(4) These constitutional rules and principles are applicable to all future times and cases in a direct, unexceptional manner.

These assumptions are here phrased broadly enough to encompass many varieties of originalism based on different types of facts and set at different levels of generality.

Despite their fierce opposition to originalism, nonoriginalists typically make some strikingly similar assumptions. They would accept assumptions 3 and 4 and modify assumptions 1 and 2 as follows:

(1) Constitutional meaning is a matter of philosophically discoverable moral fact.

(2) These facts can be determined through the examination of the best available moral philosophical theory.

These two sets of positions in constitutional theory may seem familiar to hermeneuts. Originalism and nonoriginalism parallel positions in the broader hermeneutic debate. Originalism, with its focus on the framers' intent, is a version of the authorial-intent focus of Romantic hermeneutics. Likewise, nonoriginalism has affinities with transcendental hermeneutics. What is missing in the constitutional arena is an analogue to the intermediate Gadamerian position. In a sense, that is just what this essay provides.

The exposition set out below focuses on the shortcomings of originalism, but there is a parallel critique of nonoriginalism, too. Let me group my points here under four headings—the horizontal critique, the vertical critique, precedent, and method. The contrast between the horizontal and vertical critiques relies on a distinction drawn by Jürgen Habermas and other interpretive theorists between a synchronic time slice of understanding and a diachronic historical perspective.[5] These critiques present complementary but independent perspectives on originalism and nonoriginalism.

The central problem of the horizontal critique is how to determine

---

[5]Jürgen Habermas, *Knowledge and Human Interests*, trans. Jeremy Shapiro (Boston: Beacon Press, 1971), p. 158.

the group intention whose existence originalism assumes. The historical peculiarities of the Constitution's framing and adoption make this problem particularly difficult. Whose intent counts in determining framers' intent? Just the framers' or the ratifiers', too? Unlike the case of normal legislation, these are two quite different bodies. The framers met in convention in Philadelphia during the summer of 1787 to draft the document for submission for ratification. Each of the then thirteen states had separate ratifying conventions. Whereas the framers were literally the authors of the constitutional text, it was the ratifiers' adoption that gave it its legal force. Moreover, the ratification in a number of states was contingent on the adoption of a bill of rights (which was, in turn, considered and sent to the states by the first Congress).

The record of the proceedings of the Constitutional Convention was not well kept, nor was it made public for several generations after the adoption of the Constitution. Hence, early constitutional growth occurred in an environment of some ignorance of the intent of the framers. Perhaps even more important, there is strong indication that the framers desired that their specific subjective intent regarding the provisions of the Constitution not govern subsequent interpretation and adjudication. In current terminology, the framers' interpretive intent was at war with their specific intent.

Another problem here is which statements of the framers ought to count in figuring intent and how much. They said quite different things before, during, and after the convention. Their convention statements were often brief, cryptic, and unhelpful for later interpretation. Take just one example. James Madison played a leading role at the convention and in the first Congress and was, in a very real sense, the father of both the Constitution and the Bill of Rights. He had earlier, along with Thomas Jefferson, entered the debate preceding the adoption of the Virginia Bill for Religious Liberty, an important precursor to the religion clauses of the First Amendment. Yet, his statements in the three contexts of the Virginia debates, the convention, and the first Congress were quite different (although not mutually inconsistent). Courts, and commentators have come to use his early statements in the Virginia debates to give detail and clarification to his later, briefer statements in the convention and drafting of the Bill of Rights.[6]

---

[6]The prime instance in case law is Everson v. Board of Education, 330 U.S. 1 (1947), which applied the establishment clause to the states.

The danger of proceeding in this way is that one reads into constitutional text meanings and intentions that may not be there, and certainly that were never assented to by other members of the constitutional or ratifying conventions. It is difficult enough to ascertain whether nonspeaking members of a body assent to statements made by others when those statements are made during the process of deliberation. Because those statements do not form part of the adopted text, the nonspeaking members may view them as irrelevant or innocuous. It is more questionable to read statements into the meaning of a provision when they did not even occur during the deliberation of an adopting body and may have been unknown to the other members of the body.

One way of summing up these difficulties is to say that originalism here seems to call for the existence of a group mind or, at least, a common intention. A group mind is a fuzzy, metaphysical entity that creates more problems than it can solve. What of a common intention? How similar do intentions have to be to be common? Do holders of common intentions have to recognize the mutuality of their intentions, or is mere convergence enough? How is one to determine the intention of someone who never said anything?

The most common move here to avoid these pitfalls of an intentionalistic approach to originalism is to say that the best evidence of what the framers intended is to be found in what they did, that is, the constitutional text that they enacted, rather than in what they intended.[7] This textualist approach brings only illusory relief, though. It works well enough with regard to uncontroversial constitutional provisions; most methods do. The typical example of this sort of provision is the one that requires that the president be at least thirty-five years old. Seemingly, only a change in terrestial revolution would create an interpretive problem. But it is not provisions like this that give rise to constitutional cases and controversies. And it was just the limitations of the plain meaning approach in cases involving the vague and open-ended provisions of the Constitution that led interpreters to look at intentionalism in the first place.

Some try to escape the limited purchase of textualism by using it as a burden-of-proof test.[8] True, the literal meaning of constitutional

---

[7]Justice Antonin Scalia offers a version of textualism in "Originalism: The Lesser Evil," *University of Cincinnati Law Review* 57 (1989): 849–65.

[8]E.g., William Van Alstyne in "Interpreting this Constitution: The Unhelpful Contributions of Special Theories of Judicial Review," *University of Florida Law Review* 35 (1983): 209–35.

provisions definitively resolves only some constitutional questions. But so much the worse, they say, for the bringers of controversial constitutional claims. Under this view, if a constitutional cause of action is not supported by clear constitutional language, then it simply loses.

The burden-of-proof move has a satisfying simplicity and definitiveness, but these are also the sources of its major problems. Such a method of constitutional interpretation will appeal only to those who want to greatly limit both the volume and scope of constitutional litigation today. This prudential consideration aside, textualism provides no justification for itself. It fails the test of self-reference. A textualist burden-of-proof approach to constitutional adjudication is not clearly supported by the text of the Constitution itself. In fact, it would render most of the broader constitutional provisions empty and nugatory.

What, then, of other alternatives? Even if the horizontal critique of the framers' intent fails to persuade, there is an independent vertical critique of that doctrine. It focuses on the difficulties of historical application of ancient texts. Gadamer's notion of two horizons that must be fused in understanding is relevant here.[9] The meaning of the constitutional provisions for both us and the framers depends heavily on the practical, legal, and historical backgrounds against which these provisions show up. The world of the framers of 1787 and our world today are sufficiently different to render the contemporary application of provisions enacted then problematic.

Gadamer also suggests a conversational metaphor saying, in effect, that we and the framers must become interlocutors.[10] This sort of suggestion presents great pitfalls as well as fruitful avenues for interpretation. Some constitutional theorists have posed the test of asking what the framers would do if transported to the modern day and confronted with our contemporary problems. But this maneuver can be condemned as being both irrelevant and futile. What the framers would do today is not the same as and perhaps not even relevant to the question of what they did do in enacting the constitutional provision in question. The hypothetical seance suggested just does not address this more pertinent question. But, at least this line does pose, albeit ineptly, the question of the historicity of the understanding itself.

[9]Gadamer, *Truth and Method*, pp. 267–74.
[10]Ibid., pp. 325–41.

There is a serious objection to this conversational metaphor; let me call it the Ugarte objection. Recall that in the movie *Casablanca,* in one scene Rick tells Major Strasser that he wishes to speak to Monsieur Ugarte, who had earlier stolen letters of transit from German couriers and been arrested in Rick's Cafe. Recall, too, Major Strasser's reply: "I'm afraid you would find the conversation a trifle one-sided. You see, Monsieur Ugarte is dead." The same point applies to the hermeneutic conversation metaphor and for the same reason. This objection is valid as far as it goes, but it is not fatal to the hermeneutic enterprise. True, the hermeneutic fusion of horizons and establishment of narrative lacks the give and take of face-to-face conversation, but it gains the clarity and separation that distance can provide.[11] It is a different sort of conversation, but still a dialogue.

Gadamer's notion of a fusion of horizons is crucially important here. It is consistent with, but marginalized in, the positions of new pragmatists like Fish and Richard Rorty, who are more concerned to emphasize, in contrast to traditional Platonist and Cartesian views, our embeddedness in interpretive communities or webs of belief. Gadamer would not deny this embeddedness or lay claim to some acontextual or transcendental critical position. But neither would he concede that we are hermetically sealed in our contexts. We can understand and criticize traditions, cultures, and texts from the outside—but this is not a view from nowhere, only a view from another context. This small but vital Gadamerian point is crucial for understanding the framers' intent debate and many other interpretive problems. Here it helps us see that originalism and nonoriginalism are not the only options. It also helps us see that both views suffer from similar critical shortcomings.

Both originalism and nonoriginalism find in method the answer to the question of constitutional meaning. They find in their own methods of interpretation sources of discoverable fact giving rise to sweeping principles capable of top-down application. This clarity is gained only at the price of question-begging, history-ignoring assumptions. Although they disagree over where to find it, both originalists and nonoriginalists seem to agree that we should zero in on a particular level of abstraction and source of data in determining constitutional meaning. Originalists would find it in specific historical evidence of framers' intent, whereas nonoriginalists would find it in abstract expression of moral principle. But there is no reason, other than a

---

[11]Ibid., pp. 258–67.

result-oriented one, for limiting interpretive methodology in this way at the outset. Worse yet, it gives interpretation, in both cases, a rigidity that removes the possibility of explaining change. Let us look for an alternative to these methods in paradigms and narratives.

The *Brown* Paradigm

Most disputes in contemporary constitutional theory can be recast as debates over methodology. Both originalism and nonoriginalism promise easy answers to hard cases and methodological resolution to interpretive controversy, but neither can deliver the goods. The thesis of this section is that the model for dissolution of these problems is hidden in plain sight in the form of the leading case for modern constitutional adjudication, *Brown v. Board of Education*. This is not a common view for several reasons. First, *Brown* is not an obscure case, but an all-too-obvious one. Second, *Brown* provides not a method, but a paradigm, for constitutional adjudication. I use "paradigm" here in Thomas Kuhn's sense. It is an exemplar and a disciplinary matrix, not a theory, principle, or rule.[12]

The unique status of *Brown* is in part responsible for its methodological invisibility. The result in *Brown*, declaring the unconstitutionality of public school segregation, is revered by most and accepted by all constitutional commentators, conservative as well as liberal. But the reasoning in *Brown* is, in contrast, widely disparaged. This fact, too, helps explain why it is not typically seen as a model for constitutional adjudication.

Brown allows constitutional change without constitutional amendment. It attempts to explain how a practice like public school segregation, which was not thought to run afoul of the equal protection clause in 1868, did so in 1954. The compressed historical narrative presented in *Brown* and amplified by Alexander Bickel[13] satisfies neither conservatives nor liberals. Because it departs from the specific intent of the framers, an originalist like Henry Monaghan calls this narrative bad history.[14] In contrast, a liberal like Herbert Wechsler,

---

[12]Thomas S. Kuhn, *The Structure of Scientific Revolutions*, 2d ed. (Chicago: University of Chicago Press, 1970), pp. 181–82.

[13]Alexander Bickel, "The Original Understanding and the Segregation Decision," *Harvard Law Review* 69 (1955): 1–65.

[14]Henry Monaghan, "Stare Decisis and Constitutional Adjudication," *Columbia Law Review* 88 (1988): 723, n. 3.

while applauding the result, finds that the court's decision violates the requirement that justifications be framed in terms of neutral principles of law.[15]

Both criticisms find fault in *Brown* for not presenting broad, history- or theory-based principles or rules that can deductively justify the result in this case as well as like others. What these critics see as shortcomings in *Brown*, I see as its primary merits. It is noteworthy here that *Brown* is a methodologically troubling case for both originalists and nonoriginalists, and for the same reason, too. Neither theory can abide or justify change and difference, but that is precisely what *Brown* involves. Originalists like Raoul Berger have a static view of history in which the specific intent of the framers is set at the time of the framing. But the specific evidence from the framing of the Fourteenth Amendment is that, to the extent that public school segregation was considered, it was not thought to violate the equal protection clause. So, originalists are impaled on the horns of a dilemma. They must either accept the continued constitutional validity, absent constitutional amendment, of official segregation in public schools and elsewhere, or they must abandon their originalist methodology. Berger takes the tack of making a prudential, but inconsistent, exception for *Brown*.[16]

Neither can the liberal notion of neutral principles accommodate both the manifest specific intent of the framers on segregation and the *Brown* decision. "A principled decision . . . is one that rests on reasons with respect to all the issues in the case, reasons that in their generality and their neutrality transcend any immediate result that is involved."[17] These neutral principles, a sort of legal Kantianism, remain the same in different contexts and historical settings. From this perspective, then, either *Brown* is an unjustifiable decision or the specific intent of the framers on public school segregation is not an aspect of the meaning of the equal protection clause. Neither consequence is palatable to liberals, the former because it rejects the landmark case of modern individual rights adjudication and the latter because it leaves them open to the charge of judicial legislation rather than mere interpretation.

In contrast, Chief Justice Earl Warren's opinion in *Brown* tackles both horns of the historical dilemma, saying, "In approaching this

[15]Herbert Wechsler, "Toward Neutral Principles of Constitutional Law," *Harvard Law Review* 73 (1959): 1–35.
[16]Berger, *Government by Judiciary*, pp. 412–13.
[17]Wechsler, "Toward Neutral Principles of Constitutional Law," p. 19.

problem, we cannot turn the clock back to 1868 when the amendment was adopted, or even to 1896 when *Plessy v. Ferguson* was written. We must consider public education in the light of its full development and its present place in American life throughout the Nation."[18] As Bickel writes, the view of history present in *Brown* displays "an awareness on the part of the framers that it was *a constitution* they were writing, which led to a choice of language capable of growth."[19]

What *Brown* offers is a specific narrative connecting the result of the unconstitutionality of public school segregation with the historical antecedents of the amendment's framing and the changes in public education between 1868 and 1954. This narrative claims persuasiveness, not deductive certainty from first principles or rules. This approach allows the court to maintain a flexibility and openness to change, at the same time preserving the identity and continuity of the constitutional text as well as its democratic basis. The democratic character of *Brown's* pragmatic method is twofold. First, it appeals through narrative to the text and intention of the amendment's framers. Second, it appeals to contemporary consensus or ratification.

This organic or narrative style of legal reasoning had its precursors in the legal pragmatism of judges like Justice Oliver Wendell Holmes, Jr. This is the other side of pragmatism. Dworkin and others emphasize its forward-looking utilitarian face,[20] but it also has a backward-looking narrative component.

The sort of narrative *Brown* employs is also well captured in Gadamer's notion of effective history, emphasizing context, development, and application.[21] The meaning of a constitutional provision and the nature of the practice it regulates show up only against background textual and practical configurations. What is involved here is a practical holism.[22] But context is not static. Our view must be synchronic, not merely diachronic. Putting the law into motion, we must look at it in terms of its organic development. The social change brought about through the *Brown* model in individual rights adjudication should give the lie to the transcendental charge that philosophical hermeneutics is inherently conservative.

---

[18]347 U.S. at 492–93.

[19]Bickel, "The Original Understanding and the Segregation Decision," p. 63.

[20]Ronald Dworkin, *Law's Empire* (Cambridge: Harvard University Press, 1986), pp. 95, 147–50.

[21]Gadamer, *Truth and Method*, pp. 267–78.

[22]The contrast between theoretical holism and practical holism is developed by Hubert Dreyfus in "Holism and Hermeneutics," *Review of Metaphysics* 34 (1980): 3–12.

Constitutional provisions in the *Brown* paradigm find their meaning only in successive applications in cases, rather than as top-down, mechanical deductions from preexisting rules and principles. So, paradigm meaning is not realistic in that sense. But neither is it utterly nominalistic. There is a unity and generality of meaning here that transcends individual cases. What it presents is a Peircean realism, maintaining the reality and independence of the categories of Secondness and Thirdness.[23] Identity and continuity of meaning are shown or suggested narratively, but they are ultimately supported by practice. What is at stake here is a form of life, not merely consensus or convergence as to legal principles or rules.

Let me end this section by listing four aspects of the *Brown* paradigm to contrast with the quartet of features earlier ascribed to originalism and nonoriginalism.

(1) Constitutional meaning emerges in case application. It is not a preexisting "brooding omnipresence in the sky."[24]
(2) There is no single source of constitutional meaning, nor is meaning fixed for all time.
(3) Case results flow from persuasive narratives and practical descriptions as well as deduction from rules and principles.
(4) Future decisions will turn on the relevant constitutional effective history as well as the individual case contexts.

Postmodern Jurisprudence

The practical and holistic orientation of the hermeneutic account of constitutional meaning and the *Brown* paradigm raises the possibility of a postmodern jurisprudence. But this successor study will depart in some important ways from its predecessors. For this reason (and others), it will be readily misconstrued by those still steeped in the old theoretical assumptions and expectations.

This section thematizes antireductionism as earlier sections focused on historicity and paradigms. Many philosophies of law rely on master concepts to explain law. This reliance typically leads to distortion,

---

[23]I develop this Peircean connection in "Peirce and Holmes," in *Peirce and Law*, ed. Roberta Kevelson (New York: Peter Lang, 1991), pp. 187–201.

[24]The phrase is Holmes's. He used it to criticize a certain view of the common law in *Southern Pacific v. Jensen*, 244 U.S. 205, 222 (1917).

oversimplification, and incompleteness. A postmodern jurisprudence does not substitute a new monolithic system for the old. The features it employs are neither single, masters, nor concepts. Instead, they are plural, reticulated, and practical. Other theories are not forgotten, but taken up and sublated.

An overview of what a postmodern jurisprudence might be will help contextualize my exposition. Take modern Anglo-American jurisprudence. Take, more particularly, three important thinkers in this tradition—John Austin, H. L. A. Hart, and Ronald Dworkin. Each has a master concept to explain the practice of law—commands for Austin,[25] rules for Hart,[26] and principles for Dworkin.[27] The illumination given by these notions is helpful, but only partial (as Hart argues with respect to Austin and Dworkin argues as to Hart).[28] The aim of these concepts is to achieve clarification through abstraction and reduction. But not all legal phenomena fit well in this sort of Procrustean bed. Some recognition of this is found in the fact that each succeeding theory is less starkly reductive than the one before.

Let us, then, continue the series—for it is a series—to its end. The narrative approach suggested by the *Brown* paradigm loosens and broadens jurisprudential practice yet more. But it would be a mistake to stop here. A residually theoretical approach to the *Brown* paradigm (the sort that might be taken by Joseph Rouse's Kuhn$_2$[29]) would turn *Brown* into another grand metanarrative. And, as Lyotard reminds us, postmodernism is suspicious of metanarratives.[30]

What is our alternative? The alternative is to take the *Brown* paradigm in a practical sense (much like Rouse's Kuhn$_1$). In this way, the paradigm generates not one grand, theoretical metanarrative, but an array of interpretive practices. This approach is antireductive. It does not replace or supplant commands, rules, principles, or narrative, but rather gives them a practical context in which to nest. They, in

[25]John Austin, *Lectures on Jurisprudence*, 5th ed. (London: John Murray, 1885), 1: 79–86.

[26]H. L. A. Hart, *The Concept of Law* (Oxford: Oxford University Press, 1961), pp. 77–120.

[27]Ronald Dworkin, *Taking Rights Seriously* (Cambridge: Harvard University Press, 1978), pp. 14–80.

[28]Hart, *The Concept of Law*, pp. 26–48; Dworkin, *Taking Rights Seriously*, pp. 16–39, 47–64.

[29]Joseph Rouse, *Knowledge and Power* (Ithaca: Cornell University Press, 1987), pp. 26–40.

[30]Jean-François Lyotard, *The Postmodern Condition: A Report on Knowledge*, trans. Geoff Bennington and Brian Massumi (Minneapolis: University of Minnesota Press, 1984), pp. 34–37.

turn, can then be seen as specialized legal interpretive tools, useful in some, but not all, cases. The extent and nature of their abstraction from their practical background will be the source of both their usefulness and limitation.

The context of these interpretive tools is not a Cartesian foundation, but only a background. The practical background is not different in kind from the foregrounded interpretive tools—they are all practices. The difference arises only out of a contingent purpose or focus of attention, as with the Heideggerian ready-to-hand. As purposes change and traditions evolve, different foregroundings occur. Nothing is permanently or inherently centered or marginalized.

Because the background is practical rather than theoretical, it is better approached in terms of skills (Gilbert Ryle's knowing-how or Heideggerian circumspection) rather than theoretical knowledge. So, too, constitutional meaning is better seen in terms of practical consequences than rules or principles.

It is this practical character that differentiates this postmodern jurisprudence from Fish's literary pragmatism and even Gadamer's philosophical hermeneutics, with which it otherwise has many affinities. Like them, it emphasizes context, narrative, and history. But because its interpretive scope includes actions as well as texts, it goes beyond the textual-linguistic focus of Fish and Gadamer. This has several advantages. First, it allows for a more plausible account of how contexts constrain, or at least habituate. Second, it helps explain how interpretive communities tend to be parochial and knowledge local. Finally, it helps us see how difference in meaning is dependent on difference in consequences.[31]

Let me illustrate this last point with an example of constitutional conflict. In the area of race discrimination litigation involving the equal protection clause of the Fourteenth Amendment, historically there have been two main approaches. One, the color-blind view, proscribes racial classifications generally.[32] The competing view, the two-class theory, holds that the amendment was enacted primarily to improve and safeguard the rights of blacks.[33] Which methodology best explains the meaning of the equal protection clause and the differences between these two views of it? The answer to this question is ultimately practical, and the failure to realize this point can lead to a kind of constitutional *akrasia*. The meaning of constitutional

---

[31]As with Peirce's pragmatic maxim.
[32]Plessy v. Ferguson, 163 U.S. 537, 554–55 (Harlan, J., dissenting).
[33]The Slaughter-House Cases, 83 U.S. (16 Wall.) 36, 67–72 (1872).

provisions and doctrines is most clearly shown in the actions they require, prohibit, and permit, and in what sort of cases they make hard and what sort easy.

See what happens when we apply the equal protection clause in the two best-known modern race discrimination cases—*Brown* (again) and *Regents of the University of California v. Bakke*[34] (an affirmative-action case involving a minority set-aside or quota in medical school admission). Both views of equal protection support *Brown*'s banning of officially sanctioned public school segregation, but for different reasons. On the color-blind view, school segregation violates the prohibition of race classification. On the two-class view, school segregation imposes a burden on the rights and opportunities of blacks. In contrast, the conflict between the two views prevents the court from reaching a majority opinion in *Bakke* or a clear consensus on the constitutionality of affirmative action. For although the set-asides accord with the two-class theory, they violate the color-blind view in the same way school segregation does.

Is the meaning of equal protection clear? Are the two views compatible? It depends on the case. There is no general answer. On this practical view constitutional conflict is an episodic sort of incontinence. In some situations, important and otherwise harmonious provisions or doctrines prescribe incompatible courses of action. This causes anxiety and, if a decision is reached, apparent conflict with at least one of the relevant rules. This conflict can be overcome only by altering provisions and doctrines (which may not be otherwise desirable), altering the conditions that gave rise to the situation (which may not be practical), or a procedural rather than a substantive decision procedure (as in John Rawls's contrast between pure and procedural justice).[35]

A constitutional hermeneutics is neither a therapeutic dissolution of longtime constitutional problems nor just another theory of constitutional interpretation. It lies somewhere between. It recasts problems and projects, highlighting the historical dimension and the plurality of practices involved. It provides recognition of the limitations of some constitutional approaches without claiming to fully supplant them. And, as a Peircean Third, it is a general applicable to other realms of inquiry and understanding, too.

---

[34]438 U.S. 265 (1978).
[35]John Rawls, *A Theory of Justice* (Cambridge: Harvard University Press, 1971), pp. 83–90.

CHAPTER 13

Serious Watching

Alexander Nehamas

Traditionalist critics of recent developments in American universities are fond of comparing the current situation to the past—that is, in most cases, to their own student days. Gertrude Himmelfarb, for example, recalls a time when, in contrast to today, "it was considered the function of the university to encourage students to rise above the material circumstances of their lives, to liberate them intellectually and spiritually by exposing them, as the English poet Matthew Arnold put it, to 'the best which has been thought and said in the world.' "[1] Nostalgia has colored not only Professor Himmelfarb's perception of the past but also her recollection of Arnold, who actually wrote that the "business" of criticism is "to know the best that is known and thought in the world."[2] We can dismiss Himmelfarb's other inaccuracies, but we cannot overlook her replacement of Arnold's present-tense "is" by the perfect-tense "has been." For this allows her to appeal to Arnold's authority in order to insinuate, if not to argue outright, that the university's concern is with the past and that the present, at least in connection with the humanities, lies largely outside the scope of its function.

This essay first appeared in *South Atlantic Quarterly* 89 (Winter 1990), copyright, 1990, *South Atlantic Quarterly*. It is reprinted, with minor changes, by permission of Duke University Press.

[1]Gertrude Himmelfarb, "Stanford and Duke Undercut Classical Values," *New York Times*, May 5, 1988.

[2]Matthew Arnold, "The Function of Criticism at the Present Time," in Hazard Adams, ed., *Critical Theory since Plato* (New York: Harcourt Brace Jovanovich, 1971), p. 588.

Such emphasis on the past does not exclude attention to contemporary works of fine art or philosophy, which can generally be shown to be part of what is often in this context called "the" tradition. But it does disenfranchise present-day cultural products that cannot readily be connected with that tradition. This is especially true of works of popular art, particularly television. These are either totally overlooked, as is the case in our philosophy of art, or disparaged, not only by highbrow critics like Allan Bloom[3] but also by the very people whose own livelihood depends upon them.[4] In this way, J. R. Ewing, the hero-villain of "Dallas," "the man everybody loves to hate," turns out to be the perfect metaphor for the medium that sustains him.

But though it is devoted to the past, this approach is historically blind. Its adherents consider Plato, Homer, and the Greek tragic poets equally parts of the tradition, but they fail to realize that Plato's uncompromising exclusion of the poets from the perfect state of the *Republic* proceeds from exactly the same motives and manifests precisely the same structure as their own rejection of contemporary popular culture. The paradigms of one age's high culture often began their life as entertainment for the masses of another.[5] Our seemingly unified tradition is significantly more complex and inconsistent than we tend to believe. And examining the popular artworks of our day is crucial for understanding the operations by means of which they are invested with value and the conditions under which they, too, can come to be assimilated (as some always are) into the fine arts and into high culture.

Such considerations aside, however, highbrow critics of television can also be answered in their own terms. This is the point of my essay: television rewards serious watching. Serious watching, in turn, disarms many of the criticisms commonly raised against television.

---

[3]Allan Bloom, *The Closing of the American Mind* (New York: Simon and Schuster, 1987), p. 58.

[4]An article in *Applause*, the magazine of the public television station in Philadelphia, plugging Patrick McGoohan's series *The Prisoner*, which WHYY was about to air again, closes as follows: "Watch the show when you get the chance. It's not perfect—the fashions, for example, are horribly dated. But it's very good. And for a television show, that's saying a lot." February 1987, p. 23.

[5]The argument for this view, stated dogmatically here, can be found in my "Plato on Imitation and Poetry in *Republic* 10," in J. M. E. Moravcsik and Philip Temko, eds., *Plato on Beauty, Wisdom, and the Arts* (Totowa, N.J.: Rowman and Littlefield, 1982), pp. 47–78, and, with more immediate relevance for this essay, in "Plato and the Mass Media," *The Monist* 71 (Spring 1988): 214–34.

The common criticisms of television, though they are united in their disdain for the medium, come from various directions and have differing points. Wayne Booth, for example, expresses a relatively traditional preference for primarily linguistic over mainly visual works:

> It is hard to see how anyone can eliminate the fundamental difference between media in which some kind of physical reality has established a scene *before* the viewer starts to work on it, and those like radio and print that can use language only for description—language that is always no more than an invitation to thought and imagination, never a solid presentation or finished reality. . . . The video arts tell us precisely what we should see, but their resources are thin and cumbersome for stimulating our moral and philosophical range.[6]

It is worth pointing out, but necessary to leave aside, the ironic and twisted connection between this view and the famous passage of the *Phaedrus* in which books are criticized for lacking, in comparison to the spoken word, just the features on account of which Booth praises them:

> You know, Phaedrus, that's the strange thing about writing, which makes it truly analogous to painting. The painter's products stand before us as though they were still alive, but if you question them, they maintain a most majestic silence. It is the same with written words; they seem to talk to you as though they were intelligent, but if you ask them anything about what they say, from a desire to be instructed they go on telling you just the same thing forever.[7]

This parallel is very important in its own right and should be studied in detail.[8] But what concerns me now, and what I shall be addressing soon, is simply Booth's claim that the video arts are inherently incapable of addressing serious "moral and philosophical" issues.

A related criticism is made by John Cawelti, whose celebrated study of the arts of popular culture, particularly of formulaic literature, has led him to conclude that "formulaic works necessarily stress intense and immediate kinds of excitement and gratification as opposed to the more complete and ambiguous analyses of character and

---

[6]Wayne Booth, "The Company We Keep: Self-Making in Imaginative Art," *Daedalus* 111 (Fall 1982): 42.
[7]Plato, *Phaedrus* 275d, trans. Roy Hackforth (Cambridge: 1952).
[8]See Nehamas, "Plato and the Mass Media," pp. 221–22 and notes.

SERIOUS WATCHING 263

motivation that characterize mimetic literature. . . . Formulaic works stress action and plot."[9] He also considers that a "a major characteristic of formulaic literature is the dominant influence of the goals of escape and entertainment."[10] The contrast here is one between the straightforward, repetitive, action-oriented, and entertaining formulaic works that by and large belong to popular culture—works that include the products of television—and the ambiguous, innovative, psychologically motivated, and edifying works of high art.

Finally, Catherine Belsey, who has approached the study of literature from a Marxist point of view, following the work of Louis Althusser, draws a contrast between "classic realism, still the dominant popular mode in literature, film, and television,"[11] which is characterized by "illusionism, narrative which leads to closure, and a hierarchy of discourses which establishes the 'truth' of the story,"[12] and what she calls "the interrogative text." The interrogative text, she writes,

> may well be fictional, but the narrative does not lead to that form of closure which in Classical Realism is also disclosure. . . . If it is illusionist it also tends to employ devices to undermine the illusion, to draw attention to its own textuality. . . . Above all, [it] differs from the classical realist text in the absence of a single privileged discourse which contains and places all the others.[13]

It would be easy to cite many other similar passages, but the main themes of the attack against television, on which those other passages would provide only variations, are all sounded by these three authors: (1) given its formulaic nature, television drama is simple and action oriented; it makes few demands of its audience and offers them quick and shallow gratification; (2) given its visual, nonlinguistic character, it is unsuited for providing psychological and philosophical depth; and (3) given its realist tendencies, it fails to make its own fictional nature one of its themes. It is therefore self-effacing and constructs an artificial point of view from which all its various strands can appear to be put together and unified; it thus reinforces

[9]John Cawelti, *Adventure, Mystery, and Romance* (Chicago: University of Chicago Press, 1976), p. 14.
[10]Ibid., p. 13.
[11]Catherine Belsey, *Critical Practice* (London: Methuen, 1980), p. 68.
[12]Ibid., p. 70.
[14]"Plato and the Mass Media," pp. 228–30.

the idea that problems in the world can be solved as easily as they are solved in fiction, and it domesticates its audience. These reasons are taken to show that television does not deserve serious critical attention—or that, if it does, it should be criticized only on ideological grounds.

And yet there are reasons to be suspicious of this view. They can be all based on a serious look, for example, at "St. Elsewhere"—a television drama that appears straightforward, action oriented, and realistic.

Much of discussion of "St. Elsewhere" concerns individual episodes or scenes from this show. Nevertheless, my main concern is with the series as a whole. As I have argued elsewhere,[14] the object of criticism in broadcast television drama is primarily the series and not its individual episodes. But, of course, individual episodes are all we ever see, and it is by watching them in sufficient numbers that we become familiar with the series as a whole. A large part of the dissatisfaction with television drama, I think, is due precisely to a failure to appreciate this point. By concentrating exclusively on individual episodes, the critics of television are incapable of seeing where, as it were, the impact of the medium occurs and are therefore unable to be affected by it. Character, for example, is manifested through particular occurrences in particular episodes; but each manifestation is thin and two-dimensional, until we realize that thickness and depth are added to it if (and only if) it is seen *as* a manifestation of character that can be understood and appreciated only over time and through many such manifestations. In this respect, television is not unlike the comic strip, in regard to which Umberto Eco has written:

> a structural fact that is of fundamental importance in the understanding of comics in general [is that] the brief daily or weekly story, the traditional strip, even if it narrates an episode that concludes in the space of four panels, will not work if considered separately; rather it acquires flavor only in the continuous and obstinate series, which unfolds, strip after strip, day after day.[15]

There are in fact many similarities between cartoons and at least some television series, especially those filmed before an audience, and this

---

[14]"Plato and the Mass Media," pp. 228–30.
[15]Umberto Eco, "On 'Krazy Kat' and 'Peanuts'," *New York Review of Books*, June 15, 1985.

is in my opinion partly responsible for the low regard in which many high-minded critics hold the latter. The stiffness of the poses held by the television actors, the necessity of their half facing the camera, the inability of the television image to give great detail and its lack of visual texture, the narrow angles and small groups that alone are those it can accommodate, and the staccato rhythm in which lines are often delivered with pauses for laughter or applause are all features that make of television shows cartoons that are animated, in a literal sense of the term.

Whatever its connections to the cartoon, television has always been thought to be inherently realistic, not only by high-culture intellectuals but by its own creators as well. During the first years of broadcast television, documentation seemed absolutely essential for drama as well as for comedy. For example, "Medic," the very first medical show, was, according to a recent discussion, a "highly realistic examination of surgery. The program sought to document medical case histories and used some actual hospital footage."[16] "Medic" was written by Jim Moser, a friend and ex-collaborator of Jack Webb, whose show "Dragnet," was also supposedly based on "actual files of the L.A.P.D."; the connection was responsible for "Medic" coming to be known as "Drugnet." The very first situation comedy, "Mary Kay and Johnny," which opened in 1947, starred an actual married couple, whose child, born after the show was already on the air, was incorporated into the plot and thus set the pattern made famous by Lucille Ball as well as by the Nelsons in "The Ozzie and Harriet Show." The episodes of the police show "Gangbusters" were based on "actual police and FBI files"; they concluded by airing a photograph of one of FBI's "most wanted" criminals with instructions to call the FBI or the show itself with information about them, thus anticipating the current mania for interactive programs of this sort.[17] Finally, in one of the most absurd cases of the search for verisimilitude, "Noah's Ark," produced by Jack Webb and featuring a "messianic veterinarian," was based on "actual cases" from the files of the Southern California Veterinary Association and the American Humane Society.

Whether such a mixture of documentation and fictional narrative

[16]Robert S. Alley, "Media Medicine and Morality," in *Understanding Television*, ed. Richard P. Adler (New York: Praeger 1981), p. 231.

[17]David Marc, *Demographic Vistas* (Philadelphia: University of Pennsylvania Press, 1984), p. 73.

produces or undermines realism is a complex question. For the moment I simply want to point out that in the 1960s and 1970s such obvious attempts to incorporate reality into television gave way to a more straightforward melodramatic mode. The mythical quality of melodrama, however, was soon infected with reality once again: a new realism from two new directions, which resulted from the intervention of two very different television authors.

Now, the term "author" may well seem inappropriate here, for, among all the arts, television seems to be the most authorless. Most dramatic series are written by different people, or groups of people, each week, and it is very difficult to know precisely who is to receive the credit or the blame for a show's success or failure. In an effort to determine who is finally responsible for the character of each program, Todd Gitlin has argued that whereas in the film (as André Bazin and others have claimed) this role, the *auteur*, belongs to the director, in television the relevant role is played by the producer, perhaps the only person who provides continuity in a show and who determines the overall look of the program.[18] This view is at least partly correct: "Hill Street Blues" (Gitlin's primary concern) and "L.A. Law" are indeed Steven Bochco's creatures, just as "Miami Vice" belongs to Michael Mann. If this is a view we accept, then we can say that a crucial factor in the development of American television was the work of Norman Lear, who was responsible for the nature and success of shows like "All in the Family," "Maude," "The Jeffersons," and "Mary Hartmann, Mary Hartmann" (which was actually so parodic that not even he could sell it to the networks). In his various shows Lear introduced acute social commentary and thematized complex social and political issues through the previously innocuous format of the classic situation comedy. A particularly interesting feature of Lear's work was that it was very difficult to tell where exactly his shows' sympathies lay: "Liberals and radicals tended to interpret *All In the Family* as a left-liberal critique of bigotry and conservatism, while conservative audiences tended to identify with Archie Bunker and to see the series as a vindication of Archie's rejection of his 'meathead' son-in-law's liberalism."[19] This indeterminacy of television is to a great extent dictated precisely by the medium's immense popularity and its need to appeal to an extremely heterogeneous audience. It argues against the facile charge that tele-

---

[18]Todd Gitlin, *Inside Prime Time* (New York: Pantheon, 1983), pp. 273–324.
[19]Steven Best and Douglas Kellner, "(Re)Watching Television: Notes Toward a Political Criticism," *Diacritics* 17 (Summer 1987): 104.

vision "totalizes" its narrative point of view, for, in order to be susceptible to such varying interpretations, the television "text" must be essentially incomplete and open to radical interpretation on the part of its audience (which thereby shows itself to be much more active in its reaction to the medium than our stereotypes often suggest).

Another realistic element in recent television drama is associated not with a person but with a whole production company, MTM Productions, which is behind shows like "The Mary Tyler Moore Show," "Rhoda," "Phyllis," "The Bob Newhart Show," "Lou Grant," "WKRP in Cincinnati," "Hill Street Blues," and "St. Elsewhere." MTM Productions was headed by Grant Tinker, but Tinker was not associated with the character of his many shows as directly as Lear was with his. In a serious way, credit for these programs goes to the production company rather than to any individual. And this fact in turn raises the interesting possibility not only that the television author need *not* be an individual but also that it need not always be an object of the same ontological order: both a concrete individual and an abstract entity—a company—can play the relevant role. Three features of MTM Productions are relevant to my account.

First, these shows shifted in many cases the location of the situation comedy from the home, where the genre had been truly at home, to the workplace. But the MTM workplace—a television station, doctor's office, a police precinct, a country inn, an inner-city hospital—always operates as the locus of an extended family within which individual characters face, defer, or resolve innumerable personal problems. The humor of these shows is less biting, less abusive, and less overtly political than the humor of Norman Lear. Part of their overall message seems to be that one's most real family consists not so much of the people with whom one lives but rather of the people with whom one works. Many characters have restrained personal lives; many are unhappy at home; and happy families, as in both of Bob Newhart's shows, are continuous with the family of the workplace.

Second, in contrast to earlier television drama and following the precedent established by "M*A*S*H," many of these shows allow for, and depend upon, character development. Characteristically, during the opening season of "The Mary Tyler Moore Show," the program's title song asked of its heroine, "How will you make it on your own?" In later seasons this was changed to "You're gonna make it on your own," and eventually, in line with Mary Richards's increasing independence, any reference to this issue was dropped altogether.[20]

Finally, MTM shows followed the lead of "Hill Street Blues," which was influenced by the conventions of daytime soap operas and introduced multiple story lines in individual episodes. These stories would often be carried over a number of episodes but, contrary to the situation in soap operas, they would always be resolved. The possibility of containing multiple plotlines naturally depends on the existence of a relatively large cast. Accordingly, programs like "Hill Street Blues" and "St. Elsewhere" ceased to function around a single central figure and developed into "ensemble shows" featuring many actors, each one of whom has relatively little time in front of the camera.[21]

With these ideas in mind, we can turn to "St. Elsewhere," which concerns life in a large inner-city hospital in Boston. The show seems straightforward, action oriented, and realistic. It is full of local color. It is a serious program, addressing serious medical and moral issues (it was the first television show, for example, to present a series of episodes concerning AIDS) in the liberal manner of "M*A*S*H" and "Lou Grant," but it is also bitingly, parodically funny. For example, during a title sequence a group of hospital personnel are shown hurrying a life-support machine down a corridor in what clearly seems an urgent situation. Now, television doctors do occasionally fail their patients: even Dr. Welby lost a few. But, traditionally, these were always cases of nature asserting itself over technology. Here, however, the attempt fails because, in all their dispatch and intensity, the interns clumsily stumble and end up, along with their machine, sprawled across the hospital floor. The fact that this is a scene in the title sequence and that it is repeated week after week fixes it in the mind of the program's audience and allows the incident to manifest a feature not only of St. Eligius but of hospitals in general, so that the scene appears realistic as well as funny: things like that do happen, more often than we like to think, in hospitals.

"St. Elsewhere" lacks the unrelenting technological and humanistic optimism of "Marcus Welby, M.D." Patients die there, and often there are no lessons in their deaths. The physicians not only help,

---

[20]On this and other instances of character development in MTM shows, see Jane Feuer, "The MTM Style," in Horace Newcomb, *Television: The Critical View* (New York: Oxford University Press, 1987), pp. 60–62.

[21]See Thomas Schatz, "*St. Elsewhere* and the Evolution of the Ensemble Series," in Newcomb, *Television,* pp. 85–100.

but also cheat and seduce each other. None of the ultimate positions of power in the hospital is occupied by a woman. This, in fact, becomes one of the show's themes, especially when a woman—and a Vietnamese refugee at that—replaces the obnoxious, racist, sexist but technically superb chief of surgery, Mark Craig, when he smashes his hand in a fit of pique and self-doubt. Craig's sexism, which causes a breakdown in his marriage, is consistently addressed in the show, along with his wife's efforts to find a job, a life, and a voice of her own. One of the residents is a former nurse who realized that she could do a physician's job as well as or even better than many of the men who practice medicine. The program features a very successful black doctor, a *summa cum laude* graduate of Yale and chief resident at St. Eligius, a highly motivated black orderly who moves up to paramedic and then to physician's assistant before he realizes that that is as far as he can go, and a friend of his who is content to remain an orderly. For these and many other similar reasons, "St. Elsewhere," compared with "Marcus Welby, M.D.," "Dr. Kildare," or "Ben Casey," appears to be much more true to life within the medical profession.

It is imperative, however, to note the terms of this comparison. The realism of "St. Elsewhere" is measured by comparing it not to life within a hospital, of which most of us know almost nothing, but to the standards and features of earlier shows on the same general subject. On the other hand, there does seem to be something inherently more realistic in a show that features a hospital not in some idealized suburban setting but in the middle of Boston. The fact that the Red Line runs right next to St. Eligius, moreover, places the hospital in the location of the Massachusetts General Hospital, which adds a further touch of verisimilitude—until one realizes that far from being based upon the latter, St. Eligius is constantly being contrasted with it under its fictional name of "Boston General." Boston is, indeed, a real presence a character—in this program: the governor of Massachusetts appears in one episode, the city's racial conflicts are often addressed, Harvard looms large. And yet this is a very peculiar Boston. For one thing, it contains a bar named Cheers. And, on one occasion, the show's three patriarchal figures go to this bar, whose fictional existence also involves a very "real" Boston, to drink and talk things over. To complicate matters further, in one episode a resident of St. Eligius passes by the actual bar in Boston that advertises itself as the place which inspired "Cheers" and takes his little son in after asking him, in an allusion to the theme song of that show, whether he wants to eat "where everybody knows your name."

This is, then, an impossible Boston, however realistic its representation appears. Realism in a case like this is indeed measured not by proximity to reality but by distance from fiction whose conventions we have come to see as conventions. At the time, of course, the conventions of the early medical shows were invisible, just as many of the conventions of "St. Elsewhere" will become visible only in the future, and the shows certainly seemed realistic. But even here the situation is complicated: the relationship between program and reality may be more ambiguous, and the television audience may be more aware of this ambiguity, than we are apt to suppose.

George Gerbner and Larry Gross, for example, report that over the first five years of Dr. Welby's television practice the show received roughly 250,000 letters, most of them requesting medical advice.[22] Their conclusion is that viewers consider television characters "as representative of the real world." But consider the fact that people still write letters to Sherlock Holmes at 221B Baker Street (in fact, the firm that occupies that address employs someone just to answer them); yet surely no one aware of Holmes believes that he is an actual person: rather, it is more plausible to suspect that the people writing Holmes engage in a game that exploits Holmes's ambiguous status, his fictional genius and his actual address. The same idea is also suggested by the practices of television fan magazines, which explicitly mix information about the various characters of the soap operas with information about the actors who portray them in such a way that it is difficult to separate one from the other. The television audience seems to be enjoying the equivocal interpenetration of fiction and reality. As John Fiske writes in regard to the fan magazines,

> we must be careful not to let the "cultural dope" fallacy lead us to believe that the soap fans are incapable of distinguishing between character and player. . . . This is an intentional illusion, a conspiracy entered into by viewer and journalist in order to increase the pleasure of the program. . . . The reader [is encouraged into] the delusion of realism not just to increase the pleasure of that delusion, but also to increase the activeness and sense of control that go with it.[23]

If the Boston of "St. Elsewhere" contains both the Red Line and

[22]George Gerbner and Larry Gross, "The Scary World of TV's Heavy Viewer," *Psychology Today*, April 1976, p. 44.
[23]John Fiske, *Television Culture* (London and New York: Methuen, 1987), pp. 121, 123.

the Red Sox on the one hand and Cheers on the other, it is and it is not a real city. And if this is so, then it is difficult to agree with Belsey's view that "illusionism" and lack of self-awareness are deeply characteristic of television drama. In fact, "St. Elsewhere" mixes fiction so thoroughly with life and is so sensitive to what is now being called "intertextuality" that only ignorance of the medium of television could ever have suggested that the program is naively and straightforwardly realistic. This becomes even more obvious when we realize that only someone familiar with television—a literate viewer—can understand that Cheers is explicitly fictional and that the realistic episode involving the bar and its character is doubly impossible.

Pierre Bourdieu, who objects to paying television "serious" attention, argues that aesthetic approaches to the medium mystify its cultural role and conceal its real importance. In all popular entertainment, as opposed to the fine arts, Bourdieu writes,

> the desire to enter into the game, identifying with the characters' joys and sufferings, worrying about their fate, espousing the hopes and ideals, living their life, is based on a form of *investment*, a sort of deliberate "naivety," ingenuousness, good-natured credulity ("we're here to enjoy ourselves") which tends to accept formal experiments and specifically artistic effects only to the extent that they can be forgotten and do not get in the way of the substance of the work.[24]

Similarly, Herbert Gans writes that members of lower "cultural taste groups" (to which the television audience by and large is supposed to belong) choose their form of entertainment "for the feelings and enjoyment it evokes and for the insight and information they can obtain; they are less concerned with how a work of art is created."[25] Such reactions to entertainment, according to Bourdieu, are

> the very opposite of the detachment of the aesthete who . . . introduces a distance, a gap—the measure of his distant distinction—*vis-à-vis* "first-degree" perception by displacing the interest from the "content" . . . to the "form," to the specifically artistic effects that are only appreciated

[24]Pierre Bourdieu, *Distinction: A Social Critique of the Judgment of Taste* (Cambridge, Mass.: Harvard University Press, 1984), p. 32.
[25]Herbert Gans, *Popular Culture and High Culture* (New York: Basic Books, 1974), p. 79.

relationally, through a comparison with other works which is incompatible with immersion in the singularity of the work immediately given.[26]

On the basis of this distinction between "investment" and "distance," between "immediacy" and "relationality," Bourdieu repudiates aesthetic interpretation and criticism because he considers them self-deceptive: "Specifically aesthetic conflicts about the legitimate vision of the world . . . are political conflicts (appearing in their most euphemized form) for the power to impose the dominant definition of reality, and social reality in particular."[27]

But Bourdieu's distinction between the immediate enjoyment of popular art by the lower classes and the comparative attitude of the distant aesthete cannot be maintained. The television audience is highly literate (more literate about its medium, in fact, than many high-culture audiences are about theirs) and makes essential use of its literacy in its appreciation of individual episodes or whole series. Its enjoyment, therefore, is both active and comparative. Consider the following case.

A regular secondary character on "St. Elsewhere" during the 1985 season was an amnesiac, referred to as John Doe. Having failed to regain his memory and find out who he is, Doe, who is a patient in St. Eligius's psychiatric ward, turns obsessively to television. But though his conversation is riddled with lines derived from commercials, his real interest is in the news programs: "Newscasters—*they* know who they are," he insists to his psychiatrist, Dr. Weiss. Weiss, who is concerned with Doe's state of mind, finally tells him not to watch the news any longer: "It's too depressing. I want you to watch shows that lift your soul and put a smile on your face."

Another character on this particular program is the passive-aggressive Mr. Carlin, who loves to torture Doe. Mr. Carlin, portrayed by the same actor, was a regular character in "The Bob Newhart Show," in which Newhart, a psychologist, was treating him for his (at the time) milder disorder. But Bob apparently failed, and Mr. Carlin has been committed, finding himself in a hospital in a different show.

Doe and Mr. Carlin fight over the television set in the ward lounge, incessantly switching channels. Doe finally gets reconciled to fictional shows and even tells Carlin that television is "filled with real people." "And they're only *this* tall," Carlin replies placing his thumb

---

[26]Bourdieu, *Distinction*, p. 34.
[27]Pierre Bourdieu, "The Production of Belief," in R. Collins et al., *Media, Culture and Society: A Critical Reader* (London: Jagg, 1986), pp. 154–55.

and forefinger six inches apart. "Television is the mirror of our soul," Doe insists; "we look in and we see who we really are." And as he switches from one famous program to another, he catches for a moment the very end of "The Mary Tyler Moore Show" and the logo of MTM Productions (itself a parodic reference to MGM's famous trademark, and, in its substitution of a kitten for MGM's lion, a whole parable of the relationship between film and television). MTM Productions, of course, is responsible not only for "The Mary Tyler Moore Show" but also for "The Bob Newhart Show" as well as for "St. Elsewhere" itself. As soon as he sees the MTM kitten, John Doe loudly claims that he now knows who he is: he is Mary Richards, Mary Tyler Moore's character. He instantly goes into character, dons a beret like Mary's, identifies various patients and physicians with characters from that show (Mr. Carlin, for example, becomes Rhoda, Mary's friend, though he nastily refuses to play along; Dr. Weiss, naturally enough, is Mr. Grant; Dr. Auschlander, the senior figure in the hospital and quite bald, becomes Murray, and so on), and develops, like Mary, a profound devotion to his new extended family for whom, in Mary's manner, he immediately prepares a party: "Sometimes the people you work with aren't just the people you work with," he tells Dr. Weiss, echoing the main theme not only of "The Mary Tyler Moore Show" but also of "St. Elsewhere."

Auschlander is worried about Weiss's decision to go along with Doe's fantasy and seems to be slightly embarrassed at having to appear at Doe's party as Murray. He is disdainful of the television audience in general, echoing at least some of the complaints I have introduced into this discussion. "People sit in front of their televisions," he says, "believing the characters they see there actually exist, eat, breathe, sleep." But when Weiss asks him which character *he* would like to be if he had the choice (which of course he does not, since he already is one), he unhesitatingly replies that he would like to be Trapper John, M.D.—a doctor with a reassuring manner who invariably saves his patients, the very kind of doctor "St. Elsewhere" will not allow to exist within its own fictional space and which, from within its own fiction, is thereby asserted to be more "real" than its competitors.

As part of an independent subplot, an astronaut is being treated in St. Eligius for a case of paralysis. The astronaut, however, has also announced that on his next space mission he will walk hand in hand with God. The Navy has sent one of its own medical officers to bring the astronaut to earth and to Bethesda. This Navy doctor, who has already appeared in an earlier, unrelated episode of "St. Elsewhere" and who has thus established her own "independent" identity, is portrayed by Betty White. As she is on her way to visit Dr. Weiss, she runs into Doe, who immediately exclaims, "Sue Anne! The Happy Home maker!" recognizing the actress Betty White as the character she was in "The Mary Tyler Moore Show." Betty White, naturally, responds with a blank stare and a vague "I am afraid you have me confused with someone else."

Doe's party turns out to be a success, but this causes him to start doubting his new identity: "Mary always throws lousy parties," he confesses; "maybe I am not Mary." At that point Mr. Carlin gets into a fight with another patient, and Doe runs to help him out, attacking this other patient, whom he identifies as "Mr. Coleman," the station manager who, when "The Mary Tyler Moore Show" was canceled, was supposed to have fired its main characters. "I've committed a violent act," Doe says; "Mary would never do that." Carlin, moved by Doe's friendship, abandons his nastiness and decides to play along with him: "Call me Rhoda," he suggests. But Doe responds (in a way that still mixes fiction and life), "No. I am not Mary. We've just been canceled."

The next morning Doe goes for a walk with Dr. Auschlander, who reassures him that his many friends will help him find out who he is. At the hospital's main entrance, Doe, calm, peaceful, and happy, says "I'm gonna make it after all," and in an exact parallel to the final shot of the title sequence of "The Mary Tyler Moore Show," tosses his beret in the air, replicating Mary in word and deed in the very process of liberating himself from her. Television and reality, fiction and life, character and person are intermixed through and through.

Only a literate and active audience could ever appreciate or even get the point of this ingenious use of intertextuality. Its point is not necessarily deep, though it does ask whom television characters are supposed to resemble, to what reality they correspond, and to whom—actor or character—one is responding in watching and enjoying a program. All these are questions important to ask and difficult to answer, and they make of this episode as "interrogative," self-conscious, and self-reflexive a work as any high-culture critic might possibly wish. But to be part of the high culture is not necessarily to be cultured, and to know much about literature is not necessarily to be literate.

"St. Elsewhere" lives by confounding fiction and life. During one of the show's last seasons, in an effort to improve ratings, its producers seemed to have decided that the old-fashioned hospital's seedy beige-and-brown background was failing to attract an audience getting used to the pastels made popular by shows like "Miami Vice." They brought the look of their show in line with that of other high-profile programs by means of a brilliant move: they had the problem-ridden St. Eligius bought by a private hospital chain. And the first thing the chain did was to renovate the building, which provided the show with a postmodernist set and a whole new narrative dimension.

The fictional hospital company was called Ecumena and was immensely interested in artificial heart transplants. The Humana Corporation, on which Ecumena was obviously based, objected to the whole idea, especially because Ecumena was depicted as a cold, impersonal, profit-obsessed enterprise. They succeeded in getting a disclaimer added to the closing credits, and they finally won an injunction against the use of the word "Ecumena." The name had to go. "St. Elsewhere" characteristically responded by mixing fact and fiction. Within the show, a nameless hospital company sued Ecumena on the grounds that the name was too close to its own and won. The chain is renamed Weiggert Hospitals, and as the Ecumena sign is being removed from the entrance to St. Eligius, it slips from the workers, falls to the ground, splinters into countless fragments, and almost kills the hospital administrator, a devoted and often heartless employee of the chain who looks in disgust and mutters, echoing the show's producers, "It's been that kind of day from the beginning."

In order to know where to look in order to locate the psychological power of broadcast television, we must concentrate on two features on account of which the medium has often been criticized. The first is that broadcast television works by repetition. We meet the same characters in the same general circumstances though in varying specific situations week after week over a long period of time. The second is that the television camera can cover only a small visual angle, and this, together with the low resolution of the television image, requires a large number of close-up shots. For many, this is equivalent to saying that television is visually elementary and intellectually boring.

And yet some of the medium's greatest achievements depend on these two features. For the first allows us to become acquainted with television characters gradually and over a long period of time, and the second enables us to come, in an almost physical sense, very close to them. And this closeness is not only physical. Our continuous exposure to these characters also brings us close to them in a psychological sense. Just as the characters of "St. Elsewhere" interact with one another every fictional day, so the audience comes to know them slowly, routinely, in a more or less controlled situation, not unlike the way in which they know the people they themselves work with. To a serious extent the relationship of the characters to one another replicates the relationship of these characters to their audience and the relationship of many members of that audience to the people they in turn work with. We come to know these characters, and many of the characters of television drama generally, *intimately*—in both a physical and a psychological sense. But to say that we come to know them intimately is not to say that we come to know them deeply. Their innermost nature, unlike the nature of the characters of novels, is not exposed; better put, television characters have no innermost nature. And yet, I want to suggest, the intimacy with which these not-deep characters are revealed is one of the medium's glories.

Many of the people we know best in life often move or infuriate us by some particular gesture or action the significance of which is very difficult to communicate to others because, as we say, "it has to be seen in context." The same is often the case when we try to recount a funny, moving, or nasty moment in a television program to someone who is not familiar with it. In one episode of "St. Elsewhere," for example, Donald Westphall, St. Eligius's chief of medicine, gets fired by the company representative. Mark Craig, who has always derided Westphall for being weak, boring, a do-gooder, and stubborn, continues to mock him for not apologizing and asking for his job back. When Westphall asks him why he cares whether he leaves or not, Craig, who is at the point of leaving the room, stops, turns, and, in a tone as supercilious as it is confessional, replies, "I'll miss you. Ridiculous as it may sound, you're the best friend I have." This is a moving and poignant moment, but it is difficult to say why, precisely because it is a *moment*, a small part of a complex relationship, and it is only within that relationship that it acquires whatever significance it has.

"St. Elsewhere" works through the accumulation of such moments and allows its audience to come to know its characters intimately but not deeply—just as these characters themselves know one another in the extended familial space of their workplace. Such knowledge can be extremely fine grained, but it depends essentially on long exposure. One must have learned, over time and through a large number of isolated incidents, precisely what a prude Westphall is in order to understand exactly what he does when, just before leaving the hospital and upon being told that he can have his job back provided he becomes a "team player," he turns his back and drops his pants in the face of the hospital administrator.

We might be tempted to say that even without knowledge of West-phall's character we do in fact know what he does, though we may not know exactly what it means. But this is misleading, because it suggests that there is one level on which his action is described and another on which it is interpreted, because it separates description from interpretation. It is much more nearly correct to say that we literally do not know what Westphall does on this occasion unless we see it in light of everything else he has ever done. Television, because of its serial character, highlights the essential interconnection of human actions—a psychological point—and the interdependence of their description and interpretation—a philosophical issue: is it really true to say that it is "thin and cumbersome in stimulating our moral and philosophical range"?

The serial unfolding of character and the ability of individual characters (at least in some programs) to change and develop with time have an important consequence. They render character ambiguous. By this I do not mean that television characters are difficult to understand. Rather, the point is that television can present various aspects of its characters without offering a single, all-encompassing judgment about their ultimate nature or worth. This is another sense in which television characters have no depth.

Mark Craig, the chief of surgery at St. Eligius, for example, is a terrific surgeon and a horrible sexist. "St. Elsewhere" does not account for his sexism in any way that justifies it. Craig is also brusque, selfish, insensitive, and competitive but also fiercely loyal to, and proud of, his residents. He is, in addition, insecure and more in need of others than he could possibly admit. He both loves and detests his son, who was addicted to drugs, married beneath him, and got killed in a car accident. We learn all this, and more besides, about him over a long period of time in a way not unrelated to that in which we come to know many of our friends and acquaintances. The net result of this gradual accumulation of detail is that there is no net result about Craig's character. It is difficult, perhaps impossible, and certainly not fruitful to say of him, or of most of the characters in this program, whether we like or dislike him. We may be devoted to him in the sense of wanting to know what he will be doing in the next episode, but approval or disapproval are not at issue. Do I *like* him? How can I, given his sexism, his crassness, his lack of sensitivity? Do I *dislike* him? No, because I do like his clipped manner, his pride in his work, his frightening straightforwardness. His character has too many sides for me to make a general evaluation of it. But where I see the absence of "totalization," others may not. And they may well like or dislike Craig, often for exactly the same reasons in each case. The television text is, in this sense, indeterminate. It allows its viewers to focus on different aspects of the characters it depicts and to see the same character in radically different ways, depending on their own preferences and values. It is, as John Fiske, echoing Roland Barthes, characterizes it, a "producerly" text—subject to various operations on the part of its viewers.

Similar things can be said about the show's female characters. Nurse Papandreou, for example, can be an absolute terror, nasty and full of invective. She is also unquestionably a superb nurse. She terrifies the obnoxious Victor Ehrlich, but she also brings out the best in him (the little of it there is) when she relaxes in his company at a Greek feast, invites him up to her apartment afterward, and eventually marries him. And, once married, she shows a perceptive and mature side in her relationship to him which, precisely because it does not carry over into her other interactions, makes it impossible—for me, at least—to make a general judgment about her. Is she a good or a bad character? What about most of the people with whom we live and work on a daily basis? We live and work with one another, and toward most of them we have no single unequivocal reaction.

Classical realism, according to Catherine Belsey, always creates an overarching point of view from which all the pieces of each story can be seen to fall together. I have just argued that, at least on a psychological level, "St. Elsewhere" undermines any effort to occupy such a point of view. And just for this reason, "St. Elsewhere" reveals that its medium has the resources for presenting unusual aspects of human character—unusual enough to pass completely unnoticed if we are not willing to watch seriously.

Is "St. Elsewhere," however, realistic in the further sense that its aim is to achieve "closure," to provide on a narrative level a final settlement of all the details of its plot and to put its viewers in the comfortable position of having finished *with* the story as well as simply having finished it? Jane Feuer has argued that "All in the Family" aimed at that goal: "The Lear family, however much they were divided along political lines, would each week be reintegrated in order that a new enigma could be introduced."[28] In fact, however, this was not quite true of "All in the Family." Often the show's episodes end with an extreme close-up of Archie Bunker, who has just been rendered speechless by losing an argument. But speechlessness is not accommodation. And the look on Archie's face—part admission of defeat, part stubborn reassertion of his inner conviction that he is always right—allows viewers of different political orientations to draw their own different conclusions about the very nature of the episode they have just watched.

"St. Elsewhere," however, appears to provide just the kind of closure Belsey associates with classical realism. The program was canceled at the end of the 1987–88 season. Since this was known in advance, the show's final four episodes were devoted to constructing a complete resolution of its various subplots and to disposing properly of every single one of its regular characters. Manifesting a remarkable and unusual single-mindedness, "St. Elsewhere," with the exception of those who died, created a future for all its characters and left absolutely no loose ends. Or so it seemed until the show's final scene.

Throughout the last episode, which is supposed to occur in the spring, the characters keep remarking that the temperature is dropping and that it is about to snow. At first these remarks are so out of place that they pass unnoticed until their cumulative weight makes them as impossible to ignore as they are to understand. Indeed, snow begins to fall. We see the hospital in the middle of a snowstorm, and the camera pans in order to take in the whole building—a shot that strongly disposes us to expect that the show has come to its end. But as the pan continues and the building gets progressively smaller, it also, inexplicably, begins to shake. And suddenly we realize that what we are seeing is not at all the "real" hospital but only a cardboard cutout enclosed in a glass paperweight and surrounded by "artificial" snowflakes.

Whose toy is this? It belongs to Tommy, Dr. Westphall's autistic son, who was looking at the snowfall from inside the hospital in the scene immediately preceding. Tommy, completely absorbed, is sitting on the floor shaking the paperweight. But can this be West-

[28]Jane Feuer, "Narrative Form in American Network Television," in Colin MacCabe, *High Theory/Low Culture* (Manchester: Manchester University Press, 1986), p. 107.

phall's son? He is sitting in a shabby room and not in Westphall's suburban house, and he is being watched over by Dr. Auschlander— who cannot be Dr. Auschlander, since Dr. Auschlander died of a stroke earlier on in the episode. At that point, Westphall enters: he wears a hardhat and carries a lunch box. But, of course, this is not Westphall either: he turns out to be a construction worker and the son of the man we had known as Auschlander up to that point. Having greeted his father, "Westphall" looks at his son and says, "I don't understand this autism thing, Pop. . . . He sits there all day long, in his own world, staring at that toy. What's he thinking about?" He then lifts the boy, places the toy exactly in the middle of the top of the television set, and leaves the room. The camera now closes in for the truly final shot of St. Eligius, encased—frozen—in its glass container.

Turning a story into a dream or a phantasy at the very last moment is one of the most uninteresting ways of accounting for loose ends that could not be coherently pulled together. In this case the whole show we have been watching for five years or so is made the content of the mind of an autistic boy—but only after every single one of its strands has been carefully, obsessively pulled tight. It is impossible for a story of such complexity to have been conceived by an autistic eleven-year-old. The ending is unbelievable. And it is also, since no loose ends had remained, unnecessary. Why, then, is it there?

It is there, I think, as a final reminder that the story was after all a fiction, as much a fiction as the fiction that an autistic boy could ever spin such a fiction. It is a reminder that just as the story of the boy's spinning such a fiction cannot be true, so every part of the show itself, everything that we have seen has been fiction, though it was fiction that, as we have seen, took its shape, its colors, its plot, and its very end—its death—from the demands of life. What is real, this ending asks, and what is fiction?

And the toy in which the boy was absorbed, left on top of the television set, now emerges as a metaphor for television itself and for its viewers' relation to it. It is not very flattering, if one does watch television, to see oneself described as an autistic eleven-year old. Yet this character, the show tells us, is the show's creator and is acknowledged as such by the other characters' awareness of the snow for which the boy is directly responsible. Who is it, this ending asks, who, along with life, gave the show its shape, its colors, and its end? How much has the viewer contributed? Is it a good or a bad thing to watch television, and to be part, and in part a creator, of its fiction?

These are heady questions, and there are many others like them. The fact that they are raised by a program like "St. Elsewhere" shows that the literate opponents of the popular media have no monopoly on literacy, and that the very notion of literacy needs to be examined anew. "Whoever begins at this point, like my readers," Nietzsche wrote, "to reflect and pursue his train of thought will not soon come to the end of it—reason enough for me to come to an end"[29]—and for me as well, but not before I cite one more attack on his time by an author who considered it "an age, wherein the greatest part of men seem agreed to convert reading into an amusement, and to reject every thing that requires any considerable degree of attention to be comprehended."[30] Thus David Hume. But Hume's complaint is both older and more recent: it was first made by Plato and is being repeated today by countless educated people who are unaware of its provenance. It suggests that even those with the greatest knowledge of history are not necessarily the most historical of people, and that the gesture of rejecting "every thing that requires any considerable degree of attention to be comprehended" is not peculiar to "the greatest part of men"—or, rather, that it is, except that the greatest part of men, and women, includes us all.

[29]Friedrich Nietzsche, On the Genealogy of Morals, trans. Walter Kaufmann (New York: Vintage, 1969), 1: 17.

[30]David Hume, A Treatise of Human Nature, ed. L. A. Selby-Bigge (Oxford: Oxford University Press, 1888), p. 456 (Book III, Part I, section 1).

CHAPTER 14

Hermeneutics and Genre: Bakhtin and the Problem of Communicative Interaction

THOMAS KENT

A work is only real in the form of a definitive genre.
—M. M. Bakhtin

In literary hermeneutics M. M. Bakhtin's considerable influence derives in large part from his anti-Cartesian claims concerning the public nature of discourse. For over five decades, even during the Stalinist terror when he was exiled for his beliefs, Bakhtin engaged in a sustained attack on the subjectivism of his formalist and structuralist contemporaries—important literary theorists like Victor Shklovsky, Boris Eichenbaum, Roman Jakobson, and Vladimir Propp—who promulgated the idea that meaning is produced primarily through the semiotic relations of linguistic elements.[1] According to the formalist and structuralist conception of meaning, the human language system, what Ferdinand de Saussure called *langue*, constitutes a conceptual scheme that mediates between the human subject and the world. For more extreme formalists and structuralists—I am thinking here about people like Benjamin Whorf, Claude Lévi-Strauss, and Roland Barthes—the human language system constituted all that we can know about the world, and it represented the epistemological

[1] For a good overview of the formalism and the structuralism to which Bakhtin reacted, see Lee T. Lemon and Marion J. Reis, eds., *Russian Formalist Criticism: Four Essays* (Lincoln: University of Nebraska Press, 1965), and Ladislav Matejka and Krystyna Pomorska, *Readings in Russian Poetics: Formalist and Structuralist Views* (Cambridge: MIT Press, 1971).

model for understanding every form of human endeavor.[2] Bakhtin understood clearly that when we accept this Cartesian or *internalist* conception of meaning and language—the notion that meaning is the internal business of a perceiving mind that may know the world (which includes the minds of others) only through the mediation of language—we find ourselves enclosed in what Fredric Jameson has called "the prison-house of language" where we can never escape the problems of skepticism and relativism.[3]

Bakhtin countered this internalist conception of language and meaning by endorsing an assiduously externalist position that rests on two related and, by now, well-known claims: (1) language and meaning are thoroughly holistic in nature; an utterance means something only in relation to a complex network of other utterances, and (2) utterances exist only within the dialogic and public interactions among communicants; therefore, no private language can exist. Clearly, these anti-Cartesian claims about language and meaning are not unique to Bakhtin. Appearing in different guises, these claims show up regularly in the work of language philosophers like John Dewey, Martin Heidegger, Ludwig Wittgenstein, and W. V. O. Quine, who have provided some of the most powerful and comprehensive critiques of Cartesian subjectivism.[4] Bakhtin's most important and singular contribution to this critique—and to literary hermeneutics as well—concerns, I believe, his externalist account of communicative interaction.

In his seminal essay "Speech Genres" Bakhtin argues that the most fundamental element of communicative interaction is the utter-

---

[2]See Benjamin Lee Whorf, *Language, Thought, and Reality: Selected Writings of Benjamin Lee Whorf*, ed. J. B. Carroll (Cambridge: MIT Press, 1956); Claude Lévi-Strauss, *Structural Anthropology*, vol. 2, trans. Monique Layton (New York: Basic Books, 1976); and Roland Barthes, *Elements of Semiology*, trans. A. Lavers and C. Smith (New York: Hill and Wang, 1977).

[3]Fredric Jameson, *The Prison-House of Language: A Critical Account of Structuralism and Russian Formalism* (Princeton: Princeton University Press, 1972). For an account of the problems caused by skepticism and relativism in the Cartesian view of language, see Richard Rorty, *Philosophy and the Mirror of Nature* (Princeton: Princeton University Press, 1979).

[4]No clear evidence exists demonstrating that Bakhtin was influenced significantly by philosophers such as Dewey, Heidegger, Wittgenstein, and Quine, who were writing at roughly the same time Bakhtin was writing. For many years Bakhtin worked in relative isolation, and he experienced very little contact with Continental and Anglo-American philosophy or literary theory. Nonetheless, remarkable similarities exist between Bakhtin's conception of language and the conception of language held by these philosophers, which makes Bakhtin's work all the more remarkable.

ance and not the word or the sentence, and the utterance takes form only in the shape of what he calls a "speech genre."[5] The speech genre therefore represents the starting place for every investigation of language-in-use because no more fundamental communicative unit exists. By concentrating on Bakhtin's general theory of communication developed in "Speech Genres," I argue in the discussion to follow that the speech genre, what I call for convenience simply *genre*, corresponds to an open-ended and uncodifiable strategy for hermeneutic guessing. If it can be supported, this argument requires us to rethink our notions about the possibility of describing discourse production and reception as reductive cognitive processes of one kind or another, and it requires us, as well, to relinquish the hope for hermeneutical certainty—what some have called interpretive monism—that would form the foundation for a Habermasian universal pragmatics.[6] In the discussion to follow, then, I will attempt to develop what I believe Bakhtin's externalism suggests: communication occurs through a hermeneutical guessing game engendered through genre.

The Nature of the Utterance

The importance of Bakhtin's analysis of communicative interaction goes beyond his insistence that words and sentences mean nothing until they are used. For us, this claim is a commonplace; today, no one seriously defends the idea that meaning resides exclusively in words or sentences.[7] Bakhtin understands communicative interaction

[5]M. M. Bakhtin, "Speech Genres," in *Speech Genres and Other Late Essays*, trans. Vern W. McGee, ed. Caryl Emerson and Michael Holquist (Austin: University of Texas Press, 1986). Subsequent references to this essay will be cited in the text as "SG."

[6]The goal of universal pragmatics, according to Jürgen Habermas, is to "describe exactly that fundamental system of rules that adult subjects master to the extent that they can fulfill the conditions for a happy employment of sentences in utterances, no matter to which particular language the sentences may belong and in which accidental language the utterances may be embedded." *Communication and the Evolution of Society*, trans. Thomas McCarthy (Boston: Beacon Press, 1979), p. 26). In a sense, universal pragmatics seeks to describe the *langue* of *parole*, the underlying system that allows communication to occur. I will argue that no such system can exist because of the hermeneutic nature of communicative interaction. For a discussion of what is meant by "interpretive monism," see Alexander Nehamas, "The Postulated Author: Critical Monism as a Regulative Ideal," *Critical Inquiry* 8 (1981): 133–49.

[7]The philosophers who have enunciated this position most clearly are Ludwig Wittgenstein and John Austin, but the movement of contemporary language philosophy, linguistics, and literary theory toward pragmatic externalist accounts of meaning and

to partake of what he calls the "open unity" of culture where our unified perception of the world remains always open to new signifying relations.[8] Like the open unity of culture that cannot be reduced to a Spenglerian closed circle and that demands continually new hermeneutic analyses, communicative interaction—which animates culture and gives it life—cannot be reduced to abstract systems of semantic or syntactic relations.[9] In fact, the proposition that language is an indeterminate social phenomenon may be seen as the great thematic motif that runs through Bakhtin's various commentaries on formalist and structuralist language theories; from the early "Problems of Dostoevsky's Art" to his latest essays and interviews, Bakhtin insists that language-in-use cannot be reduced to a Saussurean *langue* or to any system that seeks to codify our ability to communicate through signs. Bakhtin argues again and again that any meaningful description of language must take into account language's hermeneutic and pragmatic social nature, for no abstract model—models like those proposed by Saussure, Roman Jakobson, and Noam Chomsky—can predict the hermeneutical moves we make when we communicate.[10]

In the essay "Speech Genres" Bakhtin attempts to account for the hermeneutic dimension of language by analyzing communicative *interaction* and not language-as-system, and he sets out to identify the most fundamental element of communicative interaction, the element that gives language its ability to create effects in the world. Because this element cannot be discovered through an analysis of language-as-system, it consequently cannot be described through an analysis of either the word or the sentence, for words and sentences, as the constitutive elements of an abstract linguistic system, can mean noth-

---

away from Cartesian internalist accounts rejects fundamentally the positivistic and cognitive endeavor to locate meaning within sentences. See J. L. Austin, *How to Do Things with Words* (Cambridge: Harvard University Press, 1967), and Ludwig Wittgenstein, *Philosophical Investigations*, trans. G. E. M. Anscombe (New York: Macmillan, 1953).

[8]M. M. Bakhtin, "Response to a Question from the *Novy Mir* Editorial Staff," *Speech Genres and Other Later Essay*, p. 6.

[9]For a discussion of Bakhtin's rejection of abstract systems of semantic and syntactic relations, see Evelyn Cobley, "Mikhail Bakhtin's Place in Genre Theory," *Genre* 21 (1988): 321–38.

[10]These models are discussed in Ferdinand de Saussure, *Course in General Linguistics*, trans. Wade Baskin (New York: Philosophical Library, 1959); Roman Jakobson, *Selected Writings* (The Hague: Mouton, 1962); Noam Chomsky, *Aspects of the Theory of Syntax* (Cambridge: MIT Press, 1965).

ing until they enter into communicative interaction among the different dialogic interchanges of public life. Bakhtin moves beyond the idea of language-as-system by locating the most fundamental element of communicative interaction within these dialogic interchanges, and he calls this element the "utterance." Because Bakhtin's analysis of the utterance forms the foundation for his conception of genre and, as well, for his entire theory of communicative interaction, I would like to examine more closely what he means by this term.

Bakhtin contends that language comes into being only through "individual concrete utterances (oral and written) by participants in the various areas of human activity" ("SG," p. 60), and, in turn, through the utterance, language enters into human activity and, in a reciprocal way, human activity transforms language. The utterance, therefore, must be seen as a pragmatic element of language-in-use and not as an element of a linguistic system like the word or sentence. As an element of language-in-use, the utterance actively accounts for the other in communicative interaction, a crucial aspect of discourse production and reception that is often ignored in structuralist language theory and speech-act theory. By emphasizing the intentional role of the speaker, totalizing language theories grounded in conceptions of the word or the sentence, theories like Noam Chomsky's generative grammar or John Searle's speech acts, pay only lip service to the other, and by deemphasizing or sometimes simply ignoring the crucial importance of the other in our own individual use of language, these totalizing theories cannot escape the realm of theoretical abstraction to tell us anything concrete about how language actually communicates, how it responds to the other, how it engenders new relations with other communicants, or how it creates effects in the world.

Unlike totalizing theories of language use that pay little or no attention to the role of the other, Bakhtin's conception of the utterance accounts for the dialogic and collaborative nature of language-in-use by merging the speaker/text with the other. Within any communicative interaction, according to Bakhtin, the speaker shapes her discourse in response to the other, and in a similar fashion, the listener makes sense of another's discourse by taking a responsive and interactive stance toward the speaker/text.[11] Bakhtin argues that no mean-

[11]Bakhtin's claim that intelligible communicative interaction requires public utterances that react to the other corresponds closely, I believe, to Donald Davidson's conception of triangulation. See Donald Davidson, "The Conditions of Thought," *Le Cahier du Collège International de Philosophie* (Paris: Editions Osiris, 1989), pp. 165–71.

ingful communication can occur without a response from the other: "Any understanding is imbued with response and necessarily elicits it in one form or another: the listener becomes the speaker" ("SG," p. 68). All understanding takes place through a response to the other, and this response takes the concrete form of the utterance through which language accomplishes its work. In this formulation Bakhtin inverts the claim made by linguists like Saussure, Jakobson, and Chomsky that language-as-system makes the utterance possible; according to Bakhtin, it is the utterance that makes language-as-system possible.[12] Because no language element exists that cannot be uttered in many different communicative situations—the aspect of language that Jacques Derrida calls "iterability"—the utterance determines the nature of the elements in a language system; the language system does not determine the nature of the utterance.[13]

For Bakhtin, the utterance represents the most elemental unit of communicative interaction, and unlike the semantic and syntactic elements employed in most linguistic analyses, the utterance refutes what Bakhtin calls "graphic-schematic depictions" ("SG," p. 68). At best, schematic communication models like Jakobson's or systemic descriptions like Saussure's supply only a partial and often distorted idea about how language operates in the world because these "scientific fictions" ("SG," p. 68) cannot account for the dynamic interactive response inherent in the utterance. For example, neither Jakobson's famous schematic communication model nor Saussure's equally famous conception of paradigmatic and syntagmatic relations can capture the intricate dialogic interplay among the myriad utterances within public life where language must live.[14] Because language functions primarily to create responses or what I have been calling effects in the world, all understanding derives from the dynamic dialogic-like utterance that no graphic or schematic model can cap-

[12]The theories of language enunciated by Saussure, Jakobson, and Chomsky might be said to describe what is necessary for communicative interaction; I am arguing, however, that these descriptions are not sufficient to explain how language is used in the world. The descriptions of communicative interaction referred to here may be found in Saussure's *Course in General Linguistics*, Jakobson's *Selected Writings*, and Chomsky's *Aspects of the Theory of Syntax*.

[13]See Jacques Derrida, "Signature Event Context," *Glyph 1*, ed. Samuel Weber and Henry Sussman (Baltimore: Johns Hopkins University Press, 1977), pp. 172–97.

[14]For a discussion of some of the problems inherent in the schematic approach to communicative interaction, see Virgil Lokke, "Contextualizing the Either/Or: Invariance/Variation and Dialogue in Jakobson/Bakhtin," in *The Current in Criticism*, ed. Virgil Lokke and Clayton Kolb (West Lafayette, Ind.: Purdue University Press, 1986), pp. 201–41.

ture, for no account of language-as-system can predict the other's response to an utterance.[15] For that matter, no system can even predict what our response will be to someone else's utterance. The many different depictions of language-as-system, the depictions elaborated by Saussure, Jakobson, Chomsky, and others, form a description of only the background knowledge speakers and listeners presuppose that one another possesses, so depictions of syntagmatic-paradigmatic relations, schematic communication models, and generative grammars reveal only part of language's ability to create effects in the world. In a sense, they reveal what speakers and listeners already know; only the utterance goes beyond these scientific fictions to account for language-in-use.

As the most elemental unit of language-in-use, the utterance, according to Bakhtin, manifests three constitutive features: (1) a clearcut boundary determined by a change of speaking subjects, (2) finalization of the utterance, and (3) a specific semantic content. For the purposes of our discussion here, the most important aspect of these three features concerns their nonreductive nature. Although Bakhtin insists that the utterance is a concrete manifestation of language-in-use, he suggests that the utterance—although concrete—cannot be reduced to a systemic description that possesses predictive value. He suggests, therefore, that the utterance, as a "real unit" of language-in-use ("SG," p. 71), refutes reduction; although the utterance exists as a concrete reality, no epistemological account can describe, in any meaningful way, how the utterance does its work. In order to examine how Bakhtin's characterization of the utterance leads us to this conclusion, I would like to discuss briefly each of the three constitutive features of the utterance sketched out by Bakhtin.

As we have noted, Bakhtin insists that communication, in all its myriad manifestations, exists only in the form of concrete utterances, and although utterances dress up in many different compositional guises, all utterances nonetheless share clearly discernible features.[16] Unlike certain ambiguous terms such as "speech act" or "speech flow" that cannot be described precisely, the utterance, according to

[15]Donald Davidson addresses this issue in "Communication and Convention," *Inquiries into Truth and Interpretation* (Oxford: Clarendon Press, 1984), p. 279, where he employs the description "the ability to shift ground appropriately" to describe the dialogic-like moves we make when we communicate.

[16]According to Bakhtin, "Regardless of how varied utterances may be in terms of their length, their content, and their compositional structure, they have common structural features as units of speech communication and, above all, quite clear-cut boundaries" ("SG," p. 71).

Bakhtin, displays a clear beginning and end. These boundaries of the utterance are determined

> by a change of speaking subjects, that is, a change of speakers. Any utterance—from a short (single-word) rejoinder in everyday dialogue to the large novel or scientific treatise—has, so to speak, an absolute beginning and an absolute end; its beginning is preceded by the utterances of others, and its end is followed by the responsive utterances of others. . . . The speaker ends his utterance in order to relinquish the floor to the other or to make room for the other's active responsive understanding. The utterance is not a convention, but a real unit, clearly delimited by the change of speaking subjects, which ends by relinquishing the floor to the other, as if with a silent dixi, perceived by the listeners (as a sign) that the speaker has finished. ("SG," pp. 71–72)

Because the boundaries of the utterance are defined by language-in-use and not by idealized grammars, the utterance as a category takes in all the different forms and kinds of communicative interaction. The utterance may range from a one-syllable rejoinder to a multivolume novel. Unlike the sentence or other transformational unit, the utterance takes its identity from the dialogic-like interchanges between a communicant and the other that occur only within living language, and the constitutive marker that defines the boundaries of the utterance within the responsive interchanges of living language—a marker that no syntactic unit displays—is what Bakhtin calls the "pause" ("SG," p. 74) or what I will call hereafter the *hermeneutic pause*. Below in this discussion I consider more carefully this idea of the hermeneutic pause, but here it is important to note that no syntactic element like the sentence accounts for the hermeneutic pause that enables interpretive understanding to occur among communicants. Of course, as Bakhtin points out ("SG," p. 74), a speaker certainly may pause after a sentence to allow for a response from the other, but in this case the sentence allows the pause only because the sentence takes the completed form of the utterance, not because the completed utterance happens to take the form of a sentence. No element of communicative interaction except the utterance can account for our ability to employ a language in order to interpret the other's language, and the boundaries of the utterance are outlined by the pauses between communicants that allow the other to speak.

The second feature of the utterance is related directly to the first. Bakhtin calls this feature "finalization of the utterance," and by this idea, Bakhtin means the inner side of the change of speech subjects. This change can only take place because the speaker has said (or written) everything he wishes to say at a particular moment or under particular circumstances. When hearing or reading, we clearly sense the end of the utterance, as if we hear the speaker's concluding dixi. This finalization is specific and is determined by special criteria. ("SG," p. 76)

The most important of these criteria is the possibility of responding to the utterance ("SG," p. 76). Bakhtin seems to mean by this criterion that the pause that occurs at the end of an utterance signals a certain attitude that calls out for a response. He maintains that this attitude goes beyond simply understanding a language, for, as Bakhtin explains, "It is not enough for the utterance to be understood in terms of language. An absolutely understood and completed sentence, if it is a sentence and not an utterance comprised of one sentence, cannot evoke a responsive reaction: it is comprehensible, but it is not all. This all—the indicator of the wholeness of the utterance— is subject neither to grammatical nor to abstract semantic definition" ("SG," p. 76). As I understand Bakhtin, he means that only the completed concrete utterance and no syntactic element like the sentence can call for a response from the other, and this response, in turn, is triggered by a distinct attitude inherent in the pause occurring after the utterance. Two signifying elements—the linguistic units that make up the utterance plus the pause at the end of the utterance— constitute the "wholeness" of the utterance. Finalization, then, does not mean that the utterance closes down to become a formal and finished element of language that can be specified precisely like the sentence; finalization does not mean closure. Finalization describes the temporary "finalized wholeness of the utterance" ("SG," p. 76) that allows the other to know when to respond within the dialogic interaction of language-in-use.

What Bakhtin calls the "finalized wholeness of the utterance" that triggers a response from the other and that enables understanding to occur may be recognized by three factors: (1) semantic exhaustiveness of the theme; (2) the speaker's plan or speech will, and (3) typical compositional and generic forms of finalization. The first two of these factors are similar, and they describe the most obvious aspects of finalization. By "semantic exhaustiveness of the theme" of the utterance, Bakhtin means the range of interpretive completeness shared by speaker and listener. Some utterances may be interpreted to be exhausted of thematic content by both speaker and listener. For example, factual questions and responses, requests, orders, and other kinds of imperatives and implicatures including formulaic kinds of writing represent utterances that we recognize in everyday life as thematically exhausted; they are standardized, conventional, and automatized. Other utterances, however, may be only relatively exhausted. In what Bakhtin calls "creative spheres" ("SG," p. 77), for example, utterances of a scientific or artistic nature "do not objectively exhaust the subject, but, by becoming the theme of the utterance . . . the subject achieves a relative finalization" ("SG," p. 77). In other words, some utterances require more guesswork on the parts of both speaker and listener about the hermeneutic strategy necessary to create some effect in the world; certain utterances simply require more interpretation than other utterances.

This claim leads naturally to the second aspect of finalization posited by Bakhtin. Listening to or reading any utterance requires that "we imagine to ourselves what the speaker wishes to say" ("SG," p. 77), or, stated differently, we imagine that every speaker or text possesses a "speech plan." This speech plan is revealed through the interaction of different hermeneutic strategies available to both speaker and listener, and to make the speech plan known, the speaker naturally selects concrete elements of signification—syntactic structures, subject matter, and most importantly generic forms—that the speaker believes the listener will know. Of course, to understand the speaker, the listener also must guess about the speaker's speech plan by interpreting the concrete elements of signification employed by the speaker. In this way, communicants hermeneutically orient themselves in order to understand—to guess at—the speaker's speech plan. As Bakhtin points out, from the very beginning of an utterance, we sense its developing wholeness; we have a sense of what the utterance is and what it means. Obviously, our guesses about a speaker's speech plan may be wrong, but it is only through this hermeneutic guesswork, this paralogic sense of the utterance, that we recognize that an utterance is finalized and ready for our response.

The third and most important aspect of finalization concerns the generic form of the utterance. Because the problem of genre lies at the heart of Bakhtin's conception of the utterance, I would like to delay discussion of this aspect of finalization until I can more fully pursue it below. Here, I believe that it is enough to say that Bakhtin understands the utterance and the genre to be closely connected if not inseparable; to understand an utterance we must "guess its genre from the very first words" ("SG," p. 79), and this guesswork, as I shall argue below, cannot be reduced to a hermeneutic framework that will help us predict in advance what an utterance means. Because we must guess about the genre to which an utterance belongs in order to recognize the boundaries of an utterance and to recognize its tenuous finality, all communicative interaction derives from our ability to recognize and to generate genres, for we communicate only through the utterance as genre. Because communicative interaction cannot occur unless we recognize the generic wholeness of an utterance, the genre becomes the social realization of the utterance, and our sense of the beginnings and the endings of genres supplies us with the markers that allow us to know when an utterance is finalized.

I should emphasize again that finalization does not correspond to complete closure in that dialogic interaction is stopped.[17] Finalization corresponds only to the signal that new speakers are about to speak, and as we communicate, we require this signal provided by finalization in order to know when talk is appropriate. Finalization does not escape dialogue; it is a characteristic of dialogue. To comprehend the finalized utterance, then, we require all our background knowledge about the uses of language, and no abstract model can predict how this background knowledge might be employed. Because it may be readily comprehended but not reduced to a synchronic hermeneutic framework, finalization, like the change of speaking subjects, clearly represents an aporistic feature of the utterance that derives from language-in-use. Simply because finalization is aporistic does not mean, however, that it lacks concrete reality. Finalization represents a concrete (although linguistically indeterminate) marker that signals communicants that an utterance is complete, and as the mark of completeness (always an incomplete completeness—a tenuous "mark" of genre or absent presence), finalization also becomes a link in what Bakhtin calls the "chain of speech communion" ("SG," p. 84), a chain that holds together the dialogic interchanges that constitute communicative interaction. In its guise as the mark of completeness, finalization relates directly to Bakhtin's third feature of the utterance: the utterance as a link in the chain of speech communion.

As a link in the chain of speech communion, the utterance "is the active position of the speaker in one referentially semantic sphere or

[17]"Finalization" is, I believe, an unfortunate term for the concept Bakhtin desires to describe. It suggests that some sort of final closure may occur between communicants that ends once and for all the process of communicative interaction. Finalization might be better understood to be a pause between communicants that signals the desire for a response from the other. In no way, however, is the utterance "finished" or "final."

another" ("SG," p. 84). The utterance takes the form of the speaker's live response to the other, and this response always possesses a determinate semantic content that is governed by the speaker's speech plan and the speaker's expressive evaluative attitude. As we note above, the speech plan provides the primary semantic content of an utterance through the speaker's choice of linguistic elements available to her. In addition to the obvious words and sentences required in any utterance, an utterance also expresses "the speaker's subjective emotional evaluation of the referentially semantic content of his utterance" ("SG," p. 84). When Bakhtin claims that "there can be no such thing as an absolutely neutral utterance" ("SG," p. 84), he means that every utterance expresses more than the logical reduction of its sentential content; the utterance also relates an expressive aspect that contributes to its total meaning, an aspect of language just as important as its sentential aspect. As part of a language system— as an element of langue—the sentence possesses only a referential semantic meaning, and even when it is transposed from one context to another in an attempt to account for iterability—a technique employed by social semioticians and speech-act theorists—the sentence still remains devoid of expressive meaning. As Bakhtin explains it: "The sentence as a unit of language is . . . neutral and in itself has no expressive aspect. It acquires this expressive aspect (more precisely, joins itself to it) only in a concrete utterance" ("SG," p. 85). The sentence means nothing until it takes the form of an utterance, and as an utterance every sentence acquires an expressive aspect that joins itself to its referential aspect.

Like the speaker's or writer's speech plan, the expressive aspect of the utterance should not be regarded as a product of the language system. Bakhtin is criticized often for his neologisms and opaque explanations, but he could not be more clear in his insistence that the expressive aspect of the utterance cannot be reduced to an element of the language system:

Can the expressive aspect of speech be regarded as a phenomenon of language as a system? Can one speak of the expressive aspect of language units, that is, words and sentences? The answer to these questions must be a categorical "no." Language as a system has, of course, a rich arsenal of language tools . . . for expressing the speaker's emotionally evaluative position, but all these tools as language tools are absolutely neutral with respect to any particular real evaluation. . . . Words belong to nobody, and in themselves they evaluate nothing. But they can serve

any speaker and be used for the most varied and directly contradictory
evaluations on the part of the speakers. ("SG," pp. 84–85)

From this statement, we should not jump to the conclusion that Bakhtin means that we simply must take into account something called
context when we attempt to account for the meaning of a sentence or
word. As an attempt to describe how sentences generate different
meanings in different contexts, contextual analysis—the analytic approach to meaning employed primarily by the Halliday School, by
speech-act theorists, and by some social constructionists—cannot account for the expressive dimension of the sentence as an utterance,
nor, I believe, can it account for any important aspect of language-
in-use. In a very limited sense, contextual analysis certainly helps to
explain why a sentence—as an utterance—might be interpreted to
mean *x* in situation *y*, but contextual analysis can tell us nothing
about how the sentence came to mean *x* in situation *y*.

As Bakhtin points out, the matter is far more complicated than
simply accounting for the uses of sentences within different social
contexts. According to Bakhtin, the expressive dimension of the utterance joins with its semantic dimension to form the whole utterance
that, in turn, links up with other utterances in wholly indeterminate
ways. Within this complex interaction, all three features of the utterance work together to make communication possible: the semantic
dimension of the utterance joins with its expressive dimension to
form the whole utterance that is finalized through the semantic exhaustiveness of the theme, the speaker's plan, and the generic form
assumed by the utterance. The boundaries of the utterance are then
determined by a change of speech subjects. Because an utterance
always responds to other utterances, it is saturated in what Bakhtin
calls "dialogic overtones" ("SG," p. 92) from its responsive interaction with other utterances, and these overtones deposited by other
utterances make any specific utterance "irrational" when regarded
from the point of view of language-as-system. Bakhtin explains,
"Others' utterances and others' individual words—recognized and
singled out as such and inserted into the utterance—introduce an
element that is, so to speak, irrational from the standpoint of language as system, particularly from the standpoint of syntax" ("SG,"
p. 92). This irrational element—the dialogic overtones supplied by
the other—exists because we cannot account for the complex interaction of one utterance with another, for, as Bakhtin points out, "The
choice of all language means is made by the speaker under varying

degrees of influence from the addressee and his anticipated response" ("SG," p. 99). As a result of this dialogic give and take, we
cannot account for the linguistic versatility we acquire through the
hermeneutical guesses we make about the meaning that others might
give our utterances as well as the guesses we make about the meaning of others' utterances.

The Utterance as Genre

For Bakhtin, the utterance constitutes the lived social reality of
language-in-use, and as language-in-use, the utterance takes the historically determinate form of the genre. The genre represents the
utterance's social baggage in the sense that the utterance must take
on a determinate and public form that communicants can identify.
Consequently, the genre constitutes the public form that an utterance
must assume in order to be comprehensible. The genre assumed by
a particular utterance always responds to other forms of utterances
within the different dialogic transactions among the myriad public
discourses of social life. Bakhtin calls this response "addressivity":
"An essential (constitutive) marker of the utterance is its quality of
being directed to someone, its addressivity" ("SG," p. 95). Because
every utterance is addressed to the other and responds to the other,
the generic form of the utterance, as well as its style and composition,
depends "on those to whom the utterance is addressed, how the
speaker (or writer) senses and imagines his addressees, and the force
of their effect on the utterance" ("SG," p. 95). A genre comes into
being only through its throwness toward the other, and in its throwness—its addressivity—each genre possesses "its own typical conception of the addressee, and this defines it as a genre" ("SG," p. 95).
A genre, therefore, never stands as a synchronic category outside the
concrete reality of communicative interaction, and it cannot be reduced to a set of conventional elements that function together as a
structural or organic whole.

Because of its innate addressivity, a genre cannot be regarded as
simply another element, like the word or sentence, within a linguistic
system. A word or a sentence may be reduced to a structure of conventional elements—the word to a system of phonemes and the sentence to a system of paradigmatic and syntagmatic relations, for
example—but these structures can tell us nothing about how meaning
is conveyed when these systems are put into action. Bakhtin points

out that neither the word nor the sentence constitutes the most fundamental element of communicative interaction because neither means anything until it is directed toward the other: ''As distinct from utterances (and speech genres), the signifying units of a language—the word and the sentence—lack this quality of being directed or addressed to someone: these units belong to nobody and are addressed to nobody. . . . addressivity is inherent not in the unit of language, but in the utterance'' (''SG,'' p. 99). Since the genre is the concrete determination of the utterance, the genre takes on the character of the utterance and not the word or sentence, and like the utterance, the genre may never be exhausted in the sense that it can be reduced to a rigid taxonomy of synchronic elements. From this general description, three innate features of genre may be isolated: (1) genre is defined by addressivity and not form; (2) genre is aporistic and uncodifiable in nature, and (3) genre is the most fundamental unit of communication. I would like now to consider some of the ramifications of such a view of genre.

Addressivity and Form

Genre has been traditionally considered to be a form of discourse that derives from a set of conventions that may be codified. For example, we traditionally speak of the drama, the novel, poetry, and film as genres, and within these genres there exist subgenres like tragedy and comedy in the drama, picaresque and romance in the novel, lyric and epic in poetry, melodrama and film noir in film, and so on. The long history of these forms has been dominated by production theory, the attempt to codify the elements that constitute a genre. More specifically, production theories generally attempt to account for the rules of a genre that authors must either follow or break in order to produce texts at some historical moment.[18] When we consider the history of literary criticism, most genre studies may be classified as production theories, especially those studies dating from the Renaissance through the eighteenth century to Johann Gottfried Herder. After Herder, organicist theories of genre production developed that reacted against restrictive generic formulations like the three unities

[18]Joseph Strelka's collection of essays *Theories of Literary Genre* (University Park: Pennsylvania State University Press, 1978), and the anthology edited by Marjorie Perloff, *Postmodern Genres* (Norman: University of Oklahoma Press, 1989), supply good examples of the continuing influence of production theory on contemporary genre studies.

or doctrines of sound and sense that were popularized by critics like Pierre Corneille and Alexander Pope. Although they sought to eradicate the idea that rules existed for the production of texts, theorists like Wilhelm von Schlegel, Friedrich von Schiller, Samuel Taylor Coleridge, and William Wordsworth actually replaced one set of rules with another. Their organicist theories of genre production, which are still with us today, functioned primarily to establish the hegemony of certain ideological doctrines like the cult of the "great man" or "natural man" who somehow transcends his age. In nineteenth-century England, for example, the lyric poem was associated with certain expressive theories of the imagination and with certain evolutionary doctrines that espoused primitivism in one form or another, and these formulations were translated into prescriptions, mostly implied prescriptions, for the production of texts.[19]

In this century production theory has continued to dominate, until very recently, the study of genres. Especially in the twentieth-century Marxist tradition, production theory has held a privileged place in literary study. Georg Lukács's *Theory of the Novel*, for example, is perhaps the representative par excellence of production theory in this century.[20] Lukács attached a Marxist theory of alienation and fragmentation to the production of the novel, and in terms of approach and methodology, his account of the novel's production, with its epic contours of the human fall into fragmentation and its nostalgia for a golden past, still stands as one of the most fully realized self-conscious appraisals of the novel's origin. But the important Marxist tradition of genre study has exerted little influence on genre theory in twentieth-century Anglo-American literary criticism. Anglo-American genre study has always been marked by a pervasive antihistorical bias. Irving Babbitt, for example, in his debates with Joel Elias Spingarn and in his knee-jerk reaction to Benedetto Croce's aesthetics, called for a greater adherence to generic rules and a greater observance of both restraint and classical decorum in the production of literary texts.[21] Babbitt's pronouncements about genre became part of

[19]Wordsworth's famous definition of poetry as an overflow of powerful feeling and Coleridge's theory of the imagination are two obvious examples of organicist doctrines that have directly influenced modern generic conceptions of poetry. See William Wordsworth, *The Prose Works of William Wordsworth*, ed. W. J. B. Owen and Jane Worthington Smyser (Oxford: Clarendon Press, 1974), and Samuel Taylor Coleridge, *Biographia Literaria* (London: J. M. Dent, 1908).

[20]Georg Lukács, *The Theory of the Novel*, trans. Anna Bostock (Boston: MIT Press, 1971).

[21]For example, see Irving Babbitt, *The New Laokoön: An Essay on the Confusion of the Arts* (Boston: Houghton Mifflin, 1910).

the New Critical dogma, and with the institutionalization of the New Criticism in America, Babbitt's idealist conception of genres as transcendental categories became the law of genre in American criticism. The New Critical disciples of Babbitt, in their antihistorical approaches to a theory of literary form, did not rigorously debate genre theory.[22] Only in the curricula of American universities and high schools did a New Critical theory of generic production come into the light. Students were taught "genres" like the novel, the drama, and the short story from anthologies that incorporated the "best" or "classical" texts selected from a national literature. Of course, these texts were selected according to the aesthetic criteria authorized by the New Criticism, and these criteria, in turn, established the dominance of the intrinsic approach to the classification and the interpretation of texts.[23]

Two obvious problems exist with this reductive formalist approach to the classification of texts: the problem of infinite regress and the problem of distinguishing genres from subgenres. The problem of infinite regress in formalist accounts of genre is well known. As Tzvetan Todorov, Adena Rosmarin, and Jacques Derrida have pointed out, a generic taxonomy based on similarities among texts— the idea that texts may be classified according to the conventional formal elements they share—leads to the generation of more and more categories to cover the differences among texts.[24] For example, many different kinds of novels exist, and each time a new kind appears—which is often—a new category must be invented to account for it. Clearly, this process of generating new categories could continue indefinitely so that conceivably every new text could form its

[22]By "antihistorical" approach, I do not mean to suggest that people like T. S. Eliot or Cleanth Brooks did not possess a theory of history. (For an excellent discussion of Eliot's conception of history and tradition, see Richard Shusterman, "Essence, History, and Narrative: T. S. Eliot on the Definition of Poetry and Criticism," *The Monist* 71 [1988]: 183–96.) What I mean to suggest here is that the treatments of genre provided by theorists following Eliot, and I include Wellek and Warren's *Theory of Literature*, constitute a primarily idealized conception of literary forms that exist a priori outside of history. See René Wellek and Austin Warren, *Theory of Literature* (New York: Harcourt, Brace & World, 1970). For a discussion of New Critical theories of history, see Frank Lentricchia, *After the New Criticism* (Chicago: University of Chicago Press, 1980), pp. 103–54.

[23]For a discussion of what is meant by the "intrinsic" approach to literary study, see Jameson, *The Prison-House of Language*, p. 43.

[24]See Tzvetan Todorov, *The Fantastic: A Structural Approach to a Literary Genre*, trans. Richard Howard (Ithaca: Cornell University Press, 1973); Adena Rosmarin, *The Power of Genre* (Minneapolis: University of Minnesota Press, 1985); and Jacques Derrida, "The Law of Genre," *Critical Inquiry* 7 (1980): 55–81. Subsequent references to "The Law of Genre" will be cited in the text as "Law."

own genre. Within this kind of taxonomic system, a genre fails to achieve its raison d'être: it fails to distinguish one test from another. Because of the problem of infinite regress, formalism also cannot account adequately for hybrid texts: texts that incorporate elements from several different genres. Many highly formulaic texts like folk tales, business letters, or Harlequin romances certainly can be reduced to a system of similar conventional elements, but hybrid texts that cannot be reduced to a formula seem to form genres of their own. Northrop Frye's famous and influential genre theory, for instance, cannot account for generic deformation except to say that genres are mixed so that a specific text might be classified as a novel, confession, anatomy, and romance—all at the same time.[25] Such a classificatory system so greatly blurs distinctions among texts that, in the end, the system reveals itself as largely arbitrary; it tells us little about texts that we do not already know.

All formal classificatory systems that attempt to account for genres through an analysis of conventions or other textual elements suffer the same fate as Frye's system. On the other hand, a conception of genre steeped in the idea of addressivity avoids the problem of infinite regress by insisting that a genre is defined by its response to other utterances and not by its conventional formal elements. In this formulation a specific genre becomes a response to something within a specific social situation; it is the determinate hermeneutic form that an utterance takes. This *form*, however, should not be regarded as a synchronic ahistorical category like the novel, confession, anatomy, or romance. Instead of an ahistorical category, a genre corresponds to a hermeneutic strategy—a guessing game—that we employ in order to communicate.[26] Conceived as a hermeneutic strategy, the genre avoids altogether the problem of reductionism and the kindred problem of infinite regress, for the genre, as a hermeneutic strategy, does not correspond to a set of synchronic conventional elements. Rather, a genre—as the determinate form of the utterance—represents a response to an utterance, and as a response, the genre is the form that interpretation takes.

The Aphoristic and Uncodifiable Nature of Genre

The twin observations that communicative interaction is genre-bound and that genres may not be reduced to transcendental categor-

[25]Northrop Frye, *Anatomy of Criticism: Four Essays* (Princeton: Princeton University Press, 1957), p. 312.
[26]See Derrida, "Signature Event Context," and Davidson, "Communication and Convention."

ries have not gone unrecognized by contemporary genre theorists, and, today, most genre theorists have moved away from a production-centered approach to genre. Instead of worrying about how genres are produced, contemporary genre theorists worry about how genres are received and how they affect our interpretations of texts. For example, Jonathan Culler argues that "genres are no longer taxonomic classes but groups of norms and expectations which help the reader to assign functions to various elements in the work, and thus the 'real' genres are those sets of categories or norms required to account for the process of reading."[27] In a similar vein, Fredric Jameson tells us that "Genres are essentially contracts between a writer and his reader . . . they are literary institutions, which like the other institutions of social life are based on tacit agreements or contracts."[28] Other theorists from very different critical traditions, theorists like Hans Robert Jauss, Jacques Derrida, and even E. D. Hirsch share Culler's view that "genres are no longer taxonomic classes."[29] In our time, literary theorists generally understand genres to be sets of reading expectations held by communities of readers and writers at specific historical moments, and these expectations obviously change over time.

Although there seems to be general agreement that genres cannot be reduced to synchronic categories of conventional elements, only Derrida has traced out the ramifications of such a view. In "The Law of Genre" Derrida describes the aporistic nature of genre, and in this analysis he directly connects the concept of genre with interpretation. His argument goes like this: no genre is ever genre-less, for "every text participates in one or several genres, yet such participation never amounts to belonging" ("Law," p. 65). By participating in a genre or genres, a text or utterance marks itself as a kind, but in so doing, it also demarcates itself through its difference from all other utterances participating in the same genre or genres. This inclusion and exclusion—the simultaneous belonging and not belonging—constitutes what Derrida calls the "genre-clause:" "a clause stating at once the juridical utterance, the precedent-making designation and the law-

[27]Jonathan Culler, *The Pursuit of Signs: Semiotics, Literature, Deconstruction* (Ithaca: Cornell University Press, 1981), p. 127.

[28]Fredric Jameson, "Magical Narratives: Romance as Genre," *New Literary History* 7 (1975): 135.

[29]For example, see Hans Robert Jauss, *Toward an Aesthetic of Reception*, trans. Timothy Bahti (Minneapolis: University of Minnesota Press, 1982); Derrida, "Law" and E. D. Hirsch, Jr., *Validity in Interpretation* (New Haven: Yale University Press, 1967).

text, but also the closure, the closing that excludes itself from what it includes. . . . The clause . . . declasses what it allows to be classed" ("Law," p. 66). Through this clause, a genre always announces its own undoing, its own aporia. Therefore, an utterance—in the form of a genre—can never be placed within a rigid generic taxonomy, because it always undermines the very taxonomy to which it seems to belong. According to Derrida, the utterance as genre—through the genre-clause—always announces its own degenerescence: "Without [the genre-clause], neither genre nor literature come to light, but as soon as there is this blinking of an eye, this clause . . . at the very moment that a genre or a literature is broached, at that very moment, degenerescence has begun, the end begins" ("Law," p. 66). The genre-clause, therefore, embodies indeterminacy; it continually deconstructs itself.

Derrida's genre-clause—the "formless form" ("Law," p. 66) announced by every utterance—corresponds closely to what I have been calling a hermeneutic strategy or interpretive guessing game. When we establish the genre in which a text participates, we learn something about the hermeneutic strategy we must employ to interpret that text. When a text announces itself as a lyric poem or a grocery list, we begin to understand the kind of interpretation necessary in order to make sense of the text. Of course, the initial guess we make about how to read a text may or may not work; we may mistake a grocery list for a poem, depending on where we find it or who wrote it. More important, however, our guesses about how to read a text inevitably change as we read. As we read a text, we continually try to match our hermeneutic strategy with another's strategy as we read, even if the other is us. When we produce a text, genre is just as important. When we write something, we attempt to match our hermeneutic strategy with the strategy we think someone else may employ to interpret what we write, and, obviously, we may be wrong. So, in both the reception and the production of texts, we make hermeneutical guesses about how texts should be or will be interpreted. Within this guessing game, genre constitutes the essential interpretive element, for only through the genre—what Derrida calls the genre-clause—may we begin to formulate a hermeneutic strategy that, in turn, will enable us to make sense of an utterance. Because the genre is thoroughly hermeneutic in nature and because it comes into being only within the dialogic interchanges of public life, a specific genre cannot be treated as a linguistic element that we employ in order to make our intentions clear or to decipher the intentions of others; a genre does not constitute a predetermined framework that we choose to help us communicate. Instead, genres are hermeneutical strategies that propel the guessing games we employ in order to produce utterances and to understand the utterances of others.

Genre as the Most Fundamental Unit of Communication

From the perspective outlined above, the genre and not the word or the sentence becomes the most fundamental unit of communication. As the socially determinate realization of the utterance, the genre corresponds to a hermeneutic strategy that helps us begin to make sense of texts; neither the sentence nor the word can serve this function. The word or the sentence never relate to us how it is to be interpreted, for a word or sentence may take on different meanings depending on its use within an utterance. Clearly, a word or sentence may mean something quite different depending on its appearance in a specific genre. For example, a sentence might mean one thing in a greeting and something quite different in a joke. The genre, however, provides clues to its own meaning, so when we anticipate a text's genre, we begin to know how to interpret it. I say "begin to know" because the genre never remains fixed. It provides only the beginning place for interpretation. Unlike the word or the sentence, then, the genre represents in itself a strategy for the interpretation of discourse.

When we move away from a conception of communication grounded in the word and the sentence and move toward a conception of communication grounded in genre, both the production and the reception of discourse appear in an entirely new light. When we understand that communicative interaction takes place largely through genres and when we understand that genres are public constructs—and not internal transcendental categories—we no longer need to think of the production and the reception of discourse in terms of internal cognitive processes that, in turn, lead directly to the old Cartesian problems of skepticism and relativism. Because all communicative interaction takes place through the utterance and is consequently genre bound, both the production and the reception of discourse become thoroughly hermeneutical social activities and not the internal subjective activities of a private mind. So, Bakhtin's famous claim concerning genre—his claim that poetics should begin with genre and not end with it[30]—may be extended, for if the utterance (and, consequently, the genre) constitutes the most fundamental unit of communication, then every treatment of discourse production and discourse reception—not just poetics—should begin with the study of genre.

[30]In *The Formal Method in Literary Scholarship: A Critical Introduction to Sociological Poetics*, trans. Albert J. Wehrle (Baltimore: Johns Hopkins University Press, 1978), p. 112, Bakhtin and P. N. Medvedev write, "Poetics should really begin with genre, not end with it. For genre is the typical form of the whole work, the whole utterance. A work is only real in the form of a definitive genre. Each element's constructive meaning can only be understood in connection with genre."

CHAPTER 15

The Dialogical Self

CHARLES TAYLOR

In a sense, 'the self' is a modern phenomenon. Only in modern western culture have we begun to speak of the human person as "the self," and of people as having and being selves. But this is not to propound the absurd thesis that earlier ages had no sense of reflexivity. Of course, they did. Moreover, reflexive pronouns exist in all sorts of languages (for all I know, in all languages). So what is special about 'the self' in modern times?

The first thing to note is that we begin to use this expression only in modern times. That is, we put an article (definite or indefinite) in front of the reflexive pronoun, or we pluralize it. What does this signify? I want to argue that it reflects a description of something that has become a crucial feature of the human person for us, viz., certain powers of reflexivity.

We sometimes speak of the human person as 'a self', where our ancestors might have said 'soul'. The shift reflects a change in our understanding of what is essential. We have developed practices of radical reflexivity in the modern world. By 'radical reflexivity' I mean not only the focus on oneself, but on one's own subjective experience. To be interested in my own health, or wealth, is to be reflexively oriented, but not radically. But when I examine my own experience, or scrutinize my own thinking, reflexivity takes a radical turn.

The post-Cartesian ideal of clear, self-responsible thinking is the source of one set of disciplines of reflexivity, one in which the subject disengages himself or herself from embodied and social thinking,

This essay was read at the meeting of the American Anthropological Association, Washington, D.C., November 1989.

from prejudices and authority, and is able to think for himself or herself in a disengaged fashion. At the same time the post-Romantic ideal of self-sounding and self-expression has launched us in another whole range of practices of reflexivity, which bring into play the creative imagination.

The ideal subject of either or both of these practices cannot easily identify himself or herself with some substantive description, particularly one with the metaphysical overtones of the "soul". What she or he essentially is, is rather just this subject of reflexivity, that is, 'a self'.

What I am suggesting is that we see ourselves as selves, because our morally important self-descriptions push us in this direction or, alternatively, because we identify ourselves with this kind of description.[1]

But this definition of what is peculiar to our age suggests a description of what is perennial in human life. There is one recurrent dimension of reflexivity, which consists in the fact that humans devise, or accept, or have thrust upon them descriptions of themselves, and these descriptions help to make them what they are. Further, these self-descriptions include moral or ethical self-characterizations, that is, descriptions that situate us relative to some goods, or standards of excellence, or obligations that we cannot just repudiate. A human being exists inescapably in a space of ethical questions; she or he cannot avoid assessing himself or herself in relation to some standards. To escape all standards would not be a liberation, but a terrifying lapse into total disorientation. It would be to suffer the ultimate crisis of identity.

What do we mean by 'identity' when we speak of people defining their identity, or suffering a crisis of identity, and the like? The notion of identity is linked to that of 'who' we are. I sometimes answer the question 'who' I am by telling my function: "I am the professor for 231D"; or sometimes by stating my relationship, "I am X's brother-in-law." In this way I tell who I am by situating myself in some sort of social, professional, familial space. But the kind of identity that is crucial to having a coherent sense of self is one that relates us to ethical space. To have an identity is to know "where you're coming from" when it comes to questions of value, or issues of importance. Your identity defines the background against which you know where

---

[1] I have discussed this at greater length in "The Moral Topography of the Self," in Stanley Messer, Louis Sass, and Robert Woolfolk, eds., *Hermeneutics and Psychological Theory* (New Brunswick, N.J.: Rutgers University Press, 1988).

you stand on such matters. To have that called into question, or fall
into uncertainty, is not to know how to react, and this is to cease to
know who you are in this ultimately relevant sense.

With this in mind, we can hazard the following claims: human
beings always have a sense of self, in this sense, that they situate
themselves somewhere in ethical space. Their sense of who they are
is defined partly by some identification of what are truly important
issues, or standards, or goods, or demands; and correlative to this,
by some sense of where they stand relative to these or where they
measure up on them or both.[2] The sense of self so defined is something more than the bare reflexive awareness that they are a continuing subject, discussed for instance, by classical empiricists like David
Hume, and raised again in recent discussion by Derek Parfit.[3] This
latter awareness is quite independent of ethical assessment. That the
issue of identity should have been raised in connection with this bare
self-awareness, as against the richer sense of moral situation, is itself
a product of the disengaged perspective that has helped to shape the
modern self. I want to return to this below.

But first, I can now try to state the relation between what is perennial and what is ever changing in human life. Humans always have
a sense of self which situates them in ethical space. But the terms
that define this space, and that situate us within it, vary in striking
fashion. As we look through history, even at cultures more or less
familiar to us, we can see a range of ethical spaces that are so different
as to be often incommensurable. When we try to compare the sense
of the good which goes along with the recognition of a universe of
Forms, each of which defines its own telos and excellence, on one
hand, with the sense of the right that goes with the standard of law
that purely procedural reason gives to itself, on the other, we find it
impossible to define a common set of terms in which both these
radically different outlooks could be undistortively stated. And these
belong, after all, to the same civilization, if not the same age; neither
of them is equivalent to the space of Dharma, or of Tao. Anthropologists will have no difficulty multiplying the examples.

My claim in the opening lines above was about the particular ethical space of us moderns, one in which the excellences of radical reflexivity bulk so large that we are tempted to define ourselves as 'selves'.
This peculiar use of the reflexive pronoun belongs to our particular

---

[2]I have gone into this further in *Sources of the Self* (Cambridge: Harvard University
Press, 1989), chap. 2.
[3]See Derek Parfit, *Reasons and Persons* (Oxford: Oxford University Press, 1984).

language. In one sense, humans always have a sense of self; but we see ourselves as having or being 'a self', and that is something new.

Among the practices that have helped to create this modern sense are those that discipline our thought to disengagement from embodied agency and social embedding. Each of us is called upon to become a responsible, thinking mind, self-reliant for his or her judgments (this, at least, is the standard). But this ideal, however admirable is some respects, has tended to blind us to important facets of the human condition. There is a tendency in our intellectual tradition to read it less as an ideal than as something that is already established in our constitution. This reification of the disengaged first-person-singular self is already evident in the founding figures of the modern epistemological tradition, for instance, in René Descartes and John Locke.

It means that we easily tend to see the human agent as primarily a subject of representations: representations, first, about the world outside; and second, depictions of ends desired or feared. This subject is a monological one. She or he is in contact with an "outside" world, including other agents, the objects she or he and they deal with, his or her own and others' bodies, but this contact is through the representations she or he has "within." The subject is first of all an "inner" space, a "mind," to use the old terminology, or a mechanism capable of processing representations, if we follow the more fashionable computer-inspired models of today. The body, other people may form the content of my representations. They may also be causally responsible for some of these representations. But what "I" am, as a being capable of having such representations, the inner space itself, is definable independently of body or other. It is a center of monological consciousness.

It is this stripped-down view of the subject that motivates the discussion of identity in terms of bare self-awareness which I mentioned above. But this is a rather arcane consequence, of interest only to (some) philosophers. Of greater moment is the fact that this view of the subject has made deep inroads into social science, breeding the various forms of methodological individualism, including the most recent and virulent variant, the current vogue for rational-choice theory. It stands in the way of a richer and more adequate understanding of what the human sense of self is really like, and hence of a proper understanding of the real variety of human culture, and hence of a knowledge of human beings.

Although anthropology of all the social sciences has been founded on the recognition of deep cultural difference, perhaps even in this field a critique of monological consciousness might arouse some interest.

What this kind of consciousness leaves out is the body and the other. I want to make a brief sketch of what is involved in bringing them back in.

A number of philosophical currents in the past two centuries have tried to get out of the cul-de-sac of monological consciousness. Prominent in this century are the works of Martin Heidegger, Maurice Merleau-Ponty, Ludwig Wittgenstein.[4] What all these have in common is that they see the agent, not primarily as the locus of representations, but as engaged in practices, as a being who acts in and on a world.

Of course, no-one has failed to notice that human beings act. The crucial difference is that these philosophers set the primary locus of the agent's understanding in practice. On the mainline epistemological view, what distinguishes the agent from inanimate entities that can also affect their surroundings is the former's capacity for inner representations, whether these are placed in the "mind" or in the brain understood as a computer. What we have that animate beings do not—understanding—was identified with representations and the operations we effect on them.

To situate our understanding in practices is to see it as implicit in our activity, and hence as going well beyond what we manage to frame representations of. We do frame representations: we explicitly formulate what our world is like, what we aim at, what we are doing. But much of our intelligent action in the world, sensitive as it usually is to our situation and goals, is carried on unformulated. It flows from an understanding that is largely inarticulate.

This understanding is more fundamental in two ways: (1) it is always there, whereas we sometimes frame representations and sometimes do not, and (2) the representations we do make are comprehensible only against the background provided by this inarticulate understanding. It provides the context within which alone they make the sense they do. Rather than representations being the primary locus of understanding, they are just islands in the sea of our unformulated practical grasp on the world.

Seeing that our understanding resides first of all in our practices

[4]Martin Heidegger, *Sein und Zeit* (Tübingen: Niemeyer, 1927); Maurice Merleau-Ponty, *La Phénoménologie de la Perception* (Paris: Gallimard, 1945); Ludwig Wittgenstein, *Philosophical Investigations* (Oxford: Basil Blackwell, 1953).

involves attributing an inescapable role to the background. The connection figures, in different ways, in virtually all the philosophies of the contemporary countercurrent to epistemology, and famously, for example, in Heidegger and Wittgenstein.

But this puts the role of the body in a new light. Our body is not just the executant of the goals we frame, nor just the locus of causal factors shaping our representations. Our understanding itself is embodied. That is, our bodily know-how, and the way we act and move, can encode components of our understanding of self and world. I know my way around a familiar environment in being able to get from any place to any place with ease and assurance. I may be at a loss when asked to draw a map, or even give explicit directions to a stranger. I know how to manipulate and use the familiar instruments in my world, usually in the same inarticulate fashion.

But it is not only my grasp on the inanimate environment which is thus embodied. My sense of myself, of the footing I am on with others, are in large part also. The deference I owe you is carried in the distance I stand from you, in the way I fall silent when you start to speak, in the way I hold myself in your presence. Or alternatively, the sense I have of my own importance is carried in the way I swagger. Indeed, some of the most pervasive features of my attitude to the world and to others is encoded in the way I carry myself and project in public space, whether I am "macho," or timid, or eager to please, or calm and unflappable.

In all these cases the person concerned may not even possess the appropriate descriptive term. For instance, when I stand respectfully and defer to you, I may not have the word 'deference' in my vocabulary. Very often, words are coined by (more sophisticated) others to describe important features of people's stance in the world. (Needless to say, these others are often social scientists.) This understanding is not, or only imperfectly, captured in our representations. It is carried in patterns of appropriate action, that is, action that conforms with a sense of what is fitting and right. Agents with this kind of understanding recognize when they or others "have put a foot wrong." Their actions are responsive throughout to this sense of rightness, but the "norms" may be quite unformulated, or only in fragmentary fashion. In recent years Pierre Bourdieu has coined a term to capture this level of social understanding, the 'habitus'.[5]

---

[5]Pierre Bourdieu, *Outline of a Theory of Practice* (Cambridge: Cambridge University Press, 1977), and *Le Sens Pratique* (Paris: Minuit, 1980).

But then one can see right away how the other also figures. Some
of these practices that encode understanding are not carried out in
acts of a single agent. The example of my deference above can often
be a case in point. Deferent and deferred-to play out their social
distance in a conversation, often with heavily ritualized elements.
And indeed, conversations in general rely on small, usually focally
unnoticed rituals.

But perhaps I should say a word first about this distinction I'm
drawing between acts of a single agent (call them 'monological' acts),
and those of more than one ('dialogical' acts). From the standpoint
of the old epistemology, all acts were monological, although often
the agent coordinates his or her actions with those of others. But this
notion of coordination fails to capture the way in which some actions
require and sustain an integrated agent. Think of two people sawing
a log with a two-handed saw, or a couple dancing. A very important
feature of human action is rhythming, cadence. Every apt, coordinated gesture has a certain flow. When one loses this flow, as occasionally happens, one falls into confusion; one's actions become inept
and uncoordinated. Similarly, the mastery of a new kind of skilled
action goes along with the ability to give one's gestures the appropriate rhythm.

Now, in cases like the sawing of the log and ballroom dancing, it
is crucial to their rhythming that it be shared. These come off only
when we can place ourselves in a common rhythm, in which our
component action is taken up. This is a different experience from
coordinating my action with yours, as for instance when I run to the
spot on the field where I know you are going to pass the ball.

Sawing and dancing are paradigm cases of dialogical actions. But
there is frequently a dialogical level to actions that are otherwise
merely coordinated. A conversation is a good example. Conversations with some degree of ease and intimacy move beyond mere
coordination and have a common rhythm. The interlocutor not only
listens but participates with head nodding and "unh-hunh" and the
like, and at a certain point the "semantic turn" passes over to the
other by a common movement. The appropriate moment is felt by
both partners together in virtue of the common rhythm. The bore,
the compulsive talker, thins the atmosphere of conviviality because
he or she is impervious to this rhythm. There is a continuity between
ordinary, convivial conversation and more ritualized exchanges: lita-
nies, or alternate chanting, such as one sees in many earlier societies.[6]

[6]See the work of Greg Urban, from whom I have drawn much of this analysis; for

I have taken actions with a common rhythming as paradigm cases of the dialogical, but they are in fact only one form of these. An action is dialogical, in the sense I am using it, when it is effected by an integrated, nonindividual agent. This means that for those involved in it, its identity as this kind of action essentially depends on the sharing of agency. These actions are constituted as such by a shared understanding among those who make up the common agent. Integration into a common rhythm can be one form this shared understanding can take. But it can also come to be outside the situation of face-to-face encounter. In a different form it can also constitute, for instance, a political or religious movement, whose members may be widely scattered but who are animated together by a sense of common purpose—such as that which linked, for example, the students in TienAnMen Square and their colleagues back on the campuses, and indeed, a great part of the population of Peking. And this kind of action exists in a host of other forms, and on a great many other levels as well.

The importance of dialogical action in human life shows the utter inadequacy of the monological subject of representations which emerges from the epistemological tradition. We cannot understand human life merely in terms of individual subjects, who frame representations about and respond to others, because a great deal of human action happens only insofar as the agent understands and constitutes himself or herself as integrally part of a 'we'.

Much of our understanding of self, society, and world is carried in practices that consist in dialogical action. I would like to argue, in fact, that language itself serves to set up spaces of common action, on a number of levels, intimate and public.[7] This means that our identity is never simply defined in terms of our individual properties. It also places us in some social space. We define ourselves partly in terms of what we come to accept as our appropriate place within dialogical actions. In the case that I really identify myself with my deferential attitude toward wiser people like you, then this conversational stance becomes a constituent of my identity. This social reference figures even more clearly in the identity of the dedicated revolutionary.

At this point, the name of George Herbert Mead tends to be in-

example, "Ceremonial Dialogues in South America," *American Anthropologist* 88 (1986): 371–86.

[7]I have tried to argue this in "Theories of Meaning," in *Human Agency and Language* (Cambridge: Cambridge University Press, 1985).

voked in discussions among social scientists. But it is important to see that the dialogical view I'm propounding here is quite different from Mead's. He allows that I develop a self when I adopt the stance of the other toward myself. A person "becomes a self insofar as he can take [the] attitude of another and act towards himself as others act."[8] In the very impoverished behaviorist ontology that Mead allowed himself, this seemed to be a brilliant way to make room for something like reflexivity while remaining within the austere bounds of a scientific approach. But what we have here is something like a theory of introjection. My self is socially constituted, through the attitudes of others, as the 'me'. Mead also recognizes that this explanation cannot be the whole story, that something in me must be capable of resisting or conforming, will be in tension or harmony with what I internalize from my social world. We can't be simple functions of external demands. So Mead allows for the 'I' as well. But Mead's 'I' has no content of its own. It is a sort of principle of originality and self-assertion, which can lead at times to impulsive conduct, or to resistance to the demands of society,[9] but doesn't have an articulated nature that I can grasp prior to action. It is our previously unarticulated response to the demands of the community. We don't know what it's about until after it has acted. "The 'I' appears in our experience in memory."[10] It is obviously more closely related to the Kantian 'I' than to Erik Erikson's 'identity'. This latter has to be found in the 'me'.

What this description fails to capture is the way in which the 'I' is constituted as an articulate identity defined by its position in the space of dialogical action. Being able to take the attitude of another is an important part of growing up, of overcoming what Jean Piaget calls "egocentricity," but it is not what gives us a self in the first place. The self neither preexists all conversation, as in the old monological view; nor does it arise from an introjection of the interlocutor; but it arises within conversation, because this kind of dialogical action by its very nature marks a place for the new locutor who is being inducted into it.

Of course, our first definitions of ourselves are given by our parents and elders, because our first scenarios of dialogical action are provided by them. In this way we are initially shaped by our surround-

---

[8]George Herbert Mead, *Mind, Self and Society* (Chicago: University of Chicago Press, 1934), p. 171.
[9]Ibid., pp. 198–99, 210.
[10]Ibid., p. 196.

ings. So why object to Mead's theory of the self constituted as a 'me', which after all might just be intended to do justice to our initial passivity? But my objection is not that Mead's theory overstates the initial dependence of the child, but that it fails perspicuously to capture what happens after. The conversation between the 'I' and the 'me', or between one's own self-generated transformations of the offered scenarios and their original form, is not between an introjected identity and some unformed principle of spontaneity. It is more a matter of gradually finding one's own voice as an interlocutor, realizing a possibility that was inscribed in the original situation of dependence in virtue of its dialogical form. This is not to say that this process may not be accompanied by oppression and force: clearly it often is. It is just that the image of introjection distorts the process, whether smooth or conflictual.

This image becomes necessary for Mead, because he does not have a place in his scheme for dialogical action, and he can't have this because the impoverished behavioral ontology allows only for organisms reacting to environments. But this pushes toward a monological conception. Taking the stance of the other is another monological act, one that is causally influenced by or at best coordinated with the other, but still thoroughly mine. The only way to get the other into this behaviorist act is to introject him or her, and so that's what Mead does. One needs a richer concept of action and the self to come to grips with the formation of identity.

Introjective models abound in the human sciences, because of the hold of the monological perspective. Sigmund Freud is another source of them. Conscience as superego is the introjected voice of the parent. Once again, this image makes it difficult to understand what it might mean to develop a mature, autonomous moral outlook—except, in the form of a disengaged inner freedom from all this introjected matter, the cool distance of the scientific spirit from the messy battlefield of human emotions, an ideal that not surprisingly seems to have moved Freud.

Children plainly need recognition, confirmation, love to grow and be inducted into adult life, at the limit even to survive. But this can be conceived as a monological need, a comfort that they have to receive from others, as they depend on others for food, but that only contingently comes through conversation. Or it can be seen as a need that is essentially fulfilled in a certain form of conversation itself. The latter understanding places dialogue at the very center of our understanding of human life, an indispensable key to its comprehension, and requires a transformed understanding of language. In order to follow up this line of thinking, we need not Mead and his like, but rather Bakhtin. Human beings are constituted in conversation; and hence what gets internalized in the mature subject is not the reaction of the other, but the whole conversation, with the interanimation of its voices. Only a theory of this kind can do justice to the dialogical nature of the self.

Contributors

James F. Bohman is Associate Professor of Philosophy at St. Louis University. He is coeditor of *After Philosophy* and is the author of *New Philosophy of Social Science: Problems of Indeterminacy.*

Eloise A. Buker is Associate Professor of Political Science and Director of Women's Studies at the University of Utah. She is author of *Politics through a Looking Glass: Understanding Political Cultures through a Structuralist Interpretation of Narratives,* and she is completing a book on feminist theories and rhetoric.

Hubert L. Dreyfus is Professor of Philosophy at the University of California, Berkeley. His books include *Michel Foucault: Beyond Structuralism and Hermeneutics,* with Paul Rabinow, and *Mind over Machine,* with Stuart Dreyfus. His most recent book is *Being-in-the-World: A Commentary on Division I of Being and Time.*

Charles B. Guignon is Associate Professor of Philosophy at the University of Vermont. He is author of *Heidegger and the Problem of Knowledge,* as well as articles on Heidegger, Wittgenstein, and hermeneutics. He is editing a collection of essays on Heidegger.

David R. Hiley is Interim Dean of Liberal Arts and Professor of Philosophy at Auburn University. He is author of *Philosophy in Question: Essays on a Pyrrhonian Theme,* and he working on a book on the politics of skepticism.

DAVID COUZENS HOY is Professor of Philosophy at the University of California, Santa Cruz. He is author of *The Critical Circle: Literature, History, and Philosophical Hermeneutics,* and editor of *Foucault: A Critical Reader.* With Thomas McCarthy he is working on a book on critical theory.

THOMAS KENT is Associate Professor of English at Iowa State University. He is author of *Interpretation and Genre: The Role of Generic Perception in the Study of Narrative Texts.* He is working on a book concerning rhetoric and hermeneutics.

THOMAS S. KUHN is Laurance S. Rockefeller Professor of Philosophy at the Massachusetts Institute of Technology. His books include *The Structure of Scientific Revolutions* and *The Essential Tension.*

ALEXANDER NEHAMAS is the Edmund N. Carpenter II Class of 1943 Professor of Humanities, Professor of Philosophy and Professor of Comparative Literature at Princeton University. He is author of *Nietzsche: A Life as Literature.* His current work concerns the interaction between philosophy and literature in Plato's dialogues and the philosophical issues in mass media.

RICHARD RORTY is University Professor of Humanities at the University of Virginia. His books include *Philosophy and the Mirror of Nature* and *Contingency, Irony, and Solidarity.* Two volumes of his collected papers have recently been published.

PAUL A. ROTH is Professor of Philosophy at the University of Missouri at St. Louis. He is author of *Meaning and Method in the Social Sciences: A Case for Methodological Pluralism.* He is working on a book on narrative explanation.

JOSEPH ROUSE is Associate Professor of Philosophy and Chairman of the Science in Society Program at Wesleyan University. He is author of *Knowledge and Power: Toward a Political Philosophy of Science,* and is writing a book on modernity and postmodernity in the philosophy of science.

RICHARD SHUSTERMAN is Associate Professor of Philosophy at Temple University. He is author of *The Object of Literary Criticism* and

T. S. Eliot and the Philosophy of Criticism, and editor of *Analytic Aesthetics.* His latest book, *Pragmatist Aesthetics,* is forthcoming.

CHARLES TAYLOR is Professor of Political Science and Philosophy at McGill University. His books include *Hegel,* two volumes of his collected papers (*Human Agency and Language* and *Philosophy and the Human Sciences*), and *Sources of Self: The Making of the Modern Identity.*

JOHN J. VALAURI is Professor of Law at the Salmon P. Chase College of Law, Northern Kentucky University. He has published articles on topics in constitutional and legal theory.

SAMUEL C. WHEELER III is Professor of Philosophy at the University of Connecticut. His current project is an examination of Derrida's arguments in analytic-philosophical terms. He has recently published "Metaphor in Davidson and de Man" in *Redrawing the Lines,* edited by Reed Way Dasenbrock.

Index

Library of Congress Cataloging-in-Publication Data

The Interpretive turn : philosophy, science, culture / edited by David R. Hiley,
    James F. Bohman, and Richard M. Shusterman.
        p. cm.
    Includes bibliographical references and index.
    ISBN 0-8014-2549-2 (alk. paper).—ISBN 0-8014-9785-X (pbk. : alk. paper)
    1. Hermeneutics. I. Hiley, David R. II. Bohman, James. III. Shusterman, Richard.
BD241.I56 1991   91-55061
149—dc20